DATE			

BUSINESS/SCIENCE/TECHNOLOGY

The Black Youth
Employment Crisis

A National Bureau
of Economic Research
Project Report

The Black Youth Employment Crisis

Edited by Richard B. Freeman and
Harry J. Holzer

 The University of Chicago Press

Chicago and London

RICHARD B. FREEMAN, director of the Labor Studies
Program at the National Bureau of Economic Research and
professor of economics at Harvard University, is the author
of several books and the coeditor of *The Youth Labor
Market Problem,* published by the University of Chicago
Press. HARRY J. HOLZER is assistant professor of economics
at Michigan State University and faculty research fellow at
the National Bureau of Economic Research.

The University of Chicago Press, Chicago 60637
The University of Chicago Press, Ltd., London

95 94 93 92 91 90 89 88 87 86   5 4 3 2 1

Library of Congress Cataloging-in-Publication Data

Freeman, Richard B. (Richard Barry), 1943–
    The Black youth employment crisis.

    (A National Bureau of Economic Research project
report)
    Includes bibliographies and indexes.
    1. Afro-American youth—Employment—Congresses.
2. Unemployment—United States—Congresses.   I. Holzer,
Harry J.   II. Title.   III. Series.
HD6273.F73   1986   331.3′4125′08996073   85-20989
ISBN 0-226-26164-6

Relation of the Directors to the
Work and Publications of the
National Bureau of Economic Research

1. The object of the National Bureau of Economic Research is to ascertain and to present to the public important economic facts and their interpretation in a scientific and impartial manner. The Board of Directors is charged with the responsibility of ensuring that the work of the National Bureau is carried on in strict conformity with this object.

2. The President of the National Bureau shall submit to the Board of Directors, or to its Executive Committee, for their formal adoption all specific proposals for research to be instituted.

3. No research report shall be published by the National Bureau until the President has sent each member of the Board a notice that a manuscript is recommended for publication and that in the President's opinion it is suitable for publication in accordance with the principles of the National Bureau. Such notification will include an abstract or summary of the manuscript's content and a response form for use by those Directors who desire a copy of the manuscript for review. Each manuscript shall contain a summary drawing attention to the nature and treatment of the problem studied, the character of the data and their utilization in the report, and the main conclusions reached.

4. For each manuscript so submitted, a special committee of the Directors (including Directors Emeriti) shall be appointed by majority agreement of the President and Vice Presidents (or by the Executive Committee in case of inability to decide on the part of the President and Vice Presidents), consisting of three Directors selected as nearly as may be one from each general division of the Board. The names of the special manuscript committee shall be stated to each Director when notice of the proposed publication is submitted to him. It shall be the duty of each member of the special manuscript committee to read the manuscript. If each member of the manuscript committee signifies his approval within thirty days of the transmittal of the manuscript, the report may be published. If at the end of that period any member of the manuscript committee withholds his approval, the President shall then notify each member of the Board, requesting approval or disapproval of publication, and thirty days additional shall be granted for this purpose. The manuscript shall then not be published unless at least a majority of the entire Board who shall have voted on the proposal within the time fixed for the receipt of votes shall have approved.

5. No manuscript may be published, though approved by each member of the special manuscript committee, until forty-five days have elapsed from the transmittal of the report in manuscript form. The interval is allowed for the receipt of any memorandum of dissent or reservation, together with a brief statement of his reasons, that any member may wish to express; and such memorandum of dissent or reservation shall be published with the manuscript if he so desires. Publication does not, however, imply that each member of the Board has read the manuscript, or that either members of the Board in general or the special committee have passed on its validity in every detail.

6. Publications of the National Bureau issued for informational purposes concerning the work of the Bureau and its staff, or issued to inform the public of activities of Bureau staff, and volumes issued as a result of various conferences involving the National Bureau shall contain a specific disclaimer noting that such publication has not passed through the normal review procedures required in this resolution. The Executive Committee of the Board is charged with review of all such publications from time to time to ensure that they do not take on the character of formal research reports of the National Bureau, requiring formal Board approval.

7. Unless otherwise determined by the Board or exempted by the terms of paragraph 6, a copy of this resolution shall be printed in each National Bureau publication.

(Resolution adopted October 25, 1926, as revised through September 30, 1974)

Contents

Acknowledgments

We are indebted to the Rockefeller, Ford, and Edna McConnell-Clark Foundations for funding the collection and analysis of the NBER Inner-City Black Youth data. The role of Mathematica, Inc. in developing and administering the survey is also acknowledged. Finally, we thank the U.S. Department of Labor and the National Bureau of Economic Research for their financial support at various stages of this project.

The opinions expressed in this volume are those of the individual authors and do not necessarily reflect the views of the National Bureau of Economic Research or those of any other organization.

I The Black Youth Employment Crisis

The Black Youth Employment Crisis: Summary of Findings

Richard B. Freeman and Harry J. Holzer

Black youths have historically fared more poorly in the job market than have white youths. In the early 1960s, for example, black youths earned considerably less than otherwise comparable white youths, and they also received a lower return on their investments in schooling (Weiss 1970). Although differences between blacks and whites in skill, geographic location, and family background factors have in the past explained some of blacks' disadvantage in the job market, a large part of the observed differential was attributed to discrimination.

In recent years, with the onset of equal employment opportunity, affirmative action, and other government and private efforts to reduce market discrimination, the wages of black youths have risen relative to those of white youths. Young blacks have made advances in both occupation and education. Yet their *employment* problem has worsened, reaching levels that can only be described as catastrophic. In 1983 a bare 45 percent of black men who were aged 16 to 21 and out of school were employed, whereas 73 percent of their white counterparts were employed.[1] The heralded youth unemployment problem has taken the form not so much of joblessness among white youths as of high joblessness among black youths. In many respects, the urban unemployment characteristic of Third World countries appears to have taken root among black youths in the United States.

What are the dimensions and nature of the job crisis among black youths? What has caused the deterioration of black youth employment? What forces might reverse that deterioration?

Richard B. Freeman is director of the Labor Studies program at the National Bureau of Economic Research and professor of economics at Harvard University. Harry J. Holzer is assistant professor of economics at Michigan State University and faculty research fellow at the National Bureau of Economic Research.

Under the auspices of the National Bureau of Economic Research (NBER), ecoonomists from several universities have been engaged in extensive investigations of the problem of black youth joblessness. As part of this project, NBER researchers developed a survey to examine the situation facing black youths, the survey of Inner-City Black Youth. This survey was undertaken because existing governmental information, notably the Census Bureau's Current Population Survey (CPS), was inadequate for understanding the problem.

Basically, the CPS asks, "Are you working?" and obtains relatively little information on the activities of the jobless, particularly those out of the labor force. In addition, the census survey lacks information on certain alternatives to work that may be quite important to these youths. It is widely recognized, for example, that crime (broadly defined to include working in the "underground economy" as well as violent crime) is a major alternative to employment for youths; yet the CPS contains no questions on such activities. Finally, there is a serious "respondent bias" in the CPS, with one member of the household answering for all others. Consequently, the information obtained on the activities of youths in these households is not always accurate (Freeman and Medoff 1982).

To obtain a data set more suitable for analyzing the black youth employment crisis, NBER developed a set of questions to ask inner-city minority youths and contracted Mathematica Policy Research, Inc., to administer the survey to black men, aged 16 to 24, in Boston, Chicago, and Philadelphia. The sample was limited to men because the employment and social problems facing black women are quite different. The sample covered persons living on city blocks identified by the 1970 Census of Population as having at least 70 percent black residents and 30 percent of families living below the poverty line. Initially, the research staff was concerned whether the sampling would yield a sufficient response rate to reflect a random sample within these areas. But over 2,000 youths from the worst poverty tracts in these three U.S. cities did respond, representing an 82.6 percent response rate (see table 1).

Table 1   **General Characteristics of the NBER Survey of Inner-City Black Youths**

City	Number of Completed Interviews	Number of Attempted Interviews	Response Rate
Boston	757	939	80.6%
Chicago	800	919	87.1%
Philadelphia	801	996	80.4%
Total	2,358	2,854	82.6%

As a further check on the representative nature of the sample, we compared the characteristics of youths in our survey with those of the youths from the same geographic areas who were surveyed in the 1980 Census. Although there is some evidence that older youths and household heads may be underrepresented in our sample, we find no evidence of systematic biases in estimated relationships resulting from these differences (Bound 1986).

The topics covered by the survey ranged from standard work activities to the hourly activities of these youths in a day, their desire to work, their use of drugs, their participation in illegal activities, and their perceptions of the labor market. One set of questions had to do with their willingness to work, for example, "How willing are you to take a job at different levels of pay?" and "Would you take a full-time job right now, if it were as a laborer in a factory at——?" Various hourly wage levels were suggested in the latter question, beginning at $2.50 and rising until the respondent indicated an acceptable wage. The question also listed various potential jobs. The purpose of these questions was to gauge the "reservation wages" (the wage goals that govern the willingness to work) of these young people—again, a subject about which the CPS provides no regular information.

A second set of questions in the NBER survey dealt with some of the illegal activities in which the youths might have been involved over the previous 12 months. Although the difficulty in soliciting truthful responses to questions about criminal involvement is well known, a fair number of young people did report participation in crime; approximately one-quarter of the total income reported in the sample came from illegal activities (Hindelang, Hirschi, and Weis 1981).

A third set of questions focused on the activities of these youths in a typical day and over a 13-month period. These questions were designed to determine whether young blacks spend their time productively, especially when out of work and out of school. Questions about daily activities therefore investigated both productive ones—such as work, searching for work, school and studying, work around the house, and job training—and unproductive ones, such as crime, drug use, and recreational activities (going to movies, listening to music, "hanging out," and so forth). Similarly, the 13-month time line gauged time spent at work, in school or in training, in jail, and in other activities.

Another set of questions focused on the attitudes and family background of the youths. These included the welfare status of their families, churchgoing, residence in public housing, and jobs held by other family members.

The concentration of the NBER survey on inner-city black youths is both a strength and a weakness. The strength is that we have detailed information on the largest sample of such youths now available in social science research. One weakness is that the data cannot be used by themselves to compare the inner-city youths with other youths. Another weakness is that the NBER survey is limited to one observation in time; the only longitudinal component of the data is the retrospective "time line," for which the youths were asked what they had done in the previous 13 months. To overcome these weaknesses, many of the analysts supplemented the NBER data with other data sets, notably the youth cohort of the National Longitudinal Surveys of Labor Market Experience (NLS). The NLS surveyed a nationwide sample of white and minority youths aged 14 to 21 in 1979 and follows them in later years. The NLS also contains many questions that are similar to those asked in the NBER survey. The former was therefore well suited for a comparison of inner-city blacks with other youths.

Given the new data and a major research effort by several economists, what did the NBER analysis discover about the job crisis among black youths? Is the problem one of lack of skills and a work ethic, as some allege? Or is it one of discrimination, pure and simple? Why, in a period of overall black economic progress, have inner-city black youth suffered so much joblessness?

At the outset, it is important to state that the study has found no single factor to be *the* cause of the black youth employment problem. Rather, the various analyses in this volume identify a number of factors—on both the supply and the demand sides of the market—as contributing to the problem. Reversals or changes in these many factors, not in one single element, are needed to remedy the situation.

Among the factors that we have found to influence the employment of black youth are: the proportion of women in the labor force; the aspirations and churchgoing behavior of these youths; their willingness to accept low-wage jobs; the incentives for crime that they face; the employment and welfare status of their families; the overall state of their local labor markets; the behavior of employers and the characteristics of jobs they offer youths; the youths' performance on jobs, especially their absenteeism; and their years of education and school performance.

Because of the difficulty in determining the true "structure" by which certain factors operate, many of the studies in this volume take a "reduced form" approach to the analysis. In other words, they provide estimates of the link between factors and outcomes rather than estimates of structural parameters in complete behavioral models. Even so, the analyses provide new evidence on a broad range of causes and characteristics of the black youth employment problem that have not been seriously evaluated, to date, and without which sensible policy approaches to this problem cannot be devised.

If there is a single unifying theme in this book, it is that black male youths are quite responsive to a number of economic incentives and to their social and family environment. Thus, the magnitude of the observed employment decline in the 1970s reflects in large part the high elasticity of supply responses to negative employment incentives and to social and family developments. This finding suggests that if the society offers different incentives to young blacks in the 1980s, their employment situation should improve significantly. Developing policies that change these incentives is therefore the major challenge of any effort to improve black youth employment rates.

The Nature and Pattern of the Black Youth Employment Crisis

The striking deterioration in the employment of black youths, which motivated this study, is shown in table 2. The data show that black youth employment has declined in every age group relative to white youth employment and that unemployment rates have risen. They also show the often-forgotten and disturbing fact that the extraordinarily wide differentials have developed only in the past few decades. In 1954 approximately equal percentages of black and white youths were employed. Since that time, unemployment rates for black youths have soared and their employment rates have fallen, with especially large declines in the 1970s. This trend contrasts sharply with that of wages. Over the same period, wage differentials between young blacks and whites have narrowed dramatically, especially between subgroups having had the largest differentials in the past, such as Southerners (Bound and Freeman 1984).

What the employment numbers in the table do not reveal is that the joblessness problem is more severe among inner-city, poverty area

Table 2   **Employment and Unemployment Rates among Black and White Male Youths, 1954–81**

	Blacks and Other Nonwhites					Whites				
Age	1954	1964	1969	1977	1981	1954	1964	1969	1977	1981
	Percentage of the Population Employed									
16–17	40.4	27.6	28.4	18.9	17.9	40.6	36.5	42.7	44.3	41.2
18–19	66.5	51.8	51.1	36.9	34.5	61.3	57.7	61.8	65.2	61.4
20–24	75.9	78.1	77.3	61.2	58.0	77.9	79.3	78.8	80.5	76.9
25–54	86.4	87.8	89.7	81.7	78.6	93.8	94.4	95.1	91.3	90.5
	Percentage of the Labor Force Unemployed									
16–17	13.4	25.9	24.7	38.4	40.1	14.0	16.1	12.5	17.6	19.9
18–19	14.7	23.1	19.0	35.4	36.0	13.0	13.4	7.9	13.0	16.4
20–24	16.9	12.6	8.4	21.4	24.4	9.8	7.4	4.6	9.3	11.6
25–54	9.5	6.6	2.8	7.8	10.1	3.9	2.8	1.5	3.9	4.8

Source: Employment and Training Report of the President, 1982.

youths than among other blacks and that it is severest among those out of school.

Table 3 compares several dimensions of the employment problem among the inner-city NBER sample to the experience of all black and white youths from the National Longitudinal Survey. The comparison shows that the NBER survey correctly identified those youths facting the most severe economic problems: The inner-city black youths are much more likely to be unemployed and less likely to be employed than white youths or all black youths. They tend to have slightly lower wages than other youths and they work fewer weeks per year. In addition, these youths also have far worse family backgrounds than others. One-third of them live in public housing; almost one-half of them have a family member on welfare. Only 28 percent of them have an adult man in their household.

With respect to "socially deviant behavior," 16 percent of the NBER survey group reported having engaged in crimes; 26 percent reported drug use beyond marijuana; and 20 percent reported alcohol use. The survey responses to questions about the allocation of time show that those out of school spent only 17 percent of their time on anything that could be considered socially useful. The bulk of their days was instead spent watching television, going to movies, listening to music, or the like, in other words, on "leisure" as opposed to productive activities that might lead to work.

Table 3   **Comparison of NBER Inner-City Black Youths and All NLS White and Black Youths**

	NBER	NLS	
Characteristic	Inner-City Blacks	All Blacks	All Whites
Out-of-School Youth			
% in the Labor Force	80	90	94
% Unemployed	41	33	40
% Employed	48	61	76
Hourly Wages	$4.26	$4.29	$4.53
Weeks Worked in the Year	26	29	37
Family Background, All Youths			
% with Man in Household	28	51	69
% with Household Member			
Working or in School	41	56	71
% in Family on Welfare	45	—	—
% in Public Housing	32	10	1

Source: Tabulated from the NBER survey and the NLS.

The Dynamics of Nonemployment

Several recent analyses of joblessness have focused on the dynamics of the process, namely, the transition between the states of employment and nonemployment, the frequency with which individuals change states, and the duration of time in each of the states. For instance, people can suffer from nonemployment either because they have trouble finding jobs and are unemployed for long periods of time or because they are laid off or discharged frequently and thus hold given jobs for only short periods of time.

Analysis of the transitions in the NBER data set indicates that much of the unemployment among black youths has to do with the facts that they are out of work for very long periods of time and that, once nonemployed, they have great difficulty securing another job. They have short-term jobs followed by long spells of being out of work. Twenty percent of the sample's out-of-school youths may not be employed for over a year. Moveover, their successive jobless spells do not seem to become any shorter as time passes (Ballen and Freeman 1986).

An implication of this last finding is that the labor market problems of inner-city black youths are not likely to diminish greatly as they grow older: Although black youth employment rises with age, the increases in employment rates are relatively moderate. As a result, simple aging will not solve the problem of joblessness for black youth. Indeed, if the rate of increase in employment with age remains at the level of the 1970s, the cohort of inner-city black youths 18 to 19 years old in 1979 will not achieve a rate of employment of 80 percent until they reach their mid-thirties.[2]

One of the reasons why aging will not solve the problem is that the typical out-of-school, nonemployed youth spends his time on activities that do little to raise his employability. In the NBER time budget, the youths reported spending most of thier time on "hanging out," "TV/ movies," "listening to music," or "getting high," as opposed to searching for jobs, reading, or working around the house. Although one may regard the former set of activities as representing "leisure," the youths are not particularly satisfied with their lives and have a desire to engage in activities that could serve to improve their future.[3]

In addition to the slow transition from nonemployment to employment, the black youth employment problem is exacerbated by the frequent loss of jobs through layoffs and discharges. In a society where relatively few workers are discharged, one-quarter of the youths in the NBER survey had been fired—many because of absenteeism. Interestingly, most of the higher layoff rate among young blacks than among whites cannot be attributed to differences in human capital or broad characteristics of the workplace. However, the black youth layoff rate is reduced greatly by job tenure (Ferguson and Filer 1986; Jackson and Montgomery 1986).

Demand and Supply Causes

The potential causes of high or increasing youth joblessness can be fruitfully analyzed in terms of factors likely to affect joblessness by altering the supply of labor and the demand for labor. Although most measured variables influence both sides of the labor market, this simply dichotomy provides a useful framework for analysis.

The researchers in the NBER project analyzed a variety of factors on both sides of the market, as outlined in table 4. Because of the need to control for factors beyond the ones on which each particular study focused, nearly all variables were examined in all the studies. All told, therefore, these analyses provide a much firmer basis for assessing results than is comon in single studies. We claim as "findings" only those results occurring under different specifications and models—that is, only results that are robust.

Demand

On the demand side, the NBER survey yielded strong evidence that the state of the local labor market was a major determinant of youth

Table 4   NBER Findings on the Impact of Selected Demand and Supply Factors on Black Youth Joblessness

Variable	Effect on Black Youth Employment
State of Local Labor Market	Sizeable impact on employment.
Commuting Distance	Does not affect employment. "Race, not space."
Proportion of Women in Labor Market	The higher proportion of women in market reduces black youths' wages and employment.
Treatment of Job Seekers	Black youths treated less courteously, reducing likelihood of hire.
Layoffs	Higher rate of layoffs, due in part to absenteeism, lowers employment.
Employment of Other Family Members	Improves youths' chances of working.
Reservation wage	Higher reservation wage raises nonemployment.
Churchgoing	Improves school-going and employment; reduces socially undesirable behavior.
Career Aspirations	Improve chances of employment.
Illegal Income Opportunites	Raise crime; reduce employment.
Welfare Homes; Public Housing	Reduce employment chances.
Education	Still has significant positive effect.
Perception of Stiff Criminal Penalties	Reduces crime; improves chances of employment.

joblessness. Inner-city blacks in Boston, a city with a relatively strong labor market, had an employment rate some 10 percentage points above that of otherwise comparable youth in Chicago and Philadelphia. Confirming this, an analysis of youth employment across all Standard Metropolitan Statistical Areas (SMSAs) shows a significant portion of differences were related to geographic factors.[4]

Although the city of residence matters greatly, the particular part of a city in which youths reside appears to have only a slight effect on employment. In particular, a detailed study of the Chicago labor market strongly indicates that the youth employment problem is one of "race, not space." The Chicago area encompasses two primary residential clusterings of blacks, known as West Side and the South Side. There are many factories and jobs in the West Side; the South Side is much more exclusively residential.

On the basis of proximity to work, one might predict that youths residing on the South Side would have a much worse employment experience than those on the West Side who are closer to the jobs. But there turns out to be very little difference between their employment rates. Moveover, if one looks only at the border between the areas where blacks and whites live on the West Side, one finds that the white youths hold most of the jobs. The conclusion here is that the problem facing these black youths is not a lack of jobs in their residential neighborhoods; even when the jobs are located nearby, the white youths still obtain them more easily (Ellwood 1986).

This finding has a policy implication for cities considering the adoption of some sort of "enterprise zone" scheme: many employers might just employ white youths from elsewhere in the city. Instead, what seems to benefit black youths most is a high level of overall demand for labor in their city. This finding is consistent with the results of aggregate time-series studies that show black youth employment rates to be very sensitive to cyclical factors (Clark and Summers 1983).

Prior to the NBER study, there was considerable speculation about, but little hard evidence of, the potential effect of the rapid growth in the number of older women in the labor force on the employment prospects of young blacks. One of the most striking and surprising results from the NBER analysis of the demand for labor is the finding that cities with a high proportion of women in the labor force had the worst labor markets for young blacks. Both wages and labor participation rates were lower among blacks in those cities. We interpret this finding to mean that the rise in female participation rates in recent years has seriously hurt the job opportunities of young blacks. This interpretation suggests that women entering the job market often fill the entry-level jobs that might otherwise go to young blacks (Borjas 1986).

Despite affirmative action efforts and the elimination of blatant discrimination from the job market, our pilot "audit" project indicates that black youths still face discrimination from employers. In this project, the researchers sent out on job interviews both black and white youths who were graduating or about to graduate from high school in Newark, New Jersey. The researchers told them, in effect, "Here's a list of jobs that we've identified. We'll pay you to come back and report to us on what happened when you applied for these jobs." Ironically, and illustrative of the black-white difference in joblessness, the researchers had great difficulty finding white youths to participate; black youths were much more eager to go through this process.

On the demand side, the audit project found that the black job applicants were treated less courteously, in some respects, than the white applicants. For example, potential employers were less likely to call them "Sir." In addition, the project found that white youths had much better links to the job market but that both white and black youths were "reference poor." In other words, when filling out job applications that asked, "Who do you give as a reference for yourself?" most would list their friends at school instead of teachers or previous employers. For whites, most of whom came from families with employed members and "connections" to employers, this lack of references is not as critical a problem in finding a job as it is for blacks (Culp and Dunson (1986).

Perceived discriminatory behavior by employers seems to affect the performance of young blacks on their jobs as well as their ability to become employed. For instance, youths who claimed that their employers discriminated were more likely to be absent from their jobs. Several other job characteristics also affect absenteeism rates among black youth. These include wages and status (as measured by the Duncan index), which lower the frequency of absenteeism, and industry-specific skills, which raise it. All of these factors seem to reflect responses to incentives; the first two of these variables reflect the attractiveness of a job, while the third may reflect the employer's incentive to retain these workers despite their performance. Furthermore, absenteeism does raise the likelihood of any worker's being discharged. Thus, the performance of black youths on jobs they consider unattractive is a cause of their high discharge rate (Ferguson and Filer 1986).

The unattractive characteristics of jobs held by black youths also seem to contribute to the lengthy duration of the jobless spells they suffer. Their short and infrequent spells of employment do not reduce the duration of the periods of nonemployment they subsequently experience. Interviews with employers in low-income neighborhoods also show that the "spotty" work histories caused by unattractive jobs and high turnover rates make employers even more reluctant to hire these youths (Ballen and Freeman 1986).

Finally, as noted, young blacks also experience a serious layoff problem, due in part to their high absence rate. The cycle of layoffs or discharges and then long spells of nonemployment (in turn, partially due to spotty work histories) seems to end only when these young blacks accumulate some tenure on their jobs.

The studies examining the effects of other family members' employment indicate that young blacks were more likely to hold jobs when other members of their family were employed (Freeman 1986; Lerman 1986). It is unclear whether this represents an improved ability to find jobs because of better information or "connections" or merely a stronger work ethic instilled by the experience in the family. In either case, "family experience" factors that raise job holding and family stability among black adults may offer an important "indirect" approach for improving the job chances of black youths.

Supply

Because the NBER project surveyed the youths themselves, it gathered considerable information about supply-side behavior. Among the more interesting findings on the supply side was the result that churchgoing and "good" attitudes or aspirations are important in enabling youths to take appropriate steps toward escaping inner-city poverty. In the NBER survey, youths were asked whether they attended church and whether they were members of church groups. The reasoning behind these questions was that the church (a major social institution in the black community) might be doing things that will help these youths advance in society.

In fact, churchgoing turned out to exert a significantly positive influence. Regarding socially deviant activity, school attendance, and employment, the youths who went to church behaved differently from those who did not report going to church. But does one interpret these results as indicating the role of the church as a social institution helping youth? Or is it simply that "good kids" go to church, get jobs, stay in school, and do not commit crimes? The problem of determining causal links in nonexperimental data is a difficult one, one that different researchers treat in different ways. Although it is not possible to declare that churchgoing is truly an exogenous variable, the fact that it has different effects on youth behavior than do other family factors suggests that it does play some independent role (Freeman 1986).

Another hypothesis examined in the project was that youths with high aspirations and the "correct" outlook do better than others. Independent of churchgoing and various other objective factors, we find that attitudes play a role in youth behavior. Black youths with strong long-term career desires manage to find more work than those without such desires. The implication is that activities and factors that positively influence attitudes (ranging perhaps from role models to Operation Push activities) can help reduce the joblessness problem among black youths (Datcher-Loury and Loury 1986).

In its Fifth Annual Report to the President and the Congress, the National Commission for Employment Policy noted that one of the lacunae in understanding youth unemployment is "documentation of direct causal links between various labor market problems and illegal activities" (National Commission 1979). The NBER analysis of the relationship between youths' perceptions of market opportunities and penalties for crimes and their labor market experiences offers much of the needed documentation.

Our survey questionnaire asked the youths to compare their potential for making money on a job with their potential "on the street." A large minority saw greater opportunities for earnings "on the street": 32 percent believed there were more opportunities on the street; 58 percent believed there were more on a job; and 10 percent judged the two alternatives as offering the same earnings potential. As might be expected, this minority tended to commit (or to admit having committed) more crimes than the majority did. In fact, about one-fourth of all income reported by the inner-city black youths was from crime. Perceptions of the riskiness of crime were also found to be a major factor in whether youths chose a legitimate job or crime. The youths who perceived that the chances to make money illegally were good and who foresaw little chance of being arrested and convicted tended to commit crimes. They more often tended not to be employed, not to be in school, not to spend their time productively, and to be involved with drugs or gangs (Viscusi 1986).

Viewed in terms of supply-side behavior, the elasticities of substitution between crime and employment implied by these estimates are fairly significant. Furthermore, those engaged in criminal activity tended to perform poorly when employed and had less chance of becoming employed (Ferguson and Filer (1986). These results are striking when considered in the context of the crime literature (Freeman 1983). To date, most studies of the trade-off between unemployment and crime have found very modest linkages, as the analyses were performed using aggregate data for crime rates and unemployment rates. But the cross-sectional evidence reported above strongly suggests that poor employment opportunities lead to participation in crime, which further reduces success in the legal labor market. Nonetheless, the exact causal patterns in this cycle of crime and unemployment remain unclear.

Although no single study in the NBER project focuses on education, nearly all the analysts considered the impact of schooling on outcomes. Table 5 lists most of their findings. In spite of the poor quality of education in the inner city, staying in school longer appeared to benefit the youths, and those who did better in school had better employment records. These findings hold for a broad range of outcomes as well as a wide variety of schooling measures, and they usually remained sig-

Table 5   **NBER Findings on the Effects of Education on the Employment Outcomes of Black Youths**

Study	Finding
Freeman	Years of schooling raises the "productive hours" of youths. Also raises proportion of total time over time spent on "productive" activities.
Holzer	Graduating from high school raises youths' wages by 15% and increases weeks worked per year by 6%.
Lerman	Higher grades in school increase wages for youths: mostly A's and B's by 15%; mostly B's and C's by 39%. Also, higher grades in school reduce the likelihood that youths will drop out of school or be unemployed: mostly A's and B's by 60%; mostly B's and C's by 80%.
Datcher-Loury and Loury	Years of schooling increases wages earned per week by 11 to 14%, according to NBER study, and by 7 to 16%, according to the NLS.
Viscusi	Years of schooling reduces probability of youth participation in crime by 40 to 60%. Also reduces youths' perception of increasing income on the street.
Ferguson and Filer	Low grades increase chance that youth will be absent from work. No years-of-schooling effect found.

nificant even after controlling for many family background character-istics. Graduation from high school proved to have especially important effects, and grades in school often had effects in addition to the level of schooling. These results are consistent with those of other research-ers who have shown the positive effects of such measures as class work, test scores, and vocational training on weeks worked by black youth (Meyer and Wise 1982).

One of the more depressing results of the study is our finding that youths whose families received assistance from major public programs for disadvantaged families did worse in the job market. Youths from welfare homes with the same family income and otherwise comparable to youths from non-welfare homes had a much worse experience in the job market. If there were a natural reduction of the number of families on welfare, the odds are that the youths would benefit as well as the rest of their families. Youths living in public housing projects also did less well than youths living in private housing.

Since the loss of welfare benefits to families is slight when youths work (in the states we studied), the employment problem of youths in welfare households does not reflect family responsiveness to the pattern of benefits. Instead, their difficulties are more likely related to other factors, such as information and "connections" or attitudes and a work ethic, as noted above. It is also noteworthy that employment in female-headed households or households without an adult man present was no worse per se than in households where a man was present—if the female head was employed. The problem is therefore one of employment rather than gender (Lerman 1986; Freeman 1986).

Some direct evidence on the labor-supply responses of young black men can be found in the fact that their reservation wages were comparable to those of young white men, whereas their job prospects were worse than those of young whites. Since there were some differences in their possibilities of getting jobs, and there were some differences in the wages paid by the jobs they did get, about 30 percent of the longer period that blacks are out of employment can be explained by the fact that they *maintain* relatively high reservation wages. Black youths should not necessarily lower their expectations, nor should they accept lower wages than those offered white youths, which would be illegal discrimination by the employer. But the fact that they do not adjust their wage expectations based on their experience contributes to their joblessness. Although some blacks reported a willingness to accept low-wage or low-skilled jobs, many appeared to retain that willingness only temporarily. The fact that a large number of black youths do accept jobs at minimum-wage levels also suggests that the minimum wage may contribute to rough wage equalization between young blacks and whites in starting jobs and to the loss of some employment for the blacks (Holzer 1986).

The importance of reservation wages is underscored by the finding that a large proportion of out-of-school, not employed youths thought they could find a job relatively easily, as shown in the following:

	Very easy to find a job	Somewhat easy to find a job
Working as a laborer	18%	28%
Working at a minimum-wage job	38%	33%

Although it may be easy for a given individual to find low-paying jobs, these are the high-turnover, "dead end" jobs that youths tend to hold only temporarily. Furthermore, only a small fraction of the youths looked for and were willing to accept those jobs at any particular time. In some sense, those jobs are "shared" among youths: they work for a few months at a hamburger joint, then leave. If all of the out-of-school, nonemployed youths sought such jobs simultaneously and were willing to hold them for longer periods, it is unlikely that the jobs would be as easy to find.

An important supply-side finding running through most of our studies is that the supply of black youths is very responsive to incentives and opportunities to work or engage in other activities. If the market situation is basically unattractive and the youths see crime as a well-paying, low time-investment alternative to work, they will respond accordingly; and the converse is true if the job market is good. To indicate the magnitude of this response, we calculated a labor-supply elasticity of sorts, relating the number of individuals who reported each particular reservation wage to that wage level (and as a control, the individual's total income in the previous month). The resulting elasticity for all nonemployed black youths was 1.8, while the elasticity for those youths searching for work ranged from 2.1 to 3.2 depending on the particular reservation-wage equations—all high elasticities by any criterion.[5]

Conclusion

The NBER results are consistent with the picture of black youth employment problems provided by the recent Manpower Development Resource Corporation (MDRC) experiments with various public and private employment programs. Just as we find no single cause or single cure, the MDRC concluded that "no single program approach will work for all disadvantaged youths" (MDRC 1983). A variety of social and economic factors have contributed to the crisis. On the demand side of the market, we find evidence of several determinants, including local labor market conditions and demographics, discriminatory employer behavior, and the unattractive characteristics of the job held. On the supply side of the market, we find aspirations and churchgoing, opportunities for crime, the family's employment and welfare status, education, and the willingness to accept low-wage jobs all to be important factors. Overall, we see a picture in which many black youths face unappealing labor market choices and therefore find other ways to obtain income and spend their time. They thus are responsive to incentives posed in choosing among various market and nonmarket alternatives.

Our evidence also suggests that these factors have contributed to the deterioration of black youth employment over the last few decades: the growth of the female labor force, the rising number of welfare households, and the increasing willingness of youth to participate in crime. Evidence of the overall economic conditions in local labor markets suggests that slower growth and frequent economic downturns may have contributed to this problem as well. These local conditions have prevented inner-city black youths from realizing the improvements in wages and occupational standing that have benefited other groups of blacks as a result of government antidiscrimination efforts and improved educational levels. Nor is there any evidence that their employment problems will disappear as they age or as they witness other changes over time.

Of course, we must again stress the caveats mentioned above regarding the specific causal mechanisms by which factors such as family background and churchgoing affect black youth employment. Future research must build on our work by specifying these mechanisms and estimating models that measure these effects more precisely.

Notes

1. Tabulated from *Employment and Earnings*.
2. Calculated from Table 2.1 of Ballen and Freeman (1986), assuming a two-percentage-point rise in the employment rate per year of aging.
3. In response to the question, "Are you satisfied or dissatisfied with the way things are going in your life?" 40 percent of the total sample reported dissatisfaction, with even higher rates of dissatisfaction among the nonemployed and nonenrolled youth. In response to the question, "What is important in your life right now?" 95 percent cited being able to find steady work and 98 percent cited having a good education.
4. Specifically, the addition of a set of SMSA dummies to a regression of youth employment rates on other factors has a statistically significant effect when interacted with race.
5. Specifically, the following regression was estimated:

$$\ln N = a + b \ln ResW + c \ln Y,$$

where N is the number of individuals who would work at any particular wage or at a higher wage; $ResW$ is the reservation wage; and Y is the individual's total income in the previous month. The equations were estimated using three reservtion wages with the relevant sample for each, with the following results:

Measure of Reservation Wage/Sample	Coefficient (and Standard Error) for Elasticity of Supply
If had to get a job, What wage?	
Sample = all nonemployed	1.79 (0.45)
What wage at job sought?	
Sample = job searchers	2.09 (.058)
Lowest wage would accept?	
Sample = job searchers	3.15 (.074)

References

Studies in This Volume (1986)

Ballen, John, and Richard B. Freeman. Transitions between employment and nonemployment.

Borjas, George J. The demographic determinants of the demand for black labor.

Bound, John. Appendix.

Culp, Jerome, and Bruce H. Dunson. Brothers of a different color: A preliminary look at employer treatment of white and black youth.

Datcher-Loury, Linda, and Glenn C. Loury. The effects of attitudes and aspirations on the labor supply of young men.

Ellwood, David T. The spatial mismatch hypothesis: Are there teenage jobs missing in the ghetto?

Ferguson, Ronald, and Randall Filer. Do better jobs make better workers? Absenteeism from work among inner-city black youths.

Freeman, Richard B. Who escapes? The relation of churchgoing and other background factors to the socioeconomic performance of black male youths from inner-city poverty tracts.

Holzer, Harry J. Black youth nonemployment: Duration and job search.

Lerman, Robert. Do welfare programs affect the schooling and work patterns of young black men?

Jackson, Peter, and Edward Montgomery. Layoffs, discharges, and youth unemployment.

Viscusi, W. Kip. Market incentives for criminal behavior.

Previous Studies

Bound, John, and Richard B. Freeman. 1984. Documenting the dimensions of change. Unpublished report to the Department of Labor

Clark, Kim B., and Lawrence H. Summers. 1981. Demographic variation in cyclical employment effects. *Journal of Human Resources* 18 (1): 61–79.

Employment and Earnings. See U.S. Department of Labor, Bureau of Labor Statistics (1984).

Employment and training report of the president, 1982. See U.S. Department of Labor (1982).

Freeman, Richard B. 1983. Crime and the labor market. In *Crime and public policy*, ed. James Q. Wilson. Institute for Contemporary Studies.

Freeman, Richard B., and James L. Medoff. 1982. Why does the rate of youth labor force activity differ across surveys? In *The youth labor market problem*, ed. Richard B. Freeman and David Wise. Chicago: University of Chicago Press.

Hindelang, Michael, Travis Hirschi, and Joseph Weis. 1981. *Measuring delinquency*. Beverly Hills, Calif.: Sage.

Manpower Demonstration Research Corporation. 1983. *Findings on youth employment: Lessons from MDRC research*. New York: Manpower Demonstration Research Corporation.

Meyer, Robert, and David Wise. 1982. The transition from school to work: The experiences of blacks and whites. NBER Working Paper no. 1007. Cambridge, Mass.: National Bureau of Economic Research.

National Commission for Employment Policy. 1979. *Expanding employment opportuities for disadvantaged youth*, Report 9 (December). Washington, D.C.: Government Printing Office.

U.S. Department of Labor. 1982. *Employment and training report of the president, 1982*. Washington, D.C.: Government Printing Office.

U.S. Department of Labor, Bureau of Labor Statistics. 1984. *Employment and earnings* (January).

Weiss, Randy, 1970. The effects of education on the earnings of blacks and whites. *Review of Economics and Statistics* 52 (2): 150–59.

II The Nature and Pattern of Change

1   Black Youth Nonemployment: Duration and Job Search

Harry J. Holzer

1.1   Introduction

Total nonemployment is often decomposed for analytical purposes into two components: the *frequency* of nonemployment spells and the *duration* of an average spell. The frequency is the total number of spells and reflects the rate of employment turnover (quits and layoffs), while duration reflects the length of time before employment is gained or regained. Although most analyses of the youth employment problem among blacks and whites over the past decade have stressed job turnover and the frequency of unemployment spells, Clark and Summers (1982) showed that the duration of these spells is a crucial component of observed unemployment rates among youths and adults alike.

This study investigates why the duration of nonemployment spells experienced by young black men is generally longer than that experienced by young white men. The analysis focuses particularly on reservation wages as determinants of duration. Reservation wages, defined as the lowest wages individuals are willing to accept for employment, are stressed in the job-search literature as the key determinants of the unemployment duration chosen by individuals on the supply side of the labor market. Of course, labor demand can also affect the duration of nonemployment for young blacks. The key determinants on this side of the market are aggregate demand, skills, and discrimination. The direct effects of these forces on nonemployment duration among young blacks and whites are also considered below, as are the effects of low levels of demand on the choices of reservation wages made by each group.

Harry J. Holzer is assistant professor of economics at Michigan State University and faculty research fellow at the National Bureau of Economic Research.

The importance of analyzing the duration of nonemployment spells and reservation wages in studying black youth nonemployment (that is, unemployment or time out of the labor force) has already been demonstrated. Clark and Summers (1982) pointed out that the duration of nonemployment is significantly longer among young blacks than among young whites. They also found that differences in unemployment and nonemployment rates between young blacks and whites primarily reflect differences in probabilities of gaining employment among those without jobs, rather than differences in probabilities of becoming nonemployed. Thus, by explaining the lengthy duration of unemployment and nonemployment among young blacks, we will be able in turn to explain much of the huge rates of nonemployment among young blacks generally.

Moreover, by focusing on reservation wages as a determinant of duration, this study should shed some light on the controversy over the relative willingness to work of young blacks and whites that has arisen not only in recent studies by social scientists, but also in the popular press. In a few studies, young blacks appeared to be more willing than young whites to accept certain low-wage jobs, even after having controlled for personal and family background characteristics. But others have stressed the reluctance of young blacks to accept low-wage jobs that are considered "dead end" or "menial."[1] According to adherents of this latter view, a younger cohort of blacks developed a new consciousness or a new set of expectations as a consequence of the civil rights movement, and they now shun those low-status jobs to which large numbers of them had been relegated in the past. This point of view also stresses the role of crime as a superior source of income and status among young blacks.

Two primary issues form the basis of this analysis of reservation wages, as indicators of the willingness to accept certain kinds of work, and the duration of nonemployment among young blacks and whites. The first is the potential difference in reservation wages between young blacks and whites; the second is the impact of these reservation wages on the duration of unemployment within each group. The paper will also examine some determinants of reported reservation wages, but the study does not attempt a complete, structural model of reservation-wage formation. The data used in the analysis are from the youth cohort of the National Longitudinal Surveys (NLS) and the NBER Survey of Inner-City Black Youth.

There are four remaining sections in the paper. Section 2 presents a general model for the analysis of nonemployment duration and reservation wages; a discussion of some potential biases in the estimation; and a description of the data used for the estimation. The third section presents the empirical evidence on the reservation wages of young blacks and whites. Differences in results among the various reservation-wage measures are explained, and some evidence is presented on the relationship between reservation wages, the characteristics of the jobs individuals seek, and the kinds of low-wage, low-skilled jobs that are more readily available to black youth.

The fourth section explores the effects of reported reservation wages on subsequent labor market outcomes for young blacks and whites, namely, the duration of nonemployment spells and wages received on the next job. Some separate wage equations are also estimated for different categories of jobs ultimately received. These equations also show which of the various reported reservation wages have the most predictive power with regards to the labor market. Finally, the fifth section summarizes the results presented earlier and discusses implications for employment policy.

1.2   Models, Data, and Econometric Issues

To understand the relationship between nonemployment duration, job-search characteristics such as reservation wages and search effort, and demand more generally, the following identity is often used:

$$(1) \qquad E(DN)_t \equiv 1/P_{ne,t} \equiv 1/[P(Off)_t \cdot P(Acc|Off)_t],$$

where $E(DN)_t$ is the expected duration of a completed spell of nonemployment beginning in period t; $P_{ne,t}$ is the transition probability, or the probability that the individual will move from nonemployment to employment within the specified time period; $P(Off)_t$ is the probability of receiving a job offer; and $P(Acc|Off)_t$ is the conditional probability of accepting the offers received.

The probability of young blacks receiving offers of employment reflects, among other things, the demand for their labor that exists in the labor market. Among the factors that shift this demand is the level of aggregate demand in the local labor market, which includes the business cycle and the strength of the local economy; this factor has been shown to have strong effects on employment among both black and white youth.[2] A further determinant of the demand for young black labor may be discrimination. Blacks may be perceived as having fewer skills than whites and therefore may face greater difficulty in obtaining employment. Young blacks may also have less access to certain kinds of employment than do young whites, for the following reasons. Blacks who live in inner-city areas may have difficulty traveling to work in firms that are located in the suburbs; they may have less information about job vacancies than do young whites; they may have fewer personal "connections" in firms where vacancies arise, and finally, their actual skill levels may influence the probability of receiving offers in the labor market. Although these demand-shift factors may determine the probability of *potentially* receiving an offer, the probability of *ac-*

tually receiving one also depends on the intensity of the individual's search effort.

The probability of *accepting* offers depends exclusively on the level of the individual's reservation wage relative to the offered wage. Offered wages are embodied in a distribution $f(w^o)$ that is conditional on having received an offer and that also reflects on the demand-shift factors mentioned above. Jobs are accepted only when $w^o > w^r$, where w^r is the reservation wage. The expected duration of unemployment for an individual with search effort $SE_{i,t}$ and reservation wage $w_{i,t}^r$ is:

$$(2) \qquad E\,(DN)_{i,t} = \frac{1}{\pi(SE_{i,t}) \cdot [1 - F(w_{i,t}^r)]},$$

where π is the function relating search effort to offer probabilities, and F is the cumulative distribution function of offered wages.

This equation assumes, of course, that reservation wages and search effort will remain constant over the entire expected duration of nonemployment. If this is not the case, the transition probabilities and expected durations for subsequent periods will change and will be reflected in the observed durations of nonemployment.

Expected wages are determined for a given offered-wage distribution and reservation wage in the following manner:

$$(3) \qquad E(w)_{i,t} = \frac{_{w^r}\!\int^\infty wf(w)dw}{_{w^r}\!\int^\infty f(w)dw},$$

where each possible wage above the reservation wage is weighted by the probability of receiving it. This weighted sum is divided by the sum of the weights so that the sum of the weights equals one.

Having observed how reservation wages interact with offer probabilities and offered wages to determine the expected durations of nonemployment and received wages, let us now turn to the determinants of reservation wages. It is fairly standard in the job-search literature to show that reservation wages are in part determined by the following factors:

$$(4) \qquad w^r = w^r(\pi, f(w), y, d, H),$$

where y represents an individual's nonwage income sources, d represents his discount rate, and H represents his time horizon for working.[3] Nonwage income raises reservation wages by lowering the costs of nonemployment, while greater demand-side factors and longer horizons raise reservation wages by increasing the expected benefits of demanding a higher wage for employment. Higher discount rates should lower these expected benefits and therefore lower reservation wages. Finally, both the mean and the variance of the offered-wage distribution $f(w)$ have been shown to have positive effects on reservation wages.

This basic model can be extended in a number of ways to make it more pertinent to white and black youth. For instance, if individuals do not have rational expectations of offer probabilities and offered wages, their subjective expectations rather than the actual demand-side characteristics will determine their reservation wages; and overly optimistic expectations that adapt slowly over time may lead to high reservation wages. Furthermore, an individual's reservation wages can vary across jobs if the nonwage characteristics of these jobs vary and if these nonwage characteristics enter the individual's utility function.[4] Thus, the reservation wages for jobs with unpleasant characteristics may exhibit demands for "compensating differentials."

Models in which utility instead of income is maximized also allow tastes for leisure to affect reservation wages. These models incorporate labor-supply as well as job-search factors and can therefore be used to explain search intensity and labor-force participation.[5] Thus, the reservation wages of people who are not always actively searching for employment is yet another factor to consider.

Finally, these models often imply a declining reservation wage as the spell of nonemployment proceeds, rather than the constant one assumed above. This decline can be caused by a number of factors, including declining assets or flows of outside income, the declining marginal value of leisure, adapting expectations, and systematic search behavior, by which higher wage offers are pursued earlier and lower ones later.

The models of reservation-wage formation and nonemployment duration discussed here suggest that a set of recursive equations can be estimated empirically—equations in which the demand for individuals' labor and other factors determine their reservation wages, which in turn determine subsequent spells of nonemployment and subsequent wages. In particular, the following equations are estimated here:

$$(5) \qquad DN_{t+n} = DN(X_t, w_t^r, S_t),$$

$$(6) \qquad W_{t+n} = W(X_t, W_t^r),$$

$$(7) \qquad w_t^r = w^r(X_t),$$

where DN_{t+n} is the duration of the completed spell of nonemployment from the (1979) survey date onward; W_{t+n} is the subsequently received wage; w_t^r is the reservation at that time; S_t is a measure of search effort; and the X_t terms are the determinants of the demand for an individual's labor.

Except for these labor-demand factors, the other determinants of reservations wages outlined in the foregoing discussion are omitted from equation (7). For example, many of these factors can be considered endogenous with respect to reservation wages, such as the many sources of nonwage income ranging from government programs to illegal activities. The same can be said about earlier spells of nonemployment.[6] Including these endogenous variables as determinants in the model would lead either to serious biases or to a simultaneous-equations system with serious identification problems. For these and other reasons, the goals of this paper are simpler: to compare the reservation wages of young blacks and whites, controlling for differences in demand-side factors and to evaluate the effects of these reservation wages on the subsequent wages and nonemployment spells for each group.

Nonetheless, certain other determinants of reservation wages are examined below in order to explain differences in responses by the same individual to different reservation-wage questions. Summary and tabular data provide evidence, for instance, on occupational expectations and work horizons. The effect of nonwage job characteristics are also considered, since the surveys used below asked respondents to choose among different reservation wages. Also introduced is some outside evidence on the role of nonwage income.

It should also be noted here that equation (5) is essentially a demand function; and this recursive model achieves its identification by including direct observations of the reservation wage rather than of the received wage as the independent variable in the duration equation. The reservation wage itself is a function of the expected demand-side determinants of duration and subsequent wages, but not of subsequent duration or wages per se, thereby ensuring its exogeneity in equations (5) and (6).

The above equations are estimated separately for blacks and whites in all cases. Racial differentials in such variables as reservations wages, when controlling for personal characteristics in X_i, are obtained by using estimated coefficients from the equations for whites with mean characteristics of blacks to obtain predicted reservations wages for whites having the same characteristics as blacks. The differences between these predicted measures and the actual ones for blacks are considered estimates of the racial differential.

Most of the econometric issues associated with estimating equations (5) through (7) are discussed below in the presentation of the empirical results. But a few of the more salient problems, as well as the methods for dealing with them, deserve mention here.

For instance, in comparing the reservation wages of blacks and whites, it is crucially important that the list of determinants of the demand for an individual's labor, represented by X_i, be reasonably complete. If it is not, unobserved characteristics that are positively correlated with wages and employment but negatively correlated with being black may bias downward any measure of the black-white differential in reservation wages.

To address this problem, we include estimates of various specifications of equation (7). In some, the X_t terms reflect a set of specific determinants of wages and employment, including such human capital variables as age, experience, schooling, and "knowledge of the world of work";[7] background variables, such as household income and the presence of a library card at home; and other individual characteristics, such as region, residence in an urban area, and marital status. But since this set is bound to be incomplete, wages on the most recent job or weeks worked over the past year are used instead as controls in other equations. The former serves as a proxy for offered wages, and the latter, as a proxy for offer probabilities. Of course, received wages and weeks worked reflect expected wages and nonemployment durations, which are themselves conditional on past reservation wages. These variables are therefore instrumented on the exogenous X_t and appear only as predicted values in equation (7).

These predicted values allow the inclusion in the equations of individuals who would otherwise report wages as missing due to their lack of employment in the previous year. But since the two predicted variables are functions of the same underlying determinants, they are too highly correlated to be included together in any single equation; they therefore appear in separate versions of equation (7). The underlying X_t variables appear separately as well for purposes of identification, and the predicted wages appear in equation (6) as controls for the offered-wage distribution. Weeks worked do not appear in the equations, since wages are conditional on an offer having been received; proxies for offer probabilities are therefore not relevant here.

As for durations of subsequent spells represented in equation (6), the coefficient on the reservation wage is likely to be downward biased by the positive correlation between unobserved characteristics and reservation-wage measures and by the negative correlation between those characteristics and the durations of spells. In fact, this downward bias was serious enough to produce theoretically incorrect negative coefficients on reservation wages for whites in some versions of that equation.

It should also be noted that the source of heterogeneity in equation (5) is the correlation between unobserved characteristics and reservation wages and durations, whereas in equation (7) it is their correlation with reservation wages and race. Thus, the controls that are appropriate in the two equations may differ. In fact, an expanded group of X_t variables, described below, enters directly in equation (5); the inclusion of that group in the equation is the most successful way to rid it of downward bias. On the other hand, predicted wages and weeks worked were more successful in dealing with unobserved racial differences in equation (7). In short, the results reported below are sometimes based on equations that use different controls for labor demand; these are pointed out in each case.

A further source of downward bias in the estimated coefficients on reservation wages in equations (5) and (6) is the error that may exist in self-reported measures of reservation wages. This possibility could have very serious implications for much of the empirical work presented below, since differences in mean reservation wages are an important finding that could be undermined if the self-reported measures are not valid determinants of behavior. In fact, several of the reservation-wage measures reported below yield somewhat different results on the relative reservation wages of blacks and whites. But by estimating equations (5) and (6) separately for each of the reported measures, we can test their effects on behavior and thereby determine their "validity" or relative degrees of error as shown in section 1.4.

We must also consider some of the potential selection biases inherent in the analysis as well as the sampling techniques employed. Since spells of nonemployment observed prior or subsequent to the survey date existed only for those who were nonemployed at that time, the survey does not capture previous nonemployment spells for those currently employed and nonemployed, raising several selection issues. First, Akerlof and Main (1980) have shown that individuals with multiple spells of nonemployment in a year account for a great deal of observed nonemployment. The focus in the present analysis on one spell per person thus overlooks the issue of multiple spells. Second, Kaitz (1970) has pointed out that omission of previous completed spells can bias the estimated mean duration of spells in two directions: A "length" bias exists whereby short spells are less likely to be observed than longer ones, creating an upward bias in mean duration; and an "interruption" bias also exists whereby only a truncated part of any given spell is observed, creating a downward bias. This issue is addressed below by comparing summary evidence of current spells with evidence of previous spells that are calculated from retrospective employment histories in the NLS surveys.

Selection with respect to employment status can also bias the coefficients of all of the estimated equations. Heckman (1979) demonstrated that the correlation between the error term and the regressors of an equation induced by sampling depends on the correlation between the determinants of the sampling variable and those of the dependent variable of the analysis. Since individuals experiencing short nonemployment spells are more likely to be currently employed than those having long spells of nonemployment, spell duration can be considered a determinant of observed employment status; and since reservation wages are the hypothesized determinants of spell duration, they are also determinants of employment status. Thus, the dependent variables of equations (5) and (7) are themselves the determinants of the samples used to estimate them, and the correlation bias described above may be quite severe.

To deal with these potential biases, the analysis presents the reservation wages of both the employed and nonemployed in each racial group. The analysis also employs the inverse Mills ratio to correct for potential selection problems in some of the wage and reservation-wage equations that appear below.

A few other sampling issues remain. Students are omitted from all the estimates reported below because their labor market experiences often reflect a different set of factors than those of nonstudents. Results not reported here, however, show similar ratios of reservation wages to received wages among students and nonstudents of each racial group in the NLS; thus, the omission of students is unlikely to be a major source of selection bias.

The samples here include some individuals who had not searched for work in the month before the survey, since the discussion above indicates that search theory can be applied to those who are not always actively looking for work. Nevertheless, the relevant questions in the NLS were asked only of individuals who had searched in the past month or who intended to search in the coming year; those permanently out of the labor force are thus not included here.

A final sampling issue is the oversampling of low-income whites in the NLS. Because we are interested in estimating relationships for the black and white populations rather than those nonrandomly selected samples, and because estimated relationshps may vary across income groups, all the estimates below are weighted by sample weights to produce populationwide estimates. Although this technique may induce some heteroscedasticity, which would bias the estimated standard errors, the coefficients are unbiased estimates of populationwide relationships. The decision to weight the samples rather than stratify them by income was based on the small sample sizes used below.

As noted above, two major data sets have been used in estimating the equations: the youth cohort of the NLS and the NBER Survey of Inner-City Black Youth. The NLS conducted a nationwide survey of young men and women aged 14 through 21 in 1979. The oversampling of racial minorities in this survey yields a sufficiently large sample of young black men (1,380) for comparison, with the sample of young white men (3,081). Since the NLS also oversamples low-income whites, all the estimates here are weighted by the sample weights to achieve a true nationwide sample within each racial group.

Among the variables included in the NLS data set are reported reservation wages, search effort in the past month, and retrospective histories that give starting and ending dates for each period of employment. The 1979 and 1980 panels are both available. Thus, for individuals who were nonemployed at the time of the 1979 survey, the durations of subsequent spells and wages later received on the next job are available in the 1980 survey; these appear as the dependent variables of equations (5) and (6). Durations for previous spells are within each panel. The NLS also provides extensive information on family background and personal characteristics. Finally, occupational aspirations for the future as well as occupations currently sought are useful indicators of the accuracy of individuals' labor market expectations.

The NBER survey was conducted between November 1979 and May 1980 among 2,400 young black men, aged 16 through 24, who were living in the inner-cities of Boston, Chicago, and Philadelphia. The interviews were limited to inhabitants of city blocks with at least 70 percent black residents and 30 percent families having incomes below the poverty line. The questions in the survey focused on the daily activities of both the employed and nonemployed; their family backgrounds; their job-search behavior and experiences, including reservation wages, number of rejected offers, offered wages, and time spent and methods used while searching; their retrospective work histories for the preceding 12 months; their income sources; their participation in illegal activities; and their alcohol or drug use. The usefulness of the NBER survey as a supplement to the NLS, which provides the bulk of the black-white comparisons, lies in its focus on northern inner-city blacks, who experience the greatest youth employment problems in the nation; the direct comparability of many of the questions in the NBER survey to those in the NLS (after which some of the former were modeled); and the inclusion in the NBER survey of other questions, not duplicated elsewhere, that investigate factors that may explain the unemployment situation among young blacks. Together, the two surveys therefore allow a good comparison of young blacks and whites nationwide, as well as an additional look at a group of young blacks whose employment problems are especially severe.

1.3 Relative Reservation Wages for Blacks and Whites: Controlling for Demand Characteristics

This section presents empirical evidence from the NLS and NBER survey on the relative reservation-wage levels of young blacks and whites. Tables 1.1 and 1.2 present summary evidence comparing various reported reservation-wage measures to the received wages of young blacks and whites. These comparisons provide a crude measure of reservation wages relative to offered wages, for which we have no data. The next two tables indicate the distributions of occupations sought and held by these groups and their relationships to the reported reservation wages. They show that individuals report quite different reservation wages according to the characteristics of the jobs to which they pertain. Some differences in reservation wages also appear to result from differences in the formats of the questions used to gauge them, as decribed below. Later in this section, tables 1.5, 1.6, and 1.7 show results from the equations in which wages, weeks worked, and other characteristics control for a broad range of demand-side factors that determine the relative reservation wages of blacks and whites.

Tables 1.1 and 1.2 present summary statistics on various reported reservation-wage and received-wage measures in the NBER survey and the NLS. The first table shows the means and standard deviations of received wages and reservation wages for jobs the respondents were seeking or aspired to more generally; the histograms below also present the full distributions of many of these variables. The second table presents frequencies of the reservation wages for specific jobs, such as dishwashing and factory work, that were designated in the survey.

The reservation wages for the NLS data presented in table 1.1 reflect responses to the question, "What would the wage (or salary) have to be for you to be willing to take it?" which follows the question, "What type of work have you been looking for?" or "What type of work will you be looking for?" among those who intended to seek work in the coming year. The reported reservation wage is therefore the "job sought," where that job was allowed to vary across individuals. The responses were also open-ended: Respondents could state any wage rate they wished instead of answering "yes" or "no" to specific rates listed in the survey. The questions were asked of both the employed and the nonemployed who were seeking work or who intended to seek work that year, and the questions were asked in both the 1979 and 1980 surveys.

The reservation wages for the NBER data in table 1.1 also refer to jobs that vary across individuals. One question states, "Suppose you were offered a job of the type that you are looking for," and then states different travel times that would be necessary to get to and from work. For each time, the respondent was asked whether he would accept the job at $2.50 per hour and then at rates that increased by .50 each until the respondent found an acceptable one. Thus, unlike the NLS version of this question, the one in the NBER survey used a closed rather than open-ended format. The NBER data for "job sought" reservation wages in table 1.1 indicate the wages chosen at the lowest travel time of 30 minutes.

Another series of questions in the NBER survey read: "Say that for some reason you *had* to get (a job/another job) right now . . . what would be the best job you think you could get?" "How much per hour do you think you would earn on that job?" "If you were offered that

Table 1.1 **Means and Standard Deviations of Reservation Wages and Received Wages; NLS and NBER Samples**

	NLS					
	Reservation Wages for Job Sought		Received Wages; Most Recent Job		Ratio of Reservation to Received Wages	
	Whites	Blacks	Whites	Blacks	Whites	Blacks
Nonemployed, 1979–80	4.59 (1.96)	4.47 (2.21)	4.75 (2.76)	4.00 (2.20)	.966	1.118
North	4.73 (1.85)	4.51 (1.77)	5.05 (2.96)	3.91 (1.88)	.937	1.153
South	4.31 (2.22)	4.45 (2.54)	4.02 (1.98)	4.07 (2.45)	1.072	1.093
Employed, 1979–80	6.01 (3.05)	5.40 (2.95)	5.13 (2.25)	4.26 (1.86)	1.172	1.268
Full Year	6.18 (3.06)	5.29 (2.36)	5.32 (2.26)	4.30 (1.88)	1.162	1.226
Part Year	5.71 (3.00)	5.66 (3.83)	4.76 (2.16)	4.19 (1.82)	1.120	1.351
Nonemployed, 1979	4.39 (1.95)	4.23 (2.41)	4.23 (2.97)	3.85 (2.41)	1.038	1.099

	Reservation Wages for Job Sought		Received Wages; First Job in Subsequent Year	
	Whites	Blacks	Whites	Blacks
Nonemployed, 1979 Work in Subsequent Year	4.36 (1.86)	4.20 (2.60)	4.73 (2.37)	4.33 (2.03)

	NBER, Blacks Only			
	Reservation Wages			Received Wages
	For Job Sought	For Best Job Attainable	For Any Job	Most Recent Job
Nonemployed	3.61 (1.26)	3.64 (1.58)	3.40 (1.11)	3.98 (1.98)
Employed	4.44 (1.43)	4.59 (1.85)	3.98 (1.19)	4.34 (1.52)

	Ratio of Reservation Wages to Received Wages		
	For Job Sought	For Best Job Attainable	For Any Job
Nonemployed	.907	.915	.854
Employed	1.023	1.058	.917

Note: Only nonstudents included in both the NLS and NBER samples in all tables. Total sample sizes in the 1979–80 NLS are 1,599 for all employed whites with wages and 1,130 for those with reservation wages. Comparable numbers are 350 and 491 for nonemployed blacks. Sample weights are used in all calculations using the NLS. In the NBER Survey, sample sizes are 475 for employed and 821 for nonemployed young blacks. Reservation wages in the NLS are defined only for those who sought employment in the past month or intended to seek it in the next year. Wages received in both surveys are for those who were employed in the past year.

job tommorow would you take it if it paid $————?" In the last question, the same wage rates were used as those in the question in the preceding paragraph. Although one might expect the 30-minute travel time designated in the earlier question or the stipulation of "having to get a job right now" in the latter to bias the responses in different ways, the responses were generally quite similar.

A final question asked the respondent to list the "lowest hourly pay you'd be willing to take on any job right now," and these responses are also included in table 1.1. As was the case with reservation wages for "sought job" and "best job," responses to this question were open-ended but directly followed the others in sequence. All questions were asked of all individuals, both employed and nonemployed, in the sample.

Several interesting findings emerge from table 1.1. Perhaps the most striking is that the reported reservation wages for jobs sought by blacks in the NLS are similar to those reported by whites in an absolute sense, but blacks' are generally higher relative to their previously or currently received wages than those of whites. For the total sample of nonemployed, the ratio of reservation wages to received wages is 15.2 percent higher among blacks than whites. This black- white difference is higher in the North than in the South; but even for in the South, the ratio for the black youths is well above that for northern whites, who constitute three-fourths of the total white sample.

Of course, we would prefer to have data on offered wages rather than received wages for this comparison, but the former were not observed. As mentioned above, received wages are endogenous with respect to reservation wages because of the truncation of the offered-wage distribution from below by previous reservation wages—the higher the previous reservation wage, the higher the received wage and the lower the ratio of the two. Thus, the ratio of reservation wages to offered wages is likely to be even higher among blacks. These measures also ignore blacks' lower probability of receiving offers; therefore, the level of reservation wages relative to the overall demand for blacks is presumably even higher.

Most of the analysis in this paper concerns only those currently nonemployed, since only they had the spells of nonemployment at the time of or subsequent to our observations on reservation wages. But as noted above, selection based on employment status creates the possibility that the individuals with lower reservation wages who had shorter nonemployment spells in the past are excluded from the sample, and that the magnitude of this effect could differ between blacks and whites. The evidence presented below of shorter previous spells among the empoyed than among the nonemployed raises the possibility that selection based on employment status may be an important source of bias.

Table 1.1 also includes, therefore, the reservation and received wages of employed individuals in the NLS who were seeking or intended to seek new employment. Since we are primarily interested in the effects of reservation wages on nonemployment duration, the reservation wages of employed individuals who only do on-the-job search and who have not been nonemployed in the recent past are less relevant here. It is useful, however, to distinguish between those who have had nonemployment spells in the previous year and those who have not among those currently employed. Also, an individual's current reservation wage is not necessarily unchanged from that which determined his previous nonemployment spell, but at least the current one provides a useful first approximation to the unobserved one from the past.

The results show that the ratio of reservation wages to received wages is higher among employed blacks than among employed whites, especially among those who had nonemployment spells in the previous year. Thus, the omission of these individuals and their spells from the analysis does not appear to induce a major selection bias with regard to reservation wages.

Table 1.1 also shows that the standard deviations of received wages among both the employed and the nonemployed, as well as their means, are generally lower for blacks. Thus, the apparently higher reservation wages of blacks cannot be attributed to a higher variance in their offered-wage distributions, despite the lower means.

Finally, the reservation wages of the 1979 samples, and particularly of those who gained employment in the subsequent year, can be compared to the wages at which they gained that employment. Although a comparison of such means provides no evidence on correlations between the two measures, the comparison is at least useful as a first step toward evaluating the validity and effectiveness of self-reported reservation wages. For if these reservation wages are truncating distributions of later wages from below, we would expect the mean received wages to be somewhat higher than the reservation wages. In fact, the results here show this to be true for both groups, though the difference is not significant for blacks. Thus, either the validity of reponses or blacks' abilities to obtain these wages is more questionable for them than for whites.

Before moving on to examine other results from the NBER survey, let us briefly consider the full distributions of wages and reservation wages for blacks and whites, as well as the summary statistics presented in table 1.1. These distributions for the nonemployed, presented in figures 1.1–1.6, show that the ratios of reservation wages to received wages are higher for blacks than for whites at the medians of their respective distributions as well as at the means. The medians are 4.00 for the reservation wages and 3.00 for the received wages of nonem-

ployed blacks, and 4.00 and 3.50, respectively, for nonemployed whites.
The distributions also show that few of the jobs sought would be accepted at below the minimum wage ($2.90 in 1979 and $3.10 in 1980)
by either group, although a small fraction of received wages falls below
the minimum for each group.

Furthermore, the distributions of received wages are more prominently spiked at the minimum wage among blacks than among whites.
If this difference is true of the actual offered-wage distributions as well,
any movement of the reservation wages of blacks above the minimum
will have correspondingly greater effects on their nonemployment durations. More specifically, a greater part of blacks' wage distribution

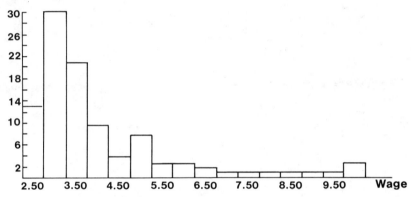

Fig. 1.1   NBER Nonemployed Blacks' Received Wages for Most Recent Job

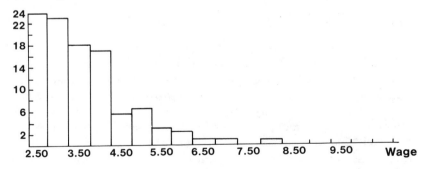

Fig. 1.2   NBER Nonemployed Blacks' Reservation Wages for Sought
Jobs

Percentage

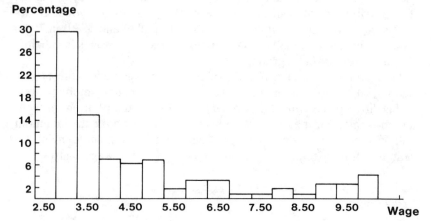

Fig. 1.3   NLS Nonemployed Blacks' Received Wages for Most Recent Job

Percentage

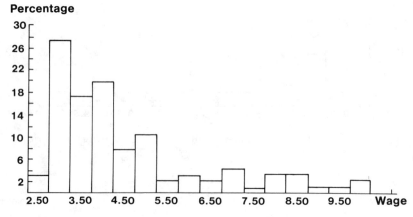

Fig. 1.4   NLS Nonemployed Blacks' Reservation Wages for Sought Jobs

will be truncated by the reservation wage, leaving a smaller fraction of the distribution that is acceptable. By differentiating equation (2), we can see this more clearly, namely, $dP_{NE}/dw^r = -\pi f(w^r)$, where P_{NE} is the transition probability, w^r is the reservation wage, and π is the offer probability. A more prominently spiked offered-wage distribution for blacks means a higher $f(w^r)$ for them and thus a larger effect on transitions and durations. This result is confirmed by estimates from the duration equations for blacks and whites below, which show larger effects of reservation wages on the durations of nonemployment spells

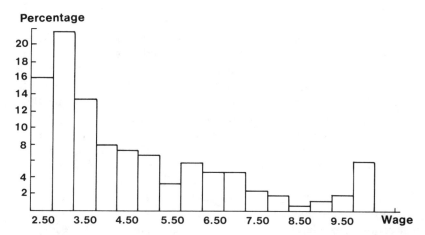

Fig. 1.5   NLS Nonemployed Whites' Received Wages for Most Recent Job

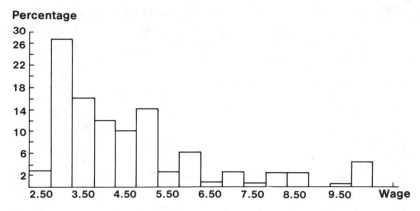

Fig. 1.6   NLS Nonemployed Whites' Reservation Wages for Sought Jobs

among blacks. The higher spiking at the minimum for blacks also confirms the evidence presented above that the variance of the offered-wage distribution appears to be lower for them and cannot be responsible for their relatively higher reservation wage.

Thus far, the evidence that has emerged is fairly consistent in indicating that the reservation wages for the sought jobs of young blacks in the NLS are higher relative to their received wages than are those of young whites. Some puzzling contradictions arise, however, in comparing the results of the NBER survey in table 1.1 with the reservation wages for specific jobs in both surveys in table 1.2. In table 1.1, the reservation wages for "sought jobs," "best jobs," and "any jobs" of young inner-city blacks are well below those of blacks and whites in the NLS, especially relative to their received wages. Furthermore, histograms on the reservation wages of the nonemployed in the NBER sample indicate that a substantial portion of the youths are willing to accept their sought jobs at below the minimum wage and that their median reservation wages are close to the minimum wage at $3.00 per hour. That the medians and means differ quite substantially here is no surprise, given the spiking of the wage distributions around the minimum and the large right-hand tails.

Other inconsistencies appear upon consideration of table 1.2. This table presents reservation wages for a list of specific jobs. In this case the format of the questions is identical in the two surveys, though the list of jobs considered in the NLS is longer. The question reads, "If you were offered a job as a ———, would you accept it at ———?" In each case the wage rates considered are $2.50, $3.50, and $5.00 an hour. Table 1.2 presents the percentages of the nonemployed who were willing to accept these jobs at each wage rate in the two surveys. Since this set of questions was asked only in the 1979 NLS, responses to the question on the job sought for that year have been rescaled to the same format and are presented here as well. The same has been done for the job-sought question in the NBER survey and for the questions on the most recently received wage in both surveys.

Several strong findings appear in table 1.2. Perhaps most important is the much greater willingness of blacks than of whites in the NLS to accept each of the specific low-skilled jobs, even though there is no such greater willingness to accept the sought jobs. This is true among those in the North as well as in the South. It is even true when comparing these reservation wages to received wages for each group. Among whites and especially among blacks, a fairly substantial number of respondents were willing to accept these jobs at below the minimum wage, even though this was not the case for either group with respect to their sought jobs.

Comparisons between the different reservation-wage measures for each group produce some interesting findings. Among whites, the cumulative percentage of respondents willing to accept such jobs as factory or supermarket work at $3.50 or $5.00 per hour is relatively close to the percentage for sought jobs at those rates, although virtually no one would accept his sought job at $2.50. But among blacks, no such convergence occurs: The percentage accepting work remains lower at each wage level for the sought jobs. The discrepancy is strongest among blacks in the South, whose reservation wages for sought jobs are higher, but for the specified jobs lower, than those of blacks in the North.

Table 1.2   **Reservation Wages for Specific Jobs: Percentage Willing to Accept Work at a Given Hourly Wage or Less, NLS and NBER Samples**

| | NLS Whites | | | | | | | | |
| | Total | | | North | | | South | | |
	$2.50	$3.50	$5.00	$2.50	$3.50	$5.00	$2.50	$3.50	$5.00
Sought Job, 1979	.02	.41	.70	.02	.40	.67	.01	.42	.76
Neighborhood									
Cleaning	.25	.44	.65	.21	.42	.59	.35	.50	.81
Cleaning	.18	.38	.62	.12	.31	.55	.32	.53	.77
Dishwashing	.17	.34	.60	.13	.28	.55	.26	.47	.68
Factory	.22	.46	.70	.20	.44	.67	.28	.52	.78
Supermarket	.17	.39	.67	.16	.35	.63	.21	.50	.78
Received Wage,									
Most Recent Job	.07	.59	.79	.06	.54	.76	.09	.72	.88

| | NLS Blacks | | | | | | | | |
| | | | | North | | | South | | |
	$2.50	$3.50	$5.00	$2.50	$3.50	$5.00	$2.50	$3.50	$5.00
Sought Job, 1979	.03	.45	.75	.03	.41	.74	.03	.50	.77
Neighborhood									
Cleaning	.31	.55	.79	.31	.54	.77	.31	.55	.79
Cleaning	.36	.60	.77	.33	.53	.68	.39	.65	.83
Dishwashing	.36	.60	.75	.36	.55	.73	.39	.68	.81
Factory	.35	.71	.86	.38	.66	.82	.33	.76	.89
Supermarket	.44	.69	.84	.40	.61	.78	.48	.76	.89
Received Wage,									
Most Recent Job	.16	.60	.82	.19	.60	.80	.12	.58	.83

| | NBER Blacks | | |
	$2.50	$3.50	$5.00
Sought Job	.24	.65	.93
Dishwashing	.15	.47	.85
Factory Labor	.26	.61	.93
Supermarket	.19	.59	.89
Received Wage,			
Most Recent Job	.11	.57	.84

Note: NLS samples are limited to the 1979 panel of the survey, since questions for specific jobs appear only in that year. Only the nonemployed are included here. NLS sample sizes are 241 for all whites and 160 for those with received wages; for all blacks they are 186 and 90 for those with wages; for blacks in the NBER survey they are 821 and 503, respectively. Reservation wages for sought job and received wages for the most recent job have been rescaled from the continuous to the discrete form.

Finally, some demands for compensating differentials can be seen among both blacks and whites in the preference of both groups for factory or supermarket jobs over such unpleasant, dead-end, or menial jobs as dishwashing or cleaning positions.

The NBER survey data show a greater consistency between reservations wages for sought jobs and those for specified jobs in factories and supermarkets. The same relative dislike as in the NLS data of such jobs as dishwashing is also evident. But reservation wages for sought jobs are lower here than for jobs like dishwashing. Furthermore, a comparison of the reservation wages for specific jobs between the inner-city blacks in the NBER survey and blacks in the NLS shows that the absolute willingness of inner-city blacks to accept these jobs is quite comparable to that of northern blacks in the NLS. If anything, the reservation-wage rates are somewhat higher for the inner-city groups, especially at the $2.50 mark. In any event, the relatively comparable responses of northern blacks across the two surveys when the question formats were the same indicate the crucial importance of these formats in determining the different responses received.

To summarize, the results from the NLS show that reported reservation wages for jobs sought relative to previously received wages are higher among blacks than among whites, whereas reservation wages for specified low-skilled jobs appear to be lower among blacks. The latter result is generally consistent with evidence from the NBER survey, in which the responses to similarly phrased questions show reservation wages for specified jobs among inner-city black youths to be somewhat higher than those of northern blacks more generally. The reservation wages of both groups indicate a demand for compensating differentials for jobs considered menial or unpleasant.

A few hypotheses will be posed here to explain why responses differ across various reservation-wage questions, and some empirical evidence will demonstrate the usefulness of those hypotheses.

Two hypotheses regarding differences in the reported reservation wages are based on the two major differences between the questions asked in each case. The first attributes the differences in the wages to differences between open-ended and closed formats in the survey questions. All but one of the NBER questions on reservation wages asked respondents whether they would accept specific dollar amounts, rather than asking them to designate their own dollar figure; and the one question that did not follow this format directly followed the others in sequence. Accordingly, tables 1.1 and 1.2 show fairly consistent responses to these questions in the NBER survey. By contrast, the "job sought" question in the NLS is open-ended, while the one for specific jobs uses specific dollar figures. The inconsistencies between responses to these two kinds of questions are much stronger in the NLS, for whites and especially for blacks, than they are in the NBER data.

One explanation for this may be that open-ended questions allow individuals to confound their wage expectations with their reservation wages.[8] This is supported by the fact that explicit wage expectations were asked of individuals in the NBER survey, and responses to these questions were substantially higher than responses to the reservation-wage questions. In fact, the mean wage expected on the "best job" obtainable by nonemployed respondents in the NBER survey is $4.88, which is substantially closer in value to the reported reservation wages of blacks in the NLS than are the reservation wages for sought jobs reported in the NBER survey. The fact that inconsistencies in the NLS are higher for blacks, especially for southern blacks, than for whites may indicate either a greater degree of confounding on their part or a greater degree of expectational error on their part.

The second hypothesis attributes differences in reported reservation wages to differences in the nature of the jobs being considered. Questions probing reservation wages for sought jobs allow those jobs to vary among individuals and racial groups. The distribution of those jobs for each group relative to what they can obtain may thus be an important determinant of reservation wages relative to received wages for each group. The jobs sought also differ from the specified jobs, which are primarily low-wage and low-skilled positions.

Furthermore, different dimensions of the various sought or specified jobs may have different implications for the relevant reservation wage. On the one hand, unpleasant nonwage characteristics of jobs that might also be considered menial may lead to higher reservation wages for those jobs; this appears to be the case for whites and blacks within the NLS as well as for blacks within the NBER survey, all of whom are more willing to accept factory or supermarket work than dishwashing or cleaning work. On the other hand, jobs sought may command higher reservation wages than low-skilled jobs for a number of reasons. For one thing, the low-skilled jobs may be regarded as more temporary because of their dead-end nature, whereas sought or desired jobs may be regarded as more permanent. As noted above, theoretical treatments of reservation wages within the job-search literature have emphasized the importance of the time horizon and its positive effects on reservation wages; and empirical evidence has shown that turnover rates are higher and employment durations lower in low-wage service occupations than in other occupations.[9]

Another reason why sought or desired jobs may carry higher reservation wages than low-skilled jobs is that higher wages may be regarded as more appropriate and therefore more equitable for the former category of jobs. A long tradition exists within the literature of labor economics that emphasizes the importance of traditional wages norms for jobs and considerations of equity and relative position with regard to comparable workers.[10] An understanding among youths that low-skilled jobs generally pay low wages may occasionally lead them to accept those jobs, particularly if they regard those jobs as being temporary and if they need the earnings temporarily while they continue to search or to aspire to longer-term positions for which they will demand higher pay. Of course, the youths' willingness to accept the low-skilled jobs even temporarily diminishes greatly when they consider those jobs unpleasant or menial, as in the case of dishwashing and cleaning.

It is therefore quite possible that the higher reservation wages in the NLS for jobs sought may reflect the characteristics of those jobs as well as a confounding of expectations with reservation wages. Again, one must ask why the willingness to accept temporary jobs would be greater among blacks in the NLS than among either blacks in the NBER survey or whites in the NLS. One answer may be that the dislike of dead-end or menial jobs is the relatively stronger effect for whites and northern, inner-city blacks. Or perhaps the expectations of blacks nationwide (including in the South) regarding attainable jobs or pay at those jobs may be more unrealistic than those of whites and of northern, inner-city blacks. Clearly, therefore, expectations about wages and jobs attainable are an important part of both of the hypotheses above, although their implications for reservation wages differ somewhat between the two explanations.

We now consider some empirical evidence on the issues of occupational expectations and time horizons, as well as their effects on the various reservation-wage measures. Table 1.3 presents distributions for jobs held, sought, and aspired to at age 35 by nonemployed blacks and whites in the 1979 NLS. Distributions for jobs held before the current spell of nonemployment as well as for those attained after the spells are both listed. Occupational aspirations are reflected by responses to the question, "What do you hope to be doing at age 35?"

Table 1.3   **Frequencies of Occupations Sought and Held by the Nonemployed, NLS**

	Job Previously Held		Job Sought		Job Attained		Job Aspired to at Age 35	
	Whites	Blacks	Whites	Blacks	Whites	Blacks	Whites	Blacks
Not Specified	.318	.451	.504	.560	.325	.352	.165	.104
White-Collar	.045	.059	.075	.062	.042	.110	.529	.556
Crafts and Operatives	.339	.185	.262	.248	.397	.248	.252	.290
Laborer and Service	.298	.305	.160	.130	.236	.290	.054	.050

Note: These are weighted frequencies for the 1979 panel of the NLS. "Job previously held" refers to the 1979 survey, and "job attained" refers to responses from the 1980 survey by those nonemployed in 1979.

The results show that the distributions of jobs sought and aspired to by young blacks and whites are remarkably similar, but the distributions of jobs held are not. More specifically, blacks are more heavily represented in the laborer and service categories as well as the white-collar category (mostly clerical), whereas whites are much more heavily represented in the crafts and operative positions. Since the latter two categories generally include more highly skilled and highly paid positions than the former, it appears that the occupational expectations of young blacks are higher than those of young whites relative to what each group ultimately obtains. This view is consistent with one presented over ten years ago by Goodwin (1973), who argued that blacks and the poor wanted the same kind of work as everyone else did, but they had no means of achieving their occupational aspirations.

Having demonstrated the relatively higher occupational expectations of young blacks, we must still seek to explain how those expectations affect their responses to the various reservation-wage questions. Table 1.4 presents the reservation wages of nonemployed blacks and whites in the NLS for jobs sought and jobs specified, disaggregated by job sought. As before, reservation wages for jobs sought appear in continuous form and as the percentage accepting work at $3.50 per hour or less; reservation wages for specified jobs appear only in the latter form.

The results show that the reservation wages of young blacks for jobs sought increase quite dramatically when the job in question moves beyond the laborer and service category. The percentage of blacks willing to accept jobs at $3.50 or less drops from over 80 percent when the job sought is from the laborer and service category to 40 percent

Table 1.4   Mean Reservation Wages by Jobs Sought of the Nonemployed, NLS-B

| | Job Sought | | | | | | | |
| | Not Specified | | White-Collar | | Crafts and Operative | | Laborer and Service | |
	Whites	Blacks	Whites	Blacks	Whites	Blacks	Whites	Blacks
Reservation Wage for Job Sought	4.51	4.49	4.04	4.28	4.76	4.24	3.62	3.28
Percentage Accepting at < $3.50/Hour								
Job Sought	.365	.409	.529	.322	.422	.371	.495	.813
Neighborhood Cleaning	.383	.558	.539	.430	.515	.543	.491	.515
Cleaning	.368	.629	.337	.118	.438	.592	.344	.669
Dishwashing	.344	.645	.303	.413	.317	.533	.400	.688
Factory	.479	.681	.479	.457	.505	.789	.348	.791

Note: Sample sizes are the same as those in table 1.2. All means are weighted.

or under in the other categories. Among whites this decline is also evident, though much less pronounced. The willingness of blacks and whites to accept the specified low-skilled jobs also shows some sensitivity to the jobs they claim to be seeking. In particular, those seeking white-collar jobs are less likely to accept specified low-skilled jobs than those seeking other jobs. But the differences in these results across the job-sought categories are far less striking than they are among blacks for the reservation wages attached specifically to the jobs sought.

This relationship becomes even stronger when one compares reservation-wage measures within each category of jobs sought. Generally, those who seek laborer or service employment have reservation wages for those sought jobs comparable to or lower than their reservation wages for the specified low-skilled jobs. But among blacks, those who seek other jobs have higher reservation wages for sought jobs than for specific ones. It is clear, then, that the jobs sought by the black non-employed affect their reservation wages for those positions, although many of those who are seeking skilled blue-collar or white-collar jobs at higher wages seem willing to accept the specified low-skilled jobs at lower wages.

The hypothesis that blacks will accept lower wages for the specified jobs because they regard them as being more temporary cannot be tested directly, but the fact that they regard them as temporary can be demonstrated on its own. The NBER survey included questions about respondents' intended time horizons for their most recently held jobs. One question asked, "Did/Do you regard this job as being long-term or temporary?" and another asked, "How long did/do you intend to stay on this job?" Table 1.5 presents responses to these questions for the different occupational groupings in the NBER sample. Turnover rates, defined as the percentage of respondents who lost or left their jobs in the previous year, are also presented for these groupings. As expected, the results show that laborer and service jobs are more often regarded as being temporary by those who hold them than are other jobs; and intended employment durations for those jobs are shorter as well. Turnover rates, which are more objectively defined, also show higher rates of movement out of (and therefore shorter employment durations in) laborer and service jobs. The evidence is thus consistent with the claim that black youths are less choosy about certain low-skilled jobs than they are about others they are seeking because they often expect the former to be temporary.

Of course, none of these results demonstrates that the responses to the open-ended reservation-wage questions for sought jobs in the NLS are *truly* reservations as opposed to just expectations about wages. It remains to be shown which of the reservation wages listed here has the greatest power to predict subsequent durations of nonemployment and wages received. This issue will be addressed in section 1.4.

Table 1.5   Time Horizons and Turnover Rates for Jobs by Occupation, NBER Blacks

	White-Collar	Crafts and Operative	Laborer and Service
Perceptions of Long-Term Potential of Job			
Long-Term	.39	.40	.29
Temporary	.53	.56	.65
Don't Know	.07	.04	.06
Intended Employment Durations:			
< 3 months	.14	.14	.19
3–6 months	.08	.12	.10
6–12 months	.02	.03	.04
Indefinite	.67	.66	.56
Turnover Rates	.64	.66	.72

Note: Calculations are for all who had employment in past year. Turnover rates are defined as the percentage of all with employment who lost or left their jobs in the past year.

For now, the analysis has shown that reservation wages for jobs sought by young blacks are higher relative to the wages they ultimately receive than are those of young whites, while the reservation wages of blacks for specific low-skilled jobs appear to be lower than those of their white counterparts. The comparisons between means (or frequencies) of reservation wages and received wages are a crude first attempt to judge the level of reservation wages of young blacks and whites relative to the potential offered wages of each group in the labor market, where offered wages reflect the demand for labor facing each group. These comparisons are of only limited use here, however.

For one thing, the comparisons include controls for offered wages but not for offer probabilities. Since black-white wage differentials have declined in recent years while employment differentials have risen, omitting the latter from the controls is likely to downward-bias the estimated black-white differentials in reservation wages. Furthermore, the endogeneity of received wages with respect to reservation wages is also likely to bias downward any measure of the latter relative to the former. This bias may be compounded by the omission from these samples of youths without any employment in the previous year, a status that may have been caused for some by their high reservation wages. On the other hand, the ratio of reservation to received wages may not be constant across all individuals within each racial group. In particular, if this ratio declines as received wages rise, the ratio of the means for whites may understate the true ratio among those whites whose characteristics are comparable to those of blacks. Thus, the black-white differential in this ratio may reflect an upward bias as well, and the net effects of these downward and upward biases are unclear.

This analysis therefore estimates different specifications of equation (7) above for blacks and for whites. These specifications are then used to calculate racial differences in reservation wages in the following manner:

$$\Delta w^r = \bar{w}^r_B - \beta_w \bar{X}_B = (\beta_B - \beta_w) \bar{X}_B$$

where the B terms are the estimated coefficients of equation (7) and the X terms are either predicted wages, weeks worked, or their underlying determinants, as described in section 1.2.[11]

The equations used to predict wages and weeks worked appear in table 1.A.1 of the appendix. Those equations were estimated using OI S and included both currently employed and nonemployed individuals in the sample. Because of the large number of individuals without wages or work over the past year, some equations were estimated using the inverse of the Mills ratio calculated from probit equations for employment in the past year. The coefficients on this variable proved to be highly sensitive to what was included in the first-stage probit equation, however, and the predicted wage values were unstable and often implausible.[12]

Table 1.6 presents the results of simple reservation-wage equations for predicted wages or predicted weeks worked in the NLS. Some equations contain the continuous reservation wage for sought jobs as the dependent variable, while others contain a dummy variable for whether or not the sought or specified jobs would be accepted at $3.50 per hour. The latter results are from equations that were estimated as linear-probability models.[13] Most of those equations for the NLS sample were estimated separately by region; these disaggregated results on the merged 1979 and 1980 samples for the continuous job-sought variable are presented here as well.

The results in table 1.6 show that the reservation wages of whites are consistently more responsive to demand-side factors than are those of blacks. The differences exist both in wages and weeks worked and in reservation wages for both sought and specified jobs. Most of the observed differences are also reasonably significant.[14] The regional breakdown indicates that the lower responsiveness is primarily a characteristic of blacks in the South, but regional breakdowns for the 1979 NLS sample (not presented here because of very small sample sizes for southern whites) also show smaller coefficients for northern blacks than for northern whites with regard to several of the specified occupations.[15]

Table 1.6   **Coefficients from Simple Reservation-Wage Equations for Predicted Wages and Weeks Worked, NLS**

Dependent Variables	Whites		Blacks	
	Wages	Weeks Worked	Wages	Weeks Worked
Reservation Wages for:				
Sought Jobs, 1979 and 1980				
Total	.623	.013	.420	.007
	(.085)	(.003)	(.120)	(.003)
South	.630	.012	.618	.013
	(.116)	(.003)	(.162)	(.004)
South	.718	.012	.260	.003
	(.175)	(.006)	(.178)	(.004)
Sought Jobs,	.716	.015	.399	.007
1979	(.153)	(.005)	(.194)	(.004)
Percentage Accepting Wages < $3.50 in 1979 for:				
Sought Jobs	− .817	− .015	− .652	− .008
	(.219)	(.007)	(.287)	(.007)
Neighborhood Cleaning	− .286	− .008	.134	.002
	(.226)	(.007)	(.239)	(.007)
Cleaning	− .574	− .019	− .285	− .002
	(.220)	(.007)	(.285)	(.007)
Dishwashing	− 1.048	− .032	− .406	− .002
	(.206)	(.006)	(.276)	(.006)
Factory	− .201	− .018	− .701	− .012
	(.231)	(.007)	(.257)	(.006)

Note: Separate equations estimated for wages and weeks worked. Independent variables are predicted values based on the equations presented in the appendix. Equations for the NLS are weighted by the sample weights. Only the nonemployed are included in the samples for the reservation-wage equations, whereas the wage and weeks-worked equations include both the employed and nonemployed. Continuous reservation-wage and predicted-wage variables appear in logs.

Table 1.7 shows the calculated racial differences in reservation wages, using the coefficients for whites from the equations in table 1.6, as well as those from equations in which the X_t variables were directly entered into the reservation-wage equation. For the sake of comparison, racial differences in mean reservation wages and in the ratios of reservation to (predicted) received wages are also included in the table.

The results here show that the reservation wages of young blacks for sought jobs are higher than those of whites, after controlling for wages and weeks worked. This result appears to reflect the greater responsiveness of whites' reservation wages to wages and weeks

Table 1.7   Black-White Differences in Reservation Wages, With and Without Various Controls, NLS

Black-White Difference	Reservation Wages For:			
	Sought Job, 1979–80			Sought Job, 1979
	Total	North	South	Total
1. Differences in Means, No Controls	−.013	−.031	.051	−.042
2. Controlling for Exogenous Determinants of Wages and Weeks Worked	−.007	−.018	−.018	−.041
3. Controlling for Wages	.094	.098	.092	.089
4. Controlling for Weeks Worked	.134	.133	.155	.149
5. Ratio of Mean Reservation Wages to Received Wages	.135	.176	.104	.149

	Percentage Accepting Wages < $3.50 in 1979 for:				
	Sought Jobs	Neighborhood Cleaning	Cleaning	Dishwash	Factory
1. Differences in Percentages, No Controls	.015	.076	.194	.279	.227
2. Controlling for Exogenous Determinants of Wages and Weeks Worked	.006	.053	.150	.203	.219
3. Controlling for Wages	−.134	.024	.081	.088	.099
4. Controlling for Weeks Worked	−.167	−.025	−.041	−.108	.013

Note: All differences are between blacks and whites. Mean received wages and weeks worked in all cases reflect predicted values here because of the large numbers of missing values for the actual variables. All means and equations are weighted. Coefficients from equations for whites are used along with mean black wages, weeks worked, or characteristics, to predict reservation wages for whites when controlling for these characteristics.

worked, as well as the lower levels of these variables for blacks. The weeks-worked control produces a larger effect than the control for wages, since the racial differential in weeks worked is larger than that in received wages; predicted values for both are shown in table 1.A.2 of the appendix. This table also shows the mean values of the underlying X_t variables for blacks and whites. Unlike predicted wages and weeks worked, the racial differences in the underlying variables and their effects on reservation wages were not strong enough to produce a racial differential in reservation wages when those variables were used as the controls. Thus, it is only the unexplained differences in wages and weeks worked between whites and blacks that cause the reservation wages of blacks to seem relatively high. Whether these unexplained differences reflect discrimination or skill differences is unclear.

The results also indicate that the racial differential suggested above by simply comparing mean reservation to mean received wages for each group is virtually identical to the one obtained from an equation that controlled for weeks worked. The various downward biases discussed above in estimating the racial differential through the means therefore seem to be almost exactly counterbalanced by the upward bias of using a constant ratio of reservation to received wages for whites—a notion rejected by the coefficients on wages for whites in table 1.6, which are significantly less than one.

The results for reservation wages for specific jobs remain generally lower for blacks than for whites even when controlling for wages. But in equations controlling for weeks worked, the willingness of young blacks and whites to accept those jobs becomes more similar. In the case of dishwashing, the control for weeks worked actually produces lower reservation wages for whites, perhaps reflecting the especially strong responses to wages and weeks worked of the reservation wages of whites for this job.

In sum, the reservation wages of young blacks for jobs sought are comparable to those of young whites in an absolute sense; but they are higher among blacks after controlling for the effect of wages on weeks worked. The same relationship appear to be true of the jobs sought by young blacks. On the other hand, blacks' reservation wages for specific low-skilled jobs are generally comparable to or lower than those of whites, even after controlling for these factors. It remains to be seen how the various reservation-wage measures affect the nonemployed durations and subsequent wages of each group.

Before moving on to this issue, a final note should be made concerning the determinants of the relatively high reservation wages of blacks. Although the discussion above presents some summary evidence on the roles of occupational expectations and job characteristics, there has been no discussion of the role of nonwage income—a factor that is central to most job-search and labor-supply models. Evidence presented elsewhere, however, indicates that reservation wages and nonwage income are positively correlated for young blacks in the NBER survey.[16] Furthermore, illegal income is a major source of nonwage income for this sample; and Viscusi (in this volume) shows that participation in illegal activities is negatively correlated with perceived labor market opportunity for this group. Thus, the outside income generated by illegal activities (and other sources) for young blacks with low skill levels may be an important source of their relatively high reservation wages.

1.4   The Effects of Reservation Wages on Labor Market Outcomes

This section uses the NLS panel data to investigate the effects of the various reported reservation-wage measures on the duration of subsequent nonemployment spells and on wages subsequently received. The estimated results of equations (5) and (6) are therefore presented and discussed below.

1.4.1   Nonemployment Duration Effects

Table 1.8 presents summary evidence on the duration of nonemployment spells among young blacks and whites in the NLS sample. The durations of three types of spells are presented here: The full, completed spell of all those who were nonemployed at the time of the 1979 survey; the incomplete portion of the spell that occurred prior to the survey; and the portion that occurred subsequent to the survey. The calculations therefore use retrospective employment histories of both the 1979 and 1980 NLS to generate the completed spells for those who were still nonemployed in 1979.

These results show that the durations of completed spells of nonemployment are about 28 percent higher among blacks than among whites, with somewhat smaller differentials for the portions of nonemployment occurring subsequent to the survey and somewhat larger for those occurring before the survey. Almost all of the differentials occur in the North as opposed to the South. Nevertheless, these numbers should be interpreted with caution, since the durations are substantially longer among southern whites than among northern whites. Thus, southern blacks also experience substantially longer spells of nonemployment than northern whites, who make up about three-fourths of the total white population and thus are primarily responsible for the aggregate results. Blacks, of course, are quite evenly split between the two regions, and the aggregate results weight both regions about equally.

Two other points should be mentioned here. First the NBER results are omitted here, since only the incomplete, prior spells are available for that cross-sectional survey. As was the case in the analyses above, the calculated results for the NBER sample are quite similar to those for northern blacks in the NLS.[17] Second, and as noted above, the issue of previous, completed spells among the currently employed must be acknowledged. The previous spells were more likely to have been missed at the time of the survey because they were likely to have been shorter. Looking only at the spells of the currently nonemployed is therefore likely to give upward-biased estimates of mean duration, especially when considering the full, completed spells (which

Table 1.8   **Durations of Nonemployment Spells: Means and Standard Deviations, NLS**

	Whites	Blacks	Black-White Difference
Current Completed Spells			
Total	317.26	406.47	.281
	(209.28)	(211.35)	
North	298.97	422.70	.414
	(204.96)	(215.63)	
South	379.29	387.84	.023
	(217.04)	(205.99)	
Spells Prior to Survey			
Total	156.93	212.10	.351
	(126.81)	(132.35)	
North	147.03	223.91	.523
	(124.24)	(130.18)	
South	189.11	198.89	.052
	(131.74)	(133.10)	
Spells Subsequent to Survey			
Total	162.64	195.29	.201
	(135.45)	(138.67)	
North	153.66	200.06	.302
	(131.00)	(141.83)	
South	194.04	190.58	− .018
	(147.85)	(135.48)	

Note: Spells calculated from retrospective employment histories in the 1979 and 1980 NLS for those who were unemployed in 1979. All spells greater than one year in length are included with a value of 365. All means are weighted using sample weights. Sample sizes are 241 for whites and 186 for blacks. The black-white difference is calculated with durations of whites as the base.

are not subject to the downward bias of truncation by the survey date). In fact, the previous, completed spells estimated from the retrospective histories are substantially shorter than any of those presented in table 1.8.[18] Nevertheless, this difference in duration is roughly the same among blacks and whites. Also, the racial differentials for these spells are in the 20 to 30 percent range, thereby reducing the case for a substantial bias in the estimated differences between blacks and whites.

Thus, given that the nonemployment rates for blacks and whites in the NLS are .396 and .196, respectively, the overall nonemployment differential is 102 percent; and differences in the durations of spells appear to account for about a third of the nonemployment rate differentials between the two groups in that sample.[19] It should be noted that this is a smaller fraction than that found by Clark and Summers (1982) or by Ballen and Freeman (in this volume), who estimated duration to account for over half of the nonemployment differential between young blacks and whites. The one-third figure can therefore be regarded as a lower bound to the true estimate.

Moving on to the estimated effects of reported reservation-wage measures on these durations, table 1.9 presents the coefficients of the duration equations that take the form of equation (5) above. The dependent variable in each case refers to the portion of the completed spell occurring subsequent to the 1979 survey date, since the reservation wage reported on that date directly determines transition probabilities and therefore expected durations from that date onward.[20]

As equation (5) specifies, the independent variables are a reservation-wage measure; a dummy variable for whether or not the respondent actively searched for work in the past month; and a set of variables to control for the labor-demand factors that determine offer probabilities and offered wages. This set of control variables includes all of the determinants of wages and weeks worked presented above, as well as dummy variables for occupation, industry, and collective bargaining for jobs held before 1979. Individuals without employment in the past year are given zero values on these variables and values of one on dummy variables for missing values.[21] Other specifications of this equation using the more limited set of demand determinants or using predicted wages or weeks worked were estimated as well. But these controls were generally insufficient to overcome the downward bias resulting from omitted personal factors in the reservation-wage coefficients,[22] and theoretically incorrect negative coefficients appeared in these equations for whites. Results for blacks were far more robust with respect to the controls used.[23]

Two other features of the results presented in table 1.9 (as well as in tables 1.10–1.12 below for subsequent wages) should be noted. Separate duration equations are estimated for each reservation-wage measure. Those measures appear in both continuous and discrete form for the job sought, and only in discrete form for specified jobs. The discrete forms appear as a pair of dummy variables that measure the willingness to accept work at $3.50 or less and at greater than $3.50 but less than or equal to $5.00. To compare the predictive power of the different reservation-wage measures with regard to outcomes, F-statistics are calculated for each set of reservation-wage dummy variables. The F-statistics can be compared with the critical F-values for joint significance at the .05 level for each sample size that appears in the table.

The results show that reservation wages for sought jobs have strong effects on the durations of nonemployment among young blacks, par-

Table 1.9   **Effects of Reservation Wages on the Duration of Subsequent Spells of Nonemployment, NLS**

Equation for:	Whites		Blacks	
	Coefficient	F-Value	Coefficient	F-Value
1. Reservations Wages for Sought Job, 1979				
Total	.112		.585	
	(.342)		(.313)	
North	.334		1.801	
	(.386)		(.726)	
South	1.001		.136	
	(1.474)		(1.442)	
Percentage Accepting Job at ≤ $3.50:				
2. Sought Job		4.75		2.86
$3.50	1.68		−.749	
	(.339)		(.339)	
$5.00	.801		−.384	
	(.348)		(.358)	
3. Neighborhood Cleaning		1.02		1.10
$3.50	−.315		−.424	
	(.244)		(.301)	
$5.00	−.042		−.221	
	(.292)		(.355)	
4. Cleaning		1.91		2.09
$3.50	−.018		−.416	
	(.258)		(.278)	
$5.00	−.484		.133	
	(.278)		(.396)	
5. Dishwashing		1.91		.33
$3.50	.142		−.047	
	(.273)		(.302)	
$5.00	−.404		−.198	
	(.288)		(.386)	
6. Factory		.07		.56
$3.50	−.080		−.355	
	(.266)		(.338)	
$5.00	.007		−.251	
	(.310)		(.427)	
Critical F.05		2.68		3.10

Note: Separate equations estimated for each reservation-wage measure. F-values are for pairs of dummy variables indicating the willingness to work at given wages. The sample includes all those nonemployed in the 1979 panel of the NLS. Controls are a dummy variable for search in the previous months; all of the determinants of wages and weeks worked used above; and dummy variables for occupation, industry, and collective bargaining. Missing values on these latter variables are given zero values and special dummy variables that take on values of one. All equations are weighted using sample weights. Sample sizes are 170 for whites and 129 for blacks. Durations of spells and continuous reservation wages are in logs. Means of the dependent variables on the total samples are 4.412 for whites and 4.738 for blacks.

ticularly among those in the North. Since both the durations and the reservation-wage measures are expressed in logs, the coefficients can be interpreted as elasticities. The results show elasticities of over 0.5 for the nationwide sample of blacks and as high as 1.8 for those in the North. The results for whites are positive but much smaller and not significant.

There are two possible interpretations for the smaller estimated coefficients for whites in these equations. As noted above, the coefficients are downward biased because certain unobserved components of demand are correlated positively with duration but negatively with reservation wages. If either of these correlations is greater among whites than among blacks, the resulting bias in their coefficients will be greater. There is, in fact, some reason to believe that both correlations are greater for whites, since several of the observed measures of personal characteristics and family background (not reported here) appear to have smaller effects on duration for blacks than for whites.[24] Furthermore, the simple equations of table 1.6 show a greater responsiveness of reservation wages to wages and weeks worked among whites than among blacks. Consequently, if the observed and unobserved components of demand have similar relationships to duration and to reservation wages, we can expect the downward bias to be greater for whites.

A second explanation of the lower estimated effects of reservation wages among whites is that the effect is, in reality, lower for them. As noted above, the partial effect of reservation wages on duration is $-\pi f(W^r)$, where π is the probability of receiving offers and $f(w^r)$ is the value of the probability density function for wages when evaluated at the reservation wage. The evidence in the appendix shows wage distributions that are more spiked around the minimum wage for blacks than for whites, as well as reservation wages that are higher relative to received wages for blacks, implying a stronger effect of blacks' reservation wages on durations. Of course, we would expect the offer probabilities to be lower among blacks, and it is not clear what the net effect on the relative magnitudes of the partials would be. As discussed below, however, it appears that the probability of *individuals'* obtaining some kind of job offer (albeit at the minimum wage) if they desired one may be quite high even among young nonemployed blacks; and thus young blacks' relatively high reservation wages for sought jobs may have strong effects on the duration of their spells of nonemployment.

Given the estimated elasticities of duration with respect to reservation wages, and given the estimated differences in these reservation wages when controlling for the demand characteristics of blacks and whites, we can estimate the overall effect of these higher reservation wages on the nonemployment durations of blacks. The estimated elasticity for blacks of .585, together with a predicted reservation-wage differential that was estimated to be as high as .135 relative to received wages for each group, implies that the higher reservation wages add as much as 7.9 percent to the nonemployment durations of blacks. Given the difference in mean durations between blacks and whites of 28 percent, as reported in table 1.8, and of over 30 percent in the dependent variable of the regression sample (see table 1.9, note), the results also suggest that a quarter to a third of the average racial difference in duration may be explained by the relatively higher reservation wages for the sought jobs of blacks than those of whites.

Since the duration of nonemployment spells appears to account for at least a third and probably over half of the higher nonemployment rates of young blacks than those of young whites, the suggestion that the reservation wages of young blacks may significantly add to their nonemployment rates is supported by the evidence. Furthermore, the estimated duration elasticity and racial differentials in reservation wages are even higher in the North than in the South, as is the difference in nonemployment durations. Although the estimated duration elasticity for the North seems implausibly high,[25] the effects of northern blacks' reservation wages on their nonemployment rates may be considerable.

Of course, these calculations use the highest estimates of both the duration elasticities and the reservation-wage differentials controlling for the demand characteristics that were estimated. It was argued earlier that in both cases the higher estimates are the more believable ones because the others are plagued by various downward biases. Even so, the effects calculated above of reservation wages on overall nonemployment durations and nonemployment rates for young blacks are likely to be upper bounds to the true effects.

A final caveat must be mentioned here with regard to the above calculations. These calculations assume that the elasticities of duration with respect to reservation wages will not change as the reservation wages change; but, as the formula for the partial derivative implies, the elasticity is itself dependent on the reservation wage. More importantly, a general decline in reservation wages should presumably lower the probabilities of receiving offers facing *individuals* if the aggregate availability of jobs is less than the number of individuals seeking work. Thus, the calculations presented above (of a quarter to a third of the racial differential explained by reservation wages) are even more likely to overstate the true contribution of reservation wages to the aggregate racial difference in durations. The power of the factors determining labor demand to explain racial differences in durations is clearly established, despite the significant effects estimated for reservation wages.

The results shown in table 1.9 indicate that the discrete measures of reservation wages for sought jobs have greater explanatory power than any of the measures of those wages for specified jobs in the equations measuring duration for blacks and whites. Nevertheless, the high joint significance level of the dummy variables for the sought jobs of whites masks the fact that the relative magnitudes of their coefficients are not "correct" since those with reservation wages above $5.00 per hour experience the shortest spells of nonemployment. Among whites, only the reservation wages for neighborhood cleaning have coefficients with sensible magnitudes, of which at least one is marginally significant; among blacks this is true of the reservation wages for neighborhood cleaning, cleaning, and factory jobs. But none of these other measures comes close to having the predictive power or magnitudes of coefficients (both relative and absolute) that the measure for sought jobs has among blacks. The belief that the measures for sought jobs are less valid than those of specified jobs because the former represent a confounding of expectations and reservations may be partially true, but the strong behavioral implications of those measures support the case for their validity.

1.4.2   Wage Effects

This section addresses the effects of reported reservation wages on subsequent wages. Consistent with the theory that received wages reflect a probability-weighted average of an offered-wage distribution truncated by reservation wages, equation (6) specifies that subsequent wages be estimated as a function of reservation wages and predicted wages, where the latter serve as a proxy for the mean of the offered wage distribution.

Table 1.10 presents the results of these equations for blacks and whites. The reservation wages for sought and specified jobs appear in the same format as in the duration equations, with separate equations and F-values presented for each measure, and with the same predicted wage as that described above. The results show very significant effects of reservation wages for sought jobs on the received wages of both blacks and whites. The effect is a bit stronger for whites, and for both groups the effects are greater in the North than in the South. In this equation, the effects of omitted components of the predicted wage should have a positive rather than negative effect on the estimated coefficients for reservation wages (since these components should be positively correlated with both reservation and received wages); these effects may be causing the higher coefficient for whites observed here.

An alternative explanation is that whites are more likely to obtain their sought jobs than are blacks, and hence their reported reservation wages for these jobs are more predictive of subsequent wages. This explanation is consistent with the results in table 1.3, which show a greater consistency between occupations sought and those received or

Table 1.10   **Effects of Reservation Wages on Received Wages at Subsequent Jobs, NLS**

Equation for:	Whites		Blacks	
	Coefficient	F-Value	Coefficient	F-Value
1. Reservations Wages for Sought Job, 1979				
Total	.554		.252	
	(.091)		(.106)	
North	.723		.643	
	(.116)		(.170)	
South	.145		.101	
	(.092)		(.141)	
Percentage Accepting Job at ≤ *$3.50:*				
2. Sought Job		21.05		5.68
$3.50	− .551		− .348	
	(.085)		(.108)	
$5.00	− .422		− .171	
	(.085)		(.112)	
3. Neighborhood Cleaning		1.78		7.51
$3.50	− .104		− .336	
	(.074)		(.089)	
$5.00	.032		− .167	
	(.088)		(.107)	
4. Cleaning		1.59		1.76
$3.50	− .142		− .161	
	(.079)		(.089)	
$5.00	− .072		− .044	
	(.082)		(.120)	
5. Dishwashing		3.93		7.66
$3.50	− .220		− .311	
	(.079)		(.095)	
$5.00	− .069		− .026	
	(.078)		(.121)	
6. Factory		2.73		2.35
$3.50	− .189		− .102	
	(.083)		(.115)	
$5.00	− .090		− .113	
	(.091)		(.133)	
Critical F.05		3.05		3.10

Note: Separate equations estimated for each reservation wage measure. F-values are for pairs of dummy variables indicating the willingness to work at given wages. The sample includes all those nonemployed in the 1979 panel of the NLS who reported wages for jobs obtained in the subsequent year. Predicted wages are included as a control variable. All equations are weighted by sample weights. Samples sizes are 143 for whites and 99 for blacks. Continuous reservation wages and received wages are in logs.

held by whites. It is also consistent with the higher estimated effects of these reservation-wage measures on the nonemployment durations of blacks, which imply that blacks' higher reservation wages relative to their offer probabilities and offered wages lead to higher nonemployment rather than higher wages for blacks.

Comparing the reservation wages for sought and specified jobs in their discrete forms, we find that sought jobs totally dominate all of the specified jobs for whites, in both magnitudes of coefficients and F-values. Among blacks, the F-values for sought jobs are a little lower than those for neighborhood cleaning and dishwashing jobs, but the magnitudes of the coefficients for sought jobs are very similar to those for neighborhood cleaning and are greater than those for dishwashing (though their standard errors are greater). Thus, the reservation wages for sought jobs serve as well as or better than those for specified jobs among both blacks and whites in explaining subsequently received wages; and again, doubts about the validity of this measure are not supported by its power to explain observed behavior. But the fact that reservation wages for specified, low-skilled jobs have relatively greater predictive power for the wages of blacks than for those of whites also suggests again that blacks are more likely to have to accept these jobs in place of their preferred ones, even if only temporarily.

This analysis also tests whether the explanatory power of the reservation-wage measures for different jobs varies according to the nature of the job ultimately received. The same wage equations are estimated for two subsamples of blacks and whites: those whose jobs received were in the laborer and service category; and those whose jobs received were in the same broad category (such as white-collar, craft and operative, or laborer and service) as their jobs sought. It was hypothesized that reservation wages for sought jobs would have relatively more explanatory power in the latter group, while reservation wages for the specified, low-skilled jobs would be more predictive in the former.

The tests are rather crude because of the broadly defined nature of the occupational aggregates and because of the much smaller sample sizes in the subsamples. Nonetheless, the tests are moderately successful, especially among whites. Table 1.11 presents results for the group with laborer and service jobs. The results show a strong increase in the explanatory power of reservation wages for dishwashing and for cleaning among whites, with a strong decline in the explanatory power of those for jobs sought relative to the results for the total sample. Among blacks the changes are less pronounced, but there is a strong increase in the explanatory power of reservation wages for factory jobs.

Table 1.12 presents results for those who obtained the kinds of jobs they had sought. The reservation wages for these jobs continue to have

Table 1.11   **Effects of Reservation Wages on Received Wages at Subsequent Jobs: Laborers and Service Workers, NLS**

Equation for:	Whites		Blacks	
	Coefficient	F-Value	Coefficient	F-Value
1. Reservations Wages for Sought Job, 1979				
Total	.735		.599	
	(.180)		(.175)	
North	—		—	
	—		—	
South	—		—	
	—		—	
Percentage Accepting Job at ≤ $3.50:				
2. Sought Job		7.59		4.92
$3.50	− .565		− .463	
	(.159)		(.172)	
$5.00	− .298		− .221	
	(.157)		(.122)	
3. Neighborhood Cleaning		1.35		6.75
$3.50	− .135		− .418	
	(.120)		(.119)	
$5.00	.059		− .219	
	(.146)		(.138)	
4. Cleaning		2.59		.45
$3.50	− .232		− .071	
	(.118)		(.133)	
$5.00	.007		.037	
	(.130)		(.155)	
5. Dishwashing		4.51		6.52
$3.50	− .336		− .358	
	(.112)		(.143)	
$5.00	− .180		.024	
	(.142)		(.125)	
6. Factory		2.07		5.77
$3.50	− .143		− .183	
	(.165)		(.149)	
$5.00	.085		.207	
	(.165)		(.211)	
Critical F.05		3.15		3.20

Note: Separate equations estimated for each reservation-wage measure. F-values are for pairs of dummy variables indicating the willingness to work at given wages. The sample is a subset of that in table 1.10 and includes only those who obtained jobs as laborers and service workers in the subsequent year. Sample sizes are 64 for whites and 47 for blacks. Continuous reservation wages and received wages are in logs.

strong explanatory power among whites, whereas those for the specified low-skilled jobs have very little. Among blacks the strongest decline is in reservation wages for factory jobs, though the magnitudes on the coefficients for these and some of the other reservation wages for specified jobs actually increase.

In summary, the reservation wages reported for sought jobs in the NLS have a large, significant effect on the duration of nonemployment among young blacks and on subsequent wages among both blacks and whites. Reservation wages for the specified, low-skilled jobs also have some effects on subsequent wages, particularly among those who obtained laborer and service jobs, and this is generally more true of blacks than of whites. The belief that reported reservation wages for sought jobs in the NLS are less valid than the others because the open-ended format of the questioning allowed confounding of expectations and reservations is not supported here, given the stronger behavioral implications of these measures. If anything, the results here suggest that young blacks do aspire to the sought jobs and the reservation wages they reported, and these measures therefore appear to contribute more to their nonemployment durations than do the measures for low-skilled jobs. The low-skilled jobs may be temporarily acceptable only when the immediate need for income is great or the nonemployment spell has been quite long.

A final issue to be addressed is that of the overall availability of jobs for young blacks. The large observed effects of reservation wages for sought jobs on nonemployment durations in this group imply that a reduction in the mean level of these reservation wages would reduce mean nonemployment durations and nonemployment rates. As noted above, the economic interpretation of the large estimated effects is that offer probabilities for lower-wage jobs are high among nonemployed blacks, that is, jobs are relatively available to those who want them or who are willing to accept them at low wages. Needless to say, this interpretation would meet with a fair amount of controversy in a community of young blacks experiencing such high rates of nonemployment. Before this strong implication can be accepted, two questions must be answered: First, is there other evidence of job availability that is more direct than simply drawing inferences from estimated duration elasticities? And second, even if these numbers of jobs are currently available to *individuals* who are willing to accept them, are they available in the *aggregate*? Or is there instead a smaller number of such jobs available that only seem plentiful to particular individuals because most other individuals will not accept them? In other words, the offer probabilities facing individuals may depend on the aggregate level of reservation wages, and also the elasticity of duration with respect to reservation wages may decline if there is an aggregate decline in those reservation wages.

Table 1.12   **Effects of Reservation Wages on Received Wages at Subsequent Jobs for Those Obtaining Jobs Sought, NLS**

	Whites		Blacks	
Equation for:	Coefficient	F-Value	Coefficient	F-Value
1. Reservation Wages for Sought Job, 1979				
Total	.402		.643	
	(.148)		(.306)	
North	—		—	
	—		—	
South	—		—	
	—		—	
Percentage Accepting Job at ≤ *$3.50:*				
2. Sought Job		5.29		3.64
$3.50	−.486		−.402	
	(.157)		(.237)	
$5.00	−.424		.315	
	(.148)		(.324)	
3. Neighborhood Cleaning		.73		4.67
$3.50	.090		−.627	
	(.203)		(.217)	
$5.00	−.204		−.200	
	(.188)		(.243)	
4. Cleaning		1.13		4.00
$3.50	.067		−.648	
	(.168)		(.229)	
$5.00	−.139		−.515	
	(.152)		(.290)	
5. Dishwashing		.07		4.00
$3.50	.024		−.603	
	(.175)		(.219)	
$5.00	.054		−.184	
	(.150)		(.318)	
6. Factory		.30		.69
$3.50	−.082		−.368	
	(.174)		(.355)	
$5.00	−.124		−.082	
	(.160)		(.421)	
Critical F.05		3.20		3.47

Note: Separate equations estimated for each reservation-wage measure. F-values are for pairs of dummy variables indicating the willingness to work at given wages. The sample is subset of that in table 1.10 and includes only those who in the subsequent year obtained the jobs they had been seeking. Sample sizes are 40 for whites and 23 for blacks. Continuous reservation wages and received wages are in logs.

These propositions may be the case, because the available jobs (or those with vacancies) are most likely to be those with high turnover rates and those not sought by the majority of workers, namely, the low-wage labor or service sector jobs. Those jobs considered menial or dead-end may be the most readily available of all because of the high turnover in and the relatively high reservation wages for these positions. The important point here is that a general lowering of reservation wages and of the level of job sought (or even of the turnover rates for these jobs) might substantially reduce the apparent availability of jobs to those who want them, leaving a more salient aggregate shortage of jobs among the nonemployed.

The empirical evidence on these larger issues is neither extensive nor conclusive. Some unique evidence from the NBER survey appears in table 1.13. The inner-city black youths were asked, "Suppose you were desperate for money. How easy would you say it would be for you to find a job working as/at ———?" and several jobs were listed afterward. The survey responses indicate that over 70 percent of the nonemployed youths in the survey believed that it would be somewhat easy or very easy to obtain some sort of job at the minimum wage, whereas for other jobs, such as laborer work, the percentage was lower (46 percent for laborer work). These data imply that nonemployed, inner-city young blacks perceive a fair number of jobs are availability at low wages, which is consistent with the high estimated elasticities of duration with respect to reservation wages for this group.

Several caveats must be mentioned with regard to these results. First, the NBER survey was conducted in late 1979 and early 1980, years that predated the recession that then plagued U.S. labor markets for the next three years. Second, the survey data are based on subjective perceptions or expectations of job availability; and as noted above, such expectations may be overly optimistic. Finally, these perceptions are clearly individual rather than aggregate and therefore tell us little about job availability if overall reservation wages were to change. The extent to which the estimated effects of reservation wages on the duration of nonemployment would hold for major changes in the aggregate remains unclear at this time.

Table 1.13   **Nonemployed Blacks' Perceived Ability to Obtain Jobs, NBER Survey**

Job	Very Easy	Somewhat Easy	Difficult	Impossible
Working as a Laborer	.184	.276	.463	.077
Working at a Minimum Wage Job	.375	.328	.227	.071

1.5 Summary

This paper has analyzed the reservation-wage differentials of young blacks and whites and the effects of those differentials on the non-employment durations and subsequent wages of both groups. The results have shown that young blacks seek jobs and wages that are comparable to those of young whites but that are at higher levels than the jobs and wages the young blacks ultimately obtain. These relatively high expectations contribute somewhat to blacks' nonemployment durations, which are already substantially higher than those of whites. On the other hand, young blacks appear at least as likely, if not more likely, than whites to take specific low-skilled jobs, although they seem to accept these only temporarily. A reluctance to take certain menial or dead-end jobs is evident among both blacks and whites.

The overall implication of these findings is that young blacks have modeled their expectations and aspirations after those of the white society around them, but their means of achieving those ends are fewer. It is not clear whether young blacks' ability to attain their expectations is the result of lower skills, fewer contacts, less information, or simply discrimination.

It does seem as though the concern expressed in recent years about a "culture of poverty" among poor blacks, namely, their lack of middle-class aspirations, is unfounded. Instead, the main problem faced by young blacks is how to achieve their aspirations.

The results also shed new light on the potential of both public and private sector strategies to create only more low-wage, dead-end jobs for young, nonemployed blacks. To the extent that many young blacks appear willing to take these jobs temporarily, they may be useful in a limited sense as a means of providing income or training. But young blacks, like their white counterparts, clearly aspire to better positions than these, even in the short run. Unless accompanied by substantial training or some other means of achieving upward movement, public service jobs or private ones created by policies like the proposed sub-minimum wage for youth are unlikely to meet the hopes and needs of the young black nonemployed.

Appendix

Table 1A.1   **Log-of-Wages and Weeks-Worked Equations, NLS**

	Whites		Blacks	
	ln Wages	Weeks Worked	ln Wages	Weeks Worked
Intercept	4.787	17.235	5.116	7.310
	(.180)	(6.598)	(.245)	(10.522)
Age	.052	.561	.024	.264
	(.010)	(.355)	(.013)	(.552)
Experience in Years	.021	1.473	.033	3.880
	(.011)	(.405)	(.016)	(.716)
Urban	.085	.144	.038	2.642
	(.020)	(.736)	(.042)	(1.832)
South	−.076	2.381	−.014	5.243
	(.021)	(.759)	(.029)	(1.246)
KWW	.019	.168	.019	.270
	(.006)	(.208)	(.008)	(.365)
Library Card	.058	1.309	.027	−1.816
at Home	(.023)	(.853)	(.070)	(1.293)
H.S. Diploma	.086	7.786	.146	5.976
	(.023)	(.805)	(.030)	(1.308)
Marital Status:				
Now Married	−.029	3.522	−.007	−.064
	(.040)	(1.581)	(.062)	(2.443)
Was Married	.168	5.572	.203	−2.131
	(.105)	(3.844)	(.186)	(13.337)
1950 Dummy Variable	.061	−.670	.051	−.192
	(.018)	(.663)	(.028)	(1.250)
Household Income,	−.002	−.016	.003	.083
Excluding Own	(.001)	(.037)	(.002)	(.079)
Household Income,	.001	5.600	.173	14.726
Listed ≤ 0	(.032)	(.947)	(.046)	(1.764)
Household Income Missing	−.040	1.041	−.024	.666
	(.025)	(1.023)	(.036)	(1.684)
R^2	.163	.160	.176	.256
N	1,891	1,936	737	832
Mean of Dependent Variable	6.140	41.086	5.953	30.105

Note: Equations estimated using OLS. Samples include all respondents reporting wages in the past year for the wage equations and all respondents (including those without work in the past year) in the weeks-worked equations. Household income (excluding own) in thousands of dollars. Knowledge of world of work (KWW) ranges from 1 to 11 for the number of questions answered correctly. Experience reflects the number of years in which the individual was employed as of one year before the survey date, starting in 1975.

Table 1.A.2 **Characteristics of the Nonemployed: Means and Standard Deviations, NLS**

	Whites				Blacks			
	1979–80		1979		1979–80		1979	
	Total	N	S	Total	Total	N	S	Total
Predicted Wages	6.054	6.105	5.913	6.007	5.878	5.989	5.860	5.816
	(.181)	(.157)	(.170)	(.168)	(.165)	(.158)	(.170)	(.145)
Predicted Weeks Worked	36.222	36.681	34.437	35.788	24.695	22.751	26.528	22.732
	(5.687)	(5.718)	(5.397)	(5.497)	(7.506)	(7.102)	(7.415)	(6.298)
Age	19.200	19.387	18.677	19.145	19.496	19.688	19.315	19.214
	(1.730)	(1.610)	(1.936)	(1.549)	(1.694)	(1.681)	(1.687)	(1.565)
Experience	1.010	1.043	.777	.785	.803	.926	.687	.578
	(1.152)	(1.204)	(.950)	(1.122)	(1.508)	(1.123)	(.980)	(.955)
Urban	.728	.821	.466	.722	.855	.952	.763	.856
	(.445)	(.383)	(.499)	(.442)	(.352)	(.213)	(.425)	(.351)
South	.263	—	—	.261	.515	—	—	.501
	(.440)	—	—	(.442)	(.500)	—	—	(.500)
KWW	5.589	5.723	5.213	5.625	4.793	4.863	4.727	4.953
	(1.790)	(1.774)	(1.780)	(1.815)	(1.709)	(1.699)	(1.715)	(1.743)
Library Card at Home	.806	.836	.722	.809	.723	.692	.753	.712
	(.396)	(.371)	(.448)	(.393)	(.447)	(.497)	(.431)	(.453)
H.S. Diploma	.499	.593	.236	.439	.452	.442	.462	.370
	(.500)	(.491)	(.424)	(.496)	(.498)	(.497)	(.499)	(.483)
Marital Status, Now Married	.051	.053	.046	.042	.073	.036	.109	.071
	(.220)	(.224)	(.209)	(.201)	(.261)	(.187)	(.312)	(.257)
Was Married	.009	.013	.000	.014	.004	.000	.007	.006
	(.096)	(.111)	(.000)	(.118)	(.061)	(.000)	(.085)	(.078)
Household Income (in dollars)	13,249	13,862	11,374	12,503	11,267	12,333	10,435	9,884
	(13,005)	(13,201)	(10,802)	(11,170)	(13,428)	(14,506)	(11,443)	(11,056)
N	420	300	120	179	296	155	141	141

Note: All means are weighted using sample weights. Predicted wages and weeks worked calculated using means from these tables and coefficients from equations presented in table 1.A.1. Sample sizes reflect those for whom reservation wages for sought jobs and all variables are defined.

Notes

1. Recent work by economists on the reservation wages of blacks and whites includes a study by Borus (1982) using only one of the available reservation-wage measures in the NLS. Using the NLS data, he found blacks more willing to work, even after controlling for personal and local labor market characteristics. A study by Anderson (1980), which employed a more sociological perspective, stressed the reluctance of young blacks to do menial work.

2. See Freeman (1979).

3. For an excellent survey of the job-search literature, see Lippman and McCall (1976).

4. For a search model based on utility maximization that allows reservation wages to vary across jobs, see Holzer (1983).

5. See Lippman and McCall (1976).,

6. The endogeneity of nonwage income with regard to reservation wages derives from the fact that participation in illegal activities or government transfer programs will be affected by employment status, which in turn may reflect reservation wages. The endogeneity of the duration of preceding spells reflects the fact that an individual's reservation wage may not vary greatly over time, and therefore current reservation wages reflect those in the past that are partly responsible for the earlier spell.

7. The "knowledge of the world of work" variable reflects the number of questions out of a possible eleven that were answered correctly, where the questions involved choosing definitions of specified occupations.

8. This possibility was first suggested to me in conversations with John Bound.

9. See, for instance, Marston (1976).

10. A classic statement of the importance of transitional wage norms and relative positions can be found in Dunlop (1957).

11. The use of white coefficients and black mean characteristics rather than vice versa for this calculation was based on two considerations. First, whites are generally considered the "baseline" group in the economy: using their coefficients along with the characteristics of other groups provides a standard by which to judge the actual behavior of the other groups. Second, table 1.6 shows that black reservation wages are less responsive to changes in their characteristics than are those of whites. Thus, using white mean characteristics with black coefficients will naturally show a smaller racial differential than vice versa.

12. Probit equations for employment in the past year included all of the determinants of wages, as well as a measure of own nonwage income and a set of dummy variables for occupational aspirations at age 35 to measure general attitudes toward work. When all of those variables were included, the coefficient on the inverse Mill's ratio in the wage equation for blacks was .420, with a standard error of .200; predicted log wages of blacks without previous employment was 6.30, which was far higher than the predicted log wages of blacks who had been employed. On the other hand, when the aspiration variables were dropped, the coefficient became $-.129$, with a standard error of .335; and the predicted log wage was 5.705, which was considered too low. The predicted values in the absence of the Mills ratio seemed intuitively most plausible.

13. Since the dependent variable here is dichotomous in value, it is more appropriate to use the logistic functional form than the linear. For the former model, $P = (1 + e^{-xb})$. Nevertheless, when some of these equations were estimated using logit, the results were extremely similar. The less expensive linear estimates were therefore used throughout the rest of the study and form the basis of the results reported.

14. The formula for the standard error of a difference between estimated parameters is $[(SE_w)^2 + (SE_b)_2 - 2cov(w,b)]^{1/2}$ where the covariance term between whites and blacks is zero.

15. In particular, the coefficients on neighborhood cleaning with respect to predicted weeks worked are $-.0087$ for northern whites and $-.0009$ for northern blacks, with standard errors of .0076 and .0089, respectively. The comparable numbers for cleaning are $-.0196$ and $-.0028$ for coefficients and .0072 and .0091 for standard errors; and for dishwashing they are $-.0361$ and $-.0077$ for coefficients with standard errors of .0065 and .0090, respectively.

16. See Holzer (1983), chap. 6.

17. The mean and standard deviation of durations of incomplete prior spells in the NBER survey are 203.89 and 142.15, respectively. Furthermore, the proportion of individuals without employment in the past year is .613, whereas it is .647 among northern blacks in the 1979–80 NLS. For northern whites this figure is .855.

18. Previous, completed nonemployment spells have means and standard deviations of 51.389 and 61.033 for whites and 64.216 and 71.803 for blacks. These durations are thus 25 percent higher for blacks, a percentage that is fairly consistent with the relative durations of current spells.

19. Since frequency and duration differentials contribute multiplicatively rather than additively, a 28 percent duration differential and a 55 percent frequency differential would constitute a 100 percent nonemployment differential.

20. Since reservation wages directly determine transitional probabilities, which in turn determine expected duration, several equations were estimated of the same form as equation (5), but the dependent variable was P_e, a dummy variable for transition probability that equals one if the subsequent nonemployment duration was 30 days or less. Results of this equation were generally consistent with those of comparable duration equations, though the coefficients were generally less significant in the former. This difference appeared to be caused by a greater variation in reservation wages within the post–30-day spells (which accounted for over 80 percent of the sample for both groups) than between the two groups of spells.

21. These extra variables were not included in the wage and weeks-worked equations because these equations were estimated for both 1979 and 1980 and because, in each of these years, the missing-value variables were endogenous with respect to wages and weeks worked. In other words, the missing-value variables were always zero if wages were earned and were always one if weeks worked were zero. This problem was not encountered in the duration equation because the missing-value variables for employment prior to 1979 were exogenous with respect to durations that occurred subsequent to 1979.

22. The formula for bias on the estimated coefficient of duration would be $b_{DN.xx} \cdot b_{xx.w} r$, where the former coefficient is the true regression coefficient on the omitted variable xx, and the latter is the auxiliary regression of the omitted on the included variable. In this case, the former would be negative and the latter positive, creating a downward bias.

23. The coefficients on reservation wages for blacks for equations using predicted wages or the more limited set of demand-side determinants as controls generally ranged from .4 to .5.

24. For instance, the coefficients on KWW, household income, and experience were significantly smaller for blacks than for whites in the duration equations.

25. The estimated duration elasticity of 1.8, together with reservation wage differentials of .176 relative to mean received wages, implies an effect of .317, which accounts for most of the racial differential in the regression sample for that region. Since sample sizes were fairly small here ($N = 71$), the results are subject to some doubt.

References

Akerlof, George, and Brian Main. 1980. Unemployment spells and unemployment experience. *American Economic Review* 70: 885.

Anderson, Elijah. 1980. Some observations of black youth unemployment. In *Youth Employment Issues and Policy,* ed. Bernard Anderson and Isabel Sawhill. New York: Prentice-Hall.

Borus, Michael A. 1982. Willingness of youth to work. *Journal of Human Resources* 17: 581.

Clark, Kim B., and Lawrence H. Summers. 1982. The dynamics of youth unemployment. In *The Youth Labor Market Problem*, ed. Richard B. Freeman and David A. Wise. Chicago: University of Chicago Press, p. 199.

Dunlop, John T. 1957. The task of contemporary wage theory. In *New Concepts in Wage Determination, ed.* G. W. Taylor and F. C. Pierson. New York: McGraw-Hill Book Co.

Freeman, Richard B. 1979. Why is there a youth labor market problem? NBER Working Paper no. 365. Cambridge, Mass.: NBER.

Goodwin, Leonard. 1973. *Do the poor want to work?* Washington, D.C.: Brookings Institution.

Heckman, James J. 1979. Sample selection bias as a specification error. *Econometrica* 47: 153.

Holzer, Harry J. 1983. Black youth nonemployment. Unpublished Ph.D. thesis. Cambridge: Harvard University.

Kaitz, Hyman B. 1970. Analyzing the length of unemployment spells. *Monthly Labor Review* 93: 11.

Lippman, Steven J., and John J. McCall. 1976. The economics of job search: A survey. *Economic Inquiry* 14: 155.

Marston, Stephen T., 1976. Employment instability and high unemployment rates. *Brookings Papers on Economic Activity,* 1: 169.

Comment   Ronald G. Ehrenberg

Holzer's paper has a number of attributes that I find very appealing. It focuses on an important topic and uses two different data bases to test the robustness of its findings. It uses alternative specifications of the variable of interest (reservation wages), examines the sensitivity of the results to alternative sets of control variables, uses a variety of statistical methods to confront a number of statistical issues, and honestly reports cases in which any of the above leads to differences in results. Finally, the paper does not claim more than the evidence warrants—a feature not present in enough academic research papers. My comments below should be taken with this overall evaluation in mind. I first raise some methodological issues and then turn to future research questions posed by the paper.

Ronald G. Ehrenberg is professor of economics at Cornell University and research associate at the National Bureau of Economic Research.

Methodological Issues

Holzer estimates a three-equation recursive model in which a vector of exogenous variables (X_i) influences an individual's reservation wage at the survey date (W_i^r); these exogenous variables and the reservation wage influence the subsequent received wage; and the exogenous variables, the reservation wage, and measures of search intensity influence the duration of a completed spell of nonemployment, dated from the time the survey was conducted. Several methodological issues are raised by his analyses.

First, we are presented with a parsimonious specification of the exogenous variables (the Xs). Missing from the list is any mention of unemployment insurance eligibility and receipt, reasons for nonemployment, whether the youths lived with their families, and variables that might influence subjective discount rates (which might vary systematically by race). These omitted variables may well bias the results.

Second, Holzer analyzes duration of "nonemployment"; there is no discussion of whether "out of the labor force status" and "unemployment status" can be meaningfully lumped into one state. Although there is disagreement in the literature on this point (compare Clark and Summers [1982] to Flinn and Heckman [1982]), Holzer's reported mean nonemployment spell durations of 317 (406) days for whites (blacks) in table 1.8 causes me to wonder about the intensity of job search that is being demonstrated by some of the youths in the sample and to question the relevance of the job-search framework.

Holzer also uses as a dependent variable the spells *from* the survey date, including the reservation wage *as of that date*. The latter is not allowed to vary with the duration of the nonemployment spell *up to* the survey date. But from the general theory of job search and the empirical work of Kiefer and Neumann (1979), among others, we know that reservation wages should be expected to vary with unemployment duration. If reservation wages *are* associated with the duration of spells up to the survey date (both because of the revision of expectations downward and the failure of the unemployed to be aware of general wage increases) and if the duration of spells prior to the survey date is correlated with race, Holzer's results will be altered accordingly.

In fact, Holzer notes in table 1.8 that spell durations prior to the survey date were some 35 percent longer for black youths than they were for white youths. One might also expect longer durations of nonemployment prior to the survey date to thwart job searchers' efforts, negatively influencing their subsequent wages and prolonging subsequent nonemployment spells. Thus, the durations of previous spells should probably enter all three equations. If this factor is omitted, the error terms are likely to be correlated across equations, and an estimation method that takes account of this fact should have been used.

Fourth, in theory the same vector of variables X should appear in all three equations in Holzer's system, otherwise it is impossible to identify the independent effect of reservation wages on the other outcomes. Holzer solves the problem by some artificial restrictions that lead to additional omitted-variables problems. If the marginal effects of these excluded variables on duration and subsequent wages differ between whites and blacks, as does their correlation with reservation wages, this might explain why the apparent effects of reservation wages differ between whites and blacks.

Finally, Holzer's data permit him to distinguish between the nonemployed who sought employment in the past month and those who intended to seek work sometime in the next year. Since the former group is more likely to contain "active" job searchers, some reanalysis of their behavior alone is probably in order. Similarly, all of Holzer's analyses pool together youths of different ages. The NLS sample covers 14- to 21-year-olds; the NBER, 16- to 24-year-olds. Since we know unemployment experience changes dramatically as youths age, separate estimations for different age groups are also in order.

Future Research Questions

The first research question posed by Holzer's study is why black youths are more willing than white youths to accept low-wage, temporary jobs. In answering this question one should distinguish between the behavior of those searching for temporary or part-time jobs and those searching for full-time career jobs. Again, the behavior of different age groups would be relevant here.

Second, Holzer presents data on reservation wages for specified hypothetical travel times to work. Future research could examine whether the compensating wage differential that black youths require for travel time to work differs from that of white youths. If it does, why should this be so, and do Holzer's results suggest such a difference will affect nonemployment durations? Also, if data are available in Holzer's samples on average travel times to work for employed black and white youths, one might compute how such differentials affect nonemployment durations. For instance, Ellwood's findings (in this volume) that young blacks in Chicago spent more than two times as much time traveling to work as young whites in 1975 might be usefully applied here.

Finally, future research should explicitly consider the role of social insurance programs. I have already mentioned unemployment insurance, but more important may be transfer payments such as Aid to Families with Dependent Children, according to which a family's grant depends on reported total family income. Do such programs discourage work effort and prolong spells of nonemployment among youths from low-income families? Are there racial differences in the effects on teenage nonemployment because the probability a teenager will be in a family eligible for AFDC may vary by race? Analyses along these lines could exploit the fact that AFDC program regulations vary across states and therefore provide a form of natural experiment.

References

Clark, K., and Summers, L. 1982. The dynamics of youth unemployment. In *The youth labor market problem: Its nature, causes, and consequences,* ed. R. B. Freeman and D. A. Wise. Chicago: University of Chicago Press.

Flinn, C. J., and Heckman, J. J. 1982. Are unemployment and out of the labor force behaviorally distinct labor force states? NBER Working Paper no. 979. Cambridge, Mass.: NBER.

Kiefer, N. M., and Neumann, G. R. 1979. An empirical job search model with a test of the constant reservation-wage hypothesis. *Journal of Political Economy* 87 (January/February): 89–109.

2   Transitions between Employment and Nonemployment

John Ballen and Richard B. Freeman

2.1   Introduction

In recent years, analyses that treat unemployment as a dynamic rather than a static phenomenon have provided important insights into the nature and causes of joblessness. One issue of concern in studying joblessness is whether unemployment is better thought of as a temporary state experienced by many individuals as part of their normal job-search process (Feldstein 1973) or as a relatively permanent state experienced by a only few (Clark and Summers 1982). Another issue is the dependence of the length of time unemployed on the number of past occurrences of unemployment (Ellwood 1982; Heckman and Borjas 1980). From the perspective of a dynamic analysis of unemployment, the factors that influence the transition between spells of employment and unemployment (or nonemployment), and thus the number of occurrences and the lengths of time in either state, are the underlying determinants of the magnitude and nature of the problem of joblessness.

This paper applies the dynamic analysis to the nonemployment problem of out-of-school inner-city black youths—the demographic group now facing the most severe joblessness in the United States. In 1980 the rate of unemployment among 18- to 19-year-old blacks, who were out of school was 36 percent, and the unemployment rate among 20- to 24-year-old blacks who were out of school was 24 percent. Because of low labor-force participation, the rate of nonemployment (unemployed + out of the labor force/population) was 64 percent among 16- to 19-year-olds and 40 percent among 20- to 24-year-olds.[1]

John Ballen is a student of law at Stanford University Law School. Richard B. Freeman is director of the Labor Studies program at the National Bureau of Economic Research and professor of economics at Harvard University.

What is the relative contribution to these high rates of long spells of nonemployment as opposed to many incidences of nonemployment? Are the labor market prospects of these youths adversely affected by previous nonemployment and positively affected by previous employment? What determines the length of spells of employment or nonemployment, and what determines the number of occurrences of each state? Does the dynamic of employment and nonemployment among black inner-city youths differ from that of other youths?

To answer these questions, we examine data on the employment and nonemployment experiences of inner-city black youths from the NBER Survey of Inner City Black Youths and data on the employment and nonemployment experiences of all black and white youths in the youth cohort of the 1979 National Longitudinal Surveys (NLS). We use the monthly time line of the NBER survey to calculate the employment and nonemployment status of inner-city black youths at two-week intervals over a year and examine the transitions between the two states. We use the questions in the NLS on activities between survey dates to calculate comparable data for a period of about two years and analyze these transitions as well. Because of the nebulous differences between the state of unemployment and the state of being out of the labor force represented in these kinds of data (Poterba and Summers 1983; Clark and Summers 1982), we concentrate on movements between employment and its converse, nonemployment. As the meaning of employment and nonemployment and the patterns of transitions are likely to be very different for youths in school from those of youths out of school, we limit our analysis to out-of-school youths.

This chapter first examines the rate of nonemployment among various groups of youths by age and over time; the number of occurrences of nonemployment and employment and the duration of nonemployment and employment spells; and the transition matrices across the two states. Next it analyzes the determinants of the transition probabilities, notably, their dependence on the past number of previous spells and the length of the most recent spell. Finally, we investigate the possible effects of incidences and spells of employment and nonemployment on wages.

2.2 Patterns of Employment Transitions

The standard analysis of employment activity over the life cycle envisages a moderate amount of time employed in the early years of working life—as youths search for the job appropriate to their talents, training, and tastes—followed by an extended period in which they hold down relatively permanent jobs.

The degree to which the normal pattern of increased employment activity with age holds for inner-city black youths is an important factor in judging their joblessness problem. If employment rises rapidly with age, reducing the gap between blacks' employment rate and that of other comparable individuals, the low rates of employment early in life may be judged less important than if employment rises slowly with age.

Table 2.1 presents evidence from the NBER and NLS data sets on the cross-sectional pattern of employment rates by age for all out-of-school inner-city black youths and for all black and white youths, by level of education. Because the employment rate (or its converse) is a limited dependent variable, varying between 0.00 and 1.00, the choice of a metric for measuring changes is an important methodological consideration. Accordingly, the table records two such measures: the absolute change and the logistic change relative to the difference between the employment rate and its upper bound.

There are two findings. First, among all out-of-school inner-city black youths, the rate of increase in employment with age is only moderate, showing no sign of a rapid movement toward the upper bound of 1.0 or toward the employment rate of whites. A similar pattern is obtained for

Table 2.1   Cross-Sectional Evidence on the Percentage of Out-of-School Youths Employed, by Age and Education

Age	Change in Odds Ratio of Employment			High School Dropouts		
	Rate of Employment (E)	Absolute Change (ΔE)	$\Delta[E/1\text{-}E]$	Rate of Employment (E)	Absolute Change (ΔE)	$\Delta[E/1\text{-}E]$
			NBER Blacks			
16–17	—	—		—		
18–19	.39	—		.38	—	
20–21	.49	.10	.16	.39	.01	.02
22–24	.51	.02	.00	.39	.00	.00
			NLS Blacks			
16–17	—	—		.25	—	
18–19	.53	—		.51	.26	.35
20–21	.65	.12	.26	.61	−.10	.20
22–24	.76	.11	.31	.50	−.11	−.28
			NLS Whites			
16–17	—	—		.58	—	—
18–19	.74	—		.69	.12	.29
20–21	.74	.00	.00	.64	−.05	−.08
22–24	.94	.20	.56	.86	.22	.61

Source: NBER survey, sample defined: not in school or military for year covered by questionnaire; sample sizes: all youths-1,067; high school dropouts-615. NLS, sample defined: male, age-16, no military hours worked in 1978, 1979, or 1980, not enrolled in school 1978-80; sample sizes: all youths-823; dropouts-415.

Note: Sample definitions and sample sizes for future tables are the same as these unless otherwise noted.

NLS black youths, with increases in the employment rate from ages 18–19 to ages 22–24 that are far below those needed to close the gap with white youths. Among whites, by contrast, there is a sharp rise in the early twenties, bringing their employment rate to .94.

Second, among black high school dropouts in the inner city, there is essentially *no* improvement in employment rates by age. Although there is some possibility this finding may be influenced by the undersampling of older black youths in the NBER survey, the evidence on sampling bias does not support such an interpretation, as indicated by Bound (in this volume). Moreover, even in the NLS, where the rate of employment by age rises for black high school dropouts from ages 16–17 to ages 18–19, the changes in the rates for the ages beyond 18–19 are insignificant. On the other hand, among white high school dropouts the rate rises considerably in the early twenties, such that the gap between blacks and whites is even greater than it was in the late teen years.

The contribution of a slow rise in employment with age to the joblessness problem of blacks 20 to 24 years old can be put another way. Given the extremely low levels of employment among teenaged black youths, an exceptionally steep relationship between age and employment is necessary for employment among youths in their twenties to reach "reasonable" levels. The data in table 2.1 show that rather than being exceptionally steep, the age–employment rate relationship flattens quickly among black youths, especially among the dropouts.

Because the cross-sectional evidence compares different persons at one specific time, it is possible that it presents a misleading picture of true longitudinal changes over the life cycle. It may be that the older youths in the sample had *lower* rates of employment when they were teenagers than the younger youths and thus greater increases in rates than implied by cross-sectional comparisons. Or it may be that the younger youths will have higher rates of employment when they are older and thus greater increases in rates than indicated by comparisons with older youths. To examine these possibilities, we have compared rates of employment for black youths of the same age over time, using published Current Population Survey (CPS) data. Those data show no greater increase in rates of employment among black teenagers in the late 1970s and no greater increase in rates of employment among blacks 20 to 24 years old in the early 1980s.[2]

To document further that rates of employment for inner-city and other black youths fail to rise substantially with age, we have tabulated employment rates for the same youths over time. In the NBER survey we compare employment rates for youths from the first month covered in the monthly time line to the last month. In the NLS we compare employment rates from 1979 to 1981. Table 2.2 records the results of this longitudinal analysis of employment with age (and time). The patterns of changes over time are quite consistent with the cross-sectional comparisons, giving no indication of extremely rapid increases in employment rates as youths age. But since the NBER data cover only one year and since the NLS sample sizes are small, we eschew detailed comparisons here.

Neither the cross-sectional nor the longitudinal comparisons isolate a pure life-cycle or age effect. The former may also reflect "cohort" effects, while the latter may also reflect pure "time" effects (notably, changes in business-cycle conditions). Still, the most plausible interpretation of the patterns in tables 2.1 and 2.2 is that part of the black youth employment problem is attributable to the failure of employment to rise with age as much as it could, or perhaps should. This interpretation, in turn, calls attention to the transition between nonemployment and employment as youths age, and to the factors underlying the transition probabilities, as important elements in the persistence of low levels of employment as black youths age.

2.2.1 Decomposition of Employment and Nonemployment

As a first step in examining the dynamics of nonemployment among inner-city black youths, we have decomposed the annual rates of employment and nonemployment into the number of times youths were in those states and the duration of time in those states. To obtain a complete accounting of youths' time over the period of concern, we include uncompleted spells in some calculations. We also examine completed spells separately, for the purpose of analyzing spells per se. Our calculations are based on the monthly time-line module of the NBER survey, which asks youths about their primary and secondary activities over a 50-week period. The NLS survey uses a work-history set of questions to determine employment status over 150 weeks. For purposes of comparison with the NBER survey, we also tabulated transitions for white youths in the NLS over a 50-week period in 1979–80.

Lines 1–4 of table 2.3 present a complete decomposition of the rates of employment and nonemployment, using the following formulas:

(1)
rate of employment = (% of youths in employment at least once)
$\times$ (# of times youths are employed)
$\times$ (average length of the employment spells)

(2)
rate of nonemployment = (% of youths in nonemployment at least once) $\times$ (# of times youths are not employed) $\times$ (average length of the nonemployment spells).

Table 2.2   Longitudinal Evidence on the Percentage of Out-of-School Youths Employed, by Age and Education, 1979–81

	NBER Blacks				NLS Blacks			NLS Whites		
Age	Rate of Employment (E)	Absolute Change (WE)	WE/1-E	Age	Rate of Employment (E)	Absolute Change (WE)	WE/1-E	Rate of Employment (E)	Absolute Change (WE)	WE/1-E
					All Youths					
18–19	.33			18–19	.53			.74		
19–20	.39	.06	.18	20–21	.67	.14	.30	.73	−.01	−.04
20–21	.50			20–21	.65			.74		
21–22	.49	−.01	−.02	22–23	.72	.07	.20	.77	.03	.12
22–24	.55			22–24	.76			.94		
24–26	.51	−.04	−.07	24–26	.64	−.12	−.50	.90	−.04	−.67
					High School Dropouts					
16–17	.18			16–17	.25			.58		
17–18	.27	.09	.11	18–19	.50	.25	.33	.65	.07	.17
18–19	.29			18–19	.51			.69		
19–20	.38	.09	.13	20–21	.64	.13	.27	.67	−.02	−.06
20–21	.35			20–21	.61			.64		
21–22	.39	.04	.06	22–23	.69	.21	.21	.67	.03	.08
22–24	.45			22–24	.50			.86		
24–26	.39	−.06	−.11	24–26	.33	−.34	−.34	.93	.07	.50

The rate of employment (nonemployment) is calculated by dividing the total number of person-weeks spent in the state by the total number of person-weeks in the sample. Thus, equations (1) and (2) are identities.

Several related aspects of the dynamics of black youth employment and nonemployment are illustrated in lines 1–4 of table 2.3. First is the remarkably large proportion (24 percent) of blacks in the NBER survey who were never in the state of employment (the converse of the percentage employed in line 2) vis-à-vis the negligible proportions of whites and blacks in the NLS who were never employed. This finding confirms the fact that the NBER survey has indeed identified youths who are, in some sense, nonparticipants in normal economic life. It also reinforces the Clark and Summers (1982) position on the concentration of nonemployment among a minority of youths: 54 percent of all the weeks in nonemployment in the NBER survey is accounted for by those youths who were *never* employed.

Second, note that the mean number of times a youth is in a state, given that he is in it at least once, varies only slightly across the groups. Third, the average duration of spells (including uncompleted spells) shows considerable differences in lengths of nonemployment spells between blacks in the NBER Survey and whites in the NLS and between blacks and whites in the NLS. The data show that blacks in both the NBER survey and the NLS remained employed for shorter periods and nonemployed for longer periods than did whites, with the biggest percentage difference in the length of time not employed.

To determine the contribution of incidences and duration of spells to the enormous differences in employment and nonemployment rates between blacks and whites, we have taken log differences between the various components of employment rates in table 2.3 and obtained the following:

	NBER blacks vs. NLS whites	NLS blacks vs. NLS whites
log difference in employment rates	−.405	−.214
ln % in state	−.244	−.031
ln # times in state	−.071	.010
ln duration	−.088	−.193
log difference in nonemployment rates	.781	.541
ln % in state	.392	.145
ln # times in state	−.043	.018
ln duration	.435	.378

Note: Totals need not add because of rounding.

Table 2.3   Number of Incidences and Durations of Spells of Employment and of Nonemployment

	One Year				Three Years			
	NBER Blacks		NLS Whites		NLS Blacks		NLS Whites	
	E	N	E	N	E	N	E	N
1. Rates for Total Sample	.52	.48	.78	.22	.63	.37	.78	.22
2. Percentage in State at Least Once	.76	.74	.97	.50	.96	.80	.99	.69
3. Number of Times in State, in State at Least Once	1.22	1.36	1.31	1.42	2.11	2.36	2.09	2.32
4. Average Duration of Spells (2-week spells)	14.1	11.9	15.4	7.7	23.3	14.8	28.3	10.11
5. Proportion of Sample with Completed Spells	.23	.15	.16	.25	.53	.54	.46	.55
6. Number of Completed Spells	1.16	1.14	1.28	1.25	2.07	2.02	2.00	1.97
7. Average Length Completed Spells (2-week intervals)	6.7	5.2	5.4	5.0	11.16	8.97	11.54	7.6

Source: Tabulated from the surveys based on number of transitions.
Notes: E = employed, N = nonemployed. The NBER sample = 1,067; the NLS sample of whites = 610; and the NLS sample of blacks = 213.

From these calculations, differences in the proportion of youths who are never employed are a major cause of the employment rate difference between blacks in the NBER survey and whites in the NLS and are a significant cause of nonemployment rate differences. Differences in the duration of spells are the dominant factor in the comparisons of blacks and whites in the NLS.

Lines 5–7 in table 2.3 examine completed spells. Because completed spells have to have begun and ended in the time period covered by the survey, the spells are necessarily short, making the mean of the completed spells noticeably smaller than the mean of the uncompleted spells. Comparison of the length of completed spells between blacks and whites in a sample like this is highly misleading, as can be seen in line 7, which shows blacks having spells of about the same length as those of whites, or longer spells. The reason for this is that many long spells of employment for whites had not ended in the period covered by the survey.

2.2.2 Transition Probabilities

Lengths of time in states and movements between them depend on transition probabilities. When the probabilities of leaving states are large, spells will be short and incidences in states numerous. When the probabilities of leaving are small—zero in the case of an absorbing state—the opposite is true. The key way to pursue a dynamic analysis of employment and nonemployment is to create matrices of transition probabilities between the two states.

Table 2.4 records the average biweekly transition probabilities between employment and nonemployment for the NBER and NLS samples. The NBER probabilities were calculated from the monthly time line. The NLS probabilities were obtained from the job-history questions about breaks in employment, organized to produce a time line, as described in appendix A. For both calculations we took averages of probabilities across youths and across time, ignoring issues of both heterogeneity among youths and the possible dependence of transition probabilities on the past history of the individual, such as his number of times and length of time in the state. Formally, if P_{ij}^{kt} is the probability that that individual k will go from state i to state j in period t, the averages in the table are:

$$(3) \qquad P_{ij..} = \sum_{tk} \sum P_{ij}^{kt} = \sum_{u} P_{ij}^{.t} = \sum_{k} P_{ij}^{k.},$$

where the dots signify averages over the relevant index.

The elements in the matrices show that P_{EN} is greatest for blacks in the NBER survey and smallest for whites in the NLS, and that P_{NE} is smallest for blacks in the NBER survey and largest for whites in the

Table 2.4 **Matrices of Transitions Between Employment and Nonemployment**

	All Youths				High School Dropouts			
	Age at the Outset							
	16–19		20–24		16–19		20–24	
	NBER Blacks							
	E	N	E	N	E	N	E	N
E	.950	.050	.967	.033	.947	.053	.955	.045
N	.041	.959	.041	.959	.039	.961	.037	.963
	NLS Blacks							
	E	N	E	N	E	N	E	N
E	.96	.04	.97	.03	.95	.05	.96	.04
N	.06	.94	.06	.94	.05	.95	.06	.94
	NLS Whites							
	E	N	E	N	E	N	E	N
E	.97	.03	.98	.02	.96	.04	.97	.03
N	.08	.92	.10	.90	.08	.92	.09	.91

Source: Tabulated as average of biweekly transition probabilities from the relevant surveys. NBER transitions based on one year; NLS transitions based on three years. Sample Sizes:

	All Youths		High School Dropouts	
	16–19	20–24	16–19	20–24
NBER blacks	307	760	234	358
NLS blacks	72	141	55	68
NLS whites	213	397	155	137

NLS. These relationships were of course, implied by the table 2.3 decomposition. In addition, note that the transition probabilities for blacks show only modest improvement with age: although P_{EN} drops, P_{NE} does not increase for blacks. Indeed, the P_{NE} transition probability is lower for older blacks than it is for younger whites. It is this pattern of transitions that underlies the sluggish improvement in the employment position of blacks as they age.

It is important to recognize that the probabilities in the table differ between blacks and whites by significant amounts; the key probabilities are the off-diagonal elements (P_{EN} and P_{NE}), and it is their ratio, rather than their absolute difference, that underlies the differential employment experiences.

The simplest way to apply the table 2.4 transition matrices to the employment and nonemployment rates is to assume that the matrices are Markovian and then to calculate the steady-state distribution of youths between employment and nonemployment generated by the equation:

(4) $s = Ps,$

where $P = (P_{ij})$ and $s = \begin{pmatrix} E \\ N \end{pmatrix}$ for the two states of employment. For the steady-state rate of employment (E) and nonemployment (N), the solution to equation (4) yields:

(5) $E = P_{EN}/(P_{EN} + P_{NE})$

$$N = 1 - E.$$

Estimates of the steady-state rates, and comparisons of these rates to the actual distributions of youths between states, are given in table 2.5. The predicted states are comparable to, but not identical to, the actual states, indicating that the table 2.4 matrices do, in fact, underly the observed patterns but that the simple Markov assumption does not strictly hold. Table 2.5 also presents the results of an experiment in which we replace the P_{EN} and P_{NE} transition probabilities for blacks with those for whites, in order to determine which transition is a greater cause of the white-black differences in employment. If the P_{EN} differences are the more important cause, the problem of nonemployment is largely one of *holding* a job. On the other hand, if the P_{NE} differences are more important, the problem is more one of *finding* a job in the first place. As can be seen in the last two columns of the table, black nonemployment rates fall much more when we replace the P_{NE} for blacks with that for whites than when we replace the P_{EN} for blacks with that for whites. These results imply that much of the differences in employment dynamics is attributable to differences in the ability to obtain work in the first place. It should be noted that these findings are consistent with those of other studies that show quit rates and turnover among blacks are not very different from quit rates and turnover among whites.[3]

2.3   Determinants of Transition Probabilities

Transition probabilities differ among persons. In this section we examine some of the potential determinants of differences among the youths in our survey to see which youths have better or worse transition probabilities. In addition, we examine the dependence of the probabilities on the individual's past work history. If a bad employment history makes escape into employment difficult, and a good employment history raises employment prospects, we will have both negative

Table 2.5   Predicted and Actual Distributions of Nonemployed Youths

	Actual	Predicted from Transition matrix	Predicted with White P_{NE}	Predicted with White P_{EN}
All Youths				
1. NBER, Black, 16–19	.59	.55	.38	.45
2. NBER, Black, 20–24	.43	.45	.25	.33
3. NLS, Black, 16–19	.46	.40	.33	.33
4. NLS, Black, 20–24	.32	.33	.23	.25
5. NLS, White, 16–19	.29	.27	—	—
6. NLS, White, 20–24	.17	.16	—	—
High School Dropouts				
7. NBER, Black, 16–19	.61	.56	.51	.56
8. NBER, Black, 20–24	.55	.55	.33	.45
9. NLS, Black, 16–19	.52	.50	.38	.44
10. NLS, Black, 20–24	.43	.40	.31	.33
11. NLS, White, 16–19	.35	.33	—	—
12. NLS, White, 20–24	.27	.25	—	—

Source: Actual distributions tabulated from NBER survey and NLS. Predicted distributions using equation (5) and the data in table 2.4. Sample sizes are the same as in table 2.4.

and positive "vicious circles." If there is no such dependence, and differences in transition probabilities are largely the result of differences among persons that existed before their entry into the labor market, the transition-to-employment problem is potentially more long-term for those individuals and thus less apt to be solved by such labor market developments and interventions as increased demand or training programs.

Because there are various ways to model the dependence of transition probabilities on past work histories, we report a variety of related tests. Some of our tests treat the entire sample of individuals. Others, designed to isolate "true" state dependence from heterogeneity among individuals, focus on smaller samples. Although the assumptions needed for any single test of the nature of transitions may render it fallible, the entire set yields consistent results, thereby strengthening our belief in the findings.

The analysis indicates that the transition-to-employment problem for young blacks is influenced by two phenomena. First, incidences of nonemployment severely limit inner-city black youths' chances for employment, apparently because employers do not trust youths with spotty work records. Second, the duration of employment does not help inner-city blacks as much as it helps whites, apparently, at least in part, because black youths tend to hold "dead end" jobs.

2.3.1   Regression Analysis

Table 2.6 presents the results of a regression analysis of the transition probabilities P_{EN} and P_{NE} on the number of incidences of the initial state in the past, the length of the ongoing state, and a host of background variables, which are both of interest in themselves and of value as controls for differences among respondents. The regression results are reported for the linear form:

$$(6) \qquad P_{ij}^{kt} = a + bT_i^{kt} + cN_i^{kt} + dX^{kt} + U_{ij},$$

where T_i represents the length of time in i up to period t, and X^{kt} signifies the background variables for the individual.

The calculations show a fairly consistent and reasonable pattern for the determination of transition probabilities. Examining the transition from employment to nonemployment first, we see that it depends as we might expect on certain background factors. For example, youths who commit illegal acts have a higher probability of leaving employment, while those with more stable family status and greater age have lower probabilities. The only difference between the samples is in time in the state, which lowers P_{EN} for blacks and whites in the NLS but not, surprisingly, for blacks in the NBER survey, where it has essentially no effect.

The regressions for the nonemployment-employment transition show a consistent pattern of negative effects of time-in-state and produce coefficients on the background variables generally opposite in sign to those found in the P_{EN} regression. Perhaps the most salient result here is the *negative* effect of age on P_{NE} for inner-city blacks, which suggests that it is more difficult for these youths to leave nonemployment as they age, a result in line with our findings about the age-employment relationship.

The second half of table 2.6 shows the means of the independent variables. Note that in some cases the means differ considerably between the transitions that began in E and those that began in N. A typical P_{EN} observation is more likely than a P_{NE} to involve a respondent who had a high school diploma or was married or the head of the household and is less likely to involve one who had engaged in illegal activities. This is another way of stating that those factors help determine the probability of a respondent being in one of the two states.

2.3.2   State Dependence

A key issue in analyzing the employment transitions is the extent to which the length of time in a spell or the incidence of spells affects transition probabilities (Ellwood, 1982 Heckman and Borjas, 1980). In seven of the eight calculations in table 2.6, we find a negative relationship between time in a state and the transition probability that is indicative of such dependence. The results obtained in the regressions could be attributed, however, to heterogeneity among persons and the sorting of them by time in the state rather than by true dependence on past work history.

To determine if the regressions results can be attributed to true dependence, we must compare the situation of the *same* respondent over time before and after he experienced a break in state, thereby eliminating heterogeneity among respondents as a possible cause of statistical significance.

Table 2.7 presents the results of four different tests of the incidence and duration dependence of transitions based on such comparisons for black and white youths. Before examining the results, recognize that

Table 2.6   **Linear Probability Estimates of the Determinants of Transition Probabilities**
(standard errors in parentheses)

	P_{EN}			P_{NE}		
	NBER Blacks	NLS Blacks	NLS Whites	NBER Blacks	NLS Blacks	NLS Whites
Mean (× 100) of Dependent Variable	3.67	2.91	2.23	4.10	5.98	9.16
Dependent Variables						
Time in State	.020 (.024)	−.056 (.009)	−.040 (.004)	−.066 (.027)	−.084 (.022)	−.083 (.028)
Age	−.17 (.09)	−.037 (.167)	−.27 (.08)	−.16 (.09)	.063 (.280)	.112 (.250)
Illegal Activities	1.40 (.40)	.15 (.39)	.84 (.22)	.38 (.40)	.71 (.73)	−1.56 (.69)
Years of School	−.17 (.18)	−.19 (.18)	−.16 (.09)	.42 (.20)	.11 (.23)	1.26 (.29)
H.S. Diploma	−1.32 (.50)	−1.37 (.52)	−1.47 (.29)	.16 (.57)	.64 (.95)	−1.69 (1.04)
Grades in School[b]	−.24 (.18)	—	—	.17 (.19)	—	—
Married	−.67 (.58)	−.93 (.57)	−.63 (.18)	.82 (.85)	.50 (1.51)	3.40 (.79)
Head of Household	−.30 (.53)	−.31 (.39)	−.13 (.18)	.51 (.71)	1.61 (.80)	2.19 (.69)
Other Controls	—[c]	—[d]	—[d]	—[c]	—[d]	—[d]

Table 2.6 (continued)

	NBER Blacks		NLS Blacks		NLS Whites	
	N	*E*	*N*	*E*	*N*	*E*
Means for the Independent Variables are:						
Time in State	9.54	10.0	16.0	24.0	11.1	26.4
Age	20.6	21.2	19.7	20.1	19.5	20.1
Illegal Activities	.27	.21	.29	.29	.31	.17
Years of School	10.8	11.3	10.1	10.9	9.9	11.0
H.S. Diploma	.33	.55	.26	.52	.31	.62
Grade in School[b]	2.86	3.02	—	—	—	—
Married	.05	.09	.05	.12	.23	.39
Head of Household	.07	.11	.29	.37	.43	.57

Note: These means are based not on persons but on transitions, so that persons count more than once. Sample sizes are NBER (P_{EN}) = 13,475, (P_{NE}) = 12,133; NLS blacks (P_{EN}) = 9,595, (P_{NE}) = 5,320; and NLS whites (P_{EN}) = 32,305, (P_{NE}) = 8,341.
[a]Because the same persons are counted several times, the standard errors are not appropriate for normal statistical tests that assume independence of errors over time.
[b]Variable not measured in NLS.
[c]Other controls for the NBER: sample were dummy variables for Chicago and Boston and for both parents present in the household at age 14.
[d]Other controls for the NLS samples were dummy variables for both parents present in the household at age 14; for residence in South at age 14; and for mother or father working when the youth was age 14.

all the tests suffer from potentially serious measurement problems. First, the sample size for some is extremely limited because of the small number of respondents who had experienced the requisite changes in state or completed spells. Second, and related, are questions about the representativeness of respondents fulfilling the conditions. When a test is limited to five percent of a sample, one is suspicious that conclusions based on that five percent are generalizable. Third are potential problems of measurement error in the tests: random measurement error is, in general, more likely to be a major problem in longitudinal analyses than in cross-sectional work.[4] Granting these problems, the tests for heterogeneity as opposed to state dependence still provide valuable information on the impact of past work history on current employment problems. The detailed calculations underlying the tests are given in appendix B.

The first test, for duration dependence, was developed by Chamberlain (1982). It is based on the idea that when there is duration dependence, various incidences of a state should occur close together in time rather than being separated by time in the other state. For

Table 2.7   **Test of Incidence and Duration Dependence of Transitions, Corrected for Heterogeneity**

	NBER Blacks	NLS Blacks	NLS Whites
Duration			
1. Chamberlain Duration Test			
P_{NE} Lowered by Duration of Nonemployment	Yes	No	No
P_{EN} Lowered by Duration of Employment	No	Yes	Yes
Incidence			
2. Counting Test Incidence			
P_{EN} Higher After Spell of Nonemployment	Yes	No	No
P_{NE} Higher After Spell of Employment	No	No	No
3. Mean Spell Test of Incidence			
P_{EN} Higher After Spell of Nonemployment	Yes	No	No
P_{NE} Higher After Spell of Employment	?	No	No
4. Heckman-Borjas Test of Incidence			
P_{EN} Higher After Spell of Nonemployment	Yes	No	No
P_{NE} Higher After Spell of Employment	Yes	No	No

Source: See appendix B for details of these tests.

example, consider the possible pattern of employment and nonemployment at six different times, such that a youth is employed four times and not employed two times. If employment duration reduces the chance of nonemployment, (P_{EN}), then it is more likely that the times the youth is employed will occur in a sequence than would be the case if employment duration has no affect on P_{EN}. Writing observed states over time in parentheses, we see that the pattern (E,E,E,N,E,N) is more likely to occur than the pattern (E,E,N,E,E,N) if there is a dependence effect.

As discussed in appendix B, we have performed a variety of tests of this sort for the three samples, examining different timing sequences. The results of these tests show a very different pattern for black youths in the NBER survey than for black or white youths in the NLS. The duration of nonemployment marginally hurts inner-city black youths—in the sense that the longer a spell of nonemployment, the lower are their chances of moving into employment—but does not hurt other youths. More strikingly, the duration of employment helps other youths significantly by reducing the probability of moving into nonemployment, but it does not help inner-city black youths.

The remaining tests in table 2.7 are for incidence dependence. They test whether a spell of nonemployment raises the chances a youth will leave employment after the spell over his chances of leaving employment before the spell. Formally, if P^0_{EN} is the transition probability before nonemployment and P^l_{EN} is the transition probability after nonemployment, the tests measure whether P^l_{EN} is less than P^0_{EN}. On the other side, the tests for incidence dependence of employment measure whether P^l_{NE} is greater than P^0_{NE}, that is, whether a spell of employment raises the chances of escaping nonemployment.

The "counting" test in line 2 of table 2.7 simply compares the lengths of spells before and after a completed intervening spell. The test compares two types of spells—completed spells before and after the intervening spell, and uncompleted spells before and after the intervening spell—based on the hypothesis that longer uncompleted spells imply longer completed spells. We do not include cases in which one spell is completed and the other is uncompleted because of potential biases. When one spell is shorter than another but uncompleted, it could become longer in the future, making mixed comparisons risky. The results of the counting tests show incidence dependence for nonemployment among inner-city black youths but not among the other groups.

The third test in the table compares the mean length of spells before and after the incidence. A parametric extension of the counting test, this test gives essentially the same results. The magnitude of the effect of an incidence of nonemployment in the NBER sample is, by the estimated regression, fairly sizable: an average spell of employment is 32 percent lower after a spell of nonemployment than it is before.

Finally, line 4 of the table presents the results of the Heckman-Borjas test of incidence dependence, which is based on comparisons of spells with various intervals. The test checks for whether nonemployment and employment are clumped together in the data. The results are generally similar to those in the other incidence tests, showing that an incidence of nonemployment hurts inner-city black youths but not other groups. There is, however, one difference between this and other tests: there is also evidence of incidence dependence in employment for NBER youths though not for other youths.

On the basis of these results, it is tempting to conclude that the transition problem of inner-city black youths is largely a result of the negative impact of nonemployment on the chances these youths will later gain jobs, and possibly to the lack of a positive impact of employment on their chances for remaining employed. Since, as we saw in table 2.5, much of the high nonemployment rate among inner-city youths in the NBER survey is due to small probabilities in the P_{NE} transition, the finding that nonemployment hurts them provides an appealing explanation of the overall dynamics of nonemployment. We are wary of drawing such a strong conclusion from these results, however. Although it is plausible that inner-city black youths are more affected by their work histories than other black youths, we would have greater faith in this conclusion if the tests for state dependence for blacks in the NLS gave results closer to those for the NBER inner-city sample than to those for whites in the NLS. As they did not, the conclusion requires additional buttressing.

2.4 Explanations of the Dependence Patterns

One way to support the finding that nonemployment among inner-city blacks reduces their chances of getting a job while employment does not increase their chances of getting a job is to examine the possible economic forces that might cause such dependence patterns. In this section we examine the possibility that the observed patterns are due, at least in part, to the job market in which the youths find themselves. In particular, we look at the effects of the employer's hiring criteria and the nature of the jobs obtained by inner-city black youths on their transition probabilities.

2.4.1 The Nonemployment-Employment Transition

To examine the incidence dependence of nonemployment, we conducted telephone interviews with 18 randomly selected employers located in a primarily black district (Roxbury) of one of the cities (Boston) in the NBER survey. The purpose of our interviews was to determine how employers react to different work histories of youths. If employers place great weight on incidences of nonemployment in choosing whom to hire, the finding that many incidences of nonemployment hurt a youth's chances of finding a job will be supported and traceable to these employers. If employers place little or no weight on the duration of the youth's last spell of nonemployment, our weak rejection of duration dependence of nonemployment will also receive support. On the other hand, if employers state that they ignore incidences of nonemployment but tend to reject job applications from youths with long spells of nonemployment, our finding will be in doubt.

Table 2.8 lists the questions we asked, and the number and percentage of employers giving various responses. Our first question concerned the candidate characteristics in which employers were most interested. As can be seen, there were essentially no skill requirements for the types of jobs of concern, and employers were primarily interested in the youths' being "good workers" in terms of dependability, namely, showing up, making an honest effort, looking presentable, and so on. Before asking about the weight placed on different aspects of a youth's work history, we asked the employers if they did in fact ask about past work records. Eighty-three percent answered "yes," and we limited the remaining questions to those employers.

The important result from our interviews, shown in table 2.8, is that most employers did regard "a casual work history with many jobs" as a negative indicator of the youths' work talents, but they did *not* regard a long period of nonemployment as being a "strike" against the youth. Sentiments expressed about youths with spotty work records ranged from "He wouldn't be working for me" to "I'm not looking for headaches." Of the employers who judged youths on their work records, all but one stated they would *never* hire a youth with many spells of unemployment or many different jobs. Managers claimed that their previous experience had indicated to them that youths with spotty work records had high absenteeism and turnover rates, because the youths were planning to work for just a short while to pick up spending money. Finally, we also asked employers if their attitudes toward youths depended on the age of the youths. Eleven employers said they would be more biased against a youth with a spotty work record if he were older than if he were younger because they believed that older youths who exhibited such work records were simply not interested in working. This last response suggests that incidence dependence interacts with age to screen out older workers who get caught in a recurring pattern of short-term jobs.

The results of the employer survey thus confirm our statistical finding about the incidence dependence and lack of duration dependence of nonemployment. At the same time, however, the reasons offered by employers for their hiring criterion—that workers with spotty work records are poor workers—suggest two possible reasons why the incidence dependence result "passed" our heterogeneity tests. One possibility is that employers engage in statistical discrimination,[5] shying away from youths with spotty records (even when the youths are potentially good workers) because of a perceived correlation between spotty records and bad personal work characteristics. The other possibility, which leads us into an entirely different point of view, is that the omitted personal attributes of youths change over time. More specifically, when a youth has numerous incidences of nonemployment, he is in fact not "really interested" in working, whereas when the same youth has few incidences, he in fact is likely to be a good employee.

Table 2.8   **Employer Selection Criteria and the Incidence of Nonemployment Effects**

Question	Answer	Responses (Out of 18)	Percentage of Responses
1. When you interview a candidate for employment, what characteristics are you most interested in?			
	Cleanliness, neatness, honesty, dependability, attitudes	11	61%
	Past education, maturity	9	50%
	Education	7	39%
	Graduation from high school	4	22%
2. Do you ask about a youth's past work record?	Yes	15	83%
3. Is it a strike against the youth if he has been out of work for a long period of time before applying for a job?	No	13	72%
	Yes, less than one year	2	11%
	Yes, greater than one year	3	17%
4. Is it a strike against the youth if he has had a casual work history with many jobs and many periods of employment?	Yes	14	78%
5. Are your attitudes toward a youth who exhibits a poor work record different if the youth is 18 or 19 from your attitudes if he were in his early twenties?	Yes	14	78%

Source: Black Youth Employers Survey, 18 Roxbury employers. See appendix C.

From this perspective, the incidences reflect potentially changeable attitudes rather than permanent personal characteristics.

2.4.2   The Employment-Nonemployment Transition

To examine the finding of a relative lack of duration dependence in employment on ensuing employment, we have explored the hypothesis that a large part of the problem results from the types of jobs held by the inner-city black youths. If these are more "dead end" jobs, with little opportunity for learning or advancement, than those of other youths, the lack of duration dependence may be attributable to the jobs themselves. Nevertheless the question why the black youths are more likely to end up in those jobs would still remain unanswered.

Table 2.9 shows the percentage of black youths in the NBER survey employed in various occupations, by age. The table shows that most of the black youths were in low-level occupations with relatively flat age-earnings profiles; a bare 5 percent were professionals or managers and just over 15 percent were in any white-collar job, whereas some 40 percent were in laborer or service jobs. That the jobs held by black youths are not the sorts of jobs to induce extended periods of employment is supported by answers to NBER survey questions regarding the nature of the work performed and the proportions who looked upon their jobs as having long-term career possibilities. As illustrated in table 2.10, relatively few inner-city youths worked in jobs that required considerable education or on-the-job training. As a result, few regarded their current jobs as having long-term possibilities and few intended to stay for an extended period. We therefore conclude that the lack of duration dependence in employment for black youths is real and due in part to the types of jobs held by these youths.

2.4.3   Wage Consequences of Initial Nonemployment

The seriousness with which one views youth nonemployment depends in large measure on whether one believes youth nonemployment creates long-term economic problems for youths or whether one believes the youths' problems diminish rapidly with age. We have seen that the increase in employment is modest with age over a short span of years and that at least one aspect of youth nonemployment has adverse consequences for the future, but we have not examined the overall consequences of nonemployment on the youths' wages. A priori, one expects wages to be adversely affected by nonemployment at this stage of youths' work life. We would expect wages to rise sharply early in the work life, so that youths who miss early work experience would suffer substantially in terms of wages, at least in the short run.

Table 2.11 presents estimates of the impact of work experience on wages in two stages of the NLS survey that enabled across-year com-

Table 2.9   **Types of Jobs Held by Black Out-of-School Youths**

	Percentage Distribution of Inner-City Black Youths, by Age		
Occupation	16–17	18–19	20–24
1. Professional, Technical and Kindred Workers	4.55	1.20	3.16
2. Managers and Administrators, except Farm	0.0	0.80	2.21
3. Sales Workers	5.68	3.20	1.90
4. Clerical and Kindred	7.95	13.60	13.27
5. Crafts and Kindred	10.23	13.60	14.53
6. Operatives, except Transport	7.96	14.00	15.96
7. Transport Equipment Operatives	2.27	2.00	6.00
8. Nonfarm Laborers	18.18	15.60	12.48
9. Private Household Workers	1.14	0.0	0.16
10. All Other Service Workers	42.04	36.00	30.33
Sample Size:	88	250	633

parisons. The table first records the results of regressions of log wages on incidences and duration of nonemployment. Second, it presents the results of regressions of first differences in wages on first differences in the same independent variables, thereby contrasting the positions of the *same* youth over time. Although the level regressions do not isolate causality, they do enable us to determine whether nonemployment is associated with low wages for the *same* youths, distinguishing the possible extent to which a specific set of youths bear the brunt of economic distress.

The level regressions in table 2.11 indeed show that youths with less work experience have lower wages later on in life. The second set of regressions eliminate heterogeneity effects by a first-differencing procedure. Although this set shows smaller effects than those in the first set, a relationship between wages and work experience for blacks is

Table 2.10   **Perceived Characteristics of the Jobs Held by Inner-City Black Youths**

Perceived Characteristic	Percentage Responding
1. This level of education needed for their job:	
Less then high school	32.2
High school graduate	14.1
Some college	1.7
College degree or more	2.1
2. Time for average person to do job:	
Less then two weeks	43.9
Two weeks to one month	22.7
One to two months	16.8
Two to six months	9.4
Six+ months	7.3
3. Regard current job/ most recent job as having long-term career possibilities:	
Long-term	24.8
Temporary	71.2
Don't know	4.0
4. Intend to stay working on job for greater or equal to:	
Less than 1 month	2.3
One month	16.4
Three months	15.9
Six months	9.7
One year	55.7

Source: NBER survey. Sample size limited to out-of-school youths who answered the questions. Sample sizes ranged from 1,540 to 1,668.

still evident. (The results for whites are contrary.) We therefore conclude that nonemployment may breed low wages as well as future nonemployment among black youths.

2.5 Conclusion

This chapter has examined the problem of black youth nonemployment from the perspective of the dynamic transition between employment and nonemployment. Subject to problems of model specification and of survey differences that make comparisons difficult, there are four substantive findings.

Table 2.11   **Effect of Nonemployment on the Wages of NLS Youth**

	Dependent Variable		
	Log Wages$_{t+1}$	$\left(\begin{matrix}\text{Log}\\\text{Wages}_{t-2}\end{matrix}\right) - \left(\begin{matrix}\text{Log}\\\text{Wages}_{t+1}\end{matrix}\right)$	
NLS Blacks			
1. Number of incidences of nonwork for those who worked period $_t$	−.09 (.05)	1. Change in number of incidences t to $t+1$	−.07 (.05)
2. Average duration of nonemployment spell in period t	−.008 (.006)	2. Change in duration t to $t+1$	−.008 (.006)
NLS Whites			
1. Number of incidences of nonwork for those who worked period t	−.03 (.03)	1. Change in number	.04 (.02)
2. Average duration of nonemployment spell in period t	−.004 (.004)		−.002 (.003)

Note: The controls are personal characteristics, as in the previous tables. The sample sizes are 394 for NLS whites and 122 for NLS blacks.

First, the "normal" increase in the rate of employment among youths as they age is severely attenuated for inner-city black youths, especially those who have dropped out of high school. Overall, the increase in the rate of employment is less for black youths than for white youths, and it is sufficiently modest to suggest that the problem of joblessness will not disappear as the youths age.

Second, much of the difference in the rates of employment and non-employment between inner-city blacks and other youths is attributable to shorter spells of employment and longer spells of nonemployment and to the large fraction of inner-city black youths who are never employed. When all black and white youths are compared, the duration of nonemployment and employment is the key component of racial differences in employment experiences.

Third, the principal difference in transition probabilities between inner-city black, all black, and all white youths lies in the transition from nonemployment to employment, rather than that from employment to nonemployment. In part, this difference seems to be the result of the fact that inner-city black youths are more adversely affected by a spotty work record, particularly past incidences of nonemployment, while other youths are not so affected. We have traced this difference to the employer hiring criterion.

Finally, whereas all black and white youths appear to have reduced chances of moving from employment to nonemployment the longer they have been employed, inner-city black youths do not appear to exhibit such duration dependence. This result is found in most, though not all, of our statistical tests, and it is attributable to the dead-end types of jobs inner-city blacks obtain.

All told, the evidence in the paper suggests that high nonemployment among inner-city black youths is likely to extract a significant cost in their future careers, because the dynamics of their transition to work are notably worse than those of other groups of youths.

Appendix A
Calculations of Time Lines

NBER Time Line

The time line is composed of point estimates of the employment state of individuals at each biweekly point. If on the first of the month an individual was working, a one was recorded; if the individual was nonemployed, a zero was recorded, and similarly for the fifteenth of every month. The time line originally comprised 13 months; however, many interviewers failed to report the last biweekly interval. For this paper, that last interval is deleted and a time line with 25 biweekly intervals is used.

NLS Time Line

The time line consists of 75 intervals, which together make up a three-year biweekly work history of employment and nonemployment for each worker. The work status for each period is derived from the yearly survey question regarding periods since the last interview (since January 1, 1978 for the 1979 survey) in which the respondent was not working or in the military. The question is asked of those workers who are at least 16 years of age and who earlier specified that they had not worked continuously since the last interview.

The 1979 question allows for the coding of six periods of no work, with the beginning and end of each period delineated by a standard week-numbering scheme. The time period covered by this question is January 1, 1978 to the date of the 1979 interview.

The 1980 question is different from the previous year in the following ways: it allows for the coding of only five periods; the beginning and end of each period is identified by month, day, and year; and the time period covered is from the previous year's interview to that year's interview. The 1981 question follows the same format.

The mechanics of deriving the employment status for each period from the questionnaire responses are as follows. Using the 1979 questionnaire responses, every other week starting with the first week in January is compared to the periods of nonemployment. If the week falls within a specified period, then it is coded appropriately. Such is the procedure until the week of the 1980 interview. Because of the increased specificity of that year's question, semimonthly rather than biweekly intervals are examined. Specific month-day responses for beginning and ending dates of periods of nonemployment are rounded to the half-month; and beginning with the rounded interview date, subsequent half-month intervals are compared to the endpoints of periods of nonemployment.

Since the 1981 question mirrors the 1980 question, the above procedure is confirmed after the 1980 interview until December 1980, at which time the desired three-year time interval is covered.

Two caveats should be mentioned in regard to this time line. First, because the questionnaire limits the number of periods of unemployment to six in 1979 and five in 1980 and 1981, respondents with greater numbers of periods of nonemployment are forced to understate the extent of their nonemployment. The effect of this limitation should be small, however, since only 15 respondents had at least six spells of nonemployment in 1979, while in 1980 and in 1981 8 had at least five spells of nonemployment.

Second, the mechanics of the time line are such that any nonemployment spell less than two weeks in duration (spells must be at least one week in duration to be coded by a respondent) is treated as if it is in fact two weeks in length. This procedure is sound, since all spells of nonemployment are picked up; however, calculations of lengths of spells are biased upward.

Appendix B
Tests of Table 2.7

Chamberlain Duration Dependence

The model proposed by Chamberlain (1982) tests whether an individual's history prior to the current spell, such as the time spent in the state, affects the distribution of time remaining in that state. The model allows each individual to have his own individual intercept and tests whether the distribution follows a Markov model. First, determine the states of each individual at preselected points during the year. Then, run through the states of each individual at these preassigned points and record whether he was employed (E) or nonemployed (N) at each particular point during the year. Finally, count and compare the number of sequences such as (E, N, E, N, N, N) with (E, N, N, E, N, N) and determine which occurs more often. Intuitively, if the first sequence is more probable than the second, we can infer that a person is either unemployed for a short period of time or unemployed for a much longer period of time. Thus, the individual does not have an equal probability of escaping nonemployment each half month. He is more likely to escape at the first point sample than at the second, and he therefore exhibits negative state dependence.

Equally spaced intervals were tested. For the NBER sample, points were selected at all possible two-, four-, six-, and then eight-week intervals. Then, the time line was searched for any of the eight patterns and the number found was recorded. For example, for the two-week intervals, states were matched to the eight patterns for weeks 2, 4, 6, 8, 10, and 12 and then weeks 4, 6, 8, 10, 12, 14, and so on until weeks 42, 44, 46, 48, 50, and 52. This process was repeated for 4-, 6-, and then 8-week intervals. The 8-week intervals compared patterns for weeks 2, 10, 18, 26, 34, and 42 and then for weeks 4, 12, 20, 28, 36, 44, and on until weeks 12, 20, 28, 36, 44, and 52.

For the NLS, equally spaced intervals were divided into three groups. The first included 2-, 4-, 6-, and 8-week intervals; the second, 10-, 12-, 14-, and 16-week intervals; and the third, 18-, 20-, 22-, and 24-week intervals.

Table 2.A.1 presents the results of the counts for the eight sequences that tell something about duration dependence. The first four sequences test duration dependence of nonemployment and the last four test duration dependence of employment. Each of the pairs of probabilities for the four tests can be used to estimate a duration-dependence parameter u. If u is one-half, which implies an equal probability for each of the two sequences in each pair, then duration dependence is rejected.

If u is significantly greater than one-half, then duration dependence is exhibited. For each of the two tests of nonemployment and employment duration dependence, two estimates are generated.

Duration dependence of employment for NLS whites and NLS blacks is the only significant result obtained (the estimate of u was significantly greater than .5). NBER blacks did not exhibit duration dependence of

Table 2.A.1   Chamberlain Duration Tests

Sequence Studied	Number of Intervening Biweekly Spells (Counts)				u	χ^2	Significance
	1–4	5–8	9–12	Total			
NBER Blacks							
Nonemployment							
ENENNN vs.	19						
ENNENN	17				.52	.11	No
NNNENE vs.	29						
NNENNE	21				.58	1.28	No
Employment							
NENEEE vs.	18						
NEENEE	22				.45	—	No
EEENEN vs.	27						
EENEEN	29				.48	—	No
NLS Blacks							
Nonemployment							
ENENNN vs.	80	235	140	455			
ENNENN	85	208	134	427	.52	.89	No
NNNENE vs.	127	185	108	420			
NNENNE	100	254	157	511	.45	—	No
Employment							
NENEEE vs.	176	426	490	1092			
NEENEE	146	392	244	846	.56	31.23	.001
EEENEN vs.	116	422	299	837			
EENEEN	139	351	289	779	.52	2.08	No
NLS Whites							
Nonemployment							
ENENNN vs.	35	101	140	276			
ENNENN	34	70	134	238	.54	2.81	No
NNNENE vs.	57	126	108	291			
NNENNE	53	149	157	369	.44	—	No
Employment							
NENEEE vs.	68	179	490	737			
NEENEE	41	150	244	435	.63	77.82	.001
EEENEN vs.	34	128	299	466			
EENEEN	43	106	289	438	.52	.868	No

Note: u = duration dependence parameter.

employment, although the NBER sample size is admittedly small. No group exhibited significant duration dependence of nonemployment. Peculiarly, all three samples exhibited negative duration dependence of nonemployment.

Counting Test of Incidence

Incidence dependence of employment implies that an intervening spell of nonemployment will shorten the second spell of employment relative to the first; and similarly, incidence dependence of employment implies that an intervening spell of employment will shorten a second spell of nonemployment relative to the first. The counting test merely registers whether the second spell is longer or shorter than the first spell after the intervening spell. If the second spell is shorter than the first, incidence dependence is present.

A problem that arises in both the NBER survey and the NLS is that if individuals have uncompleted spells in a window of time, the interview date is placed adjunct to their work histories. Thus, there are four cases: (1) both spells are completed; (2) both spells are uncompleted; (3) the first spell is completed and the second is uncompleted; and (4) the first spell is uncompleted and the second, completed.

We use only cases (1) and (2) because of potential biases in the other two cases. Consider the fourth case, when the second spell is completed and the first is uncompleted. In that situation any finding that the second spell is shorter is valid; the first spell would only be larger than registered, but that is not the case if the second spell is larger. Conversely, in the third case table 2.A.2 gives the results of all counts.

From the table of counts, only the NBER sample displayed incidence dependence. The second spells were consistently shorter than the first. In both samples it is unlikely that the bias would change the results: The NLS sample displayed no evidence of incidence dependence, whereas the NBER sample displayed very significant evidence. The χ^2 for nonemployment dependence is 12.7, while the χ^2 for employment dependence is 8.8.

Regression Test

A test for the incidence dependence of nonemployment is a test of whether an intervening spell of nonemployment affects the mean duration of the subsequent spell of employment. Information on the length of a previous spell of employment and on a subsequent spell of employment after an intervening spell of nonemployment allows unbiased estimation. The previous spell length through the first-differencing tech-

Table 2.A.2   **Incidence Dependence Counting Test**

First Spell/ Second Spell	Second Spell Shorter Than First Spell	Length of Second Spell Equals Length of First Spell	Second Spell Longer Than First Spell
	NLS Whites, Nonemployment Incidence Dependence		
C/C	36	0	47
U/U	136	22	120
C/U	58	3	53
	NLS Whites, Employment Incidence Dependence		
C/C	13	0	10
U/U	143	28	157
C/U	141	4	43
	NLS Blacks, Nonemployment Incidence Dependence		
C/C	10	0	10
U/U	55	7	58
C/U	26	1	11
	NLS Blacks, Employment Incidence Dependence		
C/C	10	0	7
U/U	48	12	57
C/U	15	2	20
	NBER Blacks, Nonemployment Incidence Dependence		
C/C	38	3	14
U/U	18	10	11
C/U	25	4	15
	NBER Blacks, Employment Incidence Dependence		
C/C	84	9	50
U/U	11	3	8
C/U	25	7	18

Note: C = completed spell; U = uncompleted spell.

nique accounts for any unobserved heterogeneity. Specifically, the following model is estimated as a test for mean incidence dependence:

(A1)
$$S_1 = a_i + BX_i + U_1 + e_1$$
$$S_2 = a_i + BX_i + U_2 + e_2,$$

where $U_1 = 0$ before the intervening spell of nonemployment and $U_2 = 1$ after the intervening spell of nonemployment. By the first-differencing technique:

(A2) $S_2 - S_1 = (a_i - a_i) + (B - B)X_i + (U_2 - U_1) + e_2 - e_1$

and yields the expected value:

(A3) $S_2 - S_1 = 1 + v,$

where S_1 = the length of the first spell of employment and S_2 = the length of the second spell of employment.

In this model a test of the mean incidence dependence of nonemployment is a test of whether the difference in the lengths of spells of employment after an intervening spell and the length of an employment spell before the intervening spell are significantly different from zero. A parameter estimate is obtained by regressing this difference on a column of 1s (ones). The criteria for selection into this test are two completed employment spells and an intervening nonemployment spell. Again, the first-differencing methodology factors away individual heterogeneity. A symmetrical test is used as a test of the restricted model for general spell dependence of employment. Specifically, the following model is tested for mean general spell dependence:

(A4)
$$S_1 = a_i + BX_i + U_1 + L_1 + e_1$$
$$S_2 = a_i + BX_i + U_2 + L_2 + e_2.$$

In addition to equation A2, $L_1 = 0$, and L_2 = the length of the intervening spell of nonemployment. By the first-differencing technique:

(A5) $$S_2 - S_1 = (a_i - a_i) + (B - B)X_i$$
$$+ (U_2 - U_1) + (L_2 - L_1) + (e_2 - e_1)$$

and yields the expected value:

(A6) $$S_2 - S_1 - 1 + (L_2) + v, \text{ where } v = 1_2 - 1_1.$$

The coefficient results for both tests are presented below; standard errors are in parentheses. Again, the only individuals included were those with both spells uncompleted or both completed.

S_2 Coefficient and Standard Error (in parentheses) for Difference in Length of Spells

Employment Incidence		
NBER blacks	−3.01	(.67)
NLS whites	.012	(.86)
NLS blacks	3.38	(2.22)
Nonemployment Incidence		
NBER blacks	−3.6	(.64)
NLS whites	2.56	(.65)
NLS blacks	2.27	(1.92)

S_2 **Coefficient and Standard Error for the Effect of Intervening Spell on Difference in Length of Spells**

	Constant		Length of Intervening Spells	
Employment Incidence				
NBER blacks	−3.74	(1.04)	.0166	(.15)
NLS whites	−.08	(1.14)	.009	(.08)
NLS blacks	3.06	(3.4)	.028	(.22)
Nonemployment Incidence				
NBER blacks	−4.49	(1.25)	.201	(.14)
NLS whites	3.16	(2.34)	−.080	(.22)
NLS blacks	2.13	(2.70)	.017	(.22)

A more general test of incidence dependence tests not only whether the incidence of an intervening spell affects the length of a second spell, but also whether the length of the intervening spell affects the length of the second spell. The test proposed is similar to the test for mean incidence dependence, but the difference in the length of a spell before and after an intervening spell is conditional upon both the incidence of an intervening spell and the length of that nonemployment spell.

Heckman-Borjas Incidence Test

To perform the Heckman-Borjas test, a semimonthly time line is calculated that indicates whether a youth is employed or nonemployed for every 15-day interval. Consider the first six intervals, or three months, of the time line. Now consider time as counting on a work clock only if the time is spent in the employment state. Thus, time spent in a nonemployment state is designated as a point interruption of employment time. Consider the case of 24 periods and three-month intervals. For the 24 periods of the sample, employment time is divided into as many three-month intervals as are possible. Thus, a worker who is employed for the entire year will have four employment intervals, while a worker with at least one employment interruption will have from one to three employment intervals. For each three-month interval, the number and the location of the nonemployment interruptions are recorded. Then, all spells with one nonemployment interruption are considered and the location of that nonemployment interruption is recorded as having occurred after the first and before the seventh interval of employment. In the absence of mean incidence dependence of nonemployment, the distribution of interruptions should be uniform. Positive incidence dependence is indicated if there are more interruptions toward the end of the three-month interval, and negative incidence dependence is indicated if there are more interruptions toward the beginning of the interval.

Intuitively, if nonemployment spells breed more nonemployment spells, an averaging over all spells should yield more interruptions toward the end of the intervals than at the beginning of the intervals. This technique is a first-difference technique in disguise, because the average length of an uninterrupted spell of employment before the first interruption is compared to the length of the employment spells after the interruption. The test for incidence dependence is again symmetrical.

The testing procedure is followed for interruptions of employment and nonemployment for various subsets of the data. The Kolmogorov-Smirnov (KS) test is used instead of the chi-square. The KS tests the cumulative distribution rather than the probability density function, and thus it has more predictive power in this analysis.

The decision to use three-month intervals was aribtrary. The effect of changing the length of the statistical interval is to select a slightly different sample to be tested each time. As the length of employment time composing one interval shortens, the youths with longer lengths of employment time who were deleted because they had two spells of unemployment in that time interval are now more likely to be included.

Table 2.A.3 presents the test of incidence dependence of nonemployment and employment. The table shows that in the NLS both employment and nonemployment incidence can be rejected, while the youths in the NBER survey exhibited both employment and nonemployment incidences.

Appendix C
Survey of Inner-City Employers

In order to test the impact of employers' screening and rejection of black youths with poor work records, John Ballen conducted a Survey of Inner-City Black Youth Employers. Telephone interviews were conducted with a randomly selected sample of employers in the Roxbury area, which comprises the Boston census tracts covered by the NBER Survey of Inner-City Black Youth. The criteria for inclusion in the sample were a Yellow Pages telephone directory listing and a Roxbury telephone exchange. All interviewees who began the survey completed it. Furthermore, over 75 percent of the managers approached agreed to answer the questionnaire. Eighteen interviews were completed with managers in charge of hiring at restaurants, grocery stores, movers, a machine shop, a food importer, a light-industry factory, and other work

Table 2.A.3 Employment and Nonemployment Incidence Tests

Length of Interval	Employment Incidence (N,E,N)					Nonemployment Incidence (E,N,E)				
	6	7	8	9	15	6	7	8	9	15
				NBER Blacks						
1	16	10	10	5	0	10	9	3	4	0
2	22	21	13	11	3	15	3	6	5	0
3	39	26	21	12	4	13	11	8	5	0
4	29	23	10	11	2	24	21	13	9	1
5	38	20	13	15	5	17	17	7	8	2
6	30	31	19	17	7	31	23	20	14	4
7		31	23		7		23	14	14	3
8			20	16	4			18	14	3
9				25	10				11	3
10					9					6
11					9					6
12					4					7
13					9					4
14					6					8
15					10					6
KS	1.5	1.3	1.4	1.68	1.64	1.6	2.1	1.98	1.74	2.18
a	.025	.05	.05	.01	.01	.02	.001	.001	.001	.001

1	26	8	5	1	15	9	5	2
2	19	8	4	1	29	20	10	3
3	15	9	8	0	31	17	9	4
4	26	18	8	0	18	8	7	2
5	19	11	5	2	30	22	13	4
6	25	12	5	1	19	16	9	0
7		12	12	5		13	9	3
8		11	7	1		14	12	4
9		16	9	3		19	6	2
10			9	1			11	3
11			8	5			9	1
12			7	1				1
13				2				1
14				1				1
15				4				1
16				1				3
17				1				3
18				2				1
19				2				1
20				3				2
21				2				2
22				2				2
23				0				
24				4				4
KS	12	1.02	.93	.56	.085	.59	.51	.11
a	>.2	>2	>.2	>.2	>.02	>.2	>.2	>.2

Table 2.A.3 (continued)

Length of Interval	Employment Incidence (N,E,N)					Nonemployment Incidence (E,N,E)				
	6	7	8	9	15	6	7	8	9	15
				NLS Whites						
1		58	26	18	3		86	32	33	7
2		42	18	16	4		83	40	37	10
3		52	25	15	3		87	46	31	6
4		52	37	18	4		86	61	32	11
5		60	22	11	0		77	48	27	14
6		70	34	16	3		79	42	29	3
7			19	23	4			53	37	11
8			28	11	1			52	31	12
9			36	17	4			57	34	10
10				16	1				26	7
11				14	0				27	10
12				21	1				40	10
13					11					11
14					2					11
15					2					7
16					1					8
17					2					5
18					5					11
19					7					5
20					4					5
21					5					8
22					2					9
23					2					8
24					4					12
KS		1.02	.78	.29	1.12		0	1.25	.39	.23
a		>.20	>.20	>.20	>.15		>.2	.10	>.2	>.20

establishments in Roxbury. In all but two of the establishments surveyed, a majority of the workers were black.

The telephone interviews sought to determine the characteristics of youths that employers queried to determine which black youths they would hire. The interview questions were phrased in an open-ended manner, and the interviews were conducted as a probing discussion. The first question was: "When you interview a candidate for employment, what characteristics are you most interested in?" and the questions followed in the order given in table 2.7.

Notes

1. These data are from the U.S. Department of Labor (1981, p. 198).
2. CPS figures do not support either of these inferences. See data in U.S. Department of Labor (1981, p. 125).
3. See Blau and Kahn (1981).
4. See Freeman (1984).
5. See Aigner and Cain (1977).

References

Aigner, Dennis, and Glen Cain. 1977. Statistical theories of discrimination. *Industrial and Labor Relations Review* 34 (4):175–225.

Becker, Brian, and Stephen Hills. 1980. The nature and consequences of teenage unemployment in the school-to-work transition period. In *Ten years of labor market experiences for young men.* Columbus: Center for Human Resource Research, Ohio State University.

———. 1980. Teenage unemployment: Some evidence of the long-term effects. *Journal of Human Resources* 15, no. 3 (1980):354–72.

Blau, Francine D., and Lawrence M. Kahn. 1981. Race and sex differences in quits by young workers. *Industrial and Labor Relations Review* 34 (4):563–77.

Brown, Charles. 1982. Dead-end jobs and youth unemployment. In *The youth labor market problem: Its nature, causes, and consequences,* ed. Richard B. Freeman and David A. Wise. Chicago: University of Chicago Press.

Chamberlain, Gary. 1980. Analysis of covariance with qualitative data. *Review of Economic Studies* 47(1), no. 146:225–38.

———. 1982. On the use of panel data. NBER Working Paper no. 1154. Cambridge, Mass.: NBER.

Clark, Kim B., and Lawrence H. Summers. 1982. The dynamics of youth unemployment. In *The youth labor market problem,* ed. R. B. Freeman and D. A. Wise. Chicago: University of Chicago Press.

Ellwood, David T. 1982. Teenage unemployment: Permanent scars or temporary blemishes? In *The youth labor market problem,* ed. R. B. Freeman and D. A. Wise. Chicago: University of Chicago Press.

Feldstein, Martin. 1973. Lowering the permanent rate of unemployment. Joint Economic Committee, 93rd Cong., 1st sess., Washington, D.C.

Freeman, Richard B. 1984. Longitudinal analyses of trade union effects. *Journal of Labor Economics* (vol. 2, no. 1), 1–26.

Freeman, Richard B., and James L. Medoff. 1982. The youth labor market problem in the United States: An overview. In *The youth labor market problem,* ed. R. B. Freeman and D. A. Wise. Chicago: University of Chicago Press.

Glasgow, Douglas G. 1980. *The black underclass.* New York: Vintage.

Heckman, James J. Heterogeneity and State Dependence, NBER Reprint no. 298. Cambridge, Mass.: NBER.

Heckman, James J., and Borjas, George. 1980. Does employment cause future unemployment? Definitions, questions and answers from a continuous time model of heterogeneity and state dependence. *Economica* 47, no. 187:247–83.

Osterman, Paul. 1979. The employment problems of black youth: A review of the evidence and some policy suggestions. In *Expanding employment opportunities for disadvantaged youth,* Special Report 37. Washington, D.C.: National Commission for Employment Policy.

Poterba, James M., and Lawrence H. Summers. 1983. Survey response variation in the Current Population Survey. NBER Working Paper no. 1109. Cambridge, Mass.: NBER.

Rosenthal, Robert, et al. 1976. *Different strokes: Pathways to maturity in the Boston ghetto.* Boulder, Colo.: Westview Press.

Stevenson, Wayne. 1978. The relationship between early work experience and future employability. In *The lingering crisis of youth unemployment,* ed. A. Adams and G. Mangum. Kalamazoo, Mich.: W. E. Upjohn Institute for Employment Research.

U.S. Department of Labor. 1981. *Employment and training report of the President.* Washington, D.C.: GPO.

Comment   Gary Chamberlain

Ballen and Freeman use incidence-dependence counting tests to examine incomplete and complete spells of nonemployment. This comment sets out some of the econometrics of these tests. Start with the one-state case in which spells of type 1 are denoted y_1, spells of type 2 are denoted y_2, and completed spells are denoted $\bar{y}_1$ and $\bar{y}_2$.

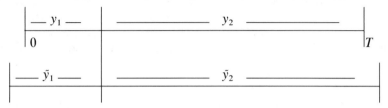

If $\bar{y}_1, \bar{y}_2$ i.i.d. $EXP(\lambda)$, then $y_1 \sim EXP(\lambda)$ and the density of y_1 conditioned on two uncompleted spells is:

$$f(y_1|I,I) = \frac{f(y_1)G(T-y_1)}{\int_0^T f(u)G(T-u)du} = \frac{\lambda e^{-\lambda y_1}e^{-\lambda(T-y_1)}}{\int_0^T \lambda e^{-\lambda u}e^{-\lambda(T-u)}du}$$

$$= \frac{e^{-\lambda T}}{e^{-\lambda T}\int_0^T du} = \frac{1}{T},$$

such that y_1 is uniformly distributed on $[0, T]$.

This formulation extends to the two-state case—an incomplete spell of type 1, a complete spell of type 2, and then an incomplete spell of type 1—as follows:

and

$$f(y_1,w|I,C,I) = \frac{\lambda e^{-\lambda y_1}g(w)e^{-\lambda(T-y_1-w)}}{\int_{u=0}^T (\int_{v=0}^{T-u} \lambda e^{-\lambda u} g(v)e^{-\lambda(T-u-v)} dv)du}$$

$$= \frac{g(w)e^{-\lambda(T-w)}}{\int_{u=0}^T [\int_{v=0}^{T-u} g(v)e^{-\lambda(T-v)} dv]du} = Ke^{\lambda w}g(w).$$

Gary Chamberlain is professor of economics, University of Wisconsin—Madison, and research associate, National Bureau of Economic Research.

The marginal density of y_1 is $f(y_1|I,C,I) = K\int_0^{T-y_1} e^{\lambda w} g(w)dw$. Now note that $y_2 = T-w-y_1$ and obtain the (y_2,w) density:

$$f(y_2, w|I,C,I) = Ke^{\lambda w} g(w) \quad (0 \leq y_2 \leq T, 0 \leq w \leq T-y_2).$$

The marginal density of y_2 is therefore $f(y_2|I,C,I) = K\int_0^{T-y_2} e^{\lambda w} g(w)dw$. Hence, y_1 and y_2 do have the same distribution, and comparing the means of these uncompleted spells is justified. But since we need y_1 and y_2 to have exponential distributions to yield this result (the distribution of the intervening spell is irrelevant), we are jointly testing for incidence dependence and duration dependence. This is true of all these tests. Thus, all the counting tests are joint tests for both forms of dependence.

3 Layoffs, Discharges and Youth Unemployment

Peter Jackson and Edward Montgomery

3.1 Introduction

The causes of the youth unemployment and nonemployment constitute one of the most troublesome labor market problems facing us today.[1] Joblessness among black youths has become increasingly acute in the past 25 years, as shown in table 3.1. The unemployment rate for black youths now stands at almost 50 percent. Further, this level has been rising relative to that of white youths. For example, the unemployment rate for young black men aged 16 to 19 was 1.2 times the rate for young white men in 1955, but it rose to 2.2 times as great by 1983. Young women have also experienced an increase in unemployment relative to that of their white counterparts, such that their rate is now 2.4 times that of white women aged 16 to 19.

In this paper we examine the importance of layoffs and discharges in explaining the high rate of unemployment among black male youths as well as the differential in black-white unemployment rates. The analysis concentrates primarily on explaining why unemployed youths lost their jobs, rather than the differences in the duration of unemployment associated with job loss. Previous work by Leighton and Mincer (1982) suggests that 60 percent of the black-white differences in unemployment rates for 16- to 19-year-olds is due to differences in the incidence of unemployment. Further, Flanagan (1978) has shown that layoffs are more common among blacks than whites.[2] Thus, an examination of the determinants of layoff or job-loss rates should shed some light on an important component of black joblessness.

Table 3.2 presents evidence from May Current Population Survey (CPS) data on youth unemployment, by reason for separation or entrant

Peter Jackson is assistant professor of economics at Rutgers University. Edward Montgomery is assistant professor of economics at Carnegie-Mellon University.

Table 3.1   Unemployment Ratios and Black-White Differentials by Race and Gender

		Unemployment Ratio, Men			Unemployment Ratio, Women		
Year	Age	Whites	Blacks	Blacks/Whites	Whites	Blacks	Blacks/Whites
1948	16–17	10.2	9.4	.92	9.7	11.8	1.22
	18–19	9.4	10.5	1.12	6.8	14.6	2.15
	20–24	6.4	11.7	1.83	4.2	10.2	2.43
1958	16–17	14.9	27.1	1.82	15.6	25.4	1.63
	18–19	16.5	26.7	1.62	11.0	30.0	2.73
	20–24	11.7	19.5	1.67	7.4	18.9	2.55
1969	16–17	12.5	24.7	1.98	13.8	31.2	2.26
	18–19	7.9	19.0	2.41	10.0	25.7	2.57
	20–24	4.6	8.4	1.71	5.5	12.0	2.18
1975	16–17	19.7	39.4	2.00	19.2	38.9	2.03
	18–19	17.2	32.9	1.91	16.1	38.3	2.38
	20–24	13.2	22.9	1.73	11.2	22.5	2.01
1979	16–17	16.1	34.4	2.14	15.9	39.4	2.48
	18–19	12.3	29.6	2.41	12.5	33.4	2.67
	20–24	7.4	17.0	2.30	7.8	20.8	2.67
1982	16–19	21.4	46.2	2.16	22.8	42.7	1.87
	20–24	15.8	31.4	1.99	12.1	27.6	2.28

Source: Handbook of Labor Statistics (1980, 69, table 32).

status. Unemployed workers are categorized as losers (laid off or discharged), leavers, entrants, and reentrants. Differences in black and white unemployment rates are explained primarily by differences in the amount of unemployment attributable to entrants and to job losers. For the younger workers, differences in unemployment among new entrants constitute the primary cause of the black-white differential. The difference in black and white unemployment rates for older youths (20 to 24 years old) is primarily the result of differences in unemployment rates for job losers and reentrants, while unemployment among new entrants is relatively unimportant.

If, as Clark and Summers (1982) have pointed out, the distinction between labor-force and non–labor-force status is a weak one, such that reentrants should be treated as losers and leavers and not as entrants, the magnitude of unemployment attributable to job loss is even greater. If reentrants are partitioned into losers and leavers in the same proportion as losers and leavers are represented in the unemployed population, job losers then account for 59 percent of the unemployment and 60 percent of the differential in black-white unemployment rates among 20- to 24-year-olds and 42 percent of the unemployment and 44 percent of the black-white differential among 18- to 19-year-olds. Clearly,

Table 3.2   Catagories of Youth Unemployment, 1969–79

Age/ Status	Blacks				Whites			
	1969	1975	1978	1979	1969	1975	1978	1979
16–17								
Total Unemployment Rate	24.6	42.4	44.0	40.8	10.7	17.7	13.8	14.4
Losers	2.7	5.6	3.4	1.3	1.4	3.3	1.5	1.1
Leavers	2.4	1.8	.8	.4	1.0	1.4	1.3	.8
Total entrants	19.6	35.1	39.8	39.1	8.2	13.0	11.0	12.3
reentrants	7.7	19.5	11.9	15.2	3.5	5.0	4.2	3.5
new entrants	11.9	15.6	28.0	23.9	4.7	8.0	6.8	8.8
18–19								
Total Unemployment Rate	18.5	36.7	38.0	36.0	5.7	15.9	9.0	10.3
Losers	5.4	13.1	4.8	6.0	1.9	7.2	2.7	1.9
Leavers	4.5	.7	2.7	3.8	.7	1.3	1.9	1.9
Total entrants	8.6	22.9	30.5	26.2	3.1	7.4	4.5	6.4
reentrants	8.1	14.1	17.8	14.8	2.5	4.8	2.9	3.8
new entrants	.5	8.8	12.7	11.4	.6	2.6	1.6	2.6
20–24								
Total Unemployment Rate	7.1	28.3	18.8	17.8	4.4	13.6	6.6	6.4
Losers	2.5	18.0	8.7	5.6	1.6	8.7	3.1	2.1
Leavers	2.7	1.7	2.2	2.5	1.0	1.0	1.2	1.4
Total entrants	2.0	8.7	7.9	9.7	1.7	4.0	2.3	2.9
reentrants	1.5	5.8	5.1	7.0	1.5	3.6	1.8	2.5
new entrants	.5	2.9	2.9	2.7	.2	.4	.5	.4

Source: For data through 1978, see Freeman and Medoff (1982 *b*). All data are weighed based on the appropriate May CPS tapes.

this high rate of job loss is a major source of unemployment among black youths.

3.2 Theory

How can we account for the high rate of job loss among black youths? The previous literature has attributed this differential to differences in seniority and unionism between black and white youths.[3] Although based on informal analysis, these conclusions are derived from the observed differences in unionism and tenure between whites and blacks. These differences can be seen in CPS data on seniority and unionism shown in table 3.3. It should be noted that these differences are greatest for older blacks aged 20 to 24, who have the highest rate of job loss. Given the negative relationship between seniority and layoffs and the positive one between unionism and layoffs that is found for mature workers, it is plausible that these differentials are a factor in explaining these differences. In addition to these parameters, differences in stocks of human capital or in concentrations in unstable industries or jobs may account for the difference in the incidence of job loss or separation between black and white teenagers. If blacks have less human capital, they are more likely to be job losers in the event of cyclical or seasonal disturbances in their industry. Moreover, concentration in occupations, industries, or geographic areas where employment is declining would also serve to generate a higher rate of job loss among blacks than among whites.

In the next section, we use a turnover model to test these propositions on the determinants of job loss among black and white youths. Our model of job loss can be derived quite simply.[4] The decision to lay off a worker depends on the value of the worker to the firm in any period of time, V_{it}, or more formally:

$$L_{it} = 1 \text{ if } V_{it} \leq 0$$

$$L_{it} = 0 \text{ if } V_{it} > 0,$$

where L_{it} indicates whether the worker is a job loser. The value of the worker to the firm is the difference between the worker's marginal product, MP_{it}, and his wage, W_{it}, or:

(1) $$V_{it} = MP_{it} - W_{it}.$$

Because of firm-specific human capital and transaction costs associated with hiring and finding new workers, the value of the worker to the firm in period t also includes a premium above the worker's current marginal product, Z_{it}, or:

Table 3.3		Seniority and Union Status, by Race	
Age	Status	Blacks	Whites
		Seniority	
16–17	1 year	114 (77.2%)	1,638 (52.4%)
	2 years	33 (22.2%)	989 (31.6%)
	3 years		498 (15.9%)
18–19	1 year	130 (60.1%)	2,548 (43.6%)
	2 years	54 (24.8%)	2,075 (35.5%)
	3 years	33 (15.1%)	1,224 (20.9%)
20–24	1 year	750 (27.2%)	8,124 (30.4%)
	2 years	959 (34.8%)	8,168 (30.5%)
	3 years	1,049 (38.0%)	10,464 (39.9%)
		Union Membership	
16–17	Yes	70 (3.9%)	1,106 (4.0%)
	No	1,774 (96.1%)	26,511 (96.0%)
18–19	Yes	506 (16.1%)	4,205 (10.3%)
	No	2,631 (83.9%)	36,808 (89.7%)
20–24	Yes	7,796 (20.7%)	19,730 (16.9%)
	No	10,717 (79.3%)	96,778 (83.1%)

Source: A subsample of employed workers included in the pension sample of the May 1979 CPS.

(2) $$V_{it} = MP_{it} - W_{it} + Z_{it}.$$

We can express the current marginal product, the wage, and the premium as a function of a vector of observable personal and job characteristics, X_{it}, that determines an individual's productivity; we also include an error term to measure the presence of unobservable individual- and firm-specific determinants of productivity, wage, and transaction costs, such that:

(3) $$MP_{it} = b(t)X_{it} + \epsilon_{it}$$

(4) $$W_{it} = g(t)X_{it} + \theta_{it}$$

(5) $$Z_{it} = h(t)X_{it} + \omega_{it}.$$

Using equations (2), (3), (4), and (5), the value of the worker to the firm in period t is thus:

(6) $$V_{it} = [b(t) - g(t) + h(t)]X_{it} + \phi_{it},$$

where ϕ_{it} is the composite error term.

If we assume that the conditional probability of job loss, L_{it}, is cumulative logistic, then the job-loss equation to be estimated is:

(7) $$\log\left(\frac{P_{it}}{1-P_{it}}\right) = \beta X_{it} + e_{it},$$

where P_{it} is the probability of a layoff. The vector X_{it} is composed of schooling, age, tenure on the job, unionism, and industry and occupational dummy variables. In some of the estimated regressions, additional job and individual characteristics, such as the wage rate, firm size, the race of the worker's supervisor, and absenteeism behavior, are added. When we estimate separate layoff and discharge equations, we expect layoffs to be more sensitive to job characteristics than are discharges because of the importance of seasonal or cyclical factors in determining temporary or indefinite layoffs. Conversely, discharges should be more sensitive to personal characteristics or behavior because of the importance of employer perceptions of an individual's productivity in discharge decisions.

To test this model we use data on individuals from three surveys: the 1979 National Longitudinal Survey of Youth (NLS), the 1979 NBER Survey of Inner-City Black Youth, and the May CPS for 1979–81. The NBER survey has detailed data on the personal characteristics of inner-city black youths and provides a large sample of black youths for detailed analysis of the determinants of black discharge and layoff experience. The NLS and CPS data sets contain detailed data on the job and personal characteristics of blacks and whites and thus allows analysis of black-white differences in turnover behavior. We use both the CPS and NLS data sets in part because of differences in the nature of the separation and unemployment questions in the two surveys.[5] Thus, by using all three data sets, we can check the robustness of our results.

3.3 Empirical Results

3.3.1 NBER Data

Previous work on youth unemployment has concentrated on explaining either the incidence or duration of unemployment. We concentrate on explaining the incidence of job loss rather than the resultant duration of spells of unemployment, in part because the incidence of spells has been shown to account for much of the black-white differences in youth unemployment. The incidence of unemployment that is the result of job loss can be related to turnover behavior by using the following expression:

(8) $P(U \text{ and } Loser) = P(Loser) \cdot P(U|Loser)$.

That is, the contribution of job losers to unemployment equals the rate of job loss multiplied by the proportion of losers who are unemployed (those who do not have new jobs lined up prior to job loss or who do not leave the labor force). To see why blacks have such a high probability of being in the P(*Loser*) category, we initially used the NBER data. The NBER sample is restricted to young black men residing in three large cities: Boston, Chicago, and Philadelphia. Since inner-city youths suffer disproportionately from unemployment, and most black youths reside in the inner city, this sample should provide insight into the determinants of job loss among black youths.

The 1979 NBER sample is restricted to respondents who had held a job in the past 12 months. The resulting sample comprised 1,549 men living in the three cities, 35 percent of whom had separated from their last job because of layoffs and 10 percent of whom had separated because of discharge. The ratio of quits to layoffs is lower in this sample (1.54) than that derived in previous work using a more representative sample (3.03).[6] This discrepancy may reflect the absence of rural youths who tend to have much lower layoff and discharge rates.

Table 3.4 presents the sample means and standard deviations, and table 3.5 presents the results of estimating logistic equations for job losers and separate layoff and discharge equations. The NBER sample is composed mainly of 16- to 19-year-olds, a large fraction of whom were still in school at the time of the survey. The extent of unionism was quite high, as over 12 percent of these inner-city young men were covered by a collective bargaining agreement. A sizable proportion of the sample, 21 percent, was employed in the heavily unionized construction and manufacturing industries. Given the fact that unionized workers tend to experience higher layoff rates and lower quit rates than those of the overall labor force, concentration in these cyclically sensitive sectors may account for the low quit-layoff ratio found in this survey. Despite the fact that 21 percent of the sample were employed in the manufacturing and construction industries, over 40 percent of the employment in the sample was in the service sector and in service occupations. Further, the mean wage for the sample was only $3.10 per hour. Thus, the majority of inner-city youths in the NBER sample tended to find employment in relatively low-paying service jobs.

The regression results isolate several important contributors to the high incidence of job loss among black youth. The importance of job tenure is evident in all of the regressions. The negative impact of tenure on both layoffs and discharges indicates that being last in the hiring queue contributes to the youth joblessness problem. Lack of seniority is important in both union and nonunion firms, as the addition of the union variable does not reduce the explanatory power of the tenure variable. Not surprisingly, tenure has a bigger impact on layoffs than on discharges. The significance of this variable in the discharge equations does, however, indicate that as blacks gain seniority, they are less likely to be job losers for any reason. The point estimate for the effect of increasing tenure is quite large. An increase in tenure of six

Table 3.4   NBER Survey Means and Standard Deviations

Independent Variable	Mean	Standard Deviation
Union	.124	.329
Hours Worked	22.15	18.45
Average Hourly Wages	3.10	2.81
Schooling	10.74	1.50
Age	19.07	2.57
Tenure (months)	20.41	9.31
Married Dummy Variable	.032	.176
Professional	.043	.203
Managerial	.009	.094
Sales	.028	.165
Clerical	.147	.354
Crafts	.099	.299
Operative	.104	.305
Transport	.031	.174
Service	.397	.490
Agriculture	.003	.050
Mining	.001	.025
Construction	.067	.249
Manufacturing	.144	.352
Transport	.034	.180
Wholesale and Retail	.224	.417
Finance	.037	.190
Service	.437	.496
Public Administration	.053	.223
Boston	.326	.469
Chicago	.335	.472
Training Dummy Variable	.081	.27
Race of Boss (Black - 1)	.278	.441
Absent Often	.012	.110
Absent Rarely	.192	.393
In School	.560	.496

months above the mean reduces the probability of job loss by 26 percent, as shown in table 3.6. The effect on layoffs is even greater than this.

These estimates of the size of the relationship between tenure and layoffs or job loss must be viewed with a degree of caution, however. Heterogeneity will bias estimates of this relationship because firms with low layoff propensities will tend to have workers with high tenure. As pointed out in Jovanovic (1979), heterogeneity may account for almost half of the observed relationship between tenure and layoffs. Nonetheless, heterogeneity only increases the observed magnitude of this relationship, it does not create it. Thus, seniority, or the lack thereof, still plays an important role in explaining black job-loss rates.

Interestingly, the effect of unionism appears to be quite weak in the layoff and job-loss equations. Both the point estimate and the signifi-

Table 3.5 **NBER Job Loss Equations**

Independent Variables	Job Losers			Layoff			Discharge		
	(1)	(2)	(3)	(1)	(2)	(3)	(1)	(2)	(3)
Constant	-2.333^{**}	-1.824^{**}	-2.109^{**}	-2.833^{**}	-2.154^{**}	-2.687^{**}	-3.113^{**}	-3.788^{**}	-3.276^{**}
	(-4.13)	(-6.20)	(-3.13)	(-4.56)	(-6.05)	(-3.57)	(-2.86)	(-8.30)	(-2.66)
Schooling	.065		.007	$.117^{**}$		.057	$-.102$		$-.128^{*}$
	(1.59)		(.15)	(2.55)		(1.16)	(-1.38)		(-1.64)
Chicago	$.273^{**}$		.076	$.243^{*}$		$-.123$	.285		.112
	(2.14)		$(-.52)$	(1.77)		$(-.79)$	(1.04)		(.39)
Boston	$.234^{*}$		$-.306^{**}$	$-.017$		$-.556^{**}$	$.854^{**}$		$.530^{*}$
	(1.79)		(-2.08)	$(-.12)$		(-3.41)	(3.36)		(1.96)
In School	$-.331^{**}$		$-.345^{**}$	$-.276$		$-.324^{**}$	$-.404$		$-.295$
	(-2.44)		(-2.33)	(-1.85)		(-2.01)	(-1.54)		(-1.08)
Age	.018		.035	.019		.024	.053		.040
	(.60)		(1.06)	(.06)		(.66)	(.96)		(.70)
Married	$-.224$		$-.091$	$-.053$		.155	$-.792$		$-.863$
	$(-.74)$		$(-.28)$	$(-.17)$		(.45)	(-1.07)		(-1.15)
Training	$-.009$		$-.115$	$-.087$		$-.245$	.209		.274
	(.04)		$(-.52)$	$(-.40)$		$(-.99)$	(.60)		(.76)

Table 3.5 (continued)

Independent Variables	Job Losers			Layoff			Discharge		
	(1)	(2)	(3)	(1)	(2)	(3)	(1)	(2)	(3)
Union		.149	.015		-.845	-.252		.637**	.687**
		(.93)	(.09)		(-.47)	(-1.36)		(2.46)	(2.56)
Tenure		-.075**	-.083**		-.081**	-.091**		-.033**	-.031*
		(-7.05)	(-7.53)		(-6.59)	(-7.16)		(-2.16)	(-1.93)
Absent Often		.546	.530		-.948	-.964		1.910**	1.830**
		(1.29)	(1.24)		(-1.49)	(-1.51)		(4.10)	(3.88)
Absent Sometimes		-.178	-.152		-.345	-.304		.331	.260
		(-.80)	(-.67)		(-1.38)	(-1.20)		(.90)	(.70)
Absent Rarely		.114	.107		.078	.069		.180	.183
		(.84)	(.78)		(.53)	(.46)		(.73)	(.73)
Race of Boss		.051	.051		.126	.011		-.212	-.126
		(.42)	(.40)		(.96)	(.74)		(-.91)	(-.53)
Industry and Occupation Control			✓			✓		✓	
Log Likelihood	-1144.10	-970.52	-959.90	-989.59	-838.82	-823.51	-421.25	-382.92	-377.39

Note: **Significant at the 5 percent level in a two-tailed test.
*Significant at 10 percent level in a two-tailed test. t-statistics in parentheses. Asymptotic t- statistics in parentheses.

Table 3.6   **Predicted Differences in Job-Loss Probabilities**

Difference	Losers	Layoff	Discharge
Base	.046	.035	.011
Union–Base	.008	− .007	.010
1 Year Tenure–Base	.040	.022	.003
2 Years Tenure–Base	− .012	− .009	.002
In School–Base	− .013	− .008	− .003
Black Boss–Base	.002	.001	− .002
Married–Base	− .004	− .005	− .006
Absent Often–Base	.030	.019	.053

Note: The base group consists of 19-year-old, nonunion members, who were out of school, with 10.8 years of schooling, no training, single, never absent, living in Philadelphia, and working as laborers in public administration, with 20 months tenure for a white boss. The predicted probabilities are based on the coefficient estimates in table 3.5.

cance level of this variable indicate that the relatively high incidence of union membership among blacks may not be at the heart of the job-loss problem. Specifically, union membership seems to increase the likelihood of discharge but reduce the likelihood of layoff.

The human capital variables also have little explanatory power in these equations. Only the dummy term for being in school is consistently significant. This negative relationship between being in school and job loss, after controlling for age and schooling, suggests that part-time jobs are more likely to end in quits than in job loss. Whether this is because part-time jobs are undesirable jobs per se or because youths leave these jobs to find better permanent jobs cannot be said. It is plausible that the in-school term is also capturing some unmeasured characteristics that are correlated with higher productivity. Youths of a given age who are still in school may have greater ability than out-of-school youths, which is leading them to invest more in human capital. Ceteris paribus, firms would thus be less likely to lay off or discharge these youths. The size of this effect indicates that examining which youths stay in school or why they do so may yield further insights into the youth unemployment problem.

It is of interest to note that the absenteeism variable is significant only in the discharge equation. Workers who are absent often have a much greater probability of discharge than those without attendance problems. This result may indicate that discharges tend to be more dependent on individual actions than are layoffs, which are primarily caused by cyclical or secular shocks. Caution should be exercised in interpreting this variable, however, because frequent absenteeism may be as much the result of undesirable job characteristics as of personal habits. Consequently, it is important to determine whether this variable is simply a proxy for unmeasured job characteristics that are correlated with discharges or instead reflects the effect of traits specific to the individual.

These job-loss equations for young inner-city black men have enabled us to isolate a few important factors that may be the root of the job-loss problem of black youth. Lack of seniority seems to be particularly important, as is the tendency of inner-city youths to drop out of school. High mean levels of unionism and the lack of training do not seem to increase significantly their job-loss probabilities. Absenteeism increased discharge frequencies but not layoff or overall job-loss rates. Some of the industry and occupational dummy variables were also significant in indicating that employment in volatile industries or occupations may also explain part of the high incidence of job loss among black youths.[7] On the other hand, schooling, marital status, and age did not seem to explain much of the job-loss problem. The human capital variables in general were less powerful than the job and occupational variables in explaining job loss. Thus, these preliminary tests indicate that differences in the types of jobs individuals hold may be relatively more important than individual characteristics in understanding the high rates of job-loss unemployment among black youths.

3.3.2   NLS Data

For comparability with the NBER results, we restricted the NLS sample to men only. The 1979 NLS is composed of 6,398 individuals, of which 1,582 are black. Table 3.7 presents the means and standard deviations for this sample. Blacks were more likely than whites to be unemployed job losers and were more likely than whites to change jobs because of job loss. The magnitude of these differences, however, is smaller than that found in the CPS results in Table 3.2, which may reflect differences in sampling (poor whites are overrepresented in the NLS) or the fact that the NLS respondents were the youths themselves, whereas the CPS respondents were household members.

In addition to differences in job-loss probabilities between blacks and whites, the NLS indicates that black youths had lower average tenure and higher unionism rates than did their white counterparts. Blacks on average were also slightly younger, were less likely to be married, and had less training than whites. Based on the NBER results, these factors would tend to lead to a higher rate of job loss among blacks than among whites. Conversely, blacks were more likely to be in school and less likely to be employed in the cyclically sensitive construction and manufacturing sectors. To distinguish the relative importance of these parameters in explaining black-white differences in job-loss probabilities, a linear probability model was estimated. The effects of human capital versus job and occupation variables are high-

Table 3.7   **NLS Summary Statistics**

Independent Variable	Whites		Blacks	
	Mean	STD	Mean	STD
Age	17.93	2.35	17.73	2.27
Education	10.43	2.06	10.20	1.87
Urban Dummy (Urban = 1)	.664	.472	.064	.245
Union	.064	.244	.064	.245
Tenure (months)	6.20	16.08	3.91	11.21
Training	.086	.281	.050	.218
In School	.576	.494	.608	.488
Married	.083	.276	.032	.177
Professional	.033	.179	.028	.121
Managerial	.025	.155	.015	.176
Sales	.061	.240	.031	.263
Clerical	.219	.254	.074	.302
Crafts	.142	.348	.101	.343
Operative	.160	.366	.136	.244
Transport	.042	.212	.064	.421
Laborer	.196	.393	.230	.194
Service	.270	.063	.310	.449
Agriculture	.076	.265	.050	.220
Mining	.008	.087	.004	.061
Construction	.080	.271	.072	.259
Manufacturing	.210	.407	.184	.388
Transport	.030	.171	.049	.217
Wholesale and Retail	.332	.471	.328	.470
Finance	.015	.123	.021	.143
Service	.226	.419	.262	.440
Public Administration	.025	.150	.028	.166
P (U and $Loser$)	5.3		6.9	
P ($Loser|Changers$)	46.8		52.2	

Note: The means are unweighted. STD = standard deviation.

lighted by estimating separate equations for each set of variables. These equations were estimated separately for blacks and whites as well as a pooled version to test for racial differences in the underlying model and the individual parameters. Tables 3.8 and 3.9 present the results of these tests.

The linear probability estimates for blacks from the NLS are generally consistent with those from the NBER sample. Being in school reduced both job-loss and layoff likelihoods. The strength of this effect was weaker in the NLS when controls for industry and occupation were entered. Nonetheless, the effect is evident among both black and white youths. Thus, youths who worked part-time or while in school were consistently less likely than others to be job losers. In addition, the coefficient on this variable is about the same size in both the black

Table 3.8 NLS Layoff Equations

Independent Variable	Blacks			Whites			Pooled
	(1)	(2)	(3)	(1)	(2)	(3)	(1)
Constant	.044 (1.04)	.0003 (.10)	.029 (.76)	.001 (.04)	.001 (.35)	-.015 (-.46)	-.0001 (.01)
Age	-.001 (-.29)		-.001 (-.49)	.003 (1.02)		.004 (1.27)	.002 (.77)
Schooling	.001 (.47)		.001 (.38)	-.001 (-.27)		-.003 (-1.16)	-.001 (-.70)
Urban	-.018** (-2.04)		-.013* (-1.71)	-.001 (-.13)		.006 (.87)	.002 (.35)
Training	-.016 (-.88)		-.008 (-.47)	-.031** (-2.75)		-.030** (-2.74)	-.028** (-3.02)
In School	-.018* (-1.69)		-.005 (-.49)	-.021** (-2.19)		-.018* (-1.90)	-.016* (-2.14)
Married	-.018 (-.38)		.046 (1.03)	.018 (.85)		.013 (.59)	.013 (.69)
Union		-.048* (-1.73)	-.050* (-1.76)		-.062** (-3.07)	-.066** (-3.19)	-.058** (-3.44)
Tenure		-.004** (-9.29)	-.004** (-9.18)		-.002** (-9.92)	-.002** (-9.60)	-.002** (-12.12)
Industry and Occupation Control		✓	✓		✓	✓	✓
SSR	12.74	8.96	8.91	58.23	49.29	48.81	59.13
$\bar{R}^2$	.01	.30	.29	.01	.14	.16	.16

Note: **Significant at the 5 percent level in a two-tailed test. *Significant at the 10 percent level in a two-tailed test. Asymptotic t-statistics in parentheses.

Table 3.9   **NLS Job-Loser Equations**

Independent Variable	Black			White			Pooled
	(1)	(2)	(3)	(1)	(2)	(3)	(1)
Constant	.021 (.60)	.0003 (.95)	.013 (.41)	−.032 (−1.39)	.0001 (.43)	−.038 (−1.58)	−.024 (−1.27)
Age	.0004 (.15)		.0003 (.13)	.004* (1.93)		.004* (1.91)	.003* (1.70)
Schooling	−.0005 (−.19)		−.0002 (−.09)	−.001 (−.54)		−.002 (−.98)	−.001 (−.96)
Urban	−.015** (−2.05)		−.010 (−1.58)	−.005 (−1.07)		−.002 (−.42)	−.004 (−.97)
Training	−.010 (−.65)		−.003 (−.20)	−.018** (−2.24)		−.017** (−2.11)	−.015** (−2.18)
In School	−.002 (−.26)		−.004 (−.47)	−.008 (−1.16)		−.006 (−.85)	−.002 (−.50)
Married	−.008 (−.21)		.036 (.95)	.014 (.91)		.015 (.92)	.015 (1.05)
Union		−.050** (−2.05)	−.049** (−1.96)		−.036** (−2.50)	−.039** (−2.65)	−.043** (−3.42)
Tenure		−.003** (−8.78)	−.003** (−8.77)		−.001** (−7.38)	−.001** (−7.21)	−.001** (−9.50)
Industry and Occupation Control		√	√		√	√	√
SSR	8.88	6.80	6.78	29.42	26.27	26.07	33.80
$\bar{R}^2$	.01	.23	.22	.01	.08	.09	.10

**Significant at the 5 percent level in a two-tailed test. *Significant at the 10 percent level in a two-tailed test. Asymptotic t-statistics in parentheses.

and the white equations. In fact, the data do not reject the restriction that this coefficient is the same for blacks and whites. Given the fact that the weighted mean value for this variable is roughly the same for blacks and whites (0.625 versus 0.652), differences in dropout rates do not seem to explain black-white differences in the likelihood of job loss. Nonetheless, these results support the view that, ceteris paribus, those who drop out of school are an important part of the high rates of job loss among black and white youths.

Increases in human capital from training reduce the likelihood of layoff or job loss for whites. Schooling also tends to reduce the probability of layoff and job loss, but its effect is insignificant. Neither of these variables, however, has any significant impact on black layoff or job-loss rates. Given the higher mean levels of schooling and training among whites than among blacks, these human capital variables should explain at least part of the lower job-loss rates among whites. Nonetheless, the equations with only the human capital variables indicate that these parameters are of minimal importance in explaining youth job-loss rates. Interestingly, a Chow test for the human capital equations does not reject the hypothesis that these variables affect blacks and whites in the same way. Given the minimal significance of these variables, this finding is not particularly surprising, but it does indicate that differences in the mean levels of these human capital variables are more important than differences in the coefficients in explaining black-white differences in job loss. Since whites on average are older, have more schooling, are more likely to be in school or married, and are more likely to receive training, these human capital results would lead us to expect lower job-loss rates among the white youths. It should be emphasized again, that the contribution of these variables to the lower job-loss rate among whites results not from differences in the parameters but from differences in the mean levels of the human capital variables.

The effect of tenure on layoff and job loss is significant for both blacks and whites. Increases in seniority lead to lower layoff and discharge rates, even after controlling for the effects of unionism. This result indicates that seniority, either because of "first in–last out" layoff rules or firm-specific human capital levels, has an important effect on youth job-loss rates. It should be noted that the size of the impact of tenure is not altered when other human capital variables are added to the regressions. Further, the data do not reject the hypothesis that the coefficients for blacks and whites are significantly different from each other.[8] In fact, the black coefficient is double that for whites, suggesting that blacks differentially gain from increased seniority. Thus, if blacks had the same mean tenure as whites, we would expect a drop in their absolute job loss rate and in the black-white job-loss differential. Since the probability of being unemployed given a separation also declines more quickly with tenure among blacks than among whites, an increase in tenure would reduce the black-white differential in the probability of being unemployed and a job loser.[9] These results indicate that the protection of seniority-based layoff rules, or the acquisition of firm-specific human capital, is a very important means to reduce the incidence of involuntary separations among young blacks.

Interestingly, unionism appears to lower job-loss and layoff rates for black and white youths. Even after controlling for industry and occupation, union membership is associated with more-stable jobs than those normally held by youths. The presence of formal rules governing layoffs and discharges may protect unionized youths from discretionary terminations. This protection for youths appears to offset the fact that unions, by reducing the employer's flexibility in adjusting labor costs, tend to be associated with higher layoff rates among adult males.[10]

The effect of being in certain industries or occupations also differs between blacks and whites.[11] Working in the construction industry or in the sales, crafts, or operative occupation has a significantly greater impact on the job-loss probabilities of blacks than of whites. That is, blacks in these fields are more likely, ceteris paribus, to lose their jobs than are white youth. Since approximately 26 percent of black youths are employed in these occupations, industry and occupation may explain part of the black-white difference in job-loss rates.

The occupation or job-type variables seem to explain black and white job-loss experience better than the demographic parameters. In other words, the types of jobs held by youths are more important than human capital differences in determining involuntary separations. This result may not be too surprising in light of the fact that the variance in the level of skills among teenagers is likely to be minimal given the amount of time they have had to invest in acquiring skills. Likewise, it is not surprising that having or obtaining a "stable" or "good" job is particularly important to the younger members of the labor force. Thus, it again seems crucial to our understanding of youth joblessness to discover which youths find these jobs and how they do so.

Despite the similarity in the coefficients for the human capital variables, the data reject the hypothesis that black and white job-loss or layoff experiences are generated by the same underlying model.[12] The differences in their experiences result from differences in the effects of job type and tenure on job-loss rates. For example, when we estimated equation (2), the data also rejected the hypothesis of no structural black-white differences in job-loss experience.[13] Either the types of jobs blacks receive have unmeasured characteristics that are correlated with job loss, or employers' treatment of black youths is fundamentally different from their treatment of whites. Thus, even though differences in the mean levels of various human capital variables and the location of black jobs explain part of the black-white differential, the results from the NLS sample indicate there are important structural differences in the determinants of black and white labor market experience.

3.3.3   CPS Data

This section examines data on the 16- to 24-year-old male labor force from the 1979, 1980, and 1981 May CPS. There are 26,969 individuals in this sample, 22,278 employed and 2,476 unemployed white men with an average unemployment rate of 10.0 percent over the 1979–81 period. Among the 1,795 employed and 420 unemployed black men in the sample, the average three-year unemployment rate was 19.0 percent.[14] Table 3.10 summarizes the characteristics of those black and white labor forces. Only small differences exist between the employed and unemployed men within the same racial group. The most noticeable exception is marital status: 24 percent of the employed white men were married, while 17 percent of the unemployed white men were married; and 18 percent of the employed black men were married, while 8 percent of the unemployed black men were married. Interestingly, the distributions of employment by industry for blacks and whites were also fairly similar. White youths were more likely to be craftsmen and less likely to be service workers, however, than were black youths.

Table 3.11 displays linear probability estimates of the unemployment, layoff, quit, and discharge equations. The results show that youths 16 to 17 years old were the least likely to be unemployed, while those 20 to 21 were the most likely. Unemployment appears to have increased with age before declining as youths reached their mid-twenties. Married men were less likely to be unemployed than were single men. In general, the probability of being unemployed was sensitive to regional, occupational, and industry variables. But even after controlling for human capital, industry, and occupation, blacks were more likely to be unemployed than white youth. Black youths were also more apt to be job losers than were whites, and the difference in discharge probabilities is also statistically significant. The positive coefficients on these dummy variables for race indicate that blacks were more likely to change jobs and significantly more likely to be discharged and unemployed. In order to obtain more precise estimates of how and why black labor market outcomes differ from those of whites, we estimated separate layoff, quit, and discharge equations for blacks and whites. We also performed Chow tests to see if the coefficients in the black and white equations were the same. Table 3.12 presents these results.

The Chow tests reject the hypothesis that the coefficients for blacks and whites will be the same in any of the estimated equations. It therefore appears that black labor market experience may not be generated

Table 3.10   CPS Summary Statistics

Independent Variable	Whites				Blacks			
	Employment		Unemployment		Employment		Unemployment	
	Mean	STD	Mean	STD	Mean	STD	Mean	STD
Age	21.9	1.1	21.9	1.0	22.0	1.0	21.7	1.0
Education	13.2	1.9	12.8	1.9	12.9	1.8	12.7	1.56
Urban	.94	.22	.98	.14	.99	.11	1.00	.07
Married	.24	.43	.17	.38	.18	.38	.08	.27
Professional	.07	.25	.04	.19	.05	.21	.03	.17
Administration	.04	.21	.02	.14	.02	.13	.01	.08
Sales	.06	.23	.03	.18	.03	.18	.03	.17
Clerical	.07	.25	.05	.22	.11	.31	.08	.28
Crafts	.19	.39	.18	.38	.11	.31	.13	.34
Operative	.15	.36	.20	.40	.16	.37	.16	.36
Transport	.05	.23	.05	.23	.06	.24	.06	.23
Laborer	.17	.37	.24	.43	.18	.39	.21	.41
Private Household	.001	.35	.001	.03	.001	.03	0	0
Service	.14	.35	.15	.36	.25	.44	.27	.45
Farm Worker	.06	.247	.03	.18	.03	.17	.02	.15
Agriculture	.08	.28	.05	.21	.05	.21	.04	.19
Mining	.02	.13	.02	.13	.01	.07	.007	.07
Construction	.11	.32	.18	.38	.08	.26	.13	.34
Manufacturing	.21	.41	.25	.43	.23	.42	.25	.43
Transport	.04	.18	.03	.18	.04	.20	.03	.17
Utility	.02	.14	.01	.12	.02	.13	.02	.14
Trade	.30	.46	.26	.44	.26	.44	.22	.41
Finance	.02	.15	.01	.10	.04	.18	.02	.14
Service	.16	.37	.16	.37	.23	.42	.24	.45
Public Administration	.02	.15	.03	.18	.05	.22	.05	.22

Note: Means are unweighted. STD = standard deviation.

Table 3.11   CPS Unemployment, Layoff, Quit, and Discharge Estimates

Independent Variable	Unemployment	Layoff	Quit	Discharge
Intercept	−41.8**	−8.7**	−2.99	−18.8**
	(9.0)	(4.6)	(1.6)	(6.5)
Black	.08**	.004	.004	.04**
	(11.3)	(1.5)	(1.3)	(8.7)
Age 16–17	−.06**	−.02**	−.02**	.06**
	(8.7)	(5.3)	(5.9)	(12.7)
Age 18–19	.003	−.1**	−.0001	−.01**
	(.6)	(2.9)	(.1)	(3.2)
Age 20–21	.01**	−.04**	.0003	.002
	(2.6)	(2.3)	(1.3)	(.8)
Married	−.05**	.002	−.01**	−.02**
	(9.4)	(1.2)	(2.9)	(6.5)
Urban	.06**	.001	.01*	.02*
	(5.5)	(.3)	(1.8)	(2.9)
Year	.02**	.004**	.002	.01**
	(9.1)	(4.6)	(1.6)	(6.5)
North Central	.01*	.01**	−.001	−.002
	(1.7)	(4.7)	(.5)	(.7)
South	−.03	−.01**	−.002	−.02**
	(4.8)	(2.5)	(.7)	(4.6)
West	−.002	−.005**	.001	.003
	(.4)	(2.1)	(.4)	(1.0)
High School	−.07**	−.01**	−.02**	−.05**
	(14.4)	(4.1)	(7.3)	(14.7)
Professional	−.06**	−.01**	−.01**	−.03**
	(−7.5)	(3.7)	(2.6)	(5.4)
Administration	.05**	−.01**	−.01	−.02**
	(5.4)	(2.3)	(1.3)	(3.4)
Sales	−.04**	−.01**	−.01**	−.02**
	(4.3)	(1.9)	2.3	(3.7)
Clerical	−.04**	−.004	−.01**	−.02**
	(5.3)	(1.3)	(2.3)	(3.8)
Crafts	−.04**	−.002	−.01**	−.01**
	(6.4)	(.8)	(2.6)	(3.4)
Operative	−.01	.01**	−.004	−.001
	(1.3)	(4.5)	(1.5)	(.5)
Transport	−.2**	.004	.003	−.001
	(2.1)	(1.1)	(.8)	(.1)
Private Household	−.10**	−.002	.02	−.03
	(2.0)	(.1)	(.9)	(.9)
Farm Worker	.01	−.01	−.001	−.01
	(.8)	(.8)	(.1)	(.5)

Table 3.11 (continued)

Independent Variable	Unemployment	Layoff	Quit	Discharge
Agriculture	− .10**	.001	− .01	− .02**
	(6.0)	(.1)	(1.1)	(2.1)
Mining	− .05**	.01	.01*	− .02**
	(2.8)	(1.5)	(1.8)	(2.2)
Construction	.01	.02**	.002	.01*
	(.6)	(4.2)	(.4)	(1.8)
Manufacturing	− .03**	.02**	.001	− .004
	(2.4)	(4.6)	(0.1)	(.5)
Transport	− .05**	.02**	− .004	− .02
	(3.3)	(2.9)	(.7)	(1.5)
Utility	− .05**	.001	.01	− .02
	(2.7)	(.1)	(1.2)	(1.6)
Trade	− .06**	.003	.003	− .01
	(5.1)	(.6)	(.6)	(.01)
Finance	− .09**	− .001	− .003	− .02**
	(5.2)	(.1)	(.5)	(2.16)
Service	− .04**	.003	.001	− .01
	(3.4)	(.7)	(.1)	(.01)
$\bar{R}^2$	.04	.02	.004	.02

Note: **Significant at the 5 percent level in a two-tailed test. *Significant at the 10 percent level in a two-tailed test. Asymptotic t-statistics in parentheses.

by the same model as is white experience. The consistency of this finding with the results from the NLS reinforces the view that there are systematic differences in how blacks and whites fare in the labor market. The individual layoff, quit, and discharge equations illustrate how these differences may arise.

In the black layoff equations, only two variables significantly influence the probability of layoff. Workers in the north-central region were less likely to be laid off than workers in the northeast region of the country, and work in manufacturing raised the probability of layoff relative to that of government work. The significance of manufacturing employment may be due to the high levels of unionism in manufacturing. Unfortunately, the direct influence of unionism is not possible to test in this data set.[15] It should be noted that none of the human capital variables are statistically significant in these regressions. Further, none of the occupation dummy variables are significant. In the white layoff equation, however, age, education, geographic location, occupation, and industry all influence the likelihood of layoff.

The same general pattern appears in the quit equations. Not only is the model generating black quit behavior different from that for whites, but the probability of quitting is also not sensitive to changes in the

Table 3.12   **CPS Separation Equations**

Independent Variable	Layoff			Quit			Discharge		
	Blacks	Whites	Pooled	Blacks	Whites	Pooled	Blacks	Whites	Pooled
Constant	3.63	9.18**	−8.16**	2.70	−3.03	−2.98	−17.64	−18.70**	−18.74**
	(.5)	(4.69)	(4.6)	(.3)	(1.53)	(1.6)	(1.26)	(6.44)	(6.4)
Age 16–17	−.01	−.02**	−.02**	−.01	−.02**	−.02**	−.14**	−.05**	−.06**
	(.7)	(5.47)	(5.5)	(1.1)	(6.02)	(6.0)	(6.56)	(10.86)	(13.4)
Age 18–19	−.01	−.01**	−.01**	.01	−.001	−.001	−.05**	−.01**	−.01**
	(1.6)	(2.50)	(3.0)	(1.4)	(.51)	(.1)	(3.0)	(2.12)	(3.6)
Age 20–21	.003	−.01**	−.005**	.005	.002	.003	−.03*	.01*	.01
	(.5)	(2.61)	(2.4)	(.6)	(1.16)	(1.3)	(1.8)	(1.72)	(.6)
Married	−.01	−.003	.002	−.01	−.01**	−.01**	−.07**	−.02**	−.02**
	(1.1)	(1.48)	(1.1)	(.7)	(2.80)	(3.0)	(4.48)	(5.15)	(7.1)
Urban	−.02	.002	.002	.02	.01*	.01*	.02	.02**	.02**
	(.6)	(.42)	(.4)	(.6)	(1.7)	(1.8)	(.3)	(2.89)	(3.2)
Year	.002	.005**	.004**	.001	.002	.002	.01	.009**	.01**
	(.5)	(4.70)	(4.6)	(.3)	(1.55)	(1.6)	(1.3)	(6.47)	(6.5)
North Central	−.03**	.01**	.01**	−.02	−.00001	−.001	.03	−.005	−.003
	(2.6)	(4.03)	(4.6)	(1.5)	(.01)	(.5)	(1.59)	(1.33)	(.8)
South	.001	−.01**	−.01**	.01	−.00004	−.001	−.01	−.02**	−.01**
	(.1)	(2.6)	(2.4)	(1.5)	(.18)	(.5)	(.9)	(4.62)	(3.6)

West	.01 (1.0)	−.01** (2.54)	−.005** (2.13)	.0001 (.01)	.001 (.60)	.001 (.4)	.02 (1.0)	.002 (.66)	.002 (.6)
High School	−.01 (.2)	−.01** (4.54)	−.01** (4.2)	−.001 (.1)	−.02** (7.75)	−.02** (7.4)	−.06** (4.68)	−.04** (13.76)	−.05** (15.1)
Professional	−.02 (1.2)	−.01** (3.55)	−.01** (3.9)	−.02 (1.51)	−.01** (2.38)	−.01** (2.7)	−.03 (.97)	−.03** (5.33)	−.03** (6.0)
Administration	−.01 (.5)	−.01 (2.24)	−.01** (2.4)	.002 (.06)	−.02 (1.25)	−.01 (1.3)	−.11** (2.20)	−.02** (2.91)	−.02** (3.9)
Sales	.0006 (.03)	−.007** (1.99)	−.01** (2.0)	−.02 (1.22)	−.01** (2.03)	−.01** (2.3)	−.05 (1.45)	−.02** (2.71)	−.02** (3.5)
Clerical	.0007 (.6)	−.006* (1.76)	−.004 (1.3)	−.02* (1.7)	−.01* (1.85)	−.01** (2.3)	−.03 (1.26)	−.02** (3.50)	−.02** (3.8)
Crafts	−.001 (.1)	−.002 (.97)	−.002 (.9)	.004 (.39)	−.01** (2.80)	−.01** (2.7)	−.02 (.85)	−.01** (3.07)	−.02** (4.0)
Operative	−.0001 (.1)	.01** (4.48)	.01** (4.4)	−.004 (.36)	−.004 (1.49)	−.004 (1.6)	−.02 (1.17)	.0001 (.03)	−.003 (.8)
Transport	.006 (.5)	.004 (1.08)	.004 (1.1)	−.004 (−.31)	.003 (.96)	.003 (.8)	.01 (.03)	−.001 (.25)	−.001 (.2)
Private Household	.01 (.1)	−.004 (.20)	−.002 (.1)	−.01 (.07)	−.02 (.93)	−.02 (.9)	.02 (.13)	−.03 (1.00)	−.03 (1.0)
Farm Worker	.001 (.1)	−.005 (.81)	−.01 (.8)	.02 (.56)	−.002 (.27)	−.001 (.1)	−.06 (1.13)	−.001 (.15)	−.01 (.5)

Table 3.12 (continued)

Independent Variable	Layoff			Quit			Discharge		
	Blacks	Whites	Pooled	Blacks	Whites	Pooled	Blacks	Whites	Pooled
Agriculture	.005	−.0003	.001	−.02	−.01	−.01	.05	−.03**	−.03**
	(.2)	(.03)	(.1)	(.03)	(.94)	(1.1)	(.98)	(2.69)	(2.5)
Mining	.01	.01	.01	−.01	.01*	.01*	.06	−.03**	−.03**
	(.2)	(1.26)	(1.5)	(.30)	(1.76)	(1.7)	(.71)	(2.60)	(2.5)
Construction	.01	.02**	.02**	−.004	.002	.002	.09**	.01	.01
	(.8)	(3.86)	(4.1)	(.21)	(.42)	(.4)	(2.87)	(.93)	(1.4)
Manufacturing	.06**	.02**	.02**	.003	.0003	.001	.02	−.01	−.01
	(3.8)	(3.65)	(4.6)	(.18)	(.06)	(.1)	(.56)	(.92)	(.8)
Transport	.01	.02**	.02**	.001	−.01	−.005	−.04	−.01	−.02*
	(.5)	(2.74)	(2.8)	(.03)	(.76)	(.7)	(.94)	(1.34)	(1.8)
Utility	−.0005	.00004	.001	.06**	.005	.01	−.02	−.02*	−.02*
	(.02)	(.01)	(.1)	(2.1)	(.64)	(1.2)	(.45)	(1.76)	(1.8)
Trade	.01	.002	.002	.01	.002	.003	.02	−.02**	−.02**
	(.7)	(.29)	(.01)	(.56)	(.38)	(.5)	(.76)	(2.36)	(2.2)
Finance	.01	−.003	−.001	.01	−.01	−.003	−.01	−.03**	−.02**
	(.4)	(.39)	(.1)	(.61)	(.76)	(.5)	(.13)	(2.39)	(2.3)
Service	.01	.002	.003	−.01	.001	.001	−.003	−.01*	.01*
	(.6)	(.41)	(.6)	(−.44)	(.25)	(.1)	(.11)	(1.83)	(.8)
SSR	40.8	375.9	417.4	47.4	382.8	430.7	151.4	829.8	987.3
R̄²	.02	.02	.02	−.001	.004	.003	.03	.02	.02
Chow Test			66.66			58.0			167.0

Note: **Significant at the 5 percent level in a two-tailed test. *Significant at the 10 percent level in a two-tailed test. Asymptotic t-statistics in parentheses.

demographic or occupational profile of blacks. For example, quits, which are presumably a worker-initiated decision, are not influenced by any of the human capital variables, including education. Moreover, industry and occupational choices have almost no influence either.

Finally, in the discharge equations, age, marital status, and education significantly affect black workers' likelihood of being fired. And again, occupational and industry variables have almost no effect on the likelihood of discharge.

3.4 Summary and Conclusions

The results from the different estimates using the NBER, NLS, and CPS data sets suggest that differences in layoff or job-loss experiences between blacks and whites cannot be explained simply by differences in schooling or the geographic and age distributions of the respective populations. Increases in schooling appear to reduce white job-loss rates but do not affect black layoff or job-loss rates. Being in school significantly reduces the probability of job loss among both blacks and whites. The aggregate importance of this effect in explaining the black-white differential, however, is probably small given the relatively small differences in dropout rates that exist between black and white teens. Of the conventional human capital variables, only tenure was consistently found to reduce job loss, layoffs, and discharges among blacks or to reduce the black-white differential in these rates. Either because of firm-specific human capital or seniority-based layoff rules, lack of tenure seems to play an important role in the high rate of job loss among blacks. Lower mean levels of tenure among blacks also help account for differences in the probability of job loss between blacks and whites.

Our estimates indicate that the distribution of employment across industries and occupations is important in understanding layoff and discharge rates among white youths. The results from the three data sets differ, however, as to the importance of these variables in determining black labor market outcomes. The CPS results showed that these parameters had no explanatory power, whereas the NLS and NBER results indicated some power.[16] Despite these differences across data sets, industry and occupation were found to be less important in explaining black layoff and discharge rates than in explaining white outcomes in all the surveys.

Unionism was found not to be a significant contributor to high rates of job loss among blacks. In fact, the NLS results indicate that blacks actually benefit from the formal layoff and discharge rules that are prevalent in unionized establishments. Thus, the higher level of unionism among blacks does not explain their high incidence of job loss.

Finally, Chow tests indicated that the structure of the model generating black layoff or job-loss behavior is different from that generating white outcomes. We obtained this result using both the NLS and CPS surveys. Further, differences in the mean levels of our measured variables accounted for only a small portion of differences in labor market outcomes between blacks and whites. It is conceivable that differences in unmeasured personal or job characteristics may explain all or part of this result. Nonetheless, the role of discrimination should not be ignored in any attempt to explain the high rate of job loss and unemployment among black youths.

Notes

1. Nonemployment refers to discouraged and other potential workers who are not seeking work. In this paper we make no attempt to measure the number of nonemployed. For a discussion of the technical aspects of movement between unemployment and nonemployment, see Clark and Summers (1982).

2. Flanagan (1978) showed that the proportion of blacks who quit in a year is equal to that of whites (0.209 versus 0.206), but the proportion of blacks who are laid off is twice as high (0.074 to 0.041).

3. See Freeman and Medoff (1982b) or Clark and Summers (1982).

4. This model borrows heavily from one developed by Altonji and Shakotko (1983) to explain layoff behavior. Their model, however, relied on the assumption that productivity evolves as a first-order autoregressive process.

5. See Freeman and Medoff (1982a).

6. See Flanagan (1978).

7. The transport and wholesale-retail sales sectors had significant coefficients, as did the operative and service occupations. The industry and occupation coefficients are available from the authors upon request.

8. The t-statistic for the restriction that the coefficients are different was 4.56.

9. See Leighton and Mincer (1982, 245).

10. See Medoff (1979).

11. The results for industry and occupation dummy variables are available from the authors upon request.

12. The F-statistics were 3.63 for the layoff equation and 4.73 for the job-loss equation.

13. The F-statistics were 5.51 for the job-loss equation and 6.49 for the layoff equation.

14. The complete sample contained over 30,000 cases; however, the results presented in this section are restricted to the experienced labor force: our reduced sample does not include people who had never worked. Thus, we have restricted the unemployed population to losers and leavers.

15. In 1979, the CPS collected union-membership data only on employed workers.

16. For a discussion of differences in the CPS and NLS surveys that may account for this discrepancy, see Freeman and Medoff (1982a).

References

Altonji, J., and R. Shakotko. 1983. Wage contracts, productivity, and turnover. New York, N.Y.: Columbia University Photocopy.

Amemiya, T. 1981. Qualitative response models: A survey. *Journal of Economic Literature* 19 (December): 1483–1536.

Clark, K. B., and L. H. Summers. 1982. The dynamics of youth unemployment. In *The youth labor market problem: Its nature, causes, and consequences,* ed. R. B. Freeman and D. A. Wise. Chicago: University of Chicago Press.

Cogan, J. 1982. The decline in black teenage employment, 1950–1970. *American Economic Review* 72 (September): 621–38.

Ellwood, D. 1982. Teenage unemployment: Permanent scars or temporary blemishes. In *The youth labor market problem: Its nature, causes, and consequences,* ed. R. B. Freeman and D. A. Wise. Chicago: University of Chicago Press.

Flanagan, R. 1978. Discrimination theory, labor turnover and racial unemployment differentials. *Journal of Human Resources* 13(2): 187–207.

Freeman, R. B. 1980. The exit voice tradeoff in the labor market: Unionism, job tenure, quits, and separations. *Quarterly Journal of Economics* 94 (June): 643–74.

Freeman, R. B., and J. L. Medoff. 1982a Why does the rate of youth labor force activity differ across surveys? In *The youth labor market problem: Its nature, causes, and consequences,* ed. R. B. Freeman and D. A. Wise. Chicago: University of Chicago Press.

Freeman, R. B., and J. L. Medoff. 1982b The youth labor market problem in the United States: An overview. In *The youth labor market problem: Its nature, causes, and consequences,* ed. R. B. Freeman and D. A. Wise. Chicago: University of Chicago Press.

Handbook of Labor Statistics. See U.S. Department of Labor.

Heckman, J., and G. Borjas. 1980. Does unemployment cause future unemployment? Definitions, questions and answers from a continuous time model of heterogeneity and state dependence. *Economica* 47 (August): 247–83.

Holzer, H. J. Black youth nonemployment: Duration and job search behavior. In *Minority youth conference volume,* ed. R. B. Freeman and H. J. Holzer. Chicago: University of Chicago Press.

Jovanovic, B. 1979. Job matching and the theory of turnover. *Journal of Political Economy* 87 (October): 972–90.

Leighton, L., and J. Mincer. 1982. Labor Turnover and Youth Unemployment. In *The youth labor market problem: Its nature, causes, and consequences,* ed. R. B. Freeman and D. A. Wise. Chicago: University of Chicago Press.

Medoff, J. 1979. Layoffs and alternatives under trade unions in U.S. manufacturing. *American Economic Review* 69 (June): 380–95.

U.S. Department of Labor, Bureau of Labor Statistics. 1980. *Handbook of Labor Statistics.* Washington, D.C.: GPO, December.

Williams, W. 1977. *Youth and minority unemployment.* Stanford, Calif.: Hoover Institution Press.

Comment   James L. Medoff

The paper by Jackson and Montgomery is a valuable discussion of job-loss unemployment among young black and white members of the labor force. Although the study provides a great deal of evidence on this subject, I believe it needs still more to resolve completely the issues at hand. In addition, the analysis would benefit from a bit more theory.

It is well known that the probability of becoming unemployed because of either a layoff or a discharge depends on both the probability of being laid off or discharged and the mean completed spell of unemployment of those who have been laid off or discharged. The authors focused on the probability of being laid off or discharged, ignoring the question of the length of spells of unemployment. Although that focus can be justified, it would be very helpful to know more about the relative importance of job-loss incidences and the mean completed spells of unemployment of job losers in explaining the very different implications.

One way the authors might shed some light on this issue is by looking at the information on mean weeks of unemployment as of a given CPS survey, which is available in the CPS data file. I recognize that mean weeks of unemployment as of a CPS survey date is not the same thing as the mean duration of completed spells of unemployment, but nevertheless the black-white ratio for the former would reflect the likely ratio for the latter. The authors could also make use of longitudinal data to draw some inferences about the relative importance of incidences and spells of job loss.

The paper would further benefit greatly from a more careful theoretical discussion of layoffs and discharges. In discussing layoffs, more attention should be paid to the importance of product-demand variation and how that variation occurs across industries. Moreover, differences in the treatment of blue- and white-collar workers must be addressed at greater length, as should the role of seniority and unions in decisions about which workers will be laid off. In discussing discharges, the theory should fully account for the fact that this form of job loss occurs with greatest frequency among new hires who undergo either explicit or implicit probationary periods in both union and nonunion settings. In the case of discharges, product-demand variation plays only a modest role. By positing these propositions the authors would provide a better understanding of the facts that layoffs and discharges are very different animals and that the probability of each depends greatly on the industrial setting and the characteristics of workers independent of either their race of human capital. It is worthwhile to discuss theoret-

James L. Medoff is associate professor of economics, Harvard University, and research associate, National Bureau of Economic Research.

ically why we expect race to have different implications for layoff probabilities than for discharge probabilities.

In light of this theoretical analysis, I would like to see a careful decomposition of the authors' results. First, exactly how much of the differentials in the probability of being unemployed due to the various forms of job loss can be explained by the human capital attributes of young blacks and whites and how much by differences in the effects of these attributes? As the authors state, in analyzing the role of human capital in a layoff equation, it is essential that the wage also be included, since what ultimately determines whether a firm decides to let go of a particular employee is the difference between the worker's value-marginal product and his wage. Nonetheless, the authors did not include the wage in any of their regressions, and they should address this omission. I would also like to see an analysis of the relative role of locational and institutional factors in explaining why the attributes of young blacks and young whites seem in some instances to mean different things in the job-loss process. We cannot tell from the results presented whether the authors' equations performed differently for black and white youths because of the youngsters' race or because they hold different types of jobs. From a policy point of view, this information would be very useful.

In sum, like the archetypical discussant, I have spent most of my time criticizing and very little time praising. Let me therefore end by saying that I learned much from Jackson and Montgomery's contribution and hope to learn still more from their future efforts.

III   Causes: Demand

4   The Spatial Mismatch Hypothesis: Are There Teenage Jobs Missing in the Ghetto?

David T. Ellwood

4.1 Introduction

Unemployment among black teenagers has reached astounding proportions. Half of all black teenagers who are out of school report themselves as looking for work but unable to find it. Another group of almost equal size say that they are neither working nor looking for work. Just 40 percent of the out-of-school black youths in this country have a job—any job. To many observers, the ghetto is the first place to look for an explanation. Even the most casual glance at the poorer sections of the nation's central cities reveals their weak economic condition. It seems quite plausible that black teenagers are trapped in blighted neighborhoods where the blue-collar, retailing, and service jobs that teenagers can perform have largely vanished. The result may be unemployment, frustration, and alienation.

This paper explores the so-called spatial mismatch hypothesis as an explanation for the poor labor market experiences of young blacks. At the core of the mismatch story is the spatial expansion of the American industrial cities. Wealthy families seeking less congestion, better services, safer neighborhoods, and a wide array of other amenities have fled the central cities, leaving behind the poor, the old, and the minorities. Industry, particularly manufacturing and retail trade, has been drawn outward by similar desires: cheaper land, better transportation networks, superior environments, wealthier customers, and to some extent, more skilled workers. What remain in the city are high-skilled white-collar jobs and low-skilled blue-collar workers. The fear is that

David T. Ellwood is associate professor of public policy at the John F. Kennedy School of Government, Harvard University, and faculty research fellow at the National Bureau of Economic Research.

the outflow of people and firms has left those least able to find and commute to employment trapped far away from the areas where new jobs are opening. In short, the young, black, urban poor struggle in a weak secondary labor market.

There are many formulations of the mismatch hypothesis. Often the formulation is influenced by its author's desired policy prescription. In this paper I hope to test whether spatially rearranging jobs in one metropolitan area would significantly improve the employment prospects of black teenagers. Logically, the question could be asked in reverse: would rearranging the residences of black teenagers in the metropolitan area improve their prospects? The problem with the latter formulation is that it would require a large number of changes. Ghetto dispersal would not only change employment accessibility, but it would also alter the social and educational environment of black teenagers. Job rearrangement would have some of these effects, but nothing like massive desegregation.

It is also important to realize that the story being tested here assumes that aggregate demand in the metropolitan area is fixed. The hypothetical experiment is not one in which new jobs are created in the ghetto. That policy would have two components: Aggregate demand in the city is increased, and the spatial distribution of employment is altered. I want to test only the effects of the latter change. The experiment is therefore one in which jobs are taken from one neighborhood and placed into another. It should be clear that whether or not the mismatch hypothesis proves to be valid, aggregate demand can affect teenage labor market performance.

This paper begins by summarizing a theoretical model that explores the necessary and sufficient conditions for the labor market outcomes of otherwise identical individuals to differ depending on their residential location within a metropolitan area. The methodological insight offered by the model is that by observing the behavior of existing workers, along with the general movement of population and industry, we can determine which groups and neighborhoods are spatially disadvantaged. The paper then explores in detail the labor market and job patterns in one metropolitan area—Chicago. Finally, this study explored in detail.

The paper shows that:
  *Low skilled jobs have been leaving the city faster than low skilled workers. As a result there are now more low skilled city residents who work in the suburbs than vice versa.
  *Young and low skilled blacks in Chicago spend far more time getting to work on the average than comparable whites.
  *Most workers, even young workers, work far outside any area that might reasonably be classified as a neighborhood.

Blacks are being gradually disadvantaged by job movements in Chicago. At the same time the fact that most workers labor far away from home hints at a more fluid labor market than might be envisioned by a mismatch theory.

This study will explore the possible labor market effects of differences in local job accessibility by examining the relationship between job proximity and labor market outcomes in Chicago's neighborhoods. The concluding section outlines the study's findings. The findings include:

*No measure of accessibility proves to have any predictive power in employment equations for young people. Black/white differences are wholly unaffected by their inclusion.

*When we allow for fixed neighborhood effects of any type, we still have no impact on this racial differential. Indeed, the data does not reject the hypothesis of their being no spatial neighborhood effects for employment at all!

*Labor market outcomes for young blacks on the West Side ghetto are remarkably similar to outcomes for those on the South Side, in spite of the dramatic differences in proximity to jobs.

*Black and white teenagers who live in the same neighborhood fare just as differently as blacks and whites who live across town from each other!

Thus we simultaneously understand the appeal of mismatch model and its failure. Blacks really are being gradually disadvantaged by job movements. However, the labor market is wide enough geographically and fluid enough that at least by 1970, neighborhood job movements could not be blamed for much of the poor performance of minorities in Chicago. Most teenagers, black and white, don't work in their neighborhoods. And in black areas where there are many jobs for youth, white youngsters tend to fill them.

This work does show that poverty and education have a very strong influence on black teenage unemployment rates, just as they do for whites. Efforts should continue to focus on these problems. Large differences remain, however, in the outcomes of measurably similar blacks and whites. Neighborhood job proximity does not seem to account for much of these differences, at least in Chicago. Race, not space, remains the key explanatory variable.

4.2   Previous Literature

In 1968, Kain published a very influential paper in which he advanced and sought to test a "mismatch hypothesis." The author argued that housing market segregation "(1) affects the distribution of Negro employment, and (2) reduces Negro job opportunities, and (3) postwar suburbanization has seriously aggravated the problem.'' He conjectured numerous links between the housing market and the labor market, links that included not only the direct effects of job accessibility, but also the influence that neighborhood characteristics might have on an employer's willingness to hire blacks. Employers with more contact and experience with blacks are presumably more disposed toward hiring them.

In his empirical work, Kain posited that there would be substantially more employment for blacks in Chicago and Detroit if neighborhoods were desegregated. That work has since come under close scrutiny. Kain's analysis clearly demonstrated that the spatial distributions of black employment and black residences were similar, confirming his first proposition. But his conclusion that black employment opportunities were therefore reduced hinged critically on his functional-form assumptions (Offner and Saks 1971). Indeed, there is something troubling about a model that predicts more employment for black workers when the number of workers used in generating the prediction is unchanged. Thus, although Kain's pathfinding work surfaced a number of tantalizing hypotheses, it left their validity largely unresolved.

Many other authors have attempted to test the mismatch hypothesis. Mooney (1969) found that nonwhite unemployment rates in different SMSAs were correlated with the percentage of area employment that was in the city and the extent of reverse commuting. But the percentage of all employment in the city would be as much affected by where the boundaries of the city were drawn as by economic forces, so that it is difficult to understand why these variables should have any predictive power. On the other side, Masters (1974) found that segregation indices did not help predict black unemployment rates in cities.[1] Although interesting, this result failed to test the mismatch hypothesis. A combination of segregation and job movement is what causes the employment problem, not merely the degree of segregation.

Most vehement in his attacks on the mismatch hypothesis has been Harrison.[2] This author has collected a variety of data that he believes show that suburbanization of employment has not increased in recent years. He has suggested that the flight of whites from the cities may even have left blacks in a stronger position for the central city jobs. Moreover, he has noted that blacks living outside the central city have incomes no higher than blacks living within the city but outside the poverty areas. This last result is difficult to interpret because Harrison explicitly selected nonpoor city blacks to compare with their suburban counterparts.

Kalachic and Goering (1970) and Danziger and Weinstein (1976) found little evidence of a wage differential between ghetto and nonghetto jobs in several cities. Recently, Straszheim (1980) has found large differentials in another city. And many other authors have looked at one or another aspect of these issues.

Because this patchwork of evidence was often derived without a strong theoretical base, it remains difficult to assess the validity of the mismatch hypothesis. Comparison between cities is dangerous, since each has its own history and since jurisdictional boundaries are largely arbitrary. The hypothesis is distinctly neighborhood-based. It implies differences in labor market outcomes depending on the neighborhood a given worker inhabits. The strategy of this paper is therefore to take that distinctly neighborhood approach in one city: Chicago. I seek to explore in detail the spatial character of the labor market, with a particular focus on teenagers. I am interested in the location of jobs and workers and changes in both over time. The complexity of even one city is almost sufficient to frustrate a comprehensive treatment of the labor market. Residential and industrial locations often reflect accidents of history as much as the workings of narrow economic forces.

4.3   Summary of a Theoretical Formulation of the Mismatch Hypothesis

In a previous paper (1981) I explored a model of the spatial mismatch between workers and jobs. Actually, the mismatch story turns most urban models on their heads. Normally in these models mobile workers choose their residences with an eye toward the location of their jobs, which are typically fixed in space. According to the mismatch story, some potential workers cannot move when the jobs they might fill move away. Because there is not space to detail the theoretical model in this paper, I shall present only its key features. The model described here can be characterized as an international trade model with a twist: People can commute between zones at a cost. Urban space is divided into a series of neighborhoods. Within each neighborhood housing prices and factor costs and rewards are identical.

Workers' utility is influenced by the housing prices in the neighborhood in which they live, the wage rate in the neighborhood in which they work, and a measure of the transportation (or search) cost associated with the workers' commute.

In the simplest form of the model, we assume there are two output sectors. The price of each good is uniform across all neighborhoods. Each sector employs labor, land, and capital. Capital costs are assumed uniform and constant across zones. Wages and industrial land rents are free to vary between zones. Finally, zones may differ in efficiency of production. (Crime, distribution, or parking costs may be higher in certain neighborhoods.)

Unemployment is not explicitly modeled in this general equilibrium treatment, but the model easily captures the influence of place of residence on labor market outcomes. The mismatch theory implies that labor market opportunities will differ among persons in different neighborhoods. We could just as easily model this relationship as very low wages (or wages net of transport costs) in some zones relative to others. And if we impose some wage rigidities in areas where equilibrium wages are low, we could instead have high wages and high unemployment.

In the context of this model, three forces will tend to equalize labor market opportunities across neighborhoods: the movement of people to new residences; the movement of capital or firms between neighborhoods; and the commuting of workers between zones. Thus, three conditions must be met for a mismatch hypothesis to have force:

1. Residential location decisions must be constrained. Free mobility of residences would equalize the utility of identical workers.
2. Conditions for business must be unfavorable due to either an excessive cost of production or a "shortage" of land in the same areas where residences are constrained. As a result, wage rates are low or else business leaves (or never enters) and few jobs are found in the neighborhood.
3. Commuting or search costs must be nontrivial for jobs outside the neighborhood. Otherwise, workers forced to live in undesirable areas would simply commute to jobs in other neighborhoods.

Because the results of these conditions are for the most part obvious, they receive only passing discussion here.

One confusion that easily arises in the mismatch hypothesis is the difference between labor market outcomes and utilities. The mismatch story could be construed to indicate that labor market outcomes will differ depending on residential location, whether or not utilities differ. Variables other than labor market outcomes enter the utility function. Areas with weak labor market opportunities may provide offsetting advantages. Indeed, if we consider job locations and wage rates to be exogenous, this model largely mimics the traditional Alonso (1964) and Kain (1962) models, in which land rents decline with distance from employment centers. Clearly, mismatch theorists have in mind labor market problems serious enough to create insufficient compensating advantages in housing markets. If that is the case, the mobility of the disadvantaged workers must be limited. Note, however, that a result showing differing labor market opportunities by neighborhood need not indicate any market failures. We should naturally expect some differences. But if people voluntarily choose to live in economically weak neighborhoods, we can be sure that there are offsetting benefits. It might still be interesting to explore the differences in labor market opportunities even if no limits were imposed on mobility, but utility variations can occur only when such limits exist.

Thus, at the very heart of the mismatch story are constraints on residential (and possibly workplace) location. Proponents of the hypothesis argue that the residential choices of blacks are particularly constrained because of discrimination in urban housing markets, and this point arouses little dispute. I know of no author who has argued that residential choices for blacks in Chicago are unconstrained, though considerable disagreement persists about whether these constraints lead to unusually high housing costs.[3] Among teenagers, the problem of mobilty leading to identical utilities even if labor market opportunities differ by location may not be serious anyway. Over 90 percent of all teenagers live at home. They have little option about their homesites. Whatever the advantages or disadvantages of the particular homesite the parents have found, they surely will not exactly offset any job accessibility differences faced by teenagers.

The foregoing discussion notwithstanding, our attention will be on the narrow question of whether identical individuals achieve "vastly" different labor market outcomes because of their residential location. We cannot pretend to be able to distinguish completely any offsetting features in other markets. If large differences in labor market outcomes are found, it will be important to consider separately the possibility of a utility difference.

Assuming residences are constrained, we must then consider under what conditions labor market outcomes will differ widely by neighborhood of residence. It is still quite plausible that mobility of firms will cause equalization of opportunity. There will naturally be pressure for the production sector to move in such a way as to equalize access to labor and wages. The geographic labor market that fails to achieve such equality must suffer from at least two other important distortions. First, the conditions for factor price equalization must not be met. Second, commuting and search costs must be nontrivial.

The best-known theorem in international trade states quite simply that if certain conditions are met, factor prices in all countries will be identical. By extension, if these assumptions are met in labor markets, wage rates (and thus opportunities) will not differ across neighborhoods. In a two-sector model the most important assumptions are that all neighborhoods allow for equally efficient production and that both goods be produced in each zone.[4]

In our model there are two particularly pertinent cases in which the theorem may break down. If efficiency does differ depending on location, the theorem fails. Or if one or another zone has a superabundance of labor relative to land or vice versa, equalization will again be thwarted. The first condition is obvious. If it is more expensive to produce one or another product in certain locations, either factor prices must fall or production simply will not take place there. There is no a priori reason to believe that higher production costs will lead to decreases only in wage rates or only in land prices. Indeed, there are unusual cases in which one factor price actually rises. In general, though, we can predict downward pressure on both land prices and wages. The lower limit on both prices naturally depends on the opportunity costs of the factors. If workers have strong opportunities in nearby neighborhoods, the wage cannot fall below the net wage received by the commuters. If land has other uses such as housing or speculation, the fall in rents will also be limited. Quite plainly, it is possible that production inefficiencies and opportunity costs of factors may be such that no production will occur in some areas.

Yet even if all areas allow for equally efficient production, where labor is very abundant in some neighborhoods relative to land or vice versa, the theorem may again fail. We noted earlier that the factor price theorem works only when production takes place in both sectors in a neighborhood. At the equalized factor prices, each sector will use a particular combination of land and labor. Equilibrium requires that all factors be exhausted. Thus, some combination of production of good X and good Y must allow for full use of resources. So long as the overall land-labor ratio in the zone falls between that implied by the equalized wage-land rental ratio for production of goods X and Y, we have no problem. That is, if our zone has three workers per acre of industrial land and good X uses four workers per acre while good Y requires two workers per acre, then by using half our land for the production of X and half for Y we will absorb all of the workers.

But should a zone have a land-labor ratio outside the bounds of production for X and Y, there is a problem. A zone with five workers per acre cannot produce both X and Y. When labor is too abundant, wages must fall and production (if it takes place at all) will be confined to the labor-intensive sector. There is nothing mystical here. When land is very scarce relative to labor, it is quickly used up. Prices for land rise and wage rates must fall or local employers cannot compete. Once again opportunity costs place a floor on the fall in factor prices. Wage rates therefore may not fall sufficiently in neighborhoods with large concentrations of labor to accommodate all nearby workers, and many residents may be forced to commute to other neighborhoods for work.

Equilibrium is achieved when the net wage of all residents is identical. Those who work nearby command less gross pay, but local employers must pay more for land so they make no excess profit. Those workers who commute receive larger paychecks but bear search and commuting costs. Either way, if efficiency differs by neighborhood or if there are very large differences in the ratio of land to labor across zones, factor prices and thus opportunities are likely to differ.

The final condition for differential labor market outcomes for identical residents of different neighborhoods is nontrivial commuting or search costs. We explicitly allow workers to search for and commute to jobs in neighborhoods outside their own. If the costs of doing so are small relative to the wage, the net effect of neighborhood differences will also be small. These search and commuting costs limit the differences in opportunity across neighborhoods. In the extreme when such costs are trivial, all persons face equal labor market opportunities. Everyone in the entire metropolitan area would be attracted to any job paying a little extra. Ultimately, it is this condition that we must explore most closely. Proximity to work does vary dramatically by neighborhood. But if such variations are important to consider when exploring the labor market outcomes of young people, search and commuting costs must be very high.

Let me summarize the conditions that must be met for a plausible mismatch theory. First, there must be constraints on the residential location decisions of workers. This condition is not essential for labor market opportunities to differ by neighborhood, but it is critical for utility levels to differ by neighborhood. Second, either neighborhoods must vary in their productive efficiency or some zones must have an overabundance of labor or land, or both; otherwise, wages will be everywhere identical. Finally, commuting costs must be nontrivial.

It can be argued very effectively that the first two conditions are met for ghetto youths. The residential choices of these youths' parents are obviously constrained. Moreover, the young people themselves are essentially constrained to live at home. It also appears that production is less efficient in the ghetto and even that usable land for industry is relatively scarce.

Production costs might be higher in the ghetto for many reasons. Theft and vandalism are unusually high. Noll (1970) argues that business expansion in ghetto areas is difficult because the acquisition of space is complicated by the need to buy land from several owners, each of whom potentially occupies a monopolistic position. Hamer (1972) reports that demolition costs are high relative to the acquisition costs of unfettered land in the suburbs. Kain (1968) points to a reluctance of skilled workers, who tend to be white, to work in undesirable areas. Parking is always a problem. Finally, a congested and outmoded transportation network often hampers the movement of goods to national markets.

There is good reason to suppose that usable land may be hard to find in the ghetto. The arguments of Noll and Hamer noted above suggest not only that production is costly, but also that usable land is limited. Population densities in urban ghettos are typically the highest of any area in the SMSA. The labor-land ratio in the ghetto is obviously many times greater than that in the suburbs.[5]

The key question, then, is whether search and commuting costs for young people in the inner city are costly. And certainly, such a scenario is plausible. Transportation costs may be very high. Cars are rarely available to poor young blacks, and the mass transportation system may not serve them well. Youths may value their leisure time very highly, implying a greater cost (relative to the wage) of commuting time than adults. An even more plausible story is one that emphasizes the high cost of initial job search outside the neighborhood. Youngsters may be unfamiliar with the transportation system they need to use to locate a job in the first place. Others may genuinely fear for their personal safety once they leave the familiar areas near home. It is widely claimed that young blacks simply will not set foot in some alien neighborhoods. Finally, the job-search process of teenagers may rely heavily on informal networks, which may dissipate with distance. I shall explore these issues in some detail later in this paper. Suffice it to say, however, it is quite plausible that commuting may impose a serious burden on many youngsters seeking work.

If the three conditions for our model are met in the ghetto, we can make three principal predictions.

HYPOTHESIS 1. *There will be downward pressure on wage rates in the ghetto.*

Whether ghetto production is less efficient or usable land is simply scarce, there will be downward pressure on wages. (For land prices, pressure will be downward if the area is less efficient and upward when land is scarce.) But wages may be constrained by the standard litany of rigidity-inducing institutions. The minimum wage, unions, government payment rules all serve to prop up wages. Firms with several plants in the region are rarely willing to offer lower wages at one or another plant. Discrimintion laws may also deter a company from offering lower wages in ghetto plants. As a result wages may not adjust downward sufficiently to provide jobs to all who seek them. Unemployment would be the inevitable result.

HYPOTHESIS 2. *Ghetto firms will tend to be labor intensive.*

The plentiful resource in a neighborhood with a depressed market is labor. The firms most likely to offset added costs of business in the ghetto are ones that can exploit this resource. The result will be more than just the obvious one that firms needing low-skilled labor will be drawn to the ghetto. This result follows from the surplus of labor in the ghetto and not from the low skills of ghetto residents. Even if all workers in metropolitan areas were identical, ghetto production—if it exists—would likely to be labor intensive.

HYPOTHESIS 3. *The ghetto will tend to export labor to other neighborhoods. Workers living in the ghetto will tend to travel farther to work than their counterparts in other metropolitan areas.*

If opportunities are more limited in the ghetto, workers will try to commute to jobs elsewhere. The greater the differential in wage rates or opportunities, the greater the incentive to commute. Thus, the weaker the opportunities in one area, the farther the marginal worker will travel for work. This result is obvious, but very important methodologically. It suggests a way of measuring accessibility by observing the journey-to-work patterns of workers. Neighborhoods with low job accessibility will tend to export workers. Those workers will travel farther to work than their counterparts in other areas.

This model illustrates the appeal of a simple mismatch story. It can generate low wages and skewed occupational distributions without re-sorting to models of discrimination or of the heterogeneity of workers. Unlike discrimination models, this formulation of the mismatch story requires no noncompetitive behavior on the part of firms. No large profits are forgone. The cost of business operation is higher in the ghetto or land is scarce, and ghetto residents suffer. Indeed, the two-sector formulation of the model used here is in most important respects similar to Becker's use of a one-sector model in his landmark book (1957) on discrimination. That similar results are generated here should be no surprise.

Of course, discrimination is not ruled out in this model. Indeed, housing market discrimination is crucial to its formulation. Discrimi-nation in the labor market could serve to exacerbate the mismatch problems. The reluctance of capital to flow into the ghetto could reflect ill feelings towards blacks rather than high real costs. If firms in or out of the ghetto refuse to hire blacks, "search costs" may indeed be high.

The appeal of the model, however, is part of the reason it is so hard to test. Low wages, skewed occupational distributions, and high un-employment can be generated by mismatch, by discrimination, and by differences among workers. The difficult task is to distinguish among these.

What is unique about the mismatch model is its emphasis on em-ployment location. In theory, ghetto firms will pay less than nonghetto firms. Those willing to commute out can command higher wages. The occupational mix of ghetto and nonghetto firms will be different. But the heterogeneity of firms and workers bedevils easy empirical testing. The strongest result is perhaps the most obvious: Persons living in neighborhoods with weak local employment opportunities will tend to commute to other neighborhoods. If that commuting imposes heavy costs—either in initial job search or in daily commuting—persons living in these areas will fare worse in the labor market.

The basic insight, then, is to observe the behavior of existing workers to determine the neighborhood's proximity to jobs. The methodology used here is to relate neighborhood employment rates to various mea-sures of job proximity based on the behavior of existing workers. Even here we must be very careful. Worker commuting patterns differ for many reasons. We must be careful to understand them.

4.4   Worksites, Homesites, and Commuting in Chicago

The theoretical model outlined above suggests that we ought to look at workers' differential residential and workplace locations and the commuting behavior these imply in our search for evidence for or against the mismatch hypothesis. We need to define a variety of proximity measures and to relate these to labor market outcomes in the neighborhoods in and around Chicago. Before embarking on that task, it is enlightening to consider briefly the broad employment, residence, and commuting patterns observed in Chicago.

During the 1960s the central city of Chicago experienced declines relative to the surrounding suburbs in both the number of jobs located there and in the number of workers living there. The city actually lost more jobs than working residents. In 1960 the city housed 59 percent of all workers in the Chicago (SMSA) and it held nearly 69 percent of all jobs. But by 1970, the figures had fallen to 48 percent and 53 percent, respectively. Thus, by 1970 the image of a central city that held the jobs for "bedroom" suburbs no longer applied to Chicago. Jobs and workers had achieved rough parity.

Of course overall parity did not translate into identical patterns of work and home locations for all occupations. Table 4.1, drawn from census data, reveals the changing workplace and residence patterns by occupation between 1960 and 1970. The table records both the percentage of all those employed in each occupation who lived in the city (rather than the suburbs) and the percentage who worked there. It also reports the ratio of these two, labeled the import ratio. In effect, the import ratio gives the ratio of jobs to workers in the city. If equal numbers of persons lived and worked there, the ratio would equal one. An import ratio of one does not of course indicate that there is no commuting, only that as many workers commute out of the city each day as commute into it. Since there are more professional jobs located in the city than there are professionals living there, on net the city imports professionals from the suburbs each day and the import ratio for that occupation exceeds one. By contrast, there are actually fewer city jobs for laborers than there are resident laborers, so each day the city is a net exporter of these workers and the ratio falls below one.

As we would expect, the city is a major net importer of professional, managerial, and sales personnel. What is somewhat surprising is the fact that Chicago is actually a net exporter of all of lower-skilled occupations. More operatives, laborers, and service workers live in the city than work there. Even more striking is the fact that the deterioration in the import ratios between 1960 and 1970 was greatest in those occupations. So although declines came in all workplace and residence

Table 4.1   **Worksites, Residences, and Central City Import Ratios for All Employed Persons, by Occupation, 1960 and 1970**

Occupation	% of All Persons Employed in Occupation Living in the City (1)	% of All Persons Employed in Occupation Working in the City (2)	Import Ratio (2) ÷ (1)
	1960		
Managerial	44.9	68.8	1.53
Professional	48.7	64.6	1.33
Sales	51.8	68.2	1.32
Clerical	63.9	74.6	1.17
Crafts	54.1	64.3	1.19
Operative	66.0	69.9	1.06
Laborer	67.6	67.9	1.01
Service Worker	66.3	66.5	1.01
Total	58.7	68.7	1.17
	1970		
Managerial	31.8	53.1	1.67
Professional	40.8	51.6	1.27
Sales	37.5	49.3	1.32
Clerical	52.7	58.3	1.11
Crafts	44.5	48.8	1.10
Operative	58.1	56.2	.96
Laborer	57.9	52.0	.90
Service Worker	57.1	53.9	.94
Total	47.9	52.6	1.10

Source: 1960 and 1970 census data.

categories, the city's biggest losses were in the residences of highly skilled, well-paid workers and in jobs for its low-skilled residents.

One portion of the mismatch hypothesis does appear to be verified, therefore, in Chicago. Low-skilled jobs are leaving faster than low-skilled workers, and those workers remaining in the city may be disadvantaged. This is particularly plausible for blacks, since roughly 90 percent of them do in fact live in the city and since as a group, they are disproportionately low-skilled. Indeed, other data do show that commuting patterns are quite different between blacks and whites. And low-skilled blacks do travel farther to work than low-skilled whites.

Table 4.2 is based on a special survey conducted by the Chicago Area Transportation Study (CATS) in 1970.[6] In general, urban theorists hypothesize that desires for land and other environmental amenities lead wealthier persons to live farther from the city (and their jobs) than those with more modest incomes. Thus, we should expect to see higher-paid professionals and managers commuting farther than lower-paid operatives and laborers. Interestingly enough, that is exactly the pattern we can observe for whites in Chicago. White managers and professionals are slightly more likely to work in the city than are whites working in lesser-skilled occupations. But they are much more likely to live in the suburbs. As a result they average 35-minute commutes each way whereas white laborers and service workers travel 25 minutes on average. The bulk of the variation in travel times seems to be caused by differences in where the members of particular occupations live, rather than in where they work.

By contrast, most of the variation in the journey-to-work times of blacks is almost entirely the result of differences in where they work. Roughly 90 percent of the workers in each occupation live in the city. But in the lower-skilled categories a sizable fraction work outside the city. As a result commuting times are actually slightly longer among these lower-skilled blacks. And they are considerably longer than the times for comparable whites. Low-skilled blacks spend as much time commuting as professional whites.

These findings are supported by yet another source: the 1975 Annual Housing Survey (AHS) for Chicago. This survey is richer in demographic detail than CATS, but it is weaker in occupational information. Table 4.3 is drawn from the AHS data. Once again we see that lower-

Table 4.2   Residence and Workplace Location Patterns, Import Ratios, and Travel Times for White and Black Workers, by Occupation, 1970

Occupation	% Living in Central City	% Working in Central City	Import Ratio	Average Travel Time
Whites				
Managerial	31.9	54.5	1.71	34.3
Professional	34.3	53.2	1.55	33.3
Sales	34.9	53.8	1.54	32.1
Clerical	45.7	57.6	1.26	31.1
Crafts	38.0	48.0	1.26	29.4
Operative	47.9	49.3	1.03	26.6
Laborer	51.6	50.0	.97	26.2
Service Worker	50.6	52.9	1.05	25.0
Blacks				
Managerial	93.8	86.9	.93	32.0
Professional	86.9	82.5	.95	33.7
Sales	86.7	86.7	1.00	31.3
Clerical	91.9	90.2	.98	31.9
Crafts	87.3	65.8	.75	36.2
Operative	86.0	73.7	.86	34.0
Laborer	79.7	64.6	.81	33.5
Service Worker	85.9	80.2	.93	34.2

Source: Calculated from 1970 Chicago Area Transportation Survey data.

skilled whites travel shorter distances and have shorter commuting times than higher-skilled whites. Perhaps most relevant for this study is the finding that white teenagers have very short travel times, averaging only 15 minutes. And again the pattern for blacks is quite different. In the lowest-skilled categories, travel times and distances are much longer for blacks than for whites. Most dramatically, black teenagers travel much farther to work and spend much longer traveling, according to this survey. Indeed, black teenage men spend more than double the time commuting of their white counterparts, on average.

We should also keep in mind that these are average and not marginal travel times. They represent the average experience of those who received jobs. In other words, they do not necessarily reflect the commuting that would be required of the next potential worker. If nearby jobs are easier to find and are filled first, excess commuting times for the marginal black teenager could in fact be much greater. Even the average figures reported in the AHS imply that in a five-day workweek, black teens spend two and one-half more hours in transit than white teens.

This glimpse at the general patterns helps illustrate why the mismatch hypothesis holds real appeal to those interested in the problems of minorities. In Chicago, at least, low-skilled jobs are in fact moving out of the city faster than low-skilled workers. Blacks do spend longer getting to work than comparable whites.[7] And the differences are most

Table 4.3   **Travel Times and Distances to Work for Whites and Nonwhites in Chicago, 1975**

	Average Time		Average Distance	
	Whites	Nonwhites	Whites	Nonwhites
	Employed Men			
All Ages	27.4		10.8	
Household Heads, Aged 30–39 with Education:				
Less than 12 Years	25.1	33.0	9.9	12.3
12 Years	27.3	27.4	11.8	9.7
Over 12 Years	31.8	33.1	13.5	12.8
Teenagers 16–19 Living at Home	15.1	36.2	4.5	9.3
	Employed Women			
All Ages	22.4	32.8	7.2	9.2
Household Heads	25.3	36.1	7.3	9.5
Wives	21.0	33.0	7.1	9.4
Teenagers 16–19 Living at Home	16.2	28.7	4.7	6.5

Source: Calculated from 1975 Annual Housing Survey.

extreme for precisely those groups we might expect to have limited mobility and haphazard job-search methods—the low-skilled and the young. Obviously, the hypothesis merits closer examination.

Although black teens spend more than twice as long as whites traveling to work, the differences need not have a sizable impact on labor market outcomes nor do they necessarily explain a large portion of the racial differences in labor market outcomes. The extra travel time amounts to just 5 percent extra work time in an eight-hour day. Transportation economists report that commuting time is typically valued at roughly half the wage.[8] If so, even an absurdly high labor-supply elasticity of, say, two would explain only five percentage points of the 50 percent difference in the employment rates of black and white teens.

Thus, we need a model that suggests youths who live farther from jobs suffer greater disadvantages than those imposed by higher commuting costs. We need a model whereby initial job search or job acquisition is severely hampered by geographic separation from jobs. If job-search costs rose, for example, exponentially with distance because of initial transportation costs, more limited information, or fear and uncertainty about neighborhoods farther from home, and if youths did not expect to stay in any particular job for an extended period, much more significant negative effects could result.

A slight modification of this notion derives from the work of Rees and Schultz (1970) in the early 1960s. They found that low-skilled workers tended to find jobs primarily through the use of informal networks.[9] It does seem plausible that such networks would dissipate proportionately with distance from home. Thus, these low-skilled black workers might be disadvantaged in their initial job search.

There is a second aspect of these results that casts doubt on the plausibility of the mismatch hypothesis. The mean distances and the variances around them are very large. A five-mile journey brings any teenager well outside almost any conception of neighborhood. Typical walking speed is roughly three miles per hour, and therefore jobs even for white youths are over one hour's walk from home. It seems unlikely that youths would be very familiar with most of the areas within a five-mile radius. And the variances in travel times and distances are very large for all groups. It is not at all uncommon for the standard deviations to be two-thirds the size of the mean. Such a wide variance indicates a far more dynamic and wide-ranging labor market than some mismatch models might suggest.

Nonetheless, it is still plausible that job accessibility differences are important. We must therefore turn to the question whether the observed differences in job accessibility do in fact explain differences in the labor market outcomes of whites and blacks and of residents of different neighborhoods in Chicago.

4.5   Methodology

In our methodological approach to the question of spatial mismatch, we are interested in two related issues. Does proximity to jobs influence labor market outcomes? And if they do, can differences in proximity explain an important part of the racial differential in the outcomes for youth—particularly employment outcomes? The natural methodological approach is to define one or several measures of job accessibility and to examine their relationship to the employment and earnings of blacks and whites in different areas of the city. Yet serious methodological problems arise when one seeks to estimate such a model. The most serious problems concern the development of appropriate measures of accessibility. Even in simple models in which workers and jobs are all identical, the fact that wage rates, labor supply, in commuting patterns are all determined simultaneously makes it difficult to select ex post a meaningful definition of accessibility, particularly if we allow for rigidity in wages and for unemployment. When the theoretical problems are combined with a rather serious shortage of individual data that provide both detailed geographic and socioeconomic information, the prospects for appropriate estimation are discouraging.

Because of these problems, the approach taken in this paper is to use three different methods to examine the potential relationship between employment and proximity. First, census tract employment rate equations will be estimated including one of many different measures of neighborhood job proximity in each. Second, census tract employment rate equations are estimated that allow for fixed neighborhood effects and that are designed to capture the impact of all unobserved neighborhood differences, including variations in job proximity. And third, natural experiments which occur within the city will be exploited by comparing the labor market outcomes of blacks who live in neighborhoods with vastly different job accessibilities and by comparing the outcomes of blacks and whites who live in the same neighborhoods.

The first method is simply an attempt to operationalize the different models described above. A large number of neighborhood proximity measures drawn from several different data sources are defined and then used as independent variables in regression models that use as the dependent variable the youth employment rate in a very small district of the city of Chicago.

The second method uses the same dependent variables but allows instead for separate intercepts for each of over 100 neighborhoods. In essence, this method controls for all neighborhood differences regardless of their origin. Thus, the fixed effects capture the impact not only of proximity differences, but also of differences in local schools, in the attitudes and tastes of local residents, and in anything else that varies over space.

The final approach is quite different. There are two ghettos in Chicago: one is the city's South Side and the other is the West Side. By every conceivable measure, blacks living in the West Side live much closer to jobs than those in the South. Just after the 1970 Census was completed, the Census Bureau conducted a series of Census Employment Surveys (CES) in low-income areas across the United States, for which the agency collected detailed labor information on relatively large samples of individuals. Two of those surveys were conducted in Chicago—fortunately, for our purposes, one in each of the ghettos. We can therefore exploit the natural experiment by comparing persons in these two areas in some detail and then explore the effects of job proximity on young blacks' employment experience.

We can also use these same CES data for another natural experiment. The West Side is actually a collection of several low-income neighborhoods, some black and some white. Thus, we can compare the labor market outcomes of blacks and whites living very close to each other. This second natural experiment allows us to examine the extent to which differential outcomes between blacks and whites can be explained by differences in proximity. If they can, blacks and whites will fare much more similarly in areas where they live close to each other.

The results of all these tests are remarkably strong and consistent. At best, proximity has a marginal impact on labor market outcomes—about as much as we might expect from the reduced real wage that results from commuting slightly farther to jobs. There is little evidence that spatial differences in job accessibility are a major explanation of the poor labor market outcomes of young blacks.

Let us begin, then, with a discussion of the methods used to examine the impact of various job proximity measures on employment rates.

4.5.1   Proximity and Employment

We might have considered the impact of accessibility on a wide variety of labor market outcomes, including employment status, wage rates, occupational attainment, and school enrollment. Ideally, we might like to use individual data on accessibility and other neighborhood variables in equations estimating labor supply, unemployment, wages, or schooling. Unfortunately, individual data with both detailed spatial identification and high-quality labor market performance measures do not exist. But using 1970 census tract data, we can relate employment rates for out-of-school youths in each tract to our measures of accessibility.

There are some 1,600 census tracts in Chicago. A series of weighted ordinary-least-squares (OLS) regressions were estimated. In all of the models the employment rate for out-of-school youths aged 16 to 21 living in the tract—labeled *EMRATE*—served as the dependent variable. This variable, along with the bulk of the independent variables, was culled from 1970 census tract data. The youth employment rate is available for both men and women. The regression results reported here are for both sexes to reduce the measurement error of the dependent variable. All have also been run separately by gender, yielding essentially similar results for the two sexes except where noted in the text.

The most critical independent variables were those designed to capture the proximity of jobs to the tract and the measure of racial composition there. We are looking for two types of results. First, a strong performance by the accessibility measures would offer support for the mismatch hypothesis. And if the inclusion of proximity measures reduces the measured coefficient on race, we will have explained a portion of the racial differential.

The proximity measures are drawn from several different sources and are discussed in section 4.5.2. The remaining independent variables were derived from census data. *PBLACK* indicates the percentage of the population who are black. *PSPANISH* provides the comparable figure for those who are Spanish speaking. In addition to the racial composition variables, a variety of human capital and socioeconomic variables were included. *PSCHOOL* is the proportion of persons aged 16 to 21 who are in school and thus is a measure of the schooling level of the out-of-school group. The greater the value of *PSCHOOL*, the later people leave school, and thus the older and better-educated are the out-of-school people. Two measures of economic well-being in the tract are also included: *FAMINC*, the average family income; and *PPOOR*, the proportion of families living below the federal poverty level. The inclusion of two income measures obviously complicates the interpretation of each one separately. *PUNDER25* indicates the percentage of the tract's residents who are under 25 years of age and is designed to capture any demographic effects. *PSING* is the percentage of children living in single-parent families.

Sample sizes vary by tract, creating heteroskedasticity in the data. OLS estimates are unbiased but inefficient. Thus, all regressions were run weighted (by the square root of the sample size) and unweighted. Both procedures yielded virtually identical results, though weighting often improved precision. The weighted results are presented here. All statistical tests (including the Fischer test described in section 4.6.1) were appropriately adjusted to account for the weighting.

4.5.2   Measuring Job Proximity

Even the most casual local observer would recognize that there is enormous variability in job accessibility across the city and SMSA of

Chicago. We shall see, for example, that by every conceivable measure there is a concentration of jobs in and around the city's West Side and there is a comparable void on the South Side. Yet finding meaningful ways to quantify those differences is a difficult task.

For both practical and theoretical reasons, accessibility should not be measured separately for each census tract. Tracts are simply too small to serve as reasonable representations of neighborhood job markets. And our limited data make it impossible to create different measures for each tract. Instead, accessibility will be defined over "neighborhoods"—the geographic concept that everyone understands but no one can define. In the 1940s, Chicago planners nonetheless accepted the task of defining zones that roughly corresponded to existing neighborhoods, and they created 76 "community areas" (or community zones). Since that time these zones have been used as basic geographic units for collecting and reporting data (and delivering services). Chicago census tracts have been chosen to be simply subdivisions of these community areas; thus, tracts can be easily aggregated to the larger zones.

These community zones seemed the logical and easiest definition of neighborhoods within the city. In the remainder of the SMSA no such convenient zones have been designated. Still, census tracts or groups of tracts often conform to municipal boundaries that in most cases have real practical significance. In the areas outside the city, census tracts were combined in such a way as to create another 40 zones. The 116 zones in and out of the city were used as neighborhoods.

Obviously, no one measure of accessibility can capture all aspects of proximity. For that reason, a variety are developed and considered here. Each captures a slightly different conception of accessibility, and each offers peculiar advantages and disadvantages. The three primary measures considered here are the following: the number of jobs within a 30-minute public transit distance from the neighborhood—either for all jobs or for particular types of jobs; the neighborhood import ratio, that is, the ratio of jobs to workers in the neighborhood—either for all occupations or for a selected subset; and the average journey-to-work travel time for workers living in the neighborhood—again, either for all workers or for a particular subset.

All three measures rely heavily on the CATS data, which provide detailed geographical information on where each worker surveyed lives and works and the mode of transit taken. In addition, the CATS group developed a "SKIMTREE" that indicates the length of time a commuter can expect to spend in traveling between any two points in the SMSA if an automobile is used or if public transit is used. We now consider each measure in turn.

4.5.3 Number of Nearby Jobs

An obvious measure of accessibility is simply the number of jobs nearby. Zones closer to more jobs would be more accessible. The time it takes to traverse a particular distance varies widely between any two points in the city; therefore, a count of jobs within 30 or 45 minutes' travel time seems most appropriate. With SKIMTREE data on travel times for mass transit or automobile between any two points in the SMSA, it is feasible to combine the tree with data on workplace location to generate measures of the number of jobs within, say, a 30-minute rapid transit commute of any neighborhood.

One serious problem with this sort of measure is that it counts only jobs and takes no account of the number of people who may be competing for those jobs. If jobs are plentiful nearby, but so are job seekers, those jobs cannot be considered readily available. Suburban workers fare poorly by this measure; low job densities and weak mass transit systems place suburban residents far from most jobs. If we include auto transit in our measure, we see no better results. Suburban residents still live close to fewer jobs. But the low population densities in suburban areas mean that even though there are fewer jobs nearby, they may be more readily available. Thus, an import ratio comparing jobs to workers in an area seems like a more appropriate measure.

4.5.4 Neighborhood Import Ratio

In a previous section we compared, for various occupations, the number of jobs in the central city to the number of workers living there. The ratio of jobs to working residents was labeled the import ratio. We found ratios far in excess of one for white-collar occupations, indicating that these workers descend en masse on the city from the suburbs each day. By contrast, the import ratio for blue-collar and service workers was less than one. These workers commute out of the city for work. It seems logical to use the same concept on a smaller scale to measure job accessibility by neighborhood. We can calculate import ratios for various types of jobs for each community zone using the CATS data. Neighborhoods with more jobs than workers will import labor and exhibit an import ratio greater than one. Those with fewer jobs than workers will exhibit the reverse.

Since our focus is on teenagers, we ought to concentrate on the relative proximity of those jobs most likely to be available to them. In principle, with sufficient data we could calculate import ratios for each neighborhood based only on teenage jobs and workers. In practice, the CATS data are too limited to allow such disaggregation with much precision. Import ratios have also been calculated for two other types of jobs and workers: first, for all occupations; and second, for blue-collar and service occupations only.

The problem with the import ratio is that it compares two stocks—workers and jobs—in a neighborhood. Yet nearby jobs may not be available to local workers. If jobs in an area are not growing, it could be argued that all existing matches between employees and employers may have already been established and that teenagers therefore cannot get local jobs. High turnover rates in manufacturing make this scenario unlikely, but it still deserves attention. Job growth is used as a measure of accessibility in this analysis, as discussed below. But an even more appropriate measure is the average travel time taken by existing workers in their journeys to work.

4.5.5   Average Travel Time

Ultimately, we seek information on the distance the marginal worker in any area must travel to find a particular job. Although we cannot calculate that distance for the marginal worker, we can for the average one. And if job turnover is high, the distinction between the average and the marginal may not be too serious.

The travel-time measure is particularly appealing because it reflects actual worker behavior. If jobs are found nearby, travel time to work will be short. If particular workers cannot find jobs in the neighborhood, their travel time will be long. The biggest measurement problems reflect the heterogeneity of the labor force. Some workers permanently attached to their firms may move far from their jobs in a search for neighborhood amenities. Their long travel times will be included in the average, even though they could find other jobs near their homes. Their travel behavior therefore may not say much about marginal accessibility. If we confine our attention to blue-collar and service workers or even to youths, among whom turnover is common, the averages are likely to be more accurate measures of accessibility.

4.5.6   Other Measures

There is a plethora of other possible measures of job accessibility. Probably the strongest candidates are those that capture job growth or decline. Employing job growth alone as a measure of job availability is inappropriate. Most jobs for teenagers are not "new" jobs; turnover and promotion create most openings. More importantly, there is a serious simultaneity bias in any job-change measure. The lack of amenities characteristic of ghettos may slowly induce firms to leave. Job decline may be the result of poverty rather than vice versa. Even when substantial employment remains, ghetto areas will look worst according to these measures.

Nonetheless, a variety of job-change variables were also tested. None performed well at all. Thus, the actual measures used and the results obtained are not reported here. The other measures that were included in the analysis are shown below. All of them are defined for community zones and were derived using 1970 CATS data on journey-to-work origins and distributions, in combination with a SKIMTREE indicating travel time, by means of transit, between all points in the area. In the regressions, these are labeled:

JOBSNEAR (ALL) = The proportion of all jobs in the SMSA that can be reached within 30 minutes of the zone by public transit.

JOBSNEAR (BCS) = The proportion of all blue-collar and service jobs than can be reached within 30 minutes of the zone by public transit.

IMPORTRATIO (ALL) = The ratio of all jobs to all workers residing in the zone.

IMPORTRATIO (BCS) = The ratio of blue-collar and service jobs to blue-collar and service workers residing in the zone.

AVTIME (ALL) = The average travel time to work of all workers living in the zone.

AVTIME (BCS) = The average travel time to work of blue-collar and service workers living in the zone.

AVTIME (TEEN) = The average travel time to work of teenage workers living in the zone.

The measures based on teenagers are included in spite of the fact that the limited sample sizes subject the estimates to considerable measurement error. The means and standard deviations of the variables used in the regressions are reported in table 4.4.

4.6   Empirical Results

4.6.1   Tract Employment Rates

Table 4.5 displays the weighted regression results, first without any accessibility measure and then with several entered individually. These particular measures are based strictly on blue-collar and service workers. Generally, the coefficients on the other independent variables are very much what we might expect. Every variable performs exactly as we would expect. The three key variables—schooing, race, and income—perform very strongly. If we increase the proportion of youngsters in school in an area from 30 to 60 percent, holding fixed all other variables, the employment rate for out-of-school youths rises four to five percentage points because, on average, those youths have more education. Poverty also shows a powerful effect. A tract where half of the families are poor suffers employment rates almost ten points lower

Table 4.4   **Means and Standard Deviations for Variables Used in Regressions**

Variable	Mean	Standard Deviation
1970 Census Tract Data		
EMRATE	0.650	0.157
FAMINC	$12,082	$3,704
PBLACK	0.222	0.380
PPOOR	0.126	0.169
PSCHOOL	0.557	0.141
PSING	0.166	0.131
PSPANISH	0.065	0.125
PUNDER25	0.542	0.089
1970 CATS Data		
AVTIME (ALL), in minutes	31.12	5.78
AVTIME (BCS), in minutes	29.58	6.3
AVTIME (TEEN), in minutes	30.60	13.9
IMPORTRATIO (ALL)	0.886	0.924
IMPORTRATIO (BCS)	1.024	1.26
IMPORTRATIO (TEEN)	0.959	1.25
JOBSNEAR (ALL)	0.048	0.043
JOBSNEAR (BCS)	0.050	0.056
1960, 1970 Where Workers Work		
IMPORTRATIO (ALL)	0.639	0.56
ΔIMPORTRATIO	0.054	0.166
ΔJOBS/WORKER	−0.004	0.146
%ΔJOBS	0.213	1.45

than one where no poverty exists. If such tracts also have an average family income of $10,000 less, the difference rises to nearly 15 points. Yet even after controlling for schooling, income, family composition, and age composition, race is the most significant variable. Tracts that are entirely black suffer employment rates 18 percentage points lower than those that are all white, all else the same. The coefficient on *PBLACK* is 18 times its standard error. Race is thus a powerful predictor of employment status in Chicago in 1970. The black-white differential to be explained is sizable.

In these results, neighborhoods with a large proportion of Spanish-speaking residents also fare poorly. The coefficient reported here is 78 percent of the black one. Quite interestingly, this is one of the two coefficients that are very different in the all-male employment rate equation. (The results in table 4.5 are for both sexes.) The estimated coefficient drops from .13 in these regressions to .07 when we consider employment for men only. One other value changes dramatically: that for *PSING*, the percentage of children in single-parent families. This coefficient also fades in significance for men only. Presumably, some women are not in the labor force because of marriage or family re-

Table 4.5   **Regression Results from 1970 Census Tract Data**

Independent Variable	Dependent Variable: *EMRATE*			
	(1)	(2)	(3)	(4)
PSCHOOL	.14 (.03)	.13 (.03)	.13 (.03)	.14 (.03)
FAMINC	$.003 \times 10^{-3}$ ($.001 \times 10^{-3}$)	$.003 \times 10^{-3}$ ($.001 \times 10^{-3}$)	$.001 \times 10^{-3}$ ($.001 \times 10^{-3}$)	$.003 \times 10^{-3}$ ($.001 \times 10^{-3}$)
PPOOR	-.16 (.04)	-.16 (.04)	-.17 (.04)	-.16 (.04)
PUNDER25	.09 (.05)	.10 (.05)	.10 (.05)	.10 (.05)
PSING	-.14 (.06)	-.14 (.06)	-.14 (.06)	-.14 (.06)
PBLACK	-.18 (.01)	-.18 (.01)	-.18 (.01)	-.18 (.01)
PSPANISH	-.13 (.03)	-.12 (.03)	-.13 (.03)	-.13 (.03)
INTERCEPT	.58 (.03)	.58 (.03)	.58 (.03)	.61 (.03)
JOSBNEAR (BCS)		-.03 (.07)		
IMPORTRATIO (BCS)			.0049 (.0024)	
AVTIME (BCS)				-.0011 (.0005)
N	1,132	1,132	1,132	1,132
Standard Error of Estimate	.094	.094	.094	.094
R²	.642	.642	.644	.644

Note: Standard errors in parentheses.

sponsibilities. It seems plausible that regarding these two coefficients, the equations for all young people are capturing both differences in labor market opportunities in the tract and differences in other factors influencing labor market participants.

Table 4.5 also plots the performance of three of the accessibility variables. *JOBSNEAR(BCS)* is the first. If the proportion of all blue-collar and service jobs within 30 minutes of the residence captures job proximity, the expected sign would be positive. Instead, we see a negative one and the variable is completely insignificant. The failure of this measure was not unexpected, since it is a better measure of proximity in the city than outside it.

IMPORTRATIO has several advantages as a measure of neighborhood job availability. It compares jobs and workers, and it is a better indicator of job accessibility in many suburban zones than in most central city ones. We would expect a positive sign; more jobs per worker should yield higher levels of employment. In fact, the coefficient is positive and just significant at conventional levels. But the coefficient is extremely small. If we could transform a neighborhood from having two workers per job to one having two jobs per worker, the employment ratio would rise only one percentage point according to these regressions!

The average travel time for blue-collar residents of the neighborhood is also signed as expected and significant. Zones where workers spend more time getting to work have lower rates of employment among young people. But here again the measured effects are very small. Reducing average travel time by two standard deviations (12 minutes) again would boost employment by only one percentage point.

The small coefficients observed are consistent with a model in which extra commuting time lowers the real wage somewhat and thereby causes a fall in labor supply. Suppose the labor supply elasticity were 1.0 and travel time were valued at one-half the wage. A one-minute extra commuting time each way would then reduce the real wage by roughly 0.2 percent in an eight-hour day ($2/480 \times 50$ percent). A 0.2 percent reduction in *EMRATE* with a mean of .65 translates into a decrease of .0013. This estimate is remarkably close to the coefficient estimate of .0011 on the average blue-collar travel-time variable. Obviously, the result is not consistent with a model in which the likelihood of finding a job is sharply reduced when jobs are not located very nearby.

Perhaps even more important is the coefficient on *PBLACK*. With or without the inclusion of accessibility variables, the coefficient is .18. None of the measures affects it in the slightest. These results show no evidence at all that black and white employment differences originate in job proximity.

Table 4.6 summarizes the results of all CATS-based measures of accessibility. The measures based on the number of jobs nearby fall flat. But the import ratio and average travel-time measures are always of the expected sign and often significant. The best single measure appears to be the import ratio for all workers. Unfortunately though, the coefficients are all very small. Pushing up employment rates just one percentage point requires massive changes in the accessibility indices. These pale in comparison to the .18 point edge enjoyed by whites over blacks. Moreover, these proximity measures are uniformly impotent with respect to the *PBLACK* coefficient. None causes it even to flinch.

Accessibility shows some minor effects here. But even these results may overstate the power of the variables. These coefficients are highly

Table 4.6   **Regression Results Showing Performance of Various Job Accessibility Measures Using 1970 Census Tract Data**

Job Accessibility Measure	Coefficient on Percent Black (Standard Error)	Coefficient on Accessibility Measure (Standard Error)	R^2 (Standard Error of Estimate)
None	− .18 (.01)		.642 (.094)
% of All Jobs Within 30 Minutes' Transit	− .18 (.01)	− .12 (.08)	.643 (.094)
% of Blue-Collar and Service Jobs Within 30 Minutes' Transit	− .18 (.01)	− .03 (.06)	.642 (.094)
Import Ratio for All Workers	− .18 (.01)	.009 (.003)	.645 (.094)
Import Ratio for Blue-Collar and Service Workers	− .18 (.01)	.0049 (.0024)	.642 (.094)
Import Ratio for Teenagers	− .18 (.01)	.008 (.002)	.646 (.094)
Average Travel Time for All Workers	− .18 (.01)	− .0009 (.0005)	.643 (.094)
Average Travel Time for Blue-Collar and Service Workers	− .18 (.01)	− .0011 (.0005)	.644 (.094)
Average Travel Time for Teenagers	− .18 (.01)	.0000 (.0002)	.642 (.094)

Source: 1970 Census Tract data (1973) and 1970 Chicago Area Transportation Study.
Note: Other variables include percent Spanish-speaking, percent high school graduates, percent of persons in tract over age 25, average family income, percent of persons in poor families, and percent of children in single-parent families.

unstable. Many more are insignificant in the male-only regressions. Other regressions using job-change data also fail to show any impact of accessibility. And the unweighted estimates are rarely significant. It is simply impossible to find strong effects with these variables.

It is plausible that accessibility is a far more important factor in black than in white households. Informal job networks may provide whites with access to jobs over a larger geographic area. Blacks are not blessed with such extensive networks and may be more at the mercy of the neighborhood job situation.

Table 4.7 provides results using tracts with greater than 50 percent blacks only. Several interesting results appear. The one of the most immediate concern is the recurrent failure of the proximity variables. Signs are often reversed, and none of the coefficients is significant. Average travel time performs best here, but once again there are only small effects. The entire arsenal of CATS-based variables are meek. Proximity as captured here explains little of the unemployment in predominantly black tracts.

There is another perhaps more telling finding, however, *PBLACK* was included because a few of the tracts had small white populations. Typically, these tracts span ghetto boundaries. The thought-provoking finding in table 4.7 is that the coefficient on *PBLACK* is almost as large as it is for all tracts. The only whites in this sample live in the ghetto or at its borders, yet tracts with more whites have better employment rates. This finding suggests that black-white differentials within neighborhoods are almost as high as differential for blacks and whites living across town, after we have controlled for income, schooling, and the like. If so, neighborhood differences cannot really explain the relatively poor performances of young blacks. We shall return to this issue momentarily.

We have tried a wide array of job accessibility variables. Most have performed poorly. Although they usually have the expected sign, their magnitudes are typically very small and many are insignificant. At best, the magnitudes seem consistent with a model that suggests extra commuting time reduces the real wage and thus reduces labor supply. Not a single one of them explains anything of the black-white differences. Surely, this performance offers little support for the hypothesis that a major reason why blacks perform poorly in the Chicago labor market is their isolation in neighborhoods with low job proximity. We are always confronted with the nagging problem, however, that we may simply have missed the true differences in accessibility across neighborhoods. It seems appropriate, therefore, to turn our focus to a more fundamental level to explore, namely, just how big the neighborhood effects of whatever origin are, once we have controlled for a few basic socioeconomic variables.

Table 4.7   **Regression Results for Tracts With 50% or More Blacks**

Job Accessibility Measure	Coefficient on Percent Black (Standard Error)	Coefficient on Accessibility Measure (Standard Error)	R^2 (Standard Error of Estimate)
None	−.15 (.07)		.488 (.100)
% of all Jobs Within 30 Minutes' Transit	−.15 (.07)	−.001 (.196)	.488 (.100)
% of Blue-Collar and Service Jobs Within 30 Minutes' Transit	−.15 (.07)	.073 (.146)	.489 (.100)
Import Ratio for All Workers	−.15 (.07)	−.003 (.008)	.488 (.100)
Import Ratio for Blue-Collar and Service Workers	−.15 (.07)	−.0002 (.0044)	.488 (.100)
Import Ratio for Teenagers	−.15 (.07)	.0048 (.0040)	.491 (.095)
Average Travel Time for All Workers	−.14 (.07)	−.0017 (.0013)	4.92 (.099)
Average Travel Time for Blue-Collar and Service Workers	−.13 (.07)	−.0017 (.0013)	.492 (.099)
Average Travel Time for Teenagers	−.15 (.07)	−.0010 (.0006)	.496 (.099)

Source: 1970 Census Tract data and 1970 Chicago Area Transportation Study.
Note: Other variables are as listed in table 4.6, n.

4.6.2   Fixed-Effects Models

When employment rates by census tract are displayed on a map, we can observe sizable differences across neighborhoods. Knowing only a youngster's neighborhood would help us greatly in making predictions about his or her likely employment status. But it would also aid us in predicting the youth's race, education, and family income. We would like to know whether significant neighborhood differences remain after having controlled for the usual list of socioeconomic variables. Indeed, we would most like to know whether the strength of such socioeconomic variables such as race or income can actually be traced to neighborhood effects that are correlated with these variables.

We can explicitly allow for fixed neighborhood effects by providing each community zone with its own intercept. These intercepts will control for all the differences between *zones*; the only information that remains comes from differences in outcomes *within* community zones. When we examine the regression results for a fixed-effects model, we are exploring only the effects of particular independent variables within neighborhoods.

The results of this experiment are astonishing. The coefficient on *PBLACK* does not fall; it actually rises to .22. There is only one possible inference: blacks and whites in the same community zone fare as differently as blacks and whites across town from each other. Remember, there are 76 community zones in the city alone. Within these small areas there is a *larger* racial differential than between the zones. No wonder the proximity measures failed to influence the *PBLACK* coefficient. Perhaps this result should not have been a surprise. After all, even in the predominatly black tracts of the earlier analyses, race seemed just as important as an explanatory variable. We can infer that no measure of accessibility, however conceived, that is defined by community area will account for black-white differences.

Perhaps the most remarkable result of all is that deriving from the traditional Fischer test for equality of coefficients, which can be used here to test whether the hypothesis of no neighborhood effects (equality of intercepts) is rejected by the data. The restriction of a uniform intercept is *not* rejected. This result is extraordinary. There are so many reasons to expect neighborhoods to differ, quite apart from accessibility, on the measured independent variable that we certainly would have expected the data to fail this test. We find small neighborhood effects from whatever origin.

Nonetheless, it is important not to overrepresent the power of this finding. The definition of neighborhood used here—community areas defined in the 1940s—may not conform well to current distinctions among neighborhoods. The fact that these neighborhoods jointly yield no significant effects does not mean some other geographic configuration would not. Nor does the result imply that none of the individual neighborhood effects is significant—they are only jointly impotent. Still, the total lack of impact on *PBLACK* and the visual and statistical failure of neighborhood effects using the city's own designations of neighborhoods cast serious doubt on the significance of the mismatch story.

We can restate the findings in another way. If a particular youth's level of schooling, family income, or race are unknown, knowing his or her neighborhood will help in predicting how they will fare in the job market, but if we do know these basic socioeconomic facts, knowing the location of their neighborhood will still not tell us very much.

The 1970 employment-rate regressions are not at all supportive of a hypothesis blaming weak the labor market performance of blacks on their segregation into neighborhoods with weak labor demand. None of the job accessibility measures serves to support that claim. Even allowing for a great many fixed neighborhood effects, we were unable to reduce the *PBLACK* coefficient, after controlling for schooling and income. These tract data therefore cast serious doubt on the mismatch story. Individual data from the Census Employment Survey (CES) controvert the hypothesis even more seriously.

4.6.3   Comparisons of the South and West Sides

According to the Northeastern Illinois Planning Commission the 11 community zones within Chicago that lie south of the Loop provided fewer than 5 percent of the city's jobs in 1970, whereas the *three* community zones in the West Side ghetto had more than three times as many jobs. Every single measure of proximity we defined also shows that the West Side has much better proximity to jobs than the South Side does. Indeed, the West Side typically offers among the best accessibility levels, and the South Side the worst, in the entire SMSA.

A drive through the black ghettos of the West and South Sides is just as revealing. From almost any block in the West Side, large, mostly industrial smoke stacks can be seen. (Not all are still in operation.) Located right in the center of the West Side, the international headquarters of Sears could be found in 1970. The complex occupied several city blocks. The company conducted office, warehousing, and sales functions all at that site. Sears moved its headquarters to the downtown Sears Tower in 1972, but even today Sears maintains the site as a warehouse and distribution center. On the eastern half of the ghetto is a large complex of hospitals, which are traditionally a good source of low-skilled jobs for service workers, such as cleaning, food preparation and distribution, and orderly services. On several borders and extending into the ghetto are old industrial parks. Brocks Candy, Westinghouse, General Electric all have manufacturing plants in and around the area. The only smoke stacks on the South Side are those of schools and churches. The South offers only two sources of employment: small commercial establishments along a few streets and the University of Chicago.

In short, the two ghetto areas present a marvelous natural experiment. For many reasons, the CES is ideal for our purposes. It was conducted right after the 1970 Census. Separate surveys were conducted on the West and South Sides of Chicago. Blacks and whites in low-income neighborhoods were surveyed, and the survey was designed particularly to gain labor market information.

We have already seen that measures of job accessibility explain little of the variation in employment rates for young people in entirely black census tracts. Since much of the variation in accessibility is between the West and South Sides, we have already implicitly exploited the

natural experiment and found little support. The CES data allow a
much more explicit test, offering a clear window through which to view
the effects of economic history.

West and South Side data were drawn from low-income census tracts.
Thus, the sampling technique corrects for the most important explanatory variable besides race. It is very revealing simply to compare the
average labor market outcomes in each area. Since we have excellent
information on individuals, we can compare not only employment rates,
but also unemployment patterns, school enrollment, occupational mix,
wage rates, and journey-to-work times between the two sides of Chicago.

Table 4.8 shows unemployment rates, employment rates, educational
attainment, and travel times for blacks in each ghetto area. The similarity in outcomes is remarkable. Half of the out-of-school youths in
each ghetto had jobs in 1970. Two-fifths of those without a high school
degree worked in each area, although the West Side does edge out the
South ever so slightly. But these figures are based on only about 100
observations in each area. Standard errors for the employment and
unemployment rates are roughly five percentage points. In these figures, the employment and unemployment rates never differ by more
than three percentage points. And we would expect the reduced real
wage on the South Side to induce small differences in labor supply.

The picture here is one of equal depression on both sides of the
Loop. Fully half of the school dropouts in both areas reported that
they were interested in work but unable to find it. School attainment

Table 4.8   **Comparison of Employment and Unemployment Rates,
Educational Attainment, and Travel Times for Out-of-School
Black Men Aged 16–21 in Very Low-Income Neighborhoods on
the South and West Sides of Chicago, 1970.**

	Ghetto Location	
Dependent Variable	South Side	West Side
Unemployment Rate		
All	.38	.35
High School Dropouts	.50	.48
Employment Rate		
All	.51	.54
High School Dropouts	.38	.41
Educational Attainment		
Proportion High School		
Dropouts	.61	.66
Travel Time		
All	36 minutes	29 minutes
High School Dropouts	35 minutes	25 minutes

Source: Census Employment Survey, 1970.

differed slightly in the two areas (the differences are not statistically significant), but roughly two-thirds of the out-of-school youths aged 16 to 21 were dropouts in both places. (This does not imply that the dropout rate was 67 percent). The problems look severe, and they look equally severe in each area.

Indeed, the only variable in the table that shows a marked difference between the two areas is travel time. Youths on the South Side spend 25 percent more time getting to work. The differences are especially pronounced for dropouts. West Side dropouts spend 25 minutes commuting to their jobs, while their South Side counterparts need 10 extra minutes to reach theirs. The earlier description of job proximity is again confirmed here. South Side residents must travel much farther to their jobs; they do, in fact, live farther away.

Occupational patterns in the two areas also appear unusually similar, as shown in table 4.9. Even though sample sizes are quite small, nearly equal proportions of young people in the two areas are working as managerial and professional workers, craftsmen, operators, transport workers, and laborers. Only the clerical and service occupations show some divergence. Sough Side workers more commonly work in clerical positions. A chi-squared test comes nowhere near rejecting the hypothesis that the areas are identical. Finally, there is the matter of wage rates. South Side residents appear to have better rather than worse jobs by this yardstick.

The differences in labor market outcomes are very small. Whether you travel south or west from the Chicago Loop, you will find similar employment problems. Considering the fact that simple journey-to-work costs vary between the areas, it is all the more surprising that

Table 4.9   **Comparison of Occupational Mix and Wage Rates for Youths 16–21 in Low-Income Neighborhoods on the South and West Sides of Chicago, 1970**

	Ghetto Location	
Occupation	South Side	West Side
Managerial and Professional	3.9%	3.5%
Crafts	9.8%	8.6%
Operative	33.3%	35.3%
Transport Worker	5.9%	4.3%
Laborer	15.7%	17.2%
Clerical	17.6%	11.2%
Service Worker	13.7%	18.1%
Other	0.0%	1.8%
Average Wage Rate:	$2.92	$2.75

Source: Census Employment Survey, 1970.

there are not at least some differences. In fact, there are some small effects. If we accept the point estimates, South Side residents do work a bit less (3 percentage points or 6 percent), attend school a little longer, and demand or command a slightly higher wage than West Side inhabitants. The differences in proximity are slightly higher than we might have expected based on the real-wage effect of a 10-minute longer travel time for South Side residents. Nevertheless, the results do not suggest that a major impact of job proximity on employment is indicated by the modest effect of transportation costs on the real wage.

More sophisticated comparisons can also be performed. I have specified human capital wage equations, conventional schooling equations, and labor-supply and unemployment models and estimated them separately for each area. Because the sample sizes are small, the coefficients tend to be somewhat unstable, but Fischer tests are rarely failed. When pooled regressions are run that include a West Side dummy variable, that variable is almost always insignificant, though it occasionally shows a slight edge for the West Side. After controlling for the conventional labor market variables, outcomes remain remarkably similar.

We have once again turned up virtually no evidence in support of the mismatch story. We had what appeared to be the purest of natural experiments: measurablly identical populations in measurably different labor markets. The labor market results were *not* measurably different.

4.6.4 Comparisons within the Same Neighborhood

There is one natural experiment that offers even more compelling evidence. Fundamentally, the mismatch story is an attempt to explain racial patterns of employment by differences in residential locations. The cleanest experiment of all, then, is to compare employment patterns for different racial groups who live in the same location. The CES once again provides the opportunity.

Poor neighborhoods in the South Side are almost entirely black. But in the West and near-northwest live both blacks and whites. The West Side survey covered both whites and blacks living in close proximity.

Table 4.10 shows the employment and unemployment rates of out-of-school men living in the surveyed low-income area. Once again, the data are quite startling. In each age group, considerably more whites than blacks have found work. Among young people the differences are particularly extreme. Nearly 80 percent of the out-of-school whites are working, whereas only just over 50 percent of comparable blacks are. Here in the West Side, the black youth unemployment rate is 35 percent, while whites suffer only 11 percent unemployment.

The table also reveals that differences cannot be attributed to the level of education. In the younger cohorts, a greater proportion of

Table 4.10   **Unemployment and Employment Rates for White and Black Out-of-School Men Living in Poor Neighborhoods on Chicago's West Side by Age, 1970**

Dependent Variable	Age			
	16–21	22–29	30–39	40–65
Unemployment Rates				
Whites	11.0%	7.6%	3.9%	4.3%
Blacks	35.1%	21.3%	11.5%	6.7%
Employment Rates				
Whites	79.4%	88.8%	91.2%	77.1%
Blacks	54.3%	73.3%	78.9%	72.3%
Percent High School Graduates				
Whites	29.4%	42.1%	33.3%	29.9%
Blacks	33.7%	57.0%	31.3%	20.9%

Source: Census Employment Survey, 1970.

blacks than whites had graduated from high school. This result may reflect greater outmigration by better-educated whites. If so, the results are all the more compelling. Those whites who remain behind are likely to be the ones least effective in their job-search behavior.

I have run regressions comparable to the census tract, employment rate equations for individuals in the CES. A simple OLS regression was run on a dichotomous employment-status variable (1 = employed). The coefficient on race (1 = black) was −.20. Controlling for everything possible given the data, being black dampened employment prospects by 20 percentage points over whites *in the same area.* The −.20 coefficient is virtually identical to the .18 coefficient we found for black versus white tracts across the SMSA. Thus, the problem isn't space. It's race.

And this result is verified by yet another source: a very recent survey conducted by Jon D. Miller for Chicago United, a socially active group of prominent business people. The survey was limited to a few low-income areas within the city. Teenagers, black and white, were surveyed in each area. The results were again startling. Using the U.S. Burear of Labor Statistics (BLS) methodology, Miller found unemployment rates of 65 percent for black youth, 29 percent for Hispanics, and 13 percent for whites all living in low-income areas. Although the figures for blacks are surely higher than we would expect in a standard BLS survey, the differences between low-income black youths and white youths in these neighborhoods are dramatic.

Perhaps the strongest piece of evidence that race, not space, explains unemployment comes from looking at maps of employment rates and racial mix. A comparison of a map showing youth employment rates by census tract and one showing the percentage of the population who are black uncovers remarkable similarities.[10] Areas with low teenage employment rates and those with predominantly black residents are almost perfectly congruent. For example, the area to the north of the eastern half of the West Side is predominantly poor white and Hispanic, and simply moving across a street to a black tract moves the unemployment rate from below 30 percent to over 60 percent. The same pattern appears at almost every border of the black areas. There is a black ribbon running from the West Side to an area just south of the Loop, and there is an identical ribbon of low teenage employment levels. The teenage employment rates are not based on very large samples, so we can expect considerable variability. That the employment rates and racial composition should be so closely matched is therefore all the more surprising. Blacks and whites in similar economic circumstances in very similar locations fare very differently.

It is no wonder that models with job accessibility measures and even fixed effects failed to budge the *PBLACK* coefficient. Where blacks live, employment rates are low. Across the street where whites reside, they are higher. No variable, however clever, can make that result disappear.

4.7 Conclusion

We have explored in detail the spatial dimensions of one labor market. Low-skilled jobs in Chicago are moving to the suburbs faster than are low-skilled workers. Young blacks do spend longer getting to work than young whites do, considerably more. And most workers, even young workers, work for outside any area that might reasonably be classified as a neighborhood. Yet all of the attempts here to find a substantial impact of job accessibility on labor market outcomes lead to the same conclusion: accessibility matters only slightly—about as much as would be expected from a slightly lower real wage caused by extra commuting time. There is no evidence that any important part of the black-white differential in employment rates can be traced to differential residential proximity to jobs. Black and white teenagers with comparable measured characteristics do just as differently when they live next to each other as when they live far apart in areas with dramatic differences in job accessibility.

Based on these results it is possible to understand both the appeal of the mismatch story and its failure. Blacks are being gradually disadvantaged by the movement of jobs—at least in Chicago. But the labor market is large enough geographically and fluid enough that these outward movements of jobs do not appear to cause substantial disadvantages to those who remain behind, except that on average they must commute farther to work.

The results here are only for one city, of course, though preliminary results from other cities suggest the results also apply elsewhere. And data from Chicago have been used by mismatch supporters in the past. Chicago has all the symptoms of the mismatch disease. The disease just does not seem to be the cause of the many labor market pains of black teenagers.

Notes

1. See also Offner and Saks (1971).
2. See especially Harrison (1972) and Harrison (1974).
3. See, for example, Kain (1980) and Berry (1976).
4. The theorem also requires that production functions be homogeneous of degree one and that the same sector always be more labor intensive than the other, regardless of the ratio of the wage to land rent. For more than two sectors, the conditions are considerably more complicated.
5. There is considerable debate over a possible inner-city land shortage. For some discussion, see Harrison (1974).
6. The sample of some 20,000 workers in the metro area is unique in that it contains detailed information on residence and workplace locations for the individuals included. When calculating import ratios for the city by profession, we find results very similar to those found in table 4.1, which are based on census data.
7. Many authors have found that blacks have longer travel times. In every category in which they reported results for blacks, Rees and Schultz (1970) showed far greater travel distances for black than for white workers in Chicago. Theirs was a nonrandom sample of firms, however. Deskins (1972) found longer travel times for blacks in Detroit. Meyer, Kain, and Wohl (1965) uncovered racial differences in Chicago and Detriot, and Greytak (1974) argued that blacks and whites behave very differently.
8. See, for example, Beesley (1973) and Hensher (1976).
9. See also Stevens (1978), Youthwork (1980), and Rosenfield (1977).
10. These maps are available from the author.

References

Alonso, William. 1964. *Location and land use: Toward a general theory of land rent.* Cambridge: Harvard University Press.

Becker, Gary. 1957. *The economics of discrimination.* Chicago: University of Chicago Press.

Beesley, Michael. 1973. *Urban transportation studies in economic policy.* London: Butterworth.

Berry, Brian. 1976. Ghetto expansion and single family housing prices: Chicago, 1968–1972. *Journal of Urban Economics* 3, no. 4 (October): 397–423.

Chicago Area Labor Market Analyses Unit. 1960, 1970, 1971, 1979. *Where workers work.* Chicago: Bureau of Employment Security, Department of Labor, State of Illinois.

Chicago Area Transportation Survey. 1977. *A summary of travel characteristics.* Chicago: CATS (August).

Chicago Area Transportation Survey. 1975. *Travel characteristics.* Chicago: CATS (August).

Chicago Area Transportation Study. 1960. *Volume II data projections.* Chicago: CATS (July).

Danziger, Sheldon, and Michael Weinstein. 1976. Employment location and wage rates of poverty area residents. *Journal of Urban Economics* 3, no. 2 (April): 127–45.

Deskins, Donald R., Jr. 1972. Race, residence, and workplace in Detroit, 1880 to 1965. *Economic Geography* 48, no. 1 (January): 79–94.

Ellwood, David T. 1981. The mismatch hypothesis: Are there teenage jobs missing in the ghetto? Unpublished Ph.D. dissertation. Cambridge: Harvard University.

Greytak, David. 1974. The journey to work: Racial differentials and city size. *Traffic Quarterly* 28, no. 2 (April): 241–56.

Hamer, Andrew. 1972. The comparative costs of location of manufacturing firms in urban areas: A Boston case study. Unpublished Ph.D. dissertation. Cambridge: Harvard University.

Harrison, Bennett. 1972. The intrametropolitan distribution of minority economic welfare. *Journal of Regional Science* 12, no. 1 (April): 23–44.

Harrison, Bennett. 1974. *Urban economic development.* Washington, D.C.: The Urban Institute.

Hensher, David. 1976. The value of travel time savings. *Journal of Transport Economics and Policy* 10, no. 2 (May): 167–76.

Kain, John. 1968. Housing segregation, negro employment, and metropolitan decentralization. *Quarterly Journal of Economics* 82, no. 2 (May): 175–97.

Kain, John. 1980. National urban policy paper on the impact of housing market discrimination and segregation in the welfare of minorities. Cambridge: Harvard University, April, Photocopy.

Kalachek, Edward, and John Goering, eds. 1970. *Transportation and central city unemployment.* St. Louis: Institute for Urban and Regional Studies, Washington University.

Masters, Stanley, 1974. A comment on John Kain's "Housing segregation, negro employment, and metropolitan decentralization." *Quarterly Journal of Economics* 88, no. 3 (August): 505–12.

Meyer, John, John Kain, and M. Wohl. 1965. *The urban transportation problem.* Cambridge: Harvard University Press.

Mooney, Joseph. 1969. Housing segregation, negro employment, and metropolitan decentralization: An alternative perspective. *Quarterly Journal of Economics* 83, no. 2 (May): 299–311.

Noll, Roger. 1970. Metropolitan employment and population distribution and the conditions of the urban poor. In *Financing the metropolis, urban affairs annual review*, vol. 4, ed. John Crecine. Beverly Hills, Calif.: Sage.

Offner, Paul, and Daniel Saks. 1971. A note on John Kain's "Housing segregation, negro employment, and metropolitan decentralization." *Quarterly Journal of Economics* 85, no. 1 (February): 147–60.

Rees, Albert, and George Schultz. 1970. *Workers and wages in an urban labor market*. Chicago: University of Chicago Press.

Rosenfield, Carl. 1977. The extent of job search by unemployed workers. *Monthly Labor Review* 100, no. 3 (March): 58–61.

Stevens, David. 1978. A re-examination of what is known about job seeking behavior in the United States. In *Labor market intermediaries*. Washington, D.C.: National Commission for Manpower Policy.

Straszheim, Mahlon. 1980. Discrimination and the spatial characteristics of the urban labor market for black workers. *Journal of Urban Economics* 7, no. 1 (January): 119–40.

U.S. Bureau of the Census. 1963. *U.S. census of population: 1960, selected area reports, Standard Metropolitan Statistical Areas*. Washington, D.C.: GPO.

U.S. Bureau of the Census. 1973. *U.S. census of population: 1970, volume I, characteristics of the population, Part 15, Illinois*. Washington, D.C.: GPO.

U.S. Bureau of the Census. 1973. *U.S. census of population and housing: 1970, census tracts Chicago, Illinois SMSA*. Washington, D.C.: GPO.

Youthwork, Inc. 1980. Learning about and seeking employment. In *School-to-Work Transition: Reviews and Synthesis of the Literature*, Youth Knowledge Development Report 2.15. Washington, D.C.: U.S. Department of Labor (May).

Comment   Jonathan S. Leonard

David Ellwood has accomplished at least three very good things here. First, he has chosen an interesting question with substantial policy implications. Second, he has gone to great lengths to assemble new

Jonathan S. Leonard is associate professor of economics at the University of California, Berkeley, and faculty research fellow at the National Bureau of Economic Research.

and appropriate data to test the question. Third, he has not rested content with one test on one set of data, but instead has carefully cross-checked his work with a variety of innovative tests on related data. It is unusual to find a paper that combines these three virtues. In my opinion, Ellwood's work is the best so far to address the mismatch hypothesis for youths, and his work will serve as a basis for further research. Given the clarity with which it poses questions and the quality of its tests, the paper provides a useful base from which to discuss, first, the difficulties of empirically analyzing urban labor markets and, second, the puzzles and paradoxes posed by the mismatch hypothesis.

In one of its forms, the mismatch hypothesis states that inner-city blacks, especially the young, suffer high unemployment in part because the jobs they are suited for are far from the ghetto. Moreover, this unemployment problem is expected to worsen as blue-collar jobs continue to move to the suburbs, as residential segregation or inadequate transportation makes it difficult for blacks to follow the jobs.

The key variable here is the number of available jobs. It would seem a simple and straightforward task to measure labor demand relative to supply. It is not. This task presents formidable theoretical and empirical challenges, not all of which have been overcome by Ellwood's analysis.

My criticisms of "The Spatial Mismatch Hypothesis" primarily concern the direct tests of the impact of job proximity and availability displayed in table 4.5. First, I suspect all of the job availability measures used here are of relatively low reliability because they are based on the Chicago Area Transportation Study. It is hard to tell how representative this sample of about 20,000 workers is. Since the job availability measures are defined for 116 zones, they are based on roughly 172 workers per zone. Of these 172, the number holding jobs that a teenager might hold must be smaller, so the analysis depends on data from small samples. Measurement error is likely to affect the dependent variable, too, since the percentage of out-of-school youths in a census tract probably numbers in the hundreds, or in the tens for a 5 percent sample. Unfortunately, Ellwood had little or no alternative to using these data, and he is to be commended for his innovative use of them. Future researchers do have an alternative, however: the 1980 Census Urban Transportation Planning Package, a data set tailor-made to extend the analysis of spatial questions, including the mismatch hypothesis, to most major urban areas in the United States.

The inevitable data problems aside, we also face a theoretical problem. How can we begin to think about the jobs available to the teenage black on the South Side of Chicago? Ellwood uses three measures of job availability, and as he notes, these average measures for the employed may not indicate the experience of the marginal worker. Consider these three measures in turn.

First is the number of nearby jobs, a count of jobs within, for example, 30 minutes of the residence. But as the author recognizes, what we need is a measure of demand relative to supply, and here arises the difficulty. One could imagine counting the number of competing workers living within the same 30-minute travel radius and calling this labor supply, but this measure could only be a flawed and rough approximation. Consider the man living on the edge of that 30-minute circle: his relevant labor demand would be given by yet another circle, a different market. We could easily go from coast to coast this way. Except for a limited class of monocentric distributions that quickly reach limits, this type of problem has largely been intractable so far.

Ellwood proceeds to two other availability measures in table 4.5. The import ratio is better than the preceeding measure, but it misses an element of choice. The logic behind this measure implies that because the suburbs export workers, the employment-population ratio there must be low and the import ratio in the central city must be high. But if there is employment discrimination, many inner-city jobs may not be available to blacks.

The third measure, travel time, again misses the issue of choice. In table 4.5, a higher average travel time is supposed to reflect the lack of local jobs, so the mismatch hypothesis predicts that zones with higher average travel times will have lower employment rates. But no one would expect, as this logic suggests, that zones of suburban whites with high travel times would have low employment rates. The same long commuting time that reflects choice on the part of suburban whites may also reflect the constraint of residential segregation affecting blacks. Although criticisms can be made of each of the availability measures used in the paper, it is far more difficult to recommend a better operational alternative.

One might also wish to see different specifications of the regressions in table 4.5, the only ones fully reported. For example, the proximity variables are defined only for groupings of the neighborhoods, but the regression is run on 1,132 tracts. (What happened to the 400 other tracts?) This specification will tend to give high standard errors on the proximity measures, since they are held fixed across tracts within neighborhoods while the employment rate varies.

As with any specification, one can argue that table 4.5 contains both too many variables and too few. If proximity affects adults as well as teenagers, we can expect the family-income variable to pick up part of the true effect of proximity. Interactions of the percentage black with the proximity and education measures might also be useful. A comparison of tables 4.5 and 4.7 shows evidence of nonlinearity: the coefficient on the percentage black is smaller, and of marginal significance, in the more heavily black neighborhoods.

The estimation of neighborhood effects may contain too many dummy variables, resulting in "fratricide," or econometric "dense pack." Should we really expect each of the neighborhoods outside the city, comprising one-half of the total, to differ from the other?

But Ellwood's conclusion does not rest on the regressions in table 4.5 alone. The author also presents a creative array of "natural" experiments, which taken together are quite compelling. Since most are based on small samples, none are claimed to be significant. For example, the CES results based on roughly 100 observations per zone can at best be suggestive.

The evidence from boundary neighborhoods, neighboring black and white districts, seems particularly telling, but one's interpretation may again depend on the underlying possibilities for choice. The comparison may be of whites who have chosen to stay near their jobs and blacks of limited residential mobility. If residential segregation constrains blacks but not whites, the movement of whites may result in lower unemployment rates in white than in nearby black districts. If there is strong employment discrimination in addition, proximity need not indicate availability. The job across the street might as well be on the moon as far as blacks are concerned.

What then do we know about the mismatch hypothesis? Ellwood's results are not unique. Using a national Current Population Survey sample, Price and Mills (1983) reached a similar conclusion. They found that only 6 percent of the black-white earnings differential could be explained by the greater concentration of blacks in the central city, whereas at least 15 percent was due to employment discrimination. Adding support to this view is Meyer and Gomez-Ibanez's (1981) review of a number of studies of transit demonstration projects funded by the federal government in the aftermath of the 1965 Watts riots. These studies tested the hypothesis that improved bus service to outlying employment centers would reduce inner-city unemployment. Meyer and Gomez-Ibanez concluded that "there was little evidence that many jobs were found because of the new bus service. . . . When compared with racial discrimination or lack of skills and education, employment decentralization and inadequate or expensive public transportation appeared to be relatively minor causes of unemployment (or underemployment) among low-income central-city residents"

The decentralization of jobs continues, and as it does inner-city employment rates, particularly for blacks, continue to fall. The situation Ellwood describes has grown worse in Chicago since 1970. In my own study (1983) of Chicago and Los Angeles between 1974 and 1980, blue-collar jobs moved farther away from the ghetto in Chicago but the average employed black moved closer. Blue-collar employment is in decline in Chicago, except in the suburbs more than five miles from the ghetto border, but the black employment share is also declining slightly outside the ghetto.

For all the mobility that Ellwood observes, the best predictor of the black employment share at a given establishment is not an indicator of employment discrimination, such as a Title VII suit, or of government pressure under affirmative action, but rather simply the distance from the ghetto. Ellwood finds that the average employed black commutes roughly 10 miles to work; but in establishments 10 miles from the ghetto, the proportion of black employees falls by half. And Chicago employment has not become more racially homogeneous across geographic zones. In that city, the impact of distance from the ghetto on the black employment share increased during the late 1970s as jobs dispersed, and the distribution of black employment came to resemble more closely the distribution of black residence, as black employment collapsed in the direction of the ghetto.

What happens to black employees when their jobs move to the suburbs? In a recent sophisticated analysis, Kain and Zax (1983) found that when an integrated firm moved from the central city to the suburbs, black employees were significantly less likely to follow and keep their jobs. Similarly, working from a complex theoretical base, Straszheim (1980) uncovered a positive wage gradient, or lower wages in the central city, for black but not for white workers with low levels of education. He concluded that this is persuasive evidence in support of Kain's view (1968) that residential segregation reduces employment opportunities for blacks.

Taking these studies together, we are still left with a paradox. Spatial considerations can explain a good deal about where blacks work, but they have not yet been shown to explain whether blacks work.

I commend Ellwood for his great efforts in framing the questions, for digging for data to answer them, and for pursuing a number of innovative tests. His paper establishes a useful framework on which future work can build, in particular by extending his analysis to other cities and other times. It seems race is important in explaining employment, even within neighborhoods. Now we must discover why that is.

References

Kain, J. 1968. Housing, segregation, negro employment, and metropolitan decentralization. *Quarterly Journal of Economics* 82 (May): 32–59.

Kain, J., and J. Zax. 1983. Feets don't fail me now: The impact of residential segregation on racial employment patterns. Photocopy.

Leonard, J. 1983. The interaction of residential segregation and employment discrimination. Berkeley: University of California. Photocopy.

Meyer, J. and J. Gomez-Ibanez. 1981. *Autos, transit and cities*. Cambridge: Harvard University Press.

Price, R., and E. Mills. 1983. Race and residence in earnings determination. Photocopy.

Straszheim, M. 1980. Discrimination and the spatial characteristics of the urban labor market for black workers. *Journal of Urban Economics* 7, no. 1 (January): 119–40.

5   The Demographic
      Determinants of the
      Demand for Black Labor

George J. Borjas

5.1 Introduction

The voluminous literature on the labor market status of blacks has concentrated mostly on the measurement of wage differentials between (statistically) similar blacks and whites.[1] Most of these studies follow the standard methodology of trying to predict what the earnings of blacks would be if they were treated as whites are in the labor market. The difference between this prediction and the actual earnings of blacks is commonly labeled discrimination. It is of some importance to note that such calculations are conducted in a theoretical vacuum: the economic theory of racial discrimination is not used and is not needed in the standard empirical framework.

A few studies have tried to incorporate theoretical insights into the empirical analysis of black-white wage differences. These studies often estimate the demand function for black labor and then test whether the variables responsible for shifts in the demand curve behave as theoretically predicted. Probably the earliest example of this approach is the work of Landes (1968), who specifically tested whether fair employment laws have had an impact on discriminatory behavior.[2] These demand-based studies differ significantly from the descriptive research summarized above because they attempt to explain *how* racial wage differentials are created.

This paper extends the demand approach to analyze how the demand function for blacks responds to changes in the demographic composition of the labor market. In other words, the labor-demand framework is used to measure the extent of labor market competition between

George J. Borjas is professor of economics at the University of California, Santa Barbara, and research associate at the National Bureau of Economic Research.

blacks and such other groups as Hispanics, immigrants, and women. The main methodological tool of the study is an estimation of the production technology in which various race, gender, and ethnic groups serve (along with capital) as inputs in the production function.[3] The parameters of the production function provide important information about the technological relationships among the various inputs. Hence, the estimated production function can be used to answer the following important policy questions: the extent to which black labor has been hampered by the growth of the Hispanic minority; the extent to which new immigrants replace black workers; and the impact of the rapid increase in female labor-force participation rates on black earnings.

The empirical analysis in this paper is based on data from the 1970 Public Use Sample of the U.S. Census. The main finding of the study is that although the demand for black labor is not adversely affected by competition from Hispanic or immigrant labor, it is adversely affected by the rapid increase in the number of women in the labor force. This finding is robust to major changes in the specification of the regression model, to changes in the definition of the labor inputs, and to whether the production technology is estimated using wage data or employment data.

Section 5.2 presents the theoretical framework used in the analysis. Section 5.3 describes the data base in detail and presents the basic estimates of the production technology. Section 5.4 replicates the main empirical analysis by focusing on the effects of labor market competition on the earnings of young blacks. In section 5.5, in which many of the assumptions underlying the model are relaxed, the main results are shown to be very robust to this type of sensitivity analysis. Section 5.6 indicates that although most existing estimates of production functions utilize wage data, it is quite easy to recover independent estimates of the production technology from information on labor-force participation. The demand function for black labor reveals qualitatively similar findings under both specifications. Section 5.7 illustrates an example of the usefulness of the model by simulating the response of the black-white wage ratio and black-white differences in labor-force participation rates to a specific change in the demographic characteristics of the labor force. Finally, Section 5.8 summarizes the results of the study.

5.2   Theoretical Framework

The analysis in this paper assumes that the production technology in the labor market can be characterized by the generalized Leontief production function (Diewert 1971), such that:

(1) $$\theta = \sum_j \sum_i \gamma_{ij}(X_i X_j)^{1/2}, \quad (i,j = 1, \ldots, n),$$

where θ is output; the X_i terms are the various inputs; and the γ_{ij} terms are the technology coefficients. It is easy to verify that the sign of γ_{ij} determines whether inputs i and j are substitutes ($\gamma_{ij} < 0$) or complements ($\gamma_{ij} > 0$). The production function in equation (1) is linearly homogeneous and restricts the values of the technology parameters so that $\gamma_{ij} = \gamma_{ji}$.[4]

The assumption that firms in this labor market maximize profits and face constant input prices leads to the following set of marginal productivity equations:

(2) $$w_i = \gamma_{ii} + \sum_{j \neq i} \gamma_{ij} (X_j/X_i)^{1/2}, \quad i, j = 1, \ldots, n,$$

where w_i is the price of input i.

The system of equations in (2) dramatically shows the usefulness of the generalized Leontief technology: the functional form in (1) leads to linear-in-parameters wage equations. Thus, the generalized Leontief technology (which is, of course, a second-order Taylor's approximation to any arbitrary production function) can provide an important link between studies of wage determination and studies of input demand theory.

Although the signs of the parameters γ_{ij} contain information about the substitution possibilities among the n inputs, it is useful to transform these parameters into Hicks partial elasticities of complementarity (Hicks 1970). These elasticities are defined by:

(3) $$c_{ij} = \frac{\theta\theta_{ij}}{\theta_i\theta_j},$$

where $\theta_i = \partial\theta/\partial X_i$, $\theta_{ij} = \partial^2\theta/\partial X_i\partial X_j$. The Hicks elasticity of complementarity measures the effect on the relative price of factor i of a change in the relative quantity of that factor, holding marginal cost and the quantities of other factors constant. Since the analysis is concerned with the effects of changes in the quantities of inputs on relative factor prices, the elasticity of complementarity (rather than its dual, the elasticity of substitution) is the natural measure to quantify this impact.[5] In the generalized Leontief technology, the elasticities of complementarity are given by:

(4a) $$c_{ij} = \frac{\gamma_{ij}}{2(s_i s_j w_i w_j)^{1/2}}$$

(4b) $$c_{ii} = \frac{\gamma_{ii} - w_i}{2(s_i w_i)},$$

where $s_i = w_i X_i / \theta$. Note that the sign of c_{ij} depends on the cross-partial from the production function. Hence, it will be positive when the inputs are complements and negative when the inputs are substitutes.

The estimation of the demand system in (2) is affected by two major econometric problems. First, equations (2) are not wage-determination functions unless (relative) supply conditions are also specified. It is not uncommon in the input-demand literature (for example, Grant and Hamermesh 1981, 355) to estimate the production technology under the assumption that input supply is exogenous. The usual justification for this assumption is that the supplies of age-specific gender and race groups are essentially fixed at any given time. Nonetheless, this assumption ignores the fact that although the total stock of specific labor inputs may be treated as fixed, its distribution across labor markets is likely to be guided by input price differentials. It is therefore unlikely that (relative) input supplies can be treated as exogenous, and the correct estimation of (2) requires a more detailed specification of supply responses to geographic wage differentials and other labor market characteristics. The exact specification of the (relative) supply equation used in the analysis will be discussed in section 5.3.

The second econometric problem that has been ignored in the labor-demand literature is the aggregation of workers into the labor inputs X_i. An implicit assumption in specifying production functions such as equation (1) is that all group i workers are homogeneous within *and* across labor markets. Of course, there are marked differences in the skill levels of individuals within each of these groups, possibly resulting in group i individuals having different average skills across different labor markets. Hence, wage differentials (or income-share differences in the more common translog model) across labor markets may simply reflect an unequal distribution of skill levels, seriously biasing the estimates of the production function.

This problem can be approached in the generalized Leontief framework by characterizing an individual's effective labor supply in terms of a fixed effect indicating the skill level of the individual. In particular, the wage paid to individual l in group i, w_{il}, depends on the market-determined wage level for the average group i person, w_i and on how the skills of individual l vary from the skills of the average group i person, f_l. Thus, in general, $w_{il} = w_{il}(w_i, f_l)$, and the individual's wage rate depends both on market forces and on his (relative) skill level.

To make this approach useful, it is necessary to add structure to the model. Two possible simplifications are $w_{il} = w_i f_l$ and $w_{il} = w_i + f_l$. The additive fixed effect assumes that the wage premium resulting from differential skills is independent of the demographic characteristics of the labor market, while the multiplicative specification allows for the possibility of such an interaction.[6] Both of these models were employed in preliminary work and the results were quite similar. For simplicity, therefore, the analysis in this paper uses the additive specification. If it is assumed that f_i can be written in terms of both observable socioeconomic characteristics, Z_l, and a random uncorrelated error, ϵ_l, the stochastic equivalent of equation (2) is given by:[7]

(5) $\qquad w_{il} = Z_l\beta_i + \sum_{j \neq i} \gamma_{ij} (X_j/X_i)^{\frac{1}{2}} + \epsilon_l, \quad i,j = 1, \ldots, n.$

Because of the definition of the skill fixed effect, the technology coefficient γ_{ii} is estimated by $\bar{Z}_i\beta_i$, where $\bar{Z}_i$ is the mean value of the socioeconomic characteristics for group i. Equation (5) specifies the wage-determination process at the individual level (given supply conditions) and will be used throughout the empirical analysis.[8]

5.3   Data and Basic Results

The data set used in this analysis is the 1970 1/100 Public Use Sample from the U.S. Census (5 percent SMSA and County Group Sample). The analysis was restricted to working-aged individuals ($18 \leq$ age ≤ 64) who were not in the military; were not self-employed or working without pay; were not residing in group quarters; and had records containing complete information on the variables used in the analysis. The local labor market is defined to be the SMSA in which the individual resided. Hence, the analysis is restricted to the 125 SMSAs identified in the census data.

There was considerable experimentation to determine the number and definition of the labor inputs to be included in the production process. It will be seen that most of the important results can be obtained from a breakdown of labor into six groups: black men *(BM)*, women *(F)*, Hispanic native men *(HNM)*, Hispanic immigrant men *(HIM)*, white native men *(WNM)*, and white immigrant men *(WIM)*. Several points should be made regarding this particular decomposition of the labor inputs. First, all women are aggregated into one group because previous research (for example, Smith 1977) suggests that earnings differentials among different types of women are much narrower than earnings differentials among different types of men. This fact implies that employer differentiation among women is likely to be less important than employer differentiation among men.[9] Second, the samples defined as "white" contain all relevant non-Hispanic, non-black observations. The "white" samples therefore include Asian immigrants, native Filipinos, and other such non-Caucasians. Finally, although the six-group decomposition is the basis for the empirical analysis presented in this paper, alternative breakdowns are presented in section 5.4 below. The results presented in this section summarize the important technological relationships among the major labor groups.

The employment data necessary for the estimation of equations (5) are obtained from the 1/100 Public Use Samples. The labor input X_i (in the SMSA) is defined as the number of individuals in group i who were of working age and participated in the labor force in 1969.[10] Since the census data are quite extensive, it is expensive to include in the estimates all the observations in each of the labor groups. The analysis therefore contains all the observations of individuals classified as black, Hispanic, or immigrants, but uses random samples of women and white native men.

Finally, the capital data used in the analysis are obtained from Grant (1979). Those data describe the capital stock in manufacturing industries in 1969 and were constructed from the Census of Manufactures and the Annual Survey of Manufactures. The capital data, of course, present serious problems for the analysis, since capital-stock calculations are well known to be subject to large measurement errors. To complicate matters, the available capital data for SMSAs are calculated for manufacturing industries only. In this paper, most of the analysis will be conducted over all industries; hence, the manufacturing capital data will lead to biased parameter estimates unless it is assumed that the aggregate capital stock in the SMSA is (roughly) proportional to the manufacturing capital stock. Because of these measurement problems, the parameter estimates of the production function will be presented in two alternate ways: with the capital variable included in and excluded from the wage equation. The latter restriction is equivalent to assuming a strong separability between capital and the various labor inputs in the generalized Leontief technology.[11]

Table 5.1 presents the means of the wage variables and socioeconomic characteristics of each of the six groups. The variables in the vector Z include years of schooling, years of labor market experience (age minus education minus 6), years of labor market experience squared, whether health limits work activity, and whether married with spouse present.[12] The two wage variables used are the 1969 wage rate and 1969 annual earnings.[13] The means in the table simply iterate what is already known about the various groups: blacks tend to do slightly worse than Hispanics, who in turn do worse than whites. It is easy to see, however, that a significant fraction of these wage differentials may be caused by major differences in educational attainment and labor market experience across the various groups.

To illustrate the types of jobs held by persons in each of the groups, table 5.1 also provides statistics summarizing the occupation and industry mix of each of the groups. There are dramatic differences in the industry mix across the groups. Blacks, for example, are overrepre-

Table 5.1   Means of Wage Variables and Socioeconomic Characteristics

Variable	BM	F	HNM	HIM	WNM	WIM
EARNINGS	6,149.7	4,147.0	6,767.1	6,321.0	9,258.3	9,310.3
WAGE	3.559	3.084	3.816	3.542	4.904	5.050
EDUC	10.423	11.349	10.063	9.434	12.358	11.447
EXPER	21.842	20.695	19.063	22.542	20.569	26.056
HLTH	.071	.052	.071	.071	.072	.063
MSP	.686	.530	.775	.729	.775	.796
Industry Mix, % in:						
Agriculture	1.5	1.0	2.8	6.1	1.1	1.3
Mining	.3	.1	.7	.3	.7	.4
Construction	9.2	.6	9.4	7.6	8.4	8.2
Manufacturing	31.2	20.6	34.1	36.8	32.7	35.7
Transportation	11.3	3.9	9.4	6.4	9.7	7.6
Trade	15.4	20.1	18.3	18.9	17.9	18.7
Finance	3.0	6.1	3.2	4.3	4.7	4.7
Business	3.6	2.7	4.0	4.1	3.7	3.5
Personal Service	3.2	12.8	2.5	4.2	1.4	2.6
Entertainment	1.0	.9	.9	1.0	1.0	.9
Professional	9.9	25.4	7.0	7.7	9.9	11.9
Public Administration	9.4	5.2	7.2	2.1	8.5	4.2

Table 5.1 (continued)

Variable	BM	F	HNM	HIM	WNM	WIM
Occupation Mix, % in:						
Professional	5.9	11.8	6.5	9.2	18.0	20.2
Managerial	2.4	1.9	3.8	3.7	10.6	8.5
Sales	2.2	5.9	3.8	3.3	7.7	5.4
Clerical	9.9	31.4	9.2	8.3	9.8	7.5
Crafts	15.6	1.7	22.4	18.8	22.6	23.6
Operative	20.5	18.9	21.3	24.1	12.8	14.7
Transport Operative	10.1	.3	8.2	4.7	5.7	3.0
Nonfarm Laborer	15.3	1.2	10.5	9.6	5.6	5.3
Farmers	.02	.01	.03	.1	.04	.04
Farm Laborer	1.0	.7	2.1	5.0	.6	.7
Service	16.2	19.0	11.8	13.1	6.8	10.8
Private Household	.4	6.8	.04	.1	.03	.2
% of Group in Population	5.5	38.9	2.0	.9	49.5	3.2
Sample Size	22,738	9,188	8,338	3,627	21,038	11,789

Note: The variables are defined as follows. *EARNINGS* = 1969 annual earnings, in dollars; *WAGE* = 1969 wage rate, in dollars; *EDUC* = Years of schooling; *EXPER* = *AGE* − *EDUC* − 6; *HLTH* = 1 if health limits working, 0 otherwise; *MSP* = 1 if married and spouse present, 0 otherwise.

sented in the public sector, while women are underrepresented in manufacturing. Similarly, the occupation-mix statistics reveal that women are crowded into clerical occupations, while all minority groups (blacks and Hispanics) tend to be overrepresented in the operative and laborer occupations.

Finally, table 5.1 also provides data on the relative size of the six labor groups examined in the analysis. Their relative sizes vary significantly. Women and white native men, for instance, make up 38.9 percent and 49.5 percent of the labor force, respectively; Hispanic groups, on the other hand, make up less than 3 percent of the labor force.

Using the 1969 wage rate as the dependent variable, equation (5) was estimated (after imposing the symmetry restrictions that $\gamma_{ij} = \gamma_{ji}$) using ordinary least squares (OLS). Table 5.2 presents the estimated technology coefficients. The top panel of the table omits the capital variable from the equation, while the bottom panel includes the manufacturing capital stock as one of the inputs. It is important to note that the OLS estimation implicitly assumes an exogenous relative supply for the various inputs in the labor market.

The results are quite interesting. Almost all entries in the γ vector are statistically significant, and many of them are numerically large. Of particular interest is the fact that only one group has a negative impact on the wage rate of blacks: women. All other groups, whether Hispanic or white male, whether immigrant or native, have actually increased the black wage rate. In the context of the generalized Leontief model, the data reveal that blacks and women are strong labor substitutes, whereas black men and all other men are complements in production. The results in table 5.2 therefore indicate that an important impediment to black economic progress has been the rapidly increasing labor-force participation of women and not, as is usually thought, the emergence of the Hispanic minority or the increased number of immigrants in the United States.[14] This finding holds in both panels of table 5.2, so that controlling for the capital stock is not an important factor in determining the production relationship between black men and other groups in the labor force.[15]

The remaining rows in table 5.2 contain a variety of interesting findings. First, women are substitutes with *all* labor inputs and seem to be weak complements with capital, though this last result is not statistically significant. Thus, the entry of women into the labor market has adversely affected all other labor inputs. But it will be seen below that the impact has been much stronger on black men than on the other groups. Second, neither Hispanic immigrants nor Hispanic natives have adversely affected the wage rates of any of the male labor inputs. Hence, the growth of the Hispanic minority (either through relatively

Table 5.2   OLS Estimates of Technology Coefficients, with the Wage Rate as the Dependent Variable

Group	F	HNM	HIM	WNM	WIM	K
			A. Omitting Capital (K)			
BM	−1.5151	.1255	.1971	1.0099	.8780	
	(−9.91)	(1.84)	(2.60)	(8.86)	(12.56)	
F		−.5902	−.2873	−1.5603	−1.3087	
		(−3.58)	(−1.46)	(−1.46)	(−7.72)	
HNM			.1421	.4799	.2445	
			(1.37)	(3.81)	(2.92)	
HIM				.2493	.1119	
				(1.65)	(1.18)	
WNM					.7134	
					(5.51)	
			B. Including Capital (K)			
BM	−1.6313	.1870	.1559	1.1075	.8670	−.0182
	(−7.20)	(2.08)	(1.57)	(5.85)	(9.50)	(−.81)
F		−.7675	−.4343	−2.1077	−1.3160	.0776
		(−3.41)	(−1.59)	(−3.68)	(−5.72)	(.95)
HNM			.2880	.5680	.0771	.0313
			(2.32)	(3.00)	(.71)	(1.30)
HIM				.3279	.0833	.0267
				(1.43)	(.74)	(1.16)
WNM					.8358	.1074
					(4.29)	(1.55)
WIM						−.0619
						(−2.48)

Note: t-ratios are in parentheses.

high fertility rates or immigration rates) has not been a major hindrance to the economic progress of most groups in the labor market. Finally, white immigrants have also not had a negative impact on the economic status of other male groups.

The most salient result in table 5.2, therefore, is that the production parameters reveal a high degree of labor market competition between men and women.[16] This result is not entirely consistent with the results of Freeman (1979) or of Grant and Hamermesh (1981), though the latter authors do find a strong degree of substitution between adult white women and youths. The results, however, are more in line with the recent findings of Berger (1983). He has shown that women are substitutes with all other labor inputs, although he did not include blacks or Hispanics as separate labor inputs in his specifications.

One serious objection to the findings in table 5.2 (and, in fact, to most of the results in the labor-substitution literature) is that the estimation technique used views (relative) labor supplies as exogenously determined. It is likely, however, that the wage differentials created across labor markets by the interactions among labor inputs lead to internal migration patterns by which the various groups move to those areas where they are likely to do relatively well. The presence of mobility costs or imperfect information suggests that the wage differentials do not vanish in the long run and that the correct estimation of the production technology requires that the supply of the inputs to labor markets be modeled more fully.

There are several ways of accounting for the endogeneity of the relative supply variables. The methodology chosen in this paper assumes that the selection of a labor market by individual l in group i is a function of a vector of socioeconomic variables. Those variables measure both individual characteristics (such as l's education) and area characteristics (such as the market's unemployment rate). Hence, relative supplies in the labor market have a reduced-form system, given by:

$$(6) \qquad (X_j/X_i)_l^{1/2} = I_l \beta_1 + A\beta_2 + \epsilon \, ,$$

where $(X_j/X_i)_l^{1/2}$ is the relative supply of group j in the area chosen by individual l of group i; I_l is a vector of individual-specific characteristics; and A is a vector of area-specific characteristics. The vector I_l includes the individual's education, age, and (if immigrant) years since immigration. The vector A includes the labor market's male and female unemployment rates, the proportions of the male and female labor force employed in the public sector, the proportions of men and women who are high school graduates, the fraction of the labor force that is employed in the manufacturing sector, the proportions of white-collar and blue-collar workers, and measures of the extent of public housing and welfare assistance in the locality.[17]

Equation (6) was estimated for each of the relative employment variables in each group. These regressions were quite successful in explaining the dependent variables: The R^2 values ranged between .3 and .6 for most of the samples. Thus, the instrument obtained, $(\overline{X_i/X_j})^{1/2}$, is not dominated by random noise. Table 5.3 presents the technology parameters estimated by using these instruments for the employment variables.

The results indicate that the very strong negative effect of female employment on black wage rates remains (in both panels), even though its magnitude and significance is attenuated. In fact, the estimates in table 5.3 reveal that even after accounting for the endogeneity of (relative) labor supply, women and all male groups remain substitutes. The one major change between tables 5.2 and 5.3 is in the relationship

Table 5.3 **2SLS Estimates of Technology Coefficients, with the Wage Rate as the Dependent Variable**

Group	F	HNM	HIM	WNM	WIM	K
		A. Omitting Capital (K)				
BM	−.7355	−.7943	.0935	.6795	1.1966	
	(−2.23)	(−4.03)	(.48)	(3.13)	(11.20)	
F		.3862	.0120	−.7325	−1.4536	
		(.87)	(.03)	(−1.28)	(−5.93)	
HNM			.3000	.0508	.2647	
			(1.45)	(.18)	(1.63)	
HIM				.0210	.1262	
				(.08)	(.92)	
WNM					.6873	
					(3.81)	
		B. Including Capital (K)				
BM	−1.4925	−.7306	.3639	1.1940	1.3121	−.0199
	(−2.82)	(−2.61)	(1.34)	(3.35)	(9.88)	(−1.32)
F		−.3936	−.1396	−1.6118	−1.7709	−.0059
		(−.63)	(−.21)	(−1.61)	(−5.09)	(−.07)
HNM			.5101	.5585	.5295	.0245
			(2.00)	(1.38)	(2.31)	(1.92)
HIM				.0008	−.0171	.0414
				(.00)	(−.08)	(3.97)
WNM					.8616	.1932
					(3.30)	(2.78)
WIM						−.0017
						(−.08)

Note: t-ratios are in parentheses.

between black men and Hispanic native men. The OLS results revealed the two inputs were complements; results in table 5.3 indicate the two inputs are strong substitutes. The two tables clearly show that of the 21 coefficients this parameter is the only one that changes signs (and remains statistically significant) in the 2SLS methodology.

Interestingly, the magnitude of the effect of women's employment on men's earnings is generally smaller (in absolute value) when labor supply is treated as endogenous. One possible explanation for this result lies in the process of labor-supply determination within the household. In particular, it is well known that the married woman's labor-force participation probability is a negative function of her husband's wage rate.[18] The regressions that fail to account for this labor-supply effect will, in estimating equation (5), yield relatively large negative effects of female employment on male wage rates, if it is true that men and women are substitutes. The correction for the endogeneity of labor supply nets out the labor-supply effect and leads to numerically smaller effects.

It should be noted that these results are obtained from wage-rate regressions, whereas most of the literature that uses the translog production function in effect uses a measure of the (relative) annual earnings of the various groups as the dependent variable. Table 5.4 presents the estimated technology coefficients from annual-earnings regressions. Both panels include capital as an input (since its exclusion does not have a major impact on the coefficients); the top panel presents the OLS estimates, while the bottom panel presents the 2SLS estimates.

The results in table 5.4 confirm all the findings from the wage-rate regressions. In the OLS regressions, for example, black men and all other men are complements, while black men and all women are sub-

Table 5.4		OLS and 2SLS Estimates of Technology Coefficients, with Annual Earnings as the Dependent Variable				
Group	F	HNM	HIM	WNM	WIM	K
			A. OLS Estimates			
BM	−2081.5	232.2	187.9	1212.3	1502.6	55.5
	(−9.28)	(2.61)	(1.92)	(6.47)	(16.63)	(2.50)
F		−715.8	−41.5	−1677.2	−2635.8	22.4
		(−3.22)	(−.15)	(−2.96)	(−11.59)	(.28)
HNM			−13.4	581.4	260.8	20.1
			(−.11)	(3.11)	(2.43)	(.85)
HIM				−19.3	484.1	4.4
				(−.09)	(4.33)	(.19)
WNM					1772.1	436.4
					(9.20)	(6.35)
WIM						−77.0
						(−3.12)
			B. 2SLS Estimates			
BM	−2882.0	−1135.5	737.8	2175.6	2351.4	−4.6
	(−5.51)	(−4.10)	(2.74)	(6.18)	(17.90)	(−.31)
F		145.9	−947.1	−3711.5	−4108.0	12.8
		(.24)	(−1.47)	(−3.73)	(−11.95)	(.16)
HNM			501.6	382.7	504.8	36.1
			(1.99)	(.95)	(2.22)	(2.86)
HIM				456.7	616.8	27.4
				(1.07)	(2.99)	(2.65)
WNM					2418.1	481.2
					(9.35)	(7.00)
WIM						1.4
						(.06)

Note: t-ratios are in parentheses.

stitutes. The instrumental variable technique again changes the sign of the relationship between black men and Hispanic native men, making them strong substitutes. In fact, a comparison of table 5.4 with the wage-rate regressions reveals a striking similarity with respect to the sign of the γ_{ij} terms.

The usefulness of the annual-earnings results is that, when translated into relevant units, they are directly comparable with the findings in the labor-substitution literature. This comparison can be made by calculating the elasticities of complementarity (see equations [4]). The elasticities calculated from the annual-earnings results in table 5.4 are presented in table 5.5. Again, the top panel presents the elasticities calculated from the OLS coefficients, while the bottom panel calculates the elasticities from the instrumental variable coefficients. All elasticities, of course, are evaluated at the mean of the relevant variables.[19]

There are several major findings revealed by the calculations in table 5.5. First, even though the female and almost all of the male inputs are substitutes, the degree of substitution (as measured by the elasticity of complementarity) is exceptionally high between women and black men. For example, the OLS results reveal an elasticity of -3.1 between women and black men, but an elasticity of only $-.6$ between women and white native men. The results therefore indicate that black men have been one of the groups particularly hurt by the entry of women into the labor market. Second, the magnitude of the calculated elasticities seems to be very sensitive to the estimation procedure used. For example, the elasticities between black men and other inputs increase (numerically) by a factor of 2 or 3 when instrumental variables are used. This difference suggests that since changes in the estimation technique lead to large fluctuations in the γ_{ij}, some caution must be used in interpreting the numerical results. Third, the large negative coefficients for the γ_{ij} terms that are associated with female employment create serious problems in evaluating the own elasticities of complementarity. Since c_{ii} is proportional to $(\gamma_{ii} - w_i)$, it is clear that the sign of the elasticity is determined by $-\left[\sum_{j\neq i}\gamma_{ij}(X_j/X_i)^{1/2}\right]$. If there are "too many" negative γ_{ij} coefficients in this summation, the own elasticity will be positive. This is precisely what happens, for example, in the case of women: The calculation of c_{ii} leads to large positive numbers, since practically all the γ_{ij} coefficients in the female wage equation are large and negative.

The fundamental problem, of course, arises from a major disadvantage of the generalized Leontief technology: the estimation procedure does not provide direct estimates of γ_{ii}. Instead, $(\gamma_{ii} - w_i)$ is calculated as a residual from the part of the wage explained by the demographic

Table 5.5   Elasticities of Complementarity, Estimated from Annual-Earnings Equations

Group	BM	F	HNM	HIM	WNM	WIM	K
			A. OLS Estimates				
BM	1.017	−3.098	.933	1.209	.717	3.468	1.417
	(3.62)	(−9.28)	(2.61)	(1.92)	(6.47)	(16.63)	(2.50)
F		2.899	−1.605	−.149	−.552	−3.396	.319
		(5.24)	(−3.22)	(−.15)	(−2.96)	(−11.59)	(.28)
HNM			−2.661	−.130	.518	.908	.773
			(−3.34)	(−.11)	(3.11)	(2.43)	(.85)
HIM				−11.985	−.027	2.686	.270
				(−4.40)	(−.09)	(4.33)	(.19)
WNM					−.033	.906	2.467
					(−.50)	(9.20)	(6.35)
WIM						1.019	−1.702
						(3.37)	(−3.12)
K							—
			B. 2SLS Estimates				
BM	.064	−4.287	−4.562	4.745	1.389	5.427	−.117
	(.01)	(−5.51)	(−4.10)	(2.74)	(6.18)	(17.90)	(−.31)
F		5.313	3.18	−3.388	−1.222	−1.078	.182
		(4.61)	(.24)	(−1.47)	(−3.73)	(−11.95)	(.16)
HNM			−10.311	4.857	.583	1.754	1.389
			(−3.67)	(1.99)	(.95)	(2.22)	(2.86)
HIM				−13.993	.649	3.422	1.682
				(−1.75)	(1.07)	(2.99)	(2.65)
WNM					.131	1.237	2.720
					(2.61)	(9.35)	(7.00)
WIM						2.452	.031
						(5.12)	(.06)
K							—

Note: The t-ratios in parentheses refer to the parameter γ^{ij} in the cross-elasticity estimates and to $(\gamma^{ii} - w^i)$ in the own-elasticity estimates. The own elasticity for K is unavailable since a capital equation was not estimated.

employment variables. This methodology is likely to lead to substantially more errors than if γ_{ii} were estimated directly, and this possibility may explain why many of the own elasticities in table 5.5 are of the unexpected sign.

In any case, the cross-elasticities presented in table 5.5 do tend to support some of the findings in recent labor-demand studies. For example, Berger (1983) estimated the elasticity of complementarity between women and men with less than a college diploma to be between $-.4$ and -1.3. This range is not too unreasonable in view of the fact that the OLS elasticity between women and white native men in table 5.5 is $-.6$.

In summary, the analysis presented in this section reveals three important findings. First, men and women are substitutes in production, with the degree of substitution between women and black men being particularly high. Second, neither of the immigrant groups, Hispanic or non-Hispanic, have had a negative impact on the earnings of black men. Finally, even though the nature of the technological relationship between different inputs is generally not affected by the method of estimation used, the numerical magnitudes of the elasticities of complementarity are quite sensitive to the specification of the labor-supply function.

5.4   The Impact of Competition on Young and Old Black Men

In the previous section the breakdown of the various labor inputs was defined along racial, gender, and native versus immigrant lines, despite the fact that most of the labor-substitution literature prefers to disaggregate labor inputs by age. The age breakdown is one way of controlling for the fact that not all individuals within a given group (such as blacks) are of equal skills. The decomposition of blacks into "young" and "old" blacks partially takes account of the within-group skill variance.

The methodology used in this paper obviously already controls for skill differences that may arise due to age differentials. It is of great policy interest, however, to investigate whether the impact of labor market competition has differentially affected the economic status of young and old black men. To consider this possibility, the black male labor input was segmented into two groups: young black men *(YBM)* and old black men *(OBM)*, defined as 24 years old or younger and over 24, respectively. The technology coefficients estimated in the black male equations are presented in table 5.6. To conserve space the table presents only a subsample of the matrix of coefficients γ_{ij}, namely, those coefficients that enter the two black male wage equations.[20] The table does include, however, the resulting estimates under various methodological assumptions. Panel A presents both the OLS and 2SLS coefficients when capital is omitted from the equation, while panel B presents the estimates from the equations that include capital.

Table 5.6 offers several interesting findings. First, women have a negative impact on the earnings of both young and old black men. The direction of this effect is unaffected by either the choice of the estimation technique (OLS or 2SLS) or the inclusion of the capital variable in the equation. Nonetheless, adding the capital measure to the young black men's regression reduces the significance of practically all the technology coefficients in that equation. The fact that these increases in the standard errors of the coefficients occur (at the same time as capital has an insignificant effect on the earnings of young black men) suggests a sizable degree of collinearity among the input variables in the young black men's equation.

A second interesting finding in table 5.6 is that the impact of immigrants seems to vary significantly between young blacks and old blacks. In the case of Hispanic immigrants, the γ_{ij} coefficients in the young black wage equations tend to be insignificant and sometimes negative, while in the case of non-Hispanic immigrants, the technological coefficients are consistently larger for older blacks. These results suggest that younger black men are more vulnerable to competition from immigrants than are older black men, although it should be emphasized that there is no evidence that any immigrant group has had a significantly adverse impact on the wages of young black men.

Table 5.7 uses the results in table 5.6 and calculates the elasticities of complementarity for the young and old samples of black men. As with the earlier results, the estimated elasticities based on the 2SLS coefficients seem to be quite sensitive and are usually significantly larger (in absolute value) than the corresponding elasticities calculated from the OLS coefficients. Table 5.7 reveals that the estimated elasticities of complementarity between women and black men tend to be larger for young men when 2SLS estimates are used, but somewhat smaller when OLS estimates are used. Thus, the calculation of the elasticities does not conclusively indicate which of the two black age groups has been most affected by the increase in female labor-force participation. This important problem will be addressed in section 5.7 below.

5.5   Extensions of the Empirical Analysis

In this section many of the restrictive assumptions underlying the earlier results are relaxed. Among the issues that will be addressed are the nature of the technological relationships within the manufacturing industry; the North-South differential in the demand function for black

Table 5.6   OLS and 2SLS Estimates of the Technology Coefficients for Young and Old Black Men

	Young Black Men (YBM)				Old Black Men (OBM)			
	OLS		2SLS		OLS		2SLS	
Group	Wage	Earnings	Wage	Earnings	Wage	Earnings	Wage	Earnings
				A. Omitting Capital				
YBM	—	—	—	—	.5026 (1.53)	80.4 (.25)	1.7416 (1.07)	749.4 (.47)
OBM	.5026 (1.53)	80.4 (.25)	1.7416 (1.07)	749.4 (.47)	—	—	—	—
F	-.6882 (-2.91)	-772.8 (-3.31)	-1.0424 (-2.04)	-1507.0 (-2.97)	-1.3744 (-7.79)	-2338.2 (-13.39)	-.3064 (-.94)	-764.9 (-2.02)
HNM	.1653 (1.32)	-6.4 (-.05)	.4429 (.98)	-163.1 (-.36)	.0644 (.76)	78.0 (.93)	-1.0324 (-3.84)	-1298.0 (-4.87)
HIM	-.1200 (-.67)	70.4 (.40)	-.6465 (-1.31)	371.3 (.76)	.2670 (2.39)	276.8 (2.50)	.3504 (1.24)	-147.8 (-.53)
WNM	.5169 (2.93)	544.9 (3.12)	.7857 (2.23)	1106.4 (3.17)	.9031 (6.85)	1581.5 (12.11)	.4163 (1.62)	779.9 (3.06)
WIM	.2644 (2.24)	320.2 (2.74)	.5291 (2.29)	503.8 (2.20)	.8052 (9.73)	1509.4 (18.4)	1.0447 (7.43)	2127.3 (3.06)

B. Including Capital (K)

YBM	—	—	—	—	.5427 (1.32)	91.0 (.22)	1.3207 (.64)	1762.8 (.86)
OBM	.5427 (1.32)	91.0 (.22)	1.3207 (.64)	1762.8 (.86)	—	—	—	—
F	-.1436 (-.38)	260.9 (-.70)	-.5226 (-1.50)	-1465.8 (-1.42)	-1.7356 (-6.48)	-2254.4 (-8.47)	-1.7537 (-2.60)	-2287.8 (-3.41)
HNM	.3039 (1.89)	-43.5 (-.27)	.3561 (.60)	-215.3 (-.37)	.0810 (.74)	268.1 (2.45)	-1.0026 (-2.79)	-1197.3 (-3.36)
HIM	-.3284 (-1.51)	-30.3 (-.14)	-1.5902 (-2.23)	52.2 (.07)	.3091 (2.23)	214.5 (1.56)	1.0471 (2.59)	699.6 (1.74)
WNM	.0464 (.15)	69.2 (.22)	-.3533 (-.50)	1116.9 (1.61)	1.2129 (5.44)	1385.5 (6.25)	1.4154 (3.07)	1766.6 (3.86)
WIM	.0671 (.44)	223.5 (1.47)	.4764 (1.72)	489.4 (1.78)	.8630 (8.06)	1472.9 (13.86)	1.1396 (6.65)	2262.8 (13.29)
K	.0301 (1.00)	39.3 (1.32)	.0053 (.30)	-20.0 (-1.16)	-.0335 (-1.36)	40.1 (1.64)	-.0239 (-1.45)	3.9 (.24)

Note: t-ratios are in parentheses. *WAGE* and *EARNINGS* are as defined in table 5.1 (n.).

Table 5.7   Elasticities of Complementarity for Young and Old Black Men, Estimated from Annual-Earnings Equations

| | Young Black Men (YBM) | | | | Old Black Men (OBM) | | | |
| | Omitting K | | Including K | | Omitting K | | Including K | |
Group	OLS	2SLS	OLS	2SLS	OLS	2SLS	OLS	2SLS
YBM	6.964	−18.720	4.557	−66.186	.682	6.360	.772	14.960
	(.75)	(−2.40)	(.93)	(−2.83)	(.25)	(.47)	(.22)	(.86)
OBM	.682	6.360	.772	14.960	1.093	−4.052	1.467	−3.306
	(.25)	(.47)	(.22)	(.86)	(2.80)	(−.53)	(2.97)	(−.53)
F	−3.436	−6.700	−1.160	−6.517	−3.705	−1.212	−3.572	−3.625
	(−331)	(−2.97)	(−.70)	(−1.42)	(−13.39)	(−2.02)	(−8.47)	(−3.41)
HNM	−.077	−1.960	−.523	−2.587	.334	−5.558	1.148	−5.127
	(−.05)	(−.36)	(−.27)	(−.37)	(.93)	(−4.87)	(2.45)	(−3.36)
HIM	1.350	7.120	−.581	1.001	1.892	−1.010	1.466	4.781
	(.40)	(.76)	(−.14)	(.07)	(2.50)	(−.53)	(1.56)	(1.74)
WNM	.962	1.953	.122	1.972	.995	.491	.872	1.111
	(3.12)	(3.17)	(.22)	(1.61)	(12.11)	(3.06)	(6.25)	(3.86)
WIM	.395	.622	.276	.604	3.714	5.234	3.624	5.568
	(2.74)	(2.20)	(1.47)	(1.78)	(18.4)	(3.06)	(13.86)	(13.29)
K	—	—	2.997	−1.525	—	—	1.090	.107
			(1.32)	(−1.16)			(1.64)	(.24)

Note: The t-ratios in parentheses refer to the parameter γ^{ij} in the cross-elasticity estimates and to $(\gamma^{ii} - w^i)$ in the own-elasticity estimates.

men; the impact of cost-of-living differences across SMSAs on the estimates; the disaggregation of the female labor input into white women and black women; the impact of outlying observations on the estimates; and the importance of the cross-equation symmetry restrictions in generating the main results of the analysis. Since the results in the previous section indicated that the breakdown of black men by age group did not essentially alter the major findings, most of the experiments in this section are conducted using the six labor groups defined in section 5.3.

5.5.1   Results for Manufacturing

The analysis in this paper has pooled all workers over all industries, whereas most of the labor-substitution literature has focused on the manufacturing sector. This sample selection is common because of the availability of data on manufacturing capital stocks. Nevertheless, such a selection may ignore important substitution effects as labor groups enter the labor market and other labor inputs are pushed out of particular industries and crowded into particular occupations.

In any case, the estimation procedure was replicated for the sub-sample of workers in the manufacturing industry. The estimated γ_{ij} coefficients in the black wage equation are presented in table 5.8. The results are by now familiar. In the OLS estimation black men and all other men are complements, while women and black men are substitutes. The 2SLS results, as before, reverse the relationship between black men and Hispanic native men, making them substitutes.

Table 5.8   **OLS and 2SLS Estimates of Black Male Technology Coefficients, Manufacturing Industry**

Group	OLS WAGE	OLS EARNINGS	2SLS WAGE	2SLS EARNINGS
F	−2.2185 (−6.51)	−2991.0 (−8.09)	−1.7805 (−2.12)	−3593.1 (−3.94)
HNM	.4179 (3.18)	455.9 (3.20)	−.5767 (−1.42)	−1136.5 (−2.57)
HIM	.1286 (.78)	269.0 (1.50)	−.0065 (−.01)	966.1 (1.91)
WNM	1.5152 (5.29)	2011.3 (6.48)	1.4759 (2.60)	2809.7 (4.56)
WIM	.9545 (7.19)	1457.8 (10.12)	1.3804 (6.87)	2305.1 (10.58)
K	−.0306 (−.92)	17.2 (.48)	−.0342 (−1.52)	8.7 (.35)

Note: t-ratios are in parentheses. WAGE and EARNINGS are as defined in table 5.1.

It is worthwhile to note the striking similarity in the results obtained in table 5.8 and those obtained earlier. Not only is the nature of the technological relationship unaffected by focusing on the manufacturing industry, but the numerical magnitude of the coefficients is roughly constant. For example, the estimated effect of female employment on black annual earnings in table 5.8 is -3593.1 (using the 2SLS results), while in table 5.4 the relevant statistic is -2882.0. Similarly, the impact of Hispanic native men on black annual earnings is -1136.5 in table 5.8 and -1135.5 in table 5.4. This similarity of estimates is remarkable given the fact that only 31 percent of black men are employed in the manufacturing industry.

5.5.2   The North-South Differential

The results in the previous sections are based on a comparison of how blacks do in different SMSAs, where the main shift variable across labor markets is the demographic composition of the labor force. Of course, it is likely that many other factors that may lead to wage differentials vary across labor markets; and to the extent that these factors are correlated with the relative supplies of the inputs, the results may be biased. To correct in part for this problem it would be useful to conduct the analysis within geographic areas where SMSAs tend to be roughly similar in such characteristics as cost of living, amenities, and industrial composition. One such breakdown is to analyze separately the demographic determinants of the demand for blacks in the South and in the North.[21]

Table 5.9 presents the technology coefficients from the black male wage equation. Due to space constraints only the OLS regressions that include capital are shown in the table; the coefficients from regressions using alternative specifications generally follow the same patterns that have been indicated throughout this analysis. The main insight provided by the results is that the relative employment variables tend to have qualitatively similar effects in both the South and the North. For example, the coefficient of the female employment variable is negative throughout. Thus, the finding that black men have been adversely affected by the entry of women into the labor market is invariant with the choice of region. The only coefficient whose sign appears to be sensitive to the region variable is the γ_{ij} between black men and white immigrant men. In the North this coefficient is numerically large and statistically significant, while in the South the effect is of smaller magnitude and sometimes reversed in sign (though it is insignificant). The main lesson from table 5.9, therefore, is that the demographic determinants of the demand for black labor are roughly similar in the North and the South. In both regions women have adversely affected the earnings of blacks, while nonblack men tend to be complements with black men.

Table 5.9   **OLS Estimates of Black Male Technology Coefficients, for South and North**

Group	South		North	
	WAGE	EARNINGS	WAGE	EARNINGS
F	− 1.8878	− 2786.4	− 1.5625	− 1955.8
	(− 2.75)	(− 4.13)	(− 5.72)	(− 7.20)
HNM	.0306	173.4	.0918	165.9
	(.12)	(.67)	(.84)	(1.53)
HIM	.5774	1051.7	.1659	73.4
	(1.95)	(3.12)	(1.27)	(.57)
WNM	1.4334	2139.1	1.1332	1206.2
	(2.81)	(4.27)	(4.92)	(5.27)
WIM	.2111	− 227.9	.6301	1156.4
	(.47)	(− .52)	(5.37)	(9.91)
K	− .1108	− 149.5	− .0510	14.6
	(− 2.20)	(− 3.02)	(− 1.76)	(.51)

Note: t-ratios are in parentheses. *WAGE* and *EARNINGS* are as defined in table 5.1.

5.5.3   Cost-of-Living Differentials

An alternative way to account for the possibility that wage differentials across SMSAs simply reflect cost-of-living differences is to use a price index, such as the consumer price index (CPI), as a deflator in the regressions. Although the CPI does not measure prices for SMSAs, the U.S. Bureau of Labor Statistics has, in recent years, constructed a cost-of-living index for 40 of the largest SMSAs in the country.[22] This index is used in the regressions reported in this section, estimated, of course, only among those observations for whom the cost-of-living index is available.

There are two ways of using the BLS cost-of-living index in the regressions. The first is to add the index, C, as one of the regressors in the wage equations. The second is to deflate the dependent variable by the index. The estimated technology coefficients for the black male OLS wage equations using both methods are presented in table 5.10. These results strongly indicate that the demographic determinants of the demand for black labor are independent of any wage differentials caused by cost-of-living differences across labor markets. The effect of female employment on black male wages remains strongly negative, while the effects of all the male groups remain positive. The results therefore show that the wage differentials that are the focus of this paper cannot be totally explained by factors unrelated to the demographic composition of the labor market. Table 5.10 clearly demonstrates that the relative employment variables have a major impact on the *real* wage rate of black men.

Table 5.10   OLS Estimates of Black Male Technology Coefficients Accounting for Cost-of-Living (C) Differentials

Group	WAGE	EARNINGS	WAGE/C	EARNINGS/C
		Dependent Variable		
F	−1.8939	−2344.7	−2.1524	−3099.9
	(−7.58)	(−9.44)	(−9.19)	(−13.29)
HNM	.1911	228.0	.2045	266.3
	(2.04)	(2.45)	(2.27)	(2.97)
HIM	.2090	227.3	.2996	486.9
	(1.88)	(2.05)	(2.85)	(4.64)
WNM	1.3543	1469.5	1.6107	2184.4
	(6.41)	(7.00)	(8.21)	(11.17)
WIM	.6546	1221.9	.3909	666.9
	(5.74)	(10.78)	(4.36)	(7.46)
K	−.0211	56.4	−.0257	36.2
	(−.86)	(2.30)	(−1.09)	(1.54)

Note: t-ratios are in parentheses. WAGE and EARNINGS are as defined in table 5.1. The regressions in the first two columns included the cost-of-living index as one of the regressors.

5.5.4 The Effects of Black Women and White Women

Up to this point the analysis has aggregated all women into a single labor input. The pooling is justified by the usual finding that wage differentials among different types of women (such as women of different races) are substantially narrower than wage differentials among different men. This finding is consistent with the hypothesis that employers tend to view women as a more homogeneous group; and thus, treating all women as a single labor input may provide a useful first-order approximation.

Nevertheless, before conducting such a pooling, the analysis experimented with various breakdowns of the female input. The changes in specification did not change the qualitative conclusions presented in the previous sections. Consider, for example, the case in which the female group (F) is divided into two labor inputs: black women (BF) and white (that is, nonblack) women (WF). The resulting technology coefficients (γ_{ij}) from the black male wage equation are presented in panel A of table 5.11. Again, for the sake of brevity the table presents only the coefficients estimated by OLS; the estimation by instrumental variables did not introduce any unusual differences.

The results show that both groups of women are substitutable with black men and that, as before, all nonblack men are complements with black men. It is of some interest to note that the impact of women on black male wages is always significantly negative for the WF input, but sometimes insignificant for the BF input. This finding suggests that the

Table 5.11   **OLS Estimates of Black Male and Black Female Technology Coefficients**

Group	WAGE (1)	WAGE (2)	EARNINGS (1)	EARNINGS (2)
A. Black Male Technology Coefficients				
BF	.1717 (.33)	−.2161 (−.33)	−522.9 (−1.01)	−1875.6 (−2.87)
WF	−1.6068 (−6.00)	−1.6751 (−4.33)	−2040.0 (−7.68)	−1756.4 (−4.56)
HNM	.1942 (1.64)	.0989 (.67)	139.7 (1.18)	277.8 (1.89)
HIM	.1844 (1.08)	.2788 (1.34)	−35.0 (−.21)	44.8 (.22)
WNM	1.1136 (5.42)	1.1921 (3.73)	1379.3 (6.76)	1029.6 (3.23)
WIM	.9903 (8.68)	.9724 (6.69)	1795.1 (15.85)	1565.7 (10.82)
K	—	−.0194 (−.73)	—	42.9 (1.63)
B. Black Female Technology Coefficients				
BM	.1717 (.33)	−.2161 (−.33)	−522.9 (−1.01)	−1875.6 (−2.87)
WF	.9800 (3.07)	1.0997 (2.45)	877.4 (2.77)	1005.9 (2.26)
HNM	−.2941 (−2.15)	−.1480 (−.87)	−277.5 (−2.05)	−334.8 (−1.98)
HIM	−.0909 (−.48)	−.2797 (−1.23)	334.7 (1.79)	148.3 (.65)
WNM	−.5789 (−2.33)	−.6880 (−1.84)	−405.8 (−1.65)	−484.0 (−1.30)
WIM	−.6221 (−4.68)	−.6296 (−3.76)	−1112.3 (−8.44)	−1055.2 (−6.34)
K	—	−.0069 (−.14)	—	−35.2 (−.73)

Note: t-ratios are in parentheses. WAGE and EARNINGS are as defined in table 5.1.

negative correlation between black male wage rates and female labor supply *cannot* be explained by the intrafamily substitution effect. Since there is a very small incidence of interracial marriage, there is little likelihood that high labor-force participation rates among white women are caused by relatively low earnings among their black male husbands. The results in table 5.11 therefore unambiguously show the major impact that the increasing labor-force participation of women has had on black male earnings.

An additional insight from the breakdown of black and white women is presented in panel B of table 5.11, which gives the γ_{ij} technology coefficients from the black female wage equation. Not surprisingly, black women are substitutes with practically all groups of men. This, of course, simply reconfirms the findings in the previous sections. What is of interest in table 5.11, however, is the relationship between black and white women. The technology coefficient is positive, indicating that these two inputs are complements. Hence, the increasing labor-force participation rate of white women has not adversely affected all blacks equally; it has been detrimental to black male economic progress, but it has not had a negative impact on black female wage rates.

5.5.5   The Impact of Outlying Observations

Since the generalized Leontief specification uses relative proportions, $(X_j/X_i)^{1/2}$, as independent variables, the independent variables are likely to take on extremely large values for observations residing in SMSAs containing few individuals of particular groups. These outlying values may lead to serious estimation problems and could, in principle, be the mechanism driving the strong results presented in this paper. A simple solution for this problem is to estimate the model for the subset of those SMSAs that contain a relatively large number of inhabitants of the relevant minority groups.

To test for the importance of this problem, the model was estimated after deleting all observations living in SMSAs where the labor force was less than either one percent Hispanic or one percent black. These deletions reduced the number of SMSAs in the analysis from 125 to 58. Table 5.12 presents the resulting black male technology coefficients, using both the wage rate and annual earnings as dependent variables. It is remarkable that the changes induced by this radical sample selection are so insignificant. The technological parameter measuring the extent of substitution between women and black men is -1.49 in table 5.12 (using the wage rate as the dependent variable) and -1.52 in table 5.2. When annual earnings are used, the coefficient estimated over the entire sample is -2082 (see table 5.4), while in the restricted sample it becomes -2661. In other words, the deletion of SMSAs that contain very few blacks or Hispanics, if anything, *reinforces* the negative impact of female labor-force participation on black male earnings.

The only coefficient in table 5.12 that has a different sign from those in the earlier results is the γ_{ij} between black men and Hispanic native men. This parameter becomes negative, but insignificant, in table 5.12. Recall, however, that this is also the coefficient that turned negative in the 2SLS regressions. The regressions therefore indicate that this parameter cannot be robustly estimated using the 1970 census data.

Table 5.12   **OLS Estimates of Black Male Technology Coefficients, Deleting Outlying Observations**

Group	Omitting Capital (K)		Including Capital (K)	
	WAGE	EARNINGS	WAGE	EARNINGS
F	− 1.4865	− 2660.6	− 1.7204	− 2793.3
	(− 5.69)	(− 10.58)	(− 4.37)	(− 7.27)
HNM	− .0749	− 126.2	− .0750	− 9.4
	(− .66)	(− 1.15)	(− .48)	(− .06)
HIM	.2905	289.5	.2873	392.4
	(2.21)	(2.29)	(1.69)	(2.36)
WNM	1.0172	1778.5	1.1894	1723.3
	(5.28)	(9.59)	(3.71)	(5.50)
WIM	.9660	1932.1	1.0057	1842.3
	(9.05)	(18.78)	(6.91)	(12.98)
K	—	—	.0011	61.7
			(.04)	(2.04)

Note: t-ratios are in parentheses. WAGE and EARNINGS are as defined in table 5.1.

5.5.6   The Symmetry Restrictions

Finally, it is worthwhile to address the question whether the results in this analysis are sensitive to the cross-equation symmetry constraints ($\gamma_{ij} = \gamma_{ji}$) that have been employed throughout. After all, given the relatively large samples used in the estimations, all tests of the null hypothesis that the symmetry restrictions hold are rejected by the data. A more fruitful approach is to investigate whether the black male labor-demand function would change substantially (in terms of the signs of the technology parameters) if the symmetry constraints were removed.

To illustrate the importance of the symmetry constraint, table 5.13 presents the unconstrained black male technology coefficients, using annual earnings as the dependent variable and including capital in the equation. The results show that, in general terms, the symmetry constraint does not play a major role in determining the qualitative nature of the conclusions of the analysis. For example, the technology parameter (using OLS) between women and black men is − 2082 when the constraint is imposed and − 2692 when it is not imposed. Roughly similar comparisons can be made for the other labor inputs, as well as for the young and old black male samples. It is safe to conclude, therefore, that the imposition of the symmetry restrictions is not hiding results that would contradict the earlier conclusions about the demographic determinants of the demand for black labor.

Table 5.13   The Impact of the Symmetry Constraint on the Technology Coefficients, with Annual Earnings as the Dependent Variable

Group	All Black Men		Young Black Men		Old Black Men	
	OLS	2SLS	OLS	2SLS	OLS	2SLS
YBM	—	—	—	—	103.4 (.12)	-945.2 (-.23)
OBM	—	—	75.1 (.16)	1982.5 (.84)	—	—
F	-2691.6 (-8.12)	-5311.6 (-5.33)	-761.6 (-1.85)	-3001.1 (-2.63)	-2735.3 (-7.63)	-4527.5 (-4.20)
HNM	396.1 (2.61)	-561.1 (-.97)	-36.9 (-.21)	233.1 (.36)	459.4 (2.76)	-677.0 (-1.09)
HIM	68.5 (.33)	1021.3 (1.52)	31.7 (.13)	235.5 (.30)	23.8 (.11)	747.6 (1.05)
WNM	1542.6 (5.62)	3655.7 (5.47)	396.4 (1.16)	2025.1 (2.63)	1069.1 (5.43)	3166.1 (4.36)
WIM	2235.0 (16.33)	3334.0 (18.74)	650.1 (3.92)	1016.3 (3.32)	2170.2 (14.08)	3158.8 (12.72)
K	40.7 (1.62)	-14.9 (-.98)	20.0 (.65)	-26.4 (-1.52)	32.4 (1.19)	-8.3 (-.49)

Note: t-ratios are in parentheses.

5.6   The Labor-Force Participation of Black Men

The analysis in the previous sections focused on the effects of labor market competition on the wage of blacks. Although the results are quite useful they do not directly address the issue of whether particular groups replace blacks in the labor market. This section directly examines the impact of other groups on the participation rate of blacks.

One important advantage of the generalized Leontief production function is its flexibility in allowing independent tests of the robustness of the results. In particular, the demand framework summarized in section 5.2 does not require data on wages for its estimation. It is possible instead to estimate the technology parameters by studying the determinants of the labor-force participation decision. The independent estimation of the technology coefficients by using participation data can thus be used to determine the robustness of the wage results described in the previous sections.

Suppose that the participation decision for individual l in group i is based on a comparison of his market wage, w_{il}, and his reservation wage, w_{il}^*. The participation decision is determined by:

$$(7) \qquad\qquad I_{il} = w_{il} - w_{il}^*.$$

The individual will participate in the labor force if $I_{il} > 0$. The generalized Leontief production function generates a linear-in-parameters wage equation. Using equation (5) and assuming that the same vector of socioeconomic characteristics, Z_{il}, helps determine the reservation-wage rate, equation (7) becomes:

$$(8) \qquad\qquad I_{il} = Z_{il}\alpha + \sum_{j \neq i} \gamma_{ij}(X_j/X_i)^{1/2} + v_i,$$

where v_i is a statistical residual. The coefficient vector α estimates the net impact of the socioeconomic characteristics on the participation decision. If it is assumed that the relative supplies of the various labor inputs do not affect individual l's reservation wage rate, the estimation of (8) identifies the technology parameters γ_{ij}. In effect, this requires that such factors as the (relative) numbers of women, immigrants, and other groups do not have an impact on the household productivity of the individual.

It is easy to understand why labor-force participation data can be used to recover information about the labor demand for specific groups. Shifts in the wage level caused by, say, an increased participation of women in the labor market will induce changes in the profitability of market work versus household work for blacks. Thus, if women and black men are strong substitutes in production, as found in the previous sections, the estimation of equation (8) should reveal that the labor-force participation of black men falls as the relative number of women in the labor market increases.

Because of the large sample sizes it is not practical to estimate the system in equation (8) using maximum-likelihood methods. The analysis therefore uses the linear-probability model. This estimation method has the additional advantage that cross-equation symmetry restrictions can be easily imposed. The basic results for the black male labor-force participation regression are presented in table 5.14.[23] The findings for the constrained regressions (the first four columns in the table) are quite interesting. The coefficients reveal that an increase in the labor-force participation rate of women will lead to lower black male participation rates. This finding holds regardless of the estimation procedure (OLS or 2SLS) and regardless of the inclusion of the capital variable in the equation. The fact that additional women in the labor market lower the black male participation rate is consistent with the findings discussed above that women and black men are substitutes in production. It is important to stress that the finding in table 5.14 suggesting that women do "take jobs away" from blacks is an entirely independent test of the robustness of the wage regressions in the previous sections.

Table 5.14 also reveals that Hispanic immigrant men and white native men are complements with black men. These results again corroborate the findings in the wage regressions. The technological relationship between Hispanic native men and black men is less clear-cut: the coefficient is positive when OLS is used, but negative when 2SLS is used.

Table 5.14   **Black Male Technology Coefficients from the Labor-Force Participation Regressions**

Group	OLS		2SLS		Unconstrained 2SLS
	(1)	(2)	(1)	(2)	(2')
F	−.0291	−.0172	−.0272	−.0777	−.2117
	(−2.90)	(−1.17)	(−1.24)	(−2.27)	(−3.07)
HNM	.0082	.0014	−.0019	−.0179	.0594
	(1.90)	(.25)	(−.15)	(−1.03)	(1.48)
HIM	.0050	.0108	.0175	.0355	.0560
	(1.01)	(1.64)	(1.36)	(1.99)	(1.20)
WNM	.0162	.0050	.0216	.0609	.1439
	(2.16)	(.41)	(1.49)	(2.63)	(3.10)
WIM	−.0035	−.0126	−.0053	−.0065	−.0108
	(−.79)	(−2.21)	(−.77)	(−.76)	(−.88)
K	—	.0023	—	−.0024	−.0024
		(1.55)		(−2.40)	(−2.26)

Note: t-ratios are in parentheses.

This switch in the sign of the coefficient also occurred in the wage regressions (see tables 5.2 and 5.3). Finally, the relationship between white immigrant men and black men suggests some substitution, though the coefficient is seldom significant. This result is not consistent with the strong complementarity found in the wage regressions and is the only major anomaly in table 5.14. Despite this problem it should be noted that, in general, the labor-force participation rate of blacks behaves in a way consistent with the technological relationships revealed by the wage analysis.[24]

Finally, the last column of table 5.14 shows the unconstrained γ_{ij} vector from the black male labor-force participation regression. For the sake of brevity only the counterpart to column 2 of the 2SLS regression is shown. The similarity in signs between the symmetry constrained and unconstrained coefficients is, on the whole, quite reasonable. For instance, the impact of women on black male labor-force participation remains strongly negative, while that of white native men and Hispanic immigrant men remains positive. The unconstrained results therefore show that the symmetry constraints are not unreasonably restricting the parameters of the black male labor-demand function.

One of the most significant labor-force changes in the postwar period has been the decline in the labor-force participation rate of young black men. For example, the participation rate of black men aged 20 to 24 dropped from 91.1 percent in 1954 to 78.0 percent in 1978. It is therefore of great interest to investigate whether the results in table 5.14 are sensitive to the breakdown of the black male input into the young and old categories defined in section 5.4. Table 5.15 replicates the labor-force participation analysis for each of the two black male samples. The results are very instructive. The effect of women on the black male participation rate is usually negative and significant in the young sample and insignificant in the older sample. The table thus reveals that the entry of women into the labor market has been an important determinant of the participation probability of young black men. It is not surprising that their effect on the labor supply of older black men is insignificant, since it is well known that prime-aged men have relatively inelastic labor-supply functions.

The estimates in table 5.15 indicate that these findings are not sensitive to the method of estimation used, to the inclusion of the capital measure in the regressions, or to the imposition of the symmetry constraints. The table leaves little doubt that the rapid entry of women into the labor force has been an important factor causing the decline of the labor-force participation rate of young black men.

It should be noted that the qualitative nature of the labor-force participation results are robust to the variety of sensitivity tests carried out in section 5.5. Although space constraints prohibit a complete rep-

Table 5.15		Technology Coefficients from Labor-Force Participation Regressions Young and Old Black Male Samples			
	OLS		2SLS		Unconstrained
Group	(1)	(2)	(1)	(2)	(2SLS)

			A. Young Black Male Coefficients		
OBM	−.1077	−.0888	.0420	.2267	.3160
	(−5.56)	(−3.57)	(.42)	(1.81)	(2.25)
F	−.0404	−.0234	−.0687	−.1209	−.1907
	(−2.96)	(−1.09)	(−2.17)	(−1.90)	(−2.75)
HNM	−.0050	.0046	.0274	.0423	.0754
	(−.67)	(.48)	(.97)	(1.17)	(1.93)
HIM	.0391	.0383	.0150	.0329	.0419
	(3.61)	(2.93)	(.49)	(.75)	(.87)
WNM	.0239	.0065	.0419	.0955	.1418
	(2.35)	(.37)	(1.92)	(2.24)	(3.04)
WIM	.0082	−.0031	.0051	−.0229	−.0295
	(2.35)	(−.35)	(.35)	(−1.36)	(−1.60)
K	—	.0038	—	−.0015	−.0016
		(2.16)		(−1.43)	(1.54)

			B. Old Black Male Coefficients		
YBM	−.1077	−.0888	.0420	.2267	.0124
	(−5.56)	(−3.57)	(.42)	(1.81)	(.04)
F	−.0069	−.0066	.0112	.0059	−.0985
	(−.60)	(.39)	(.44)	(1.14)	(−1.35)
HNM	.0122	−.0005	.0112	−.0492	.0124
	(2.20)	(−.07)	(.44)	(−2.12)	(.30)
HIM	−.0141	−.0085	−.0151	.0137	.0141
	(−1.97)	(−.95)	(−.86)	(.53)	(.29)
WNM	.0024	.0028	.0112	−.0009	.0669
	(.28)	(.20)	(.60)	(−.03)	(1.36)
WIM	−.0080	−.0116	−.0026	.0014	−.0106
	(−1.46)	(−1.66)	(−.15)	(.12)	(−.64)
K	—	.0004	—	−.0018	−.0020
		(.24)		(−1.62)	(−1.75)

Note: t-ratios are in parentheses.

lication of the various models in that section, the labor-force partici-pation analogue to the wage models generally confirmed the results of the wage regressions. Thus, for example, women "take jobs away" from black men in the South and in the North, and both white and black women adversely affect the participation rate of black men. The labor-force participation results therefore provide a strong independent confirmation of the validity of the results discussed in the previous sections.

5.7 The Impact of Women on Black Earnings and Participation Rates

To illustrate the implications of the results presented earlier, it is useful to investigate the future behavior of black male earnings as the entry of women into the labor market continues. In 1970, the proportions of the six basic groups in the labor market were $p_{BM} = .055$, $p_F = .389$, $p_{HNM} = .020$, $p_{HIM} = .009$, $p_{WNM} = .495$ and $p_{WIM} = .032$, where p_i is the percentage of the labor force belonging to group i. Since the generalized Leontief technology estimated in this paper imposes constant returns to scales, all that is needed for a simulation of the black male wage rate is a prediction of the employment shares for each of the groups. By 1980 the proportion of women in the labor force had increased to .424. If the same rate of increase continues over the next decade, p_F will exceed .45 by 1990.

Of course, it is even harder to predict what will happen to the relative shares of the male groups, except that, as a whole, they must decline. A reasonable approximation to these p_i's can be obtained if the purpose of the simulation is to isolate how the rise in the female labor-force participation rate will affect black male wage rates. A natural experiment would hold constant the ratio $p_i/p_j\,(i,j\,=\,BM,\,HNM,\,HIM,\,WNM,\,WIM)$ across the five male groups. Hence, none of the male groups will increase its relative importance in the labor force. Under these conditions the predicted employment vector is given by: $p_{BM} = .050$, $p_F = .450$, $p_{HNM} = .018$, $p_{HIM} = .008$, $p_{WNM} = .446$, $p_{WIM} = .029$.

Using these employment shares and the regression results in section 5.3, we can easily predict what will happen to the wages of black men as women become a more significant part of the labor force. The top panel of table 5.16 summarizes the results of such simulations, throughout which the regressions that omit capital were used.

The first column of the table reveals that in OLS regressions, the black male wage rate will drop 14.7 percent as the labor-force participation of women increases. The 2SLS estimates moderate this decline to 7 percent. Similar magnitudes appear in the annual-earnings analysis. Of course, these numbers may not be very meaningful, since the estimates of the production function revealed that all the male groups are likely to suffer from increased female employment. The last two columns control for this fact by considering how the ratio between black male and white native male wages responds to the changing employment shares. These statistics also show a decline in (relative) black male economic status. The OLS results predict about a 10 percent decline in relative black wages, while the 2SLS results predict a 4 percent drop.

The remaining two panels in table 5.16 repeat the simulation analysis for each of the two black age groups.[25] The impact of the increased

Table 5.16   **Predicted Changes in Black Male Wages Resulting from Women's Increased Participation in the Labor Force**

Estimation METHOD	% Change in Wage Levels		% Change in BM/WNM Wage Ratio	
	WAGE	EARNINGS	WAGE	EARNINGS
		A. All Blacks		
OLS	−14.7	−13.0	−10.8	−10.2
2SLS	−7.0	−6.6	−4.1	−4.4
		B. Young Blacks		
OLS	−18.8	−17.3	−15.7	−15.2
2SLS	−22.4	−31.9	−24.9	−30.7
		C. Old Blacks		
OLS	−14.1	−13.3	−10.8	−11.1
2SLS	−4.1	−4.5	−2.6	−2.7

Note: WAGE and EARNINGS are as defined in table 5.1.

labor-force participation of women will obviously be particularly adverse for young black men. For example, the simulation using the OLS estimates reveals that the relative wage of young black men will drop by about 15 percent, while that of older black men will drop only 11 percent. These differences are, of course, exaggerated when the 2SLS estimates are used in the simulation. The table then shows that the relative wage of young black men will drop about 25 percent, while that of older black men will fall by only 3 percent.

The simulation results presented in table 5.16 therefore reveal that increased female employment is an important factor in the determination of the black relative wage. In fact, the magnitudes suggested by the simulation indicate that the increased labor-force participation of married women in the postwar period may well have prevented the equalization of black and white wage rates in the U.S. labor market.

The analysis in the previous sections has also indicated that the entry of women into the labor force is partly responsible for the decline in the labor-force participation rates of black men. It is thus of interest to investigate how the black participation rate would respond to the assumed change in the demographics of the labor market. The first column of table 5.17 presents the labor-force participation rates calculated from the census data, and the remaining columns present the predicted labor-force participation rates. Again, the simulation reveals that the increased labor-force participation of women will have a major impact on the participation rate of young black men but only a negligible impact on the participation rate of older black men. In particular, the results indicate that the labor-force participation rate of young black men will drop about 5 percentage points by 1990 if current trends in female labor-force participation continue. The sizable magnitude of this change indicates that the entry of women into the labor market in the postwar period may have been the most important factor causing the declining participation rates of young black men.

5.8 Summary

This paper has attempted to estimate how the demand for black labor is affected by changes in the demographic characteristics of the local labor market. The main tool of the analysis was the use of the generalized Leontief production technology. This functional form has the advantage of yielding linear-in-parameters marginal productivity equations, so that wage regressions at the individual level can be interpreted in terms of a labor-demand framework. From data in the 1970 Public Use Samples of the U.S. Census, several important empirical results were obtained.

First, women are strong substitutes for black men in the production process. In fact, women tend to be substitutes for all groups of men, but black men are particularly vulnerable to the increased entry of women in the labor market.

Second, black men have not been adversely affected by the entry of immigrants in the labor market. This complementarity holds for both Hispanic and non-Hispanic immigrants.

Third, these results are not sensitive to major changes in the specification, samples, or estimation methodology. Thus, the adverse effect on black earnings of increased female employment, for example, is true both for wage rates and annual earnings, in the North and in the South, among young black men and older black men, and in the manufacturing sector.

Table 5.17   **Predicted Changes in the Black Male Labor-Force Participation Rate Resulting from the Increased Participation of Women**

Group	Actual Participation Rate	Predicted Participation Rate	
		OLS	2SLS
All Black Men	.915	.902	.905
Young Black Men	.835	.788	.782
Old Black Men	.939	.938	.942

Fourth, the analysis shows that estimates of the production-function parameters can also be obtained by studying the labor-force participation of individuals. These employment regressions indicate that women do "take jobs away" from black men, since increased female employment leads to lower black male participation rates.

Fifth, the simulation of the estimated production function reveals that the current trends in female labor-force participation will result in a 4 to 10 percent decline in the black male wage (relative to the white native male wage).

Finally, the simulation analysis also reveals that the continuing entry of women into the labor market will have a particularly adverse impact on the earnings and labor-force participation rates of young black men. In fact, much of the decline in the participation rates of young black men in the postwar period can be directly attributed to the rapid increase in the number of working women.

Of course, it is important to stress that much further study needs to be conducted before the demographic determinants of the demand for black labor are fully understood. For example, future research should determine whether the time-series paths of female employment and black wage rates are consistent with the technological relationships suggested by this paper. Similarly, researchers should investigate how the entry of women into the labor market affects the job distribution of black men along narrowly defined occupation and industry categories. The insights from these future studies should indicate that much can be gained by the introduction of economic theory in the empirical study of blacks' performance in the labor market.

Notes

1. See, for example, the recent studies by Gwartney and Long (1978), Haworth, Gwartney, and Haworth (1975), Smith (1977), and Weiss and Williamson (1972).

I am grateful to James Grant for providing me with the capital data used in the analysis, to Richard Freeman and Daniel Hamermesh for comments and suggestions made on previous drafts of this paper, and to Wei Jang Huang for her highly skillful research assistance. The research support provided by the Rockefeller Foundation and the National Bureau of Economic Research is gratefully acknowledged.

2. More recent examples in this tradition include the work of Ashenfelter (1972), Butler and Heckman (1977), Borjas (1982), Freeman (1981), and Smith and Welch (1977). Each of these papers attempts to determine whether exogenous factors (such as the unionization of the firm's workers, passage of the 1964 Civil Rights Act, or the racial prejudices of voters) determine black-white wage differentials.

3. Thus, the analysis in this paper is closely related to the emerging literature that estimates empirically tractable production technologies. Examples of this work are Berger (1983), Borjas (1983), Freeman (1979), and Grant and Hamermesh (1981). An instructive survey of the main results in the literature is given by Hamermesh and Grant (1979). It should be noted that only two recent papers (Grant and Hamermesh 1981;

Borjas 1983) treat black labor as a separate input in the production process. The findings in these and related studies will be discussed below.

4. Another restriction implied by the functional form in equation (1) is that diminishing marginal productivity for input l requires that not all γ_{lj} $(j = 1, \ldots, l - 1, l + 1, \ldots, n)$ be negative. In other words, some inputs must be complements with input l. It turns out that a somewhat similar restriction is implied by the second-order conditions of the profit-maximization model in terms of the elasticities of complementarity (defined below): not all cross-elasticities can be negative. For a discussion of these issues see Diewert (1971) and Sato and Koizumi (1973). Several studies discussing the properties of a variety of multifactor production functions, including the generalized Leontief, are contained in Fuss and McFadden (1978).

5. Recall that the elasticity of substitution measures the effect of a change in the relative price of a factor on the relative quantity of that factor, holding output and the prices of other factors constant. See Sato and Koizumi (1973) for an extended discussion of the duality between the elasticity of substitution and the elasticity of complementarity.

6. Note that the definition of the fixed effect requires that $E(f_l) = 1$ in the multiplicative specification and that $E(f_l) = 0$ in the additive model.

7. An alternative derivative of equation (5) can be easily obtained. Suppose we pool all i observations within and across the m labor markets and estimate the regression:

(n1)
$$ w = Z\beta + M\delta + \upsilon, $$

where $M = (M_1 \ldots M_m)$, $\delta = (\delta_1 \ldots \delta_m)'$, $M_l = 1$ if the individual lives in labor market l, and the subscript i for the group is omitted for simplification. The vector of coefficients δ will measure geographic differences in group i's wage rate *net of any skill differentials*. The demand framework outlined in this section predicts that the vector δ depends on the demographic characteristics of the labor market, $\bar{X}$, so that:

(n2)
$$ \delta = \bar{X}\gamma + u. $$

Substituting equation (n2) into equation (n1) yields:

(n3)
$$ w = Z\beta + (M\bar{X})\gamma + \epsilon. $$

Since the vector M is of the form $(0 \ldots 0\ 1\ 0 \ldots 0)$, the term $M\bar{X}$ will yield the values of the demographic variables for the labor market where the individual resides. By appropriate specification of $\bar{X}$, equation (n3) is therefore equivalent to equation (5) in the text.

8. It is worth noting that the wage-generating equation predicted by the generalized Leontief model differs substantially from the log-linear specification derived in the human capital framework. The human capital model does not account, however, for any employer objectives in its derivation; it is entirely based on an accounting equation defining earnings growth over time and the individual's incentive to invest less in human capital as he ages. Moreover, of all commonly used production functions only the Cobb-Douglas leads to a linear-in-parameters log wage equation. Unfortunately, the Cobb-Douglas builds in a unitary elasticity of substitution among the various inputs.

9. Further, the results in Freeman (1979) suggest a high degree of substitution among women of different age groups. Thus, the aggregation of women into one labor input can be viewed as a reasonable first-order approximation.

10. An alternative definition of X_i would be based on the number of working-aged persons in the SMSA rather than on the number of labor-force participants in the SMSA. In the case of male groups the difference between the two definitions is minimal. The introduction of women as a separate labor input, however, would lead to serious biases in the measurement of the (relative) employment variables if a population-based measure of X_i were used.

11. Grant (1979) constructed the capital stock index for only 84 of the 125 SMSAs identified in the 1970 census data. The inclusion of the capital variable therefore introduces an important sample restriction. Furthermore, the 84 SMSAs Grant selected are not a random sample of the 125 markets available in the data. Rather they tend to include only the largest SMSAs in the United States.

12. In the female sample, the vector Z also includes whether the woman is an immigrant and the number of years since her immigration. In the Hispanic and white immigrant samples the vector Z includes the number of years since immigration.

13. Actually, because of the particular construction of the census data, the 1969 wage rate is defined in terms of weeks worked in 1969 and hours worked last week (in 1970).

14. The complementarity between Hispanics and blacks confirms the results obtained by Borjas (1983) using the 1976 Survey of Income and Education.

15. It is of some interest to compare these results with those obtained from a more conventional analysis that simply adds the employment proportions to the typical human capital earnings function. The estimated equation for the black male (ln) wage rate (t-ratios in parentheses) is given by:

$$\ln(WAGE) = Z\beta \underset{(-7.1)}{- 2.12 p_F} \underset{(-4.9)}{- 1.36 p_{HNM}} + \underset{(.32)}{.11 p_{HIM}}$$

$$+ \underset{(3.2)}{.45 p_{WNM}} + \underset{(21.0)}{5.27 p_{WIM}}, \quad R^2 = .11,$$

where p_i is the proportion of group i individuals in the SMSA's labor force, and p_{BM} is the omitted proportion. Note that female employment has the strongest negative impact on black male wage rates, so that the generalized Leontief results parallel those obtained from this descriptive regression.

16. The very strong negative coefficients in the female equation are actually somewhat troublesome, since they will certainly lead, in the generalized Leontief framework, to perversely sloped labor-demand curves for women. As was noted earlier an important requirement for concavity of the production function in equation (1) is that not all γ_{ij} variables in the marginal productivity equation be negative. The women's wage equation clearly contradicts this restriction, and this fact will lead to severe problems in the calculation of own elasticities of complementarity below.

17. Most of these aggregate variables were constructed from the Census 1/100 data. The exceptions were the measures of public housing and welfare assistance, which were obtained from the 1976 Survey of Income and Education. See Borjas (1983) for details.

18. See, for example, Ashenfelter and Heckman (1974) and Schultz (1980).

19. The calculation of the elasticities of complementarity requires data on the value of average product. It is defined by the gross national product per person in the labor force in 1969. This quantity was $11,105.

20. The remaining coefficients in the matrix are available from the author.

21. The labor market is defined to be in the South if the SMSA is located *entirely* in the census definition of the South; otherwise the SMSA is defined to be in the North.

22. The August 1973 cost-of-living index is available in U.S. Department of Labor (1975). Note that although the wage data are for 1969, the deflator is for 1973. This difference in dates is not likely to cause major problems, since cost-of-living differences across SMSAs are correlated over time.

23. The participation variable is obtained from the "Employment Status Recode" variable in the Public Use Samples. It is set equal to unity if the individual was in the labor force during the reference week and zero otherwise. To ensure that the sample contained only individuals who seriously considered employment as an alternative, the labor-force participation regressions were restricted to persons who had worked at some point since 1959. The mean participation rate in the black male sample was .92.

24. The labor-force participation analysis has the additional advantage of avoiding the problems arising from the fact that cost-of-living differentials across labor markets create spurious wage differentials. Since behavior is invariant to changes in the nominal price level, any nonzero effects of the relative employment variables must reflect the impact of demographic characteristics on the real wage rate.

25. To conduct these simulations it is assumed that the relative proportions of blacks in the two age groups remain fixed after the entry of women in the labor force occurs. In other words, p_{YBM}/p_{OBM} is constant over the period of simulation.

References

Ashenfelter, Orley. 1972. Racial discrimination and trade unionism. *Journal of Political Economy* 80: 435–64.

Ashenfelter, Orley, and James J. Heckman. 1974. The estimation of income and substitution effects in a model of family labor supply. *Econometrica* 42: 73–85.

Berger, Mark C. 1983. Changes in labor force composition and male earnings: A production approach. *Journal of Human Resources* 18: 177–96.

Borjas, George J. 1982. The politics of employment discrimination in the federal bureaucracy. *Journal of Law and Economics* 25: 271–99.

———. 1983. The substitutability of black, hispanic, and white labor. *Economic Inquiry* 21: 93–106.

Butler, Richard, and James J. Heckman. 1977. Government's impact on the labor market status of black Americans: A critical review. In *Equal rights and industrial relations,* 235–81. Madison, Wis.: Industrial Relations Research Association.

Diewert, W. E. 1971. An application of the Shephard duality theorem: A generalized Leontief production function. *Journal of Political Economy* 79: 481–507.

Freeman, Richard B. 1979. The effect of demographic factors on age-earnings profiles. *Journal of Human Resources* 14: 289–318.

———. 1981. Black economic progress after 1964: Who has gained and why? In *Studies in labor markets,* ed. Sherwin Rosen, 247–94. Chicago: University of Chicago Press.

Fuss, Melvyn, and Daniel McFadden, eds. 1978. *Production economics: A dual approach to theory and applications,* vols. 1 and 2. Amsterdam: North-Holland.

Grant, James H. 1979. Substitution among labor, labor and capital in U.S. manufacturing. Ph.D. dissertation. East Lansing: Michigan State University.

Grant, James H., and Daniel S. Hamermesh. 1981. Labor market competition among youths, white women and others. *Review of Economics and Statistics* 63: 354–60.

Gwartney, James D., and James E. Long. 1978. The relative earnings of blacks and other minorities. *Industrial and Labor Relations Review* 31: 336–46.

Hamermesh, Daniel S., and James H. Grant. 1979. Econometric studies of labor-labor substitution and their implications for policy. *Journal of Human Resources* 14: 518–42.

Haworth, J. G., J. D. Gwartney, and C. Haworth. 1975. Earnings productivity and changes in employment discrimination during the 1960's. *American Economic Review* 65: 158–68.

Hicks, John. 1970. Elasticity of substitution again: Substitutes and complements. *Oxford Economic Papers* 22: 289–96.

Landes, William. 1968. The economics of fair employment laws. *Journal of Political Economy* 76: 507–52.

Sato, Ryuzo, and Tetsunori, Koizumi. 1973. On the elasticities of substitution and complementarity. *Oxford Economic Papers* 25: 44–56.

Schultz, T. Paul. 1980. Estimating labor supply functions for married women. In *Female labor supply: Theory and estimation,* ed. James P. Smith, 25–89. Princeton, N.J.: Princeton University Press.

Smith, James P., and Finis R. Welch. 1977. Black-white male wage ratios, 1960–1970. *American Economic Review* 67: 323–38.

Smith, Sharon. 1977. *Equal pay in the public sector: Fact or fantasy?* Princeton, N.J.: Princeton University Press.

U.S. Department of Labor, Bureau of Labor Statistics. 1975. *Handbook of labor statistics 1975—Reference edition*. Bulletin 1865. Washington, D.C.: GPO.

Weiss, L., and J. G. Williamson. 1972. Black education, earnings, and interregional migration: Some new evidence. *American Economic Review* 62: 372–83.

Comment   Daniel S. Hamermesh

There has been far too little empirical work on the demand for labor, in general, and on labor-labor substitution, in particular. Borjas's paper is a major addition to these literatures, a contribution that is at least as important as its implications regarding how minorities fare in the labor market. Borjas's primary contribution to the literature on demand is his confirmation of results explicit in Grant and Hamermesh (1981) and implicit in Freeman (1979) on the q-substitutability of women and other workers with relatively little human capital (youths and minorities). Although three empirical studies do not a fact make, I am fairly confident that this result will be robust to tests using other sets of data and methods using other specifications. Since there are very few established facts characterizing the demand for labor, this contribution is important.

The accretion to our knowledge of the position of minorities in the labor market is twofold. Clearly, Borjas's finding of q-substitution between women and black men, and especially between women and young

Daniel S. Hamermesh is professor of economics, Michigan State University, and research associate, National Bureau of Economic Research.

black men, is important, as he stresses. Just as important is the remarkable confirmation of his earlier results (Borjas 1983) on the lack of q-substitution between blacks and Hispanics. Although the methods employed are the same in both papers, the data sets are quite different, as are the periods during which they were collected. This replication quite strongly suggests that attempts to enhance employment opportunities for one of the two largest minority groups in the United States will not necessarily hurt the economic status of the other.

Borjas is to be commended for the extreme care he has taken to address the problems of estimating systems of equations based on cost or production functions. He is one of the few scholars studying labor demand who actually consider whether labor is separable from capital. (It is gratifying to see that ignoring capital changes his labor-labor substitution parameters little, even if he does not formally test for strong substitutability). Borjas is, in fact, the first to address the simultaneity problem in estimating relations of this sort. His attempts to use standard simultaneous-equations methods to solve the problem are most worthwhile. Despite his valiant effort, however, I do not believe the standard approach to the problem will be very fruitful. We may have good models specifying labor supply at the microeconomic level, but equations characterizing supply responses across geographic areas are quite poorly specified. Thus, although Borjas does include the standard variables in his first-stage equations explaining X_i/X_j, it seems unlikely that much of the simultaneity is removed or that the variation that is removed necessarily should be. The problem will not be solved unless the units of observation used in estimating cost or production relations are very small, particularly at the level of establishments. Let me stress, though, that the problem is with the entire literature, not simply with Borjas's study.

This important objection not withstanding, part of the study's contribution is its exposition of a number of useful paths for future research on the subject, using different sets of data and examining competition among subgroups in the labor force disaggregated differently from those used here. Also, by stressing the ease of using the generalized Leontief specification, Borjas succeeds in reversing the reliance on the translog specification. This should help further in producing some consensus about the signs of substitution parameters, and perhaps even about their magnitudes.

References

Borjas, George J. 1983. The substitutability of black, hispanic, and white labor. *Economic Inquiry* 21: 93–106.

Freeman, Richard B. 1979. The effect of demographic factors on age-earnings profiles. *Journal of Human Resources* 14: 289–318.

Grant, James H., and Daniel S. Hamermesh. 1981. Labor market competition among youths, white women and others. *Review of Economics and Statistics* 63: 354–60.

6 Brothers of a Different Color: A Preliminary Look at Employer Treatment of White and Black Youth

Jerome Culp and Bruce H. Dunson

6.1 Introduction

The high levels of youth unemployment that began in the 1960s and have continued into the 1970s and 1980s have created a large body of data and analyses attempting to explain the unemployment experienced by both black and white youths.[1] Many authors have concentrated on the more serious black youth unemployment problem.[2]

The explanations for the large racial differences in unemployment levels fall into two broad categories: demand and supply causes. According to the demand view, the principal reason for this large differential is discrimination. According to the supply view, the principal reason is the differential mix of skills and aspirations in the two groups.

For reasons of theory and data availability, most social scientists, particularly economists, have focused on supply questions—in particular, why black youths seem to be incompatible with the labor market they seek to enter. Some have attributed this incompatibility to young blacks' lack of labor market information; lack of educational skills; low productivity; and inappropriate work attitudes, speech, and dress (Wilson 1982). Investigators have concentrated on these supply issues because it is difficult to explain theoretically how long- run discrimination can persist in a competitive labor market. Since there is some evidence that the labor market is competitive, it seems reasonable to blame unemployment differences on the inability of black youths to bring to the job market labor of equal quality to whites'.

This view is especially inapplicable to the employment of young people, since entry-level jobs are most likely to be noncompetitive. A

Jerome Culp is associate professor of law at Duke University Law School. Bruce H. Dunson is associate professor and chairman of the Department of Economics and Finance at Prairie View A & M University.

large number of young people seek and acquire employment in small establishments, where the discriminatory preferences of owners and supervisory personnel are not subject to effective governmental regulation and where some measure of monopsony power among employers may exist.[3]

In addition to these theoretical assumptions, there are limitations in the data on employment that are commonly collected. None of the longitudinal or other survey data permits us to ask how employers treat similarly situated black and white labor. Previous investigators have focused most of their attention on the impact of existing employment information on individual employees. This individual information permits a direct investigation of the influence of race and poverty on the individual employee.

This paper is a modest attempt to investigate the other side of the employment picture—the demand side. It will attempt to measure the extent to which employer activities contribute to the plight of black youths in the labor market.

6.2   The Audit Technique and Questionnaire

The research methodology employed in this study is an audit technique. In our audit we sent out teams of job seekers to look for jobs. Members of each team were matched as closely as possible according to such characteristics as family income and general appearance; their only obvious difference was in skin color. The audit was originally designed to send all members of each team to the same firm, at closely spaced intervals, looking for similar jobs; but as noted below, for logistic reasons this was not always possible.

Each audit team in this project was composed of one white and at least two black high school graduates from the class of 1983 in Newark, New Jersey. Each "auditor" recorded his treatment by the potential employer on standard forms immediately after the visit. The items in the audit questionnaire (see appendix B) can be grouped into five categories (each of which contains 25 to 40 items): the courtesy of the job interviewer; the stated terms and conditions of employment; the information requested by the interviewer; the information volunteered by interviewer; and the final outcome of the interview.

This information was then analyzed in an effort to answer the following question: Do blacks experience differential treatment in the interview process? This investigation is thus a first step in determining whether black youths encounter discrimination when searching for a job.

6.3   Previous Studies and Sample Selection

A number of studies have used variants of this audit technique, usually either a correspondence test or an actor test. In correspondence testing, fictitious résumés or applications are sent to prospective employers. In actor testing, actors play the role of job applicants to prospective employers. McIntosh and Smith (1974), for example, employed both methods in a study in Great Britain. They carried out 305 correspondence tests for white-collar jobs in six different towns. Each test involved a pair of matched applications: one for an English person, and the other for an Italian, a West Indian, or a Pakistani. The two résumés always listed similar (British) qualifications and experience.

The second part of the study contracted actors to carry out tests for two kinds of job searches: personal applications for unskilled or semi-skilled manual jobs; and telephone inquiries concerning skilled manual jobs advertised in newspapers. Two sets of actors were used, each of which consisted of a white British, a West Indian, an Indian, a Pakistani, and a Greek actor. Two actors from each set participated in each of the two job searches; one of the pair was always the white British actor, while the other was one of the other four. McIntosh and Smith found evidence of substantial discrimination against racial minorities who were viewed as immigrants and evidence that this discrimination was greater than that against white immigrants to Great Britain.

Another correspondence test, by Firth (1981), investigated the British job market for accountants and financial executives. Firth sent out fictitious applicant letters in response to job advertisements in newspapers. The applicants represented seven different nationalities but otherwise had identical qualifications and work experiences. Firth found that considerable discrimination based on race, nationality, and language remains in the British labor market; more specifically, employers treated similarly qualified applicants differently based on differences in their nationality.

In the United States, Newman (1978) studied discrimination in recruitment by analyzing variations in responses from 207 companies to unsolicited résumés from fictitious black and white applicants. The employer responses strongly indicated discriminatory behavior, in favor of blacks at some firms and whites at others, with the black applicants the beneficiary slightly more often than the whites. But as pointed out by McIntyre, Moberg, and Posner (1980), not all of the differential responses that Newman found were necessarily based on racial discrimination. Some responses might have been the result of artifacts of the experiment, such as responses lost in the mail or misdirected to an inappropriate individual or office, or flaws in selection systems independent of race. An example of the latter would be lack of standardization in the process of assessing or responding to applications.

One important distinction should be drawn between these studies and our audit reported here. Our study fundamentally differs from any previous audit studies in its observation of people who were actually searching for jobs. A consequence of this was that we could not control as accurately for individual background characteristics as audit studies that use either résumés or actors. Nonetheless, by selecting similar youths and by using standard statistical techniques to control for differences where they existed, we believe we have adequately controlled for background factors.

Two other sample biases in our study may, however, be significant. First, the auditors were self-selected to the extent that they were willing to talk to the authors (and their schools were willing to permit us to talk to them). It is not clear how large this bias is or in what direction it lies. Second, we sent the auditors on interviews with the largest employers in the Newark area. Those employers may not have been a random sample of employer behavior (particularly toward young workers). Although it was not possible to eliminate these biases, our sample suggests, as discussed below, that it is more typical than we might have hoped.

To determine whether we had appropriately assured the difference between the individuals, we performed two tests. First, we videotaped all of the students and then examined the tapes with the aid of an outside reviewer who had had extensive experience as an employer.[4] Second, we submitted the personnel data of the auditors, after deleting information on race and high school, to a group of nine experienced employers (primarily in the public sector). The results of this second test are shown in table 6.1. We asked each employer to rate the students for potential managerial and maintenance jobs on a scale of 1 to 5, where 5 was "must hire" and 1 was "never hire."[5] The black and white potential auditors were rated very similarly; the rating employers did not perceive them as being very different.[6]

6.4   Demographics of the Sample Area

This study was conducted in Essex County, New Jersey. Table 6.2 presents the demographics of this county. As of 1980, the total population was 851,116. Whites were the largest racial group with 57 percent of the total population. They were followed by blacks with 37 percent and by the "other" category with 6 percent of the total population. The age distributions of the two major races clearly demonstrate that the blacks were, on average, younger than the whites. For example, 17.4 percent of the total white population were 14 years old or younger,

Table 6.1   **Employer Ratings of Potential Auditors**

	Average Score for Managerial Job	Average Score for Maintenance Job
All Auditors	2.4	3.1
Blacks	2.4	3.1
Whites	2.3	3.1

		Distribution of Ratings, by Score				
		1	2	3	4	5
Managerial Job	Blacks	34%	20%	25%	17%	2%
	Whites	37%	17%	30%	9%	7%
	All Auditors	36%	19%	27%	15%	5%
Maintenance Job	Blacks	6%	23%	34%	29%	8%
	Whites	9%	22%	30%	30%	9%
	All Auditors	7%	23%	33%	29%	8%

Note: The average scores reflect a possible range from 1 = "never hire" to 5 = "must hire."

whereas 28.9 percent of blacks were in the same age cohort, according to the 1980 Census.

The unemployment rate of individuals 16 years of age and over by race and gender are also presented in table 6.2. Consistent with national patterns, the 1980 unemployment rates for blacks were higher than those of their white counterparts. For example, whereas the unemployment rate for white men was 5.5 percent, the rate for black men was 13.4 percent. Similarly, the unemployment rate for black women was greater than that for white women, by almost six percentage points.

Important differences existed in both the racial composition and the unemployment rates in different localities within Essex County. An example of this diversity is the City of Newark, as shown in table 6.3. Newark, with a total population of 329,248 in 1980, is a black city with a significant white population (a third of whites are of Hispanic origin). By contrast, Essex County is a predominantly white area with a significant black population.

The labor-force status of individuals 16 years old and over by race and gender are also presented in table 6.3. Salient in these data is, first, the difference in the magnitudes of the unemployment rates between Newark and the county as a whole. For example, 8.7 percent of Newark's white men in the labor force were unemployed, whereas only 5.54 percent of the white men in Essex County were without a job. Second is the difference in the magnitudes of unemployment rates between blacks and whites in the city and the county. In Newark, the black male unemployment rate was almost twice the white male rate. On the other hand, in Essex County as a whole the black male un-

Table 6.2   **Demographic and Labor-Force Characteristics of Essex County, New Jersey**

	Population in Households	
	Number	Percent
Whites	482,193	57
Blacks	316,440	37
Others	52,483	6
Total	851,116	100

	Population, by Age and Race			
	Whites		Blacks	
Age	Number	Percent	Number	Percent
0–14	83,425	17.3	91,207	28.9
15–54	308,460	64.0	183,599	58.0
55+	90,308	18.7	41,634	13.1
Total	482,183	100.0	316,440	100.0

	Percentage Unemployed	
Race	Men	Women
Whites	5.5	6.3
Blacks	13.4	12.2

Source: 1980 Census, General Population Characteristics, 32-406, New Jersey.

Table 6.3   **Demographic and Labor-Force Characteristics of Essex County and Newark, New Jersey**

	Essex County		Newark	
	Number	Percent	Number	Percent
Total	851,116		329,248	
Whites	490,199	57	107,465	31
Blacks	316,648	37	191,968	58
Other	30,175	6	26,471	11

	Unemployment Rates (percent)			
	Essex County		Newark	
Race	Men	Women	Men	Women
Whites	5.5	6.3	8.7	10.9
Blacks	13.4	12.2	16.5	15.1

Source: 1980 Census.

employment rate was a little more than two and one-half times greater than the white male rate.

The information presented in table 6.4 illustrates that differences also existed between the two areas in the distribution of workers across occupations and industries. In Newark, the three primary occupations were administrative support, including clerical (19.9 percent); operators, fabricators, and laborers (19.5 percent); and service, except protective and household (17.9 percent of total employment).

Essex County is relatively prosperous; the mean family income of whites in 1979 was $30,000. But in Newark that mean was $17,860. Among blacks the mean family income in 1979 was only $13,283 in the county and a slightly higher $15,682 in Newark. The ratio of black to white mean family income in Essex County (.52) was thus lower than that in Newark (.74).

6.5   The Sample

To conduct the audit, we selected a sample of black and white non-Hispanic teenagers who were to graduate from high school in June 1983. These teenagers were students in four high schools in the Newark area. All of the students selected had to express disinterest in continuing their educational experiences in college or other forms of higher education.

Initially, we attempted to enlist black and non-Hispanic white teenagers from the same high schools. But white flight to private schools and residential segregation has left the Newark school system almost entirely black and Hispanic. We called almost all of the high schools in the Newark area, looking for male students who were graduating and who needed to find full-time employment. We had little difficulty finding blacks who fit this profile, but we could find few whites who wanted to participate in the study. In fact, the high school nearest our office (about a half-mile away), Harrison High School, is entirely white and Hispanic. There we met with a group of some 12 non-Hispanic white seniors, none of whom was willing to take the eight-block walk to our office to collect $5.00 and possibly a job, or at least some job prospects.[7] But we had some problems gaining access to students in all locations. It never took fewer than three phone calls to reach an individual who could provide access to the school. Easter holidays, spring recess, and the senior prom all slowed down the responsiveness of the high schools and their students to our requests.

Of the 21 Newark high school seniors who finally participated in the audit, all were male; 14 were black and seven were white. Table 6.5 shows that the social class of these auditors, as indicated by whether the income of their parents was above or below the poverty level in

Table 6.4   **The Distribution of Total Employment, by Occupation and Industry, Essex County and the City of Newark, New Jersey**

	Percentage in:	
Occupation/Industry	Newark	Essex
Employed Persons 16 Years Old and Over, by Occupation		
Managerial and Professional Speciality:		
Executive, Administrative, Managerial,	4.8	11.1
Professional Speciality	7.5	13.6
Technical, Sales, Administrative Support:		
Technicians and Related Support	1.9	2.5
Sales	4.7	8.6
Administrative Support Including Clerical	19.9	21.4
Service:		
Private Household	0.8	0.8
Protective Service	2.9	2.5
Service, Except Protective and Household	12.9	9.9
Farming, Forestry, and Fishing	0.3	0.4
Precision Production, Craft, and Repair	10.2	9.5
Operators, Fabricators, and Laborers:		
Machine Operators, Assemblers, Inspectors	19.5	10.8
Transportation and Material Moving	6.0	4.1
Handlers, Equipment Cleaners, Helpers, Laborers	8.3	4.7
Employed Persons 16 Years Old and Over, by Industry		
Agriculture, Forestry, Fisheries	0.1	0.3
Construction	4.1	3.7
Manufacturing:		
Nondurable Goods	13.9	11.2
Durable Goods	17.2	13.3
Transportation	6.6	5.3
Communication, Other Public Utilities	2.4	3.1
Wholesale Trade	3.7	4.5
Retail Trade	10.3	12.8
Finance, Insurance, and Real Estate	6.8	8.9
Business and Repair Services	4.7	5.2
Personal, Entertainment, and Recreation Services	3.7	3.6
Professional and Related Services:		
Health Services	8.3	8.9
Other Professional and Related Services	3.8	5.2
Public Administration	6.5	5.4

Source: 1980 Census, Detailed Occupation of Employed Persons by Sex, Race and Spanish Origin

1983, was similar to the metropolitan Newark averages in one respect: more blacks were below the poverty level than whites. In our sample 86 percent of the black and only 29 percent of the white youths were from families with incomes below the national poverty level. These percentages were higher, however, than the percentages for the population of the City of Newark who lived below the poverty line. Based on 1979 income 37.7 percent of all blacks and 29 percent of all whites were reported as living with incomes below the poverty level. Our sample is therefore overrepresentative of poor blacks and whites.

Table 6.5 also indicates that the black auditors were more likely than the white auditors to reside in single-parent households. They were also from less-educated families than those of their white counterparts. This difference suggests a potential problem with inferring discrimination based simply on differences in employer treatment of blacks and whites. Unlike audit studies that examine matched pairs of actors, ours examines the experiences of actual job seekers. The auditors obviously differed in many respects.

In fact, as shown in table 6.6, the white auditors were four times as likely as the black auditors to be employed full time by 31 July 1983 and only one-tenth as likely to be unemployed as of that date. The remainder of this paper will attempt to distinguish the differences in treatment by potential employers based on race and those differences based on other specific factors.

6.6   The Firms

We started with a list of the private firms with more than 200 employees in Essex County in 1978. This list presented two methodological problems. First, in recent years Newark and Essex County have experienced a large drop in employment, particularly in the manufacturing sector. A substantial number of firms on our list had therefore ceased operations. Second, when this study began in March 1983, the country was in the deepest recession since the Great Depression of the

Table 6.5   **Socioeconomic Characteristics of Auditors**

Characteristic	Blacks (%)	Whites (%)
Family Income		
At or Below Poverty Level	86	29
Above Poverty Level	14	71
Living Arrangements		
Two-parent household	57	86
Other	43	14
Parents' Education Level		
Mother	10.7	10.4
Father	11	13.2
Sample Size	14	7

Source: Audit survey data (see appendix A).

Table 6.6   Auditors' Employment Status as of Week of 31 July 1983, by Race

	Whites		Blacks	
Status	Number	Percent	Number	Percent
Enrolled in School Full-Time	1	14.3	2	.143
Military	1[a]	14.3	0	0
Employed Full-Time	2[b]	28.5	1[c]	.071
Employed Part-Time	1[d]	14.3	2[e]	.143
Unemployed	1	14.3	6	.428
Unreachable	1	14.3	3	.214
Total	7		14	

[a]Job in the Coast Guard in Virginia.
[b]A unionized supermarket job at the wage of $7.75 per hour and a job under father's employ.
[c]Job as a guard secured through the auspices of this study.
[d]Job in a fast-food restaurant.
[e]Jobs in government job-creation programs.

1930s. New Jersey weathered the recession better than the nation as a whole, however. In July 1983, the statewide unemployment rate was only 8.4 percent, well below the national and regional averages. Nonetheless, of the 190 public and private firms we approached, only 32 were hiring recent high school graduates or accepting applications from such applicants. These 32 were not evenly distributed throughout the county. The auditors were first sent to those of the firms in the immediate Newark area. We then supplemented the list of large firms with firms that advertised in the Newark *Star Ledger* in March and May 1983. But of the numerous firms we queried, only four or five said they would accept applications from recent high school graduates.

The recession may have influenced our measure of discrimination in several ways. If the recession requires rationing of scarce opportunities in a market undergoing temporary disequilibrium, the measured level of discrimination could be much higher than normal because the firms would have greater freedom to exercise hiring prejudices. On the other hand, a poor labor market may encourage some potential job applicants who want a job out of high school to exit the labor market either as full-time enrolled students or simply as temporary labor market dropouts. It is possible that these influences would not affect white and black graduates in the same way. If white graduates are more likely to go to school in a recession than are similarly situated black graduates, the sample of students in the labor market will be biased, which in turn will skew our perception of employer responses. We partially controlled for these sampling differences by carefully selecting the students.

We chose to sample large firms instead of small retail or service firms, such as McDonald's, because large firms are less likely to rely on internal referrals of family and friends in selecting employees. If we had sent auditors to small firms, we would have been less sure whether applicant failure was based on employers' hiring internal referrals. Accordingly, we expect our measurement of treatment differences to be an underestimate of the average effect if all firms were included.

6.7   Attitudes Toward Jobs and Reservation Wages

This section examines the auditors' responses to two questions from our audit background survey (appendix A), which was designed to investigate the attitudes of the auditors toward the world of work. The first question queried job preferences and the second, reservation wages.

The first question asked, "What is most important to you for a permanent job? Wages? Safety? Promotion prospects? Enjoyment of the job? Status of the job in the community?" The implication suggested by table 6.7, which displays the results for this question, is that black and white youths differ in what they want from a job. Whites were concerned with the more tangible aspects of a job. Forty-three percent of the white youths in our sample listed wages as their primary concern; 14 percent checked promotion prospects; and 43 percent chose enjoyment of the job. Among the black youths in the sample, 7 percent listed wages; 21 percent, safety; 14 percent, promotion prospects; 43 percent, job enjoyment; and 14 percent, status of the job as their primary concern.

Although this evidence suggests that blacks are more concerned with the nonfinancial aspect of employment than are their white counterparts, such a conclusion would be incorrect. For example, some of the black auditors were later questioned as to their preferences for a specific job generally thought to be held in high status but to pay low wages versus a more undesirable job paying a high wage. In each case the high wage was chosen. Further conversations suggested that wages were also important to the young black men, but they had lower expectations than their white counterparts of obtaining employment at a high wage. It seems that as a result of their low wage expectations, they focus their sights instead on the prestige of the job. Further indirect support for this conjecture is provided by their response to the second

Table 6.7   **Characteristics of Jobs Desirable to Black and White Auditors**

Characteristic	Blacks (%)	Whites (%)
Wages	7	43
Safety	21	0
Promotion Prospects	14	14
Enjoyment	43	43
Status	14	0

Source: Audit survey data (see appendix A).

question of relevance here, namely, "What is the minimum wage at which you would consider accepting a job." The mean acceptance wage for blacks was $3.75, whereas for whites it was $4.26.

Different reservation wages between whites and blacks is a factor commonly believed to influence differential rates of unemployment between the two races. Both Osterman (1980) and Stephenson (1976), using different data sets, found no evidence to support this hypothesis, though Holzer (in this volume) does find major reservation wage effects.

To investigate this issue using our sample, we estimated a simple equation. The results of this estimation appear in table 6.8. The independent variables were the high school grade-point average, previous job experience in months, and race. Initially, poverty status was also included in the equation, but it was almost perfectly related to race, making the estimates highly unstable. The results show that for our sample minimum acceptance wages, though slightly less for blacks, statistically speaking were equivalent for the two races. The only variable that shows any effect is the number of months of previous work experience.

6.8   Personal References

We asked the auditors to give us three personal references whose names they would have provided to a potential employer. Table 6.9 illustrates their responses to that question and offers two very interesting results. First, both white and black students rely inordinately on friends and relatives as references. One white student gave only one reference—his mother. It is clear that all the auditors, but particularly the black auditors, were reference poor. For example, eight of the 14 black and one of the seven white auditors had some experience with a summer youth employment program, but none of these students could give one person associated with these programs as a reference. Most could not remember the name of anyone they had worked for,

Table 6.8	Determinants of Auditors' Reservation Wages	
Variables	Coefficients	t-Statistics
Black	−.213	(.509)
Grade Point Average		(.342)
in High School	.118	
Job Experience	.027	(1.43)
Constant	3.55	
R^2	.23	

Source: Audit survey data (see appendix A).

and the one person who came up with a name did not know how to reach that reference.

This finding suggests at least one reason why poor and black youths are unable to translate their summer job experiences into future employment. How can a hardworking young person convince a potential employer that he knows how to work when he can provide no corroboration from a previous employer? There is no obvious reason why, as an adjunct to the income-transfer function of government jobs programs (probably their most important function), these programs cannot be better designed to encourage youths to maintain contact with their supervisors.

Most of the literature on references has to do with who referred the successful applicant to his job. The U.S. Department of Labor (1980) has collected data for more than 15 years on methods used to look for jobs, data summarized in table 6.10. This focus on methods fails to distinguish between the issue of youths' lack of references and the issue of how they find jobs. Among those who do find jobs, a significant majority rely on familial and job experience ties to obtain employment. Black men are more likely than white men to try to get job information through the public sector of the job market, and they are one-third more likely to use public and private employment agencies. Black men

Table 6.9   **References Given by Potential Auditors**

Type of Reference/ Number Given	Black Students		White Students	
	Percent	Number	Percent	Number
Friends				
0	35.71	5	28.57	2
1	42.86	6	28.57	2
2	21.43	3	0	0
3	0	0	0	0
Relatives				
0	57.14	8	65.71	6
1	28.57	4	14.29	1
2	14.28	2	0	0
Teachers				
0	35.71	5	65.71	6
1	28.57	4	14.29	1
2	21.43	3	0	0
3	14.29	2	0	0
Previous Employers	92.86			
0	7.14	13	31.43	5
1	0	1	0	0
2	0	0	28.57	2

Source: Audit survey data (see appendix A).

246 Jerome Culp/Bruce H. Dunson

are less likely than white men to apply directly to an employer or to count on the help of relatives or friends. Since information on which employers to approach is generally likely to come from friends, blacks' overlooking of friends as a source of information may reflect a lack of information on employment in the black community.

An example of how important this lack is emerged in our research. A large, semipublic employer was seeking several employees for maintenance jobs at the time of our study. The firm did not publish its openings because doing so would have produced, in the words of its personnel manager, a line of applicants that would stretch around the block. Instead, the employer posted the jobs internally and relied on word-of-mouth referrals to solicit applicants. None of our auditors was aware of these jobs. These procedures obviously work against those who are information poor and whose friends and relatives are information poor. It appears from the responses of our auditors that not only do they have trouble producing job references, but they also have difficulty acquiring job market information.

The second interesting result from our question about references was the failure of white students to use teachers as references. Only one white student in this sample used teachers as a reference, and he used only one. Nine of the 14 black students used at least one teacher as a reference and five used at least two. This difference could be caused simply by the better access that white youths have to job market information through parents and friends. Nonetheless, it is hard to understand why the white auditors, who like the blacks had spent a majority of their time in school, had no references from school. When giving references to the companies audited, the students also gave their potential employer a similar selection of teachers and relatives as references.

Our tentative conclusion is that white students who are not going to college or other advanced educational institutions are more alienated from society than black students. The guidance counselors in the three

Table 6.10   Job-Search Methods Used by Unemployed Male Job Seekers Nationwide, 1979

Percent Using	Black	White
Public employment agency	35.7	26.4
Private employment agency	7.0	6.3
Employer directly	68.7	73.3
Friends or relatives	15.5	16.4
Placed or answered ad	23.1	29.2
Other	7.1	8.1
Average No. Methods Used	1.6	1.60

Source: U.S. Department of Labor (1980, 90, table 43).

predominantly white high schools we visited invariably had had to discipline the white students who fit into this category. Less discipline was required in the high schools visited that were predominantly black. Theoretically, a black high school graduate is as likely to go to college as a white high school graduate. This means either that the tails of the two distributions of high school students differ in their approach to work and work habits or that we are not in fact examining the tail of the black distribution.

It is clear from this analysis that black and white youths are not able to bring much in the way of personal references to the job market. All of the auditors relied primarily on friends and relatives, and among the black auditors, on teachers, as references.

6.9 Aspirations

A frequent explanation for the poor labor market outcomes of black youths is their "unrealistic" expectations for high paying jobs. In our limited sample, we found no expectation that could be characterized as "unrealistic." When asked what jobs they wanted, the black youths tended to be very general in their responses: for example, "a well-paying job" or "a job with prestige." But when pressed about what jobs they would accept, the black auditors almost without exception were willing to take any job that paid the minimum wage. This shift in their answers is consistent with other recent research findings that have shown that the way the reservation-wage question is asked of black youths influences the nature of their responses (Holzer, in this volume).

The minimum wage seems to play a curious role in the formation (Holzer 1984) of job expectations. Almost all of the auditors knew approximately what the minimum-wage level was. A few thought it was slightly higher than its actual level ($3.50 instead of $3.35 per hour). They used the existence of the minimum wage as a rationale for not accepting a lower wage. This suggests that even if the purpose of the minimum wage is to redistribute income, young people use it to help form their reservation wages. We found no interest in jobs paying less than the minimum wage, even if they had significant promotion possibilities. Nor should this be surprising. Some part-time jobs at the minimum wage do exist for black youths in their neighborhoods. But any minimum-wage job that requires a significant investment in travel time (the average commuting time in Newark is 27 minutes) and bus or train fare is unlikely to be worthwhile to any job seeker.

6.10 Audit Results

Having established that our subsamples of black and white youths were in many respects similar to each other, we now turn to the question whether they were treated similarly in their search for employment. In undertaking this phase of our study, the attrition rate for our original group of 21 individuals posed some difficulty. After we selected the original group of auditors, we sought to send them on interviews with various employers. But the addresses and telephone numbers of the students often changed, so that we could not reach many members of our sample. Furthermore, after having been referred to employers, many of the white students, in particular, were no longer interested in using our services as employment brokers or had already obtained jobs (as indicated in table 6.6). We ultimately sent five students, of whom one was white, to a total of 45 audits. The types of industries and frequencies with which they were audited are presented in panels A and B, respectively, of table 6.11. We constructed an index of treatment for each employment application, based on the sum of the number of times an auditor responded in the affirmative to questions 12(a) through 12(c) and 15(a) through 15(f) in appendix B. These questions elicited information on the employer's treatment of the auditor during the job interview.

For example, question 12(a) asked, "Did anyone in the office tell you of other job openings?" and 12(b) asked, "Did anyone in the office engage you in a conversation?" A mean treatment value for each auditor was computed, and these values are presented in the second half of table 6.11. As expected, the mean treatment varied across auditors.

Table 6.11   Treatment Indexes: Means and by Selected Industries

A. Index of Treatment

Auditor	Mean Treatment	Number of Audits
Auditor 1	2.00	18
Auditor 2	2.40	5
Auditor 3	1.27	11
Auditor 4	1.33	3
Auditor 5 (white)	2.87	8

B. Index of Treatment, by Selected Industries

	Retail Trade	Finance, Insurance, and Real Estate	Manufacturing
Auditor 1	2.85	2.20	1.89
Auditor 2	2.00	2.67	
Auditor 3	1.00	2.00	1.20
Auditor 4		1.33	
Auditor 5 (white)	5.33	1.4	

Source: Audit survey data (see appendix B).

It should be noted, however, that the mean treatment index for the white auditor was slightly higher than that of the four black auditors.

An interesting finding was that differences in treatment varied by auditor across the major industry categories. Ranking those industries by the average hourly wage, we find that differential treatment by race was greater for those industries with jobs paying closer to the minimum wage. For instance, the February 1983 average hourly wage in retail trade was $5.71, and in finance, insurance, and real estate it was $7.75. The differential treatment indexes for the former were more pronounced than those for the latter industry.

The discussion of treatment effects has so far been very general. Although data limitations severely reduced the usefulness of more refined statistical procedures, a more precise measurement of differences in treatment was desired. The variance in treatment can be thought of as consisting of two principal kinds: one arising from individual-specific effects, and the other arising from industry- or firm-specific effects.

We first estimated an equation in which the dependent variable was the index of treatment by a particular firm. The independent variables were individual-specific dummy variables, with the white auditor as the excluded category. The results are in table 6.12. Although differences did exist among the blacks in each instance, the four black auditors on average were treated less favorably than the white auditor. Moreover, the magnitude of the difference in treatment in each instance was greater between the blacks and the white auditor than among the black auditors. Since the auditors did not all interview with the same employers, if some employers typically treated job applicants with less courtesy, part of the difference attributed to differences in individuals was caused by these employer or industry effects.

The audited firms were then grouped into five industry types: retail trade; manufacturing; transportation; public institutions; and finance, insurance, and real estate. These dummy variables, coupled with the individual-specific dummies, were placed into one equation and our treatment effects reestimated. The excluded industry category was retail trade. The results were generally as expected. The magnitude of the individual-specific coefficients in all but one instance decreased. The one exception resulted from the fact that auditor 4 did not have any interviews in retail trade. The major point nevertheless remains. The black auditors, although not significantly so, in most instances were treated less courteously than the white auditor.

6.11 Conclusions

Despite the very limited sample that we have been able to gather, we believe we can draw a number of tentative conclusions from this study.

Table 6.12   Regression Estimates of Treatment Effects

Variable	Individual-Specific Effects	Individual and Industry Effects
Constant	2.87	3.35
Auditor 1	−.75	−.587
	(1.24)	(.770)
Auditor 2	−.475	−.428
	(.505)	(.461)
Auditor 3	−1.60	−1.37
	(2.07)	(1.67)
Auditor 4	−1.54	−1.62
	(1.38)	(1.45)
Public Sector	—	.547
		(.530)
Transportation	—	−2.37
		(1.60)
Finance and Insurance	—	−.864
		(1.22)
Manufacturing	—	−.837
		(1.07)
R^2	.114	.24

Note: t-statistics in parentheses.

First, the black auditors were treated with less courtesy by the potential employer than the white auditor. They were less likely to be addressed as "Mr.", to be informed of job prospects, or to be asked to be seated.

Second, black and white youths who are seeking jobs without the benefit of a college education appear, absent race, to be similar in their potential attractiveness to employers. Nevertheless, some differences did exist between blacks and whites in this study, namely, blacks typically had less work experience.

Third, retail establishments treated the white auditor better than the black auditors, but manufacturing establishments treated the two races similarly.

Fourth, the black auditors did not seem to have unreasonable expectations or aspirations. They stated they were willing to work at any job that paid the minimum wage.

Fifth, the difficulty in finding white youths to participate in the audit in itself suggests that black and white youths, at least in Newark, New Jersey, do not face the same job prospects.

Sixth, both the white and black auditors were reference poor, that is, they were unable to name appropriate-personal references to give to potential employers. White auditors were reluctant to use teachers as references.

Finally, although nine of the auditors had extensive experience in summer youth employment programs in Newark, none of them could provide a person from the program who could give them a reference. Summer jobs programs do not appear to teach youths to cultivate references as a critical part of the employment process.

Researchers often ask for more information in order to examine in greater detail the results of their studies. We urge others to continue the efforts that we and others have made to determine if racial discrimination in employee selection still exists. The results of black youth unemployment are obvious, as is its simple existence, as recorded in everything from social science research to decisions of the Supreme Court.[9] Yet many observers believe that demand issues can be safely ignored. If nothing else, this paper suggests that employer behavior is an important topic that begs further inquiry by research on black youth unemployment.

Appendix A
Auditor Survey

1. High school presently attending _____
   Course of study _____
   High school class standing _____
   Total number in senior class _____

2. List references (specify relationship)
   (Check one)
   _____ Friend __ Relative __ Teacher__ Employer __
   (Telephone) _____
   _____ Friend __ Relative __ Teacher__ Employer __
   (Telephone) _____
   _____ Friend __ Relative __ Teacher__ Employer __
   (Telephone) _____

3. Where did you go to sixth grade? _____

4. Family income per week _____

5. Highest grade in school of: Father _____
                                 Mother _____

6. What jobs are you looking for and at what wage per hour? (List jobs)
   _____   _____
   _____   _____

7. What is most important to you for a permanent job? (Check one)
    (a) Wages _____
    (b) Safety _____
    (c) Promotion prospects _____
    (d) Enjoyment of the job _____
    (e) Status of the job in community _____

8. What is the lowest wage you would accept for permanent em-
    ployment? (Check one)
    $2.00_____ $3.00_____ $4.00_____ $5.00_____
    $2.50_____ $3.50_____ $4.50_____ $5.50_____
    Other (Specify $/Hour)_____

9. Father employed?   yes _____   no _____
    Mother employed?   yes _____   no _____
    Father's occupation _____
    Mother's occupation _____

10. Your education _____

11. Living status: a. at home _____
                     b. with other relative _____
                     c. with nonrelated friend _____
                     d. alone _____

12. Family   a. both parents present _____
             b. mother absent _____
             c. father absent _____
             d. both parents absent _____

13. # of other children _____

14. # of persons in the household _____

15. Your age _____

16. Married?   Yes _____
                No _____

17. # of your children _____

18. Residence   Town _____
                Ward _____

19. Do you have any training?
                Yes _____
                No _____
    If yes, specify _____

Vocational?   Yes _____
              No _____
If yes, specify _____
Summer Youth?   Yes _____
                No _____

If yes, specify _____
Other _____

20.   Place of birth (State) _____

21.   Previous job experience

Employer	Job Title	Wages/Hour	Length of Time
_____	_____	_____	_____
_____	_____	_____	_____
_____	_____	_____	_____
_____	_____	_____	_____

22.   Do you have access to a car?

              Yes _____
              No _____

23.   Race   Black _____
                White _____
                Hispanic _____
                Asian _____
                Other _____

Appendix B
Job Practices Audit Survey

Employer Name _____
Address _____
Telephone _____

Auditor Name _____
Auditor # _____

1.1   *Timing and Logistics*

1.   Date of audit _____

2.   Did you telephone first?   Yes _____   No _____

3.   If yes, did the person say:
     (a)   They were hiring?_____
     (b)   Taking applications _____

    (c)   They weren't taking applications and you could leave your
          name and telephone number _____
    (d)   They weren't taking applications but they would not take
          your name and telephone number _____

4.   How did you get to the interview?
      Your car _____   Bus _____
      Friend's car _____   Walked _____
      Taxi _____   Subway _____

5.   How long did it take to go to the job interview?
      Number of minutes _____

6.   Where did you leave from to go to the audit?
    (a)   Home _____
    (b)   School _____
    (c)   Other (specify) _____

7.   Time of the day and day of the week you arrived at interview
      (Specify A.M. or P.M.) _____

1.2   *Office Interaction*

8.   When you entered employer's office were you:
    (Check all applicable items)
    (a)   Welcomed by secretary or receptionist and referred to per-
          sonnel manager (interviewer) _____
    (b)   Welcomed by secretary or receptionist and told there are
          no jobs _____
    (c)   Welcomed by the interviewer _____
    (d)   Had to start conversation _____
    (e)   Other (Specify) _____

9.   From when you entered the personnel office how long before
    you were interviewed? (In minutes) _____

10.   How many employees were visible in the office? _____

11.   Were any of these employees black? _____
    If yes, how many? _____

12.   Did anyone in the office:
    (a)   Tell you of other job openings
          Yes _____   No _____
    (b)   Engage you in a conversation
          Yes _____   No _____

    (c)   Ask you to be seated
          Yes _____   No _____
    (d)   Offer you some water or a beverage
          Yes _____   No _____
    (e)   Other act of courtesy (Specify) _____

13.   How many other job applicants were there in the office?_____
      How many of the applicants were: Black _____
                                     Female _____

  1.3 *Interview*

14.   Who interviewed you?
      Name _____
      Job Title _____

15.   Did the interviewer:
    (a)   Give his/her name when introduced to you
          Yes _____   No _____
    (b)   Give you business card
          Yes _____   No _____
    (c)   Ask your name
          Yes _____   No _____
    (d)   Address you as Mr.
          Yes _____   No _____
    (e)   Offer you a seat
          Yes _____   No _____
    (f)   Shake your hand
          Yes _____   No _____
    Other acts of courtesy (Specify) _____

16.   Did the interviewer request any of the following information?
    (a)   Previous employment
          Yes _____   No _____
    (b)   Job training
          Yes _____   No _____
    (c)   High School
          Yes _____   No _____
    (d)   Location of home (where you are from)
          Yes _____   No _____
    (e)   Special job skills (Typing, etc). (Specify) _____
          Yes _____   No _____
    (f)   Parents' occupation
          Yes _____   No_____

(g) Parents' income
   Yes _____   No _____
(h) Your marital status
   Yes _____   No _____

17. What was the race and sex of the interviewer? _____
_____

18. Did the interviewer request any of the following:
   (a) References
      Yes _____   No _____
      If yes, specify who you gave:
      Teacher _____ Employee of interviewer _____
      Friend _____ Employer _____
      (b) Telephone number
      Yes _____   No _____
   (c) Address
      Yes _____   No _____
   (d) Date of availability
      Yes _____   No _____
   (e) Other (Specify) _____

19. How did the interviewer take this information:
   (Check relevant items)
   (a) Permitted you to complete an application
      Yes _____   No _____
   (b) Interviewer took notes
      Yes _____   No _____
   (c) Interviewer completed a form
      Yes _____   No _____
   (d) Made no apparent notation
      Yes _____   No _____
   (e) Permitted you to write down your name and address but
      not on a standard application form:
      Yes _____   No _____

20. What jobs did the interviewer say were available:
_____
_____

   Were any of these jobs covered by union contract?
   Yes _____   No _____

21. Did the interviewer make it clear that you could apply for all
   these jobs?
   Yes _____   No _____

22.   Specify any wage rates and jobs that were explicitly mentioned during the interview:
      Dollars/Hour _____

      _____

23.   Did you get a job offer?   Yes _____   No _____
      If yes, for how much? (Specify Dollars/Hour) _____

24.   Did the interviewer mention whether blacks worked at this job-site now?
      Yes _____   No _____

25.   If so, was the mention positive _____
                    or
      Negative _____ (Specify) _____

26.   Did the interviewer make any comments about race using code words? (Specify)

      _____

      _____

27.   What was the approximate age of the interviewer? _____

28.   When did the interviewer tell you that you were likely to hear whether you got the job? (Time) _____

29.   Did the interviewer say he would contact you or that you should contact them? _____

30.   How would you evaluate how well you did during the interview? (Circle one)
      1   2   3   4   5   6   7   8   9   10
      Poor   Excellent

31.   What qualifications do you think the employer found most important? (Check all relevant ones)
      (a)   High school you attended _____
      (b)   Parent's job _____
      (c)   Previous job experience _____
      (d)   Race _____
      (e)   Personality _____
      (f)   Grades _____
      Other (Specify) _____

1.4   *Other Comments about the interview*

      _____

      _____

      _____

[For Office Use Only]

32.   One month after audit did you get an:
      (a)   Interview? Yes _____   No _____
            If yes, did you go? Yes _____   No _____
      (b)   Job? At what wage?_____

33.   Two months after audit did you get an:
      (a)   Interview? Yes _____   No _____
            If yes, did you go? Yes _____   No _____
      (b)   Job? At what wage? _____

34.   June 1. Did you get an:
      (a)   Interview? Yes _____   No _____
            If yes, did you go? Yes _____   No _____
      (b)   Job? At what wage? _____

Notes

1. See, for example, Freeman and Wise (1982).
2. See Freeman and Wise (1982). These studies by and large have concentrated on the role of unemployment. Differentials for teachers have not adequately been explained. But see Wallace (1975).
3. Title VII of the 1964 Civil Rights Act, 42 U.S.C. § 2000E *et seq.*, which prohibits discrimination in hiring, does not apply to employers of 15 or fewer employees. In addition, there is effectively little enforcement for the smallest employers who are covered by Title VII because of the statistical difficulty in proving group discrimination in small groups and because of the larger costs associated with bringing such suits against a small employer.
4. We would like to thank Art Hilson, who at the time of the study was Executive Director of a New York City agency and had more than ten years' experience in hiring, and Steven Brown and Rodney Stenlake for their assistance in this project.
5. See appendix B, which contains the survey instrument used, and question 7 of auditor survey, contained in appendix A.
6. Some characteristics that we did not control for were height, weight, and other personal characteristics. Some of these, but not all, were partially controlled for by the use of the videotapes. None of the auditors who went on interviews were particularly tall, heavy, or handsome (or, conversely, short, thin, or ugly).
7. Two Harrison High School students signed up to come to Professor Culp's office, but they did not keep their appointments.
8. For further discussion of the audit study method in the housing context, see Wienk, Reid, and Simonson (1979).
9. See Wilson (1982) and Texas Department of Community Affairs v. Burdine, 450 U.S. 248 (1981).

References

Firth, Michael. 1981. Racial discrimination in the British labor market. *Industrial and Labor Relations Review* 34 (January): 265–72.

Freeman, Richard B., and David A. Wise. 1982. *The youth labor market problem: Its nature, causes, and consequences.* Chicago: University of Chicago Press.

McIntosh, Neil, and David S. Smith. 1974. The extent of racial discrimination. Vol. 40, broadsheet no. 547. London: Social Science Institute.

McIntyre, Shelby J., Dennis J. Moberg, and Larry Z. Posner. 1980. Discrimination in recruitment: An empirical analysis; Comment. *Industrial and Labor Relations Review* 33 (July): 543–47.

Newman, Jerry. 1978. Discrimination in recruitment: An empirical analysis. *Industrial and Labor Relations Review* 32 (October): 15–24.

Osterman, Paul. 1980. *Getting started: The youth labor market problem.* Cambridge, Mass.: MIT Press.

Stephenson, Stanley P., Jr. 1976. The economics of youth job search behavior. *Review of Economics and Statistics* 58 (February): 104–11.

U.S. Department of Labor, Bureau of Labor Statistics. 1980. *Handbook of labor statistics.* Washington, D.C.: GPO.

Wallace, P. 1975. *Pathways to work.* Lexington, Mass.: D.C. Heath.

Wienk, Ronald E., Clifford E. Reid, and John Simonson. 1979. *Measuring racial discrimination in the American housing market.* Washington, D.C.: U.S. Department of Housing and Urban Development.

Wilson, William Julius. 1982. *The declining significance of race.* Chicago: University of Chicago Press.

Comment   Paul Osterman

Virtually all studies of racial differences in labor market outcomes treat discrimination as a residual. That is, all legitimate factors that might explain a particular difference in wages or unemployment are given their full due and any unexplained remaining difference is attributed to discrimination. The problem with this indirect technique is that there is always uncertainty whether omitted considerations might reduce the residual or, from another perspective, whether the weight given some of the "legitimate" explanatory variables might really proxy a discriminatory pattern.

The paper by Culp and Dunson is an effort to overcome this uncertainty by employing a technique often used in housing studies. By sending teams of matched blacks and whites to real estate agents, apartment owners, or employers, actual differences in treatment can be observed. Virtually all studies of the housing market that have employed this procedure have found considerable discrimination. As Culp

Paul Osterman is associate professor of economics at Boston University.

and Dunson note there have been few comparable labor market studies, and the difficult issue of employment differentials between black and white youths is a promising topic to examine along these lines.

The research strategy the authors employed seems to me a good one, although I find their case for using actual job seekers instead of actors unconvincing. Unfortunately, in the end only five youths participated and only one of these was white. Given this sample size few conclusions can be drawn from this effort. Nonetheless, the authors did conduct more extensive interviews with a larger group of 21 youths, and these provide some insight into the youth employment problem and racial differences in outcomes.

Most striking from these interviews is the paucity of references black youth can bring to the job market. Other studies have asked employed youths how they located their jobs, and their responses have suggested that black youths are forced to rely on formal employment systems, such as job training programs, since their parents and relatives are in no position to help help. Culp and Dunson improve on this research by avoiding the selection bias inherent in data drawn only from youths who have been successful in finding work. When young job seekers are asked about who they can draw upon, the situation of blacks appears even more serious. It seems that most cannot even turn to formal government programs such as schools and training programs. This suggests a rethinking of the placement activities of those institutions.

The interviews also confirm earlier findings that racial differences in reservation wages and aspirations are not important explanatory variables. It is also striking that many of the white youths the authors sought to enlist were sufficiently confident about their job prospects that they were reluctant to participate, despite financial incentive for participating. The considerable attrition in the white sample also speaks to this point.

In summary, the authors undertook a commendable effort and have reported their results clearly and honestly. Although somewhat disappointing, the experiment was successful enough that others might consider replicating it on a large scale.

7   Do Better Jobs Make Better Workers? Absenteeism from Work Among Inner-City Black Youths

Ronald Ferguson and Randall Filer

7.1   Introduction

Employed black youths earn roughly the same wages as white youths (Freeman and Wise 1982). Thus, at least as far as wages are concerned, the disadvantage faced by black youths in the labor market is not that they obtain worse jobs than white youths do, but that white youths seem to be able to find jobs with greater ease (Clark and Summers 1982). Counter to conventional wisdom, Ellwood (in this volume) has shown that this difference does not arise from patterns of residential and employment location. Rather, it appears that a good deal of the explanation has to do with the relative position of black youths in the hiring queue: they are more often at the rear or excluded altogether. This study will investigate some possible reasons why black youths may appear less attractive to employers and will also suggest possible methods of improving their relative standing.

Justifiable or not, black youths have a collective reputation as the least dependable and least productive demographic group in the labor force. Analysis of data in the Current Population Survey shows that there is a statistically significant difference in absenteeism between black and white youths, with the black youths absent more often.[1] Thus, even in the absence of a residual preference for hiring white youths, it is not surprising that black youths might appear less attractive to potential employers, other things being equal. If their negative reputation as a group plays an important role in the treatment of individual black youths, information that aids employers in the screening process

Ronald Ferguson is assistant professor of public policy at the John F. Kennedy School of Government, Harvard University. Randall Filer is assistant professor of economics at Brandeis University.

should reduce this statistical discrimination, thereby helping deserving black youngsters to be treated more fairly. Similarly, measures that induce black youngsters collectively to improve their conduct might gradually erode their negative reputation and their poor position in the queue.

Some analysts (Anderson 1980, for example) argue that the conduct of inner-city black youths is more sensitive to the quality of the jobs they hold than is the behavior of other youths. Thus, it is reasoned, various forms of job upgrading may go a long way toward producing more job commitment and conformity to accepted standards of conduct on the part of black youths. Others (Banfield 1974, for example), however, are highly sceptical of that view and believe that the employment behavior of inner-city youths is too tied to educational deficiencies and environmental factors for job quality to have a substantial influence. There is little scientific evidence (especially in the economics literature) regarding the sensitivity of this population's behavior to various incentives, including the attractiveness of the jobs they hold.

Absenteeism is one of a range of behaviors that reflect a worker's attitude and commitment to his job and perceptions of his value as an employee. This study attempts to gauge the effects of job characteristics and personal background factors on absenteeism from work among inner-city black men between the ages of 16 and 24. The study places central emphasis on the effect of job quality. The results provide strong evidence that job quality does affect absenteeism, but in a more complicated way than is usually supposed.

The results show that many direct and indirect job benefits, such as the wage paid and the amount of prestige attached to the job, reduce the incidence of absenteeism markedly. On the other hand, both theoretical and empirical results suggest that a rational worker may be absent more often, other things being equal, the greater the marketability of the skills he has learned on the job and the greater the value of his experience as a signal to future employers. Hence, if a "dead end" job is defined as one that adds little or nothing to a worker's stock of human capital, less dead-end jobs may in fact produce less reliable workers.

For empirical purposes, less dead-end jobs will be represented by jobs in which there is a higher probability of a long-term attachment to the *industry* in which the worker is employed. The presumption is that among occupations held by inner-city black youths, those that lead to a high level of industry attachment do so by developing industry-specific human capital and hence more security and mobility within the industry. There is, of course, an alternative interpretation, namely, the lack of interindustry mobility could imply a more dead-end job if the job holder is stuck in the same job with no opportunity for change or advancement. This explanation seems unlikely, however, since industry retention rates are in fact highly positively correlated with the desirable characteristics of both jobs and workers. Given this definition, developed and defended below, reducing the dead-end nature of a job will enhance the worker's welfare but may increse his absenteeism.

Finally, it is found that the various job characteristics discussed above (as well as the length of the commuting time to the job and the style of supervision) are as important as, and perhaps more important than, employee characteristics in determining absenteeism. Among employee characteristics, directly measured personality and aptitudes have significant explanatory power. But once these are controlled for, more general environmental and family background variables appear to add little to our ability to understand absenteeism.

Data for the study come from the 1979–80 NBER Survey of Inner-City Black Youth. The survey provides a myriad of data on the daily activities, personality, family, environment, academic background, and labor market of each of over 2,300 black men aged 16 to 24. The youths surveyed were randomly selected from city blocks that, according to the 1970 Census, had at least 70 percent black residents and 30 percent families below the poverty line in income. Those studied for the present report are the approximately 70 percent who held regular jobs for ten days or more at some time during the year preceding the interview. Absenteeism on the most recent job is the primary subject of analysis.

Other data sets that contain measures of absenteeism are not nearly as rich as the NBER youth data in their coverage of important job and worker characteristics. Thus, the NBER data enable the elimination of more sources of possible omitted-variables bias. Still, the NBER data are less than ideal and impose certain constraints on the scope and method of the analysis. First, the measure of absenteeism is ordinal rather than cardinal: each respondent was asked whether he was never, rarely, sometimes, or often absent not because of illness; absent due to illness; or tardy. Although the current study focuses on absenteeism not due to illness, estimates for absenteeism due to illness and tardiness will also be discussed.

The second limitation imposed by the data is that, since they cover only black men between 16 and 24 years of age, important comparisons with other demographic groups are not possible. Third, the data are cross-sectional, so the same worker cannot be observed in different employment settings. This leaves the interpretation that there is a strong causal link between job characteristics and absenteeism open to the criticism that some part of the influence we attribute to job characteristics is really the result of unobserved worker characteristics that affect both absenteeism and the quality of the job that the individual can obtain.[2] Arguments presented later explain why it is highly unlikely that unobserved worker characteristics are an important source of bias in this study.

There are very few absenteeism studies by economists with which to compare the current undertaking.[3] This is somewhat surprising, since roughly as many hours are lost each year due to absenteeism as from strikes and layoffs in the U.S. economy. Allen (1981b) conducted a study of absenteeism, using the 1972–73 Quality of Employment Survey (QES), in which he included race as one of several personal characteristics in a cross-sectional analysis. His results were similar to those of this study insofar as he found that job characteristics affect absenteeism and that "most easily observable personal characteristics [were] unrelated to work attendance" when important job characteristics were held constant. Allen also found that race had no statistically significant impact on absenteeism. This finding, he claimed, was "not at all consistent with 'vicious circle of poverty' or 'ghetto pathology' theories of nonwhite vocational behavior." Observed differences between white and nonwhite adults could largely be accounted for by differences in marginal earnings, scheduling flexibility, and health. Although there were differences in the specific job characteristics analyzed, Allen's finding that job characteristics play a decisive role in affecting employee behavior is consistent with the findings reported below. Unfortunately, the QES data set used by Allen did not include sufficient numbers of youths to judge whether his findings would extend to young people as well as adults.

This paper proceeds first through a simple expositional model, then presents comparative statics that describe the effects of variations in wages, status, and security on absenteeism. From there, variables used in the empirical analysis are defined, and a summary is given of parts of the analysis for which quantitative results are not reported here. In particular, a long list of personality and environmental variables that did not affect absenteeism directly is summarized. Empirical estimates are then given for both ordinary least squares (OLS) and ordered probit coefficients from the absenteeism equation. The quantitative effect on absenteeism of variation in each of the independent variables is discussed. Job quality and worker characteristcs are found to be of similar quantitative importance. Finally, the major findings are reviewed and some of their implications are discussed.

The decision to skip work is a time allocation decision reflecting a balancing of the costs and benefits of alternative uses of time. Some common inducements for employees to skip work are that they are sick, they have other "business" (such as a job search or other income opportunities) to take care of, they wish to engage in some form of leisure, or they desire to avoid some unpleasantness in the work environment. On the other hand, incentives to avoid, or the costs of, absenteeism include lost pay, the possible embarrassment of later being questioned or reprimanded, a lower probability of promotion, and the possibility of being fired from the job. The conceptual foundation and empirical analysis of this paper rests on all of these costs and benefits of absenteeism. For expository simplicity, however, the theoretical model in the next section will focus on leisure consumption as the benefit from increased absenteeism and forgone earnings and the risk of job loss as the costs. In addition, explicit consideration of variations in tastes and environments will be deferred until after the following section, which may be passed over by the less technically inclined reader.

7.2   A Theoretical Model of Absenteeism

The view of the labor market underlying the behavioral model presented in this section is best characterized as a job search–turnover model. The distribution of workers across jobs at any given time results from matches made in the past. Due to imperfect information, costs of adjustment, and risk aversion, recontracting does not take place continually in order to adjust instantaneously to every change in market conditions.[4] Thus, at any particular time, identical people may not achieve exactly identical levels of utility, and every worker may not be employed at what would be his or her globally optimal position if the conditions of the standard competitive model held absolutely.

This analytical perspective highlights the fact that even when differences in tastes and personality can be effectively controlled, there may remain differences in job situations that can lead to differences in behavior. Youths with similar tastes and abilities may differ in how well they like their jobs. Thus, there may be behavioral differences that are unrelated to tastes and personal characteristics.

An approach that would be consistent with a static competitive model would be to assume that a worker chooses simultaneously his job and his expected behavior on that job. The model here, however, assumes that these choices are basically sequential, with the worker first taking the best available job that he knows of (providing, of course, that that job is above his reservation standard of acceptability) and then deciding on appropriate behavior on that job as a function of how much he likes the job and how much he would mind losing it. The quality of the best available job is measured in terms of the wage it pays, the status it offers, the skills it teaches, and so on and is not a choice variable (aside from conventional considerations of optimal length and intensity of search). It is given by current market conditions and employers' impressions of the applicant, each of which the applicant has no real control over in the short run. The following model therefore abstracts from the choice of job, takes job characteristics as given, and focuses on the decision regarding how much to be absent as a function of the three job characteristics most commonly examined in studies of minority youth employment problems: wages, status, and the dead-end nature of jobs (or the opportunity to acquire useful human capital).

7.2.1   A Two-Period Model

The rewards of work include psychic benefits and income that enables the worker to purchase commodities to enhance the quality of leisure time. Additionally, there are various ways in which working in the present helps to enhance prospects for a happy future. To look more closely at aspects of the labor-leisure decision that will be at the center of the empirical analysis, let us consider a two-period model in which a worker wishes to maximize the sum of present plus future utilities. Currrent-period consumption of leisure in this model is balanced against two categories of costs: forgone income and a reduction in the expected value of future utility.

On most jobs there is some agreement, usually explicit, regarding how many hours per week a worker is expected to work unless he is ill. Say that this number is 40 and that 40 is the maximum number of hours one can work on the job under consideration. In this model, when a worker chooses to work fewer than 40 hours, he risks forfeiting the chance to work for his current employer in the future, that is, he risks being fired. If he loses his job he will either find another job or become unemployed.

An objective function can be specified to represent the sum of present plus expected future utilities. Let U_{1a} represent the current-period utility, which captures the enjoyment that comes from current consumption of leisure (L), status (S), and income (Y). Income (Y) is the product of the hourly wage rate (w) and the number of hours (T) per week that the worker chooses to work, such that $T = 40 - L$. If K represents the degree to which the job teaches specific skills, then U_{1a} becomes:

$$U_{1a} = U_{1a} (L|w,S,K).$$

The expected value of future utility is the sum of two terms. U_{2b} is the utility the worker will experience in the future if he loses his job and has to find another or becomes unemployed.[5] There is a known probability (P) that a worker will lose his job. P can be influenced by his behavior on the job and may also be a function of job characteristics. If the worker is not laid off or fired, and if the second-period utility (U_{2a}) of staying with his current employer exceeds U_{2b}, then he will remain with his first employer. This will occur with probability $1 - P$. Hence, the two terms whose sum represents the expected value of the second-period or future utility are: PU_{2b} and $(1 - P)U_{2a}$. Some rearrangement allows the sum to be written: $U_{2a} - P(U_{2a} - U_{2b})$. Comparative statics will be carried out below under the assumption that $U_{2a} > U_{2b}$. U_{2a} and U_{2b} will be treated as exogenous insofar as they will be unaffected by the worker's choice of how much leisure to consume in the first period. On the other hand, various exogenous forces can cause U_{2a} and U_{2b} to change in ways that affect the intertemporal trade-off embodied in the current period labor-leisure decision, thereby affecting the optimal choice of first-period leisure, L^*.

For expository ease assume that the worker's rate of time preference is zero, so that his two-period expected utility can be expressed as:

(1) $$E(U) = U_{1a} + U_{2a} - P(U_{2a} - U_{2b}).$$

Maximization by choice of current leisure (L) gives the following first-order condition, where superscripts will be used throughout to indicate the variable(s) with respect to which the derivatives have been taken:

(2) $$E^L(U) = U^L_{1a} - U^Y_{1a}w - P^L(U_{2a} - U_{2b})$$
$$= 0 \text{ when } L = L^*,$$

where $U^L_{1a} > 0$, $U^Y_{1a} > 0$ and $P^L > 0$. (Assume that U_{1a} is quasi-concave and that P^{LL} is nonnegative. This ensures that $E^{LL} < 0$.)

The first-order condition in equation (2) can now be totally differentiated to explore the impact of exogenous forces on the optimal level of leisure consumption in period 1. The following three comparative static experiments provide a basis for several of the interpretations in the empirical section that follows.

7.2.2 Comparative Statics

From the perspective of a youth who has found a job that satisfies or exceeds his minimal requirements, the characteristics of the job can be taken as given parameters. This subsection will examine the comparative static implications of changes in three job characteristics of particular interest. The wage, status, and skill contents of a job are probably the three most important aspects of job quality determining attractiveness to inner-city black youths. Discussions of the demeaning aspects of "menial" jobs focus on the facts that these jobs pay low wages, attract little respect from society at large, and teach few skills that might lead to employment security and upward social mobility.[6]

Advocates of the provision of better jobs for minority youths argue that jobs with higher wages, greater status, and more training will induce more stable and acceptable behavior. The following comparative static experiments examine whether or not these predictions hold true for utility-maximizing youths.[7]

Case 1. Wages

In this case we analyze the impact on L^* of an increase in wages (w). The question that interests us here is how a worker's optimal leisure might differ on two jobs that differ only in that one pays a slightly higher wage both in the present and the future. Both U_{1a} and U_{2a} are thus affected.

If we apply the implicit-function theorem to equation (2) and assume that the appropriate second-order condition ($E^{LL} < 0$) holds, the sign of L^{*w}, which gives the direction of the impact of w upon L^*, must be the same as the sign of E^{Lw}. Hence, we need only to examine the following equation:

$$(3) \quad sgn\, L^{*w} = sgn[U_{1a}^{LY}T - U_{1a}^{YY}wT - U_{1a}^{Y}$$
$$- P^{L}U_{2a}^{w} - P^{Lw}(U_{2a} - U_{2b})].$$

This expression does not have an unambiguous sign. U_{1a}^{LY} is positive because an increase in income enhances the marginal utility of leisure, and $- U_{1a}^{YY}wT$ is positive under the usual assumption of the diminishing marginal utility of income. These two terms together represent forces pushing toward more consumption of leisure (absenteeism) at higher wages. In situations in which these terms dominate, workers are said to be on the backward-bending portion of their labor-supply curves. Readers who believe that most inner-city youths work to achieve target current incomes with little or no concern for future earnings should expect these terms to exceed the sum of the absolute values of the other terms in equation (3) and therefore to produce an empirical finding that higher wages lead to greater consumption of leisure.

Forces pulling in the opposite direction are captured by $- U_{1a}^{Y}$ and $- P^{L}U_{2a}^{w}$ and probably by $- P^{Lw}(U_{2a} - U_{2b})$. If a nonzero rate of time preference were in the model, it would multiply the last two terms. The greater a worker's concern for the future relative to the present, the stronger the influence of $- P^{L}U_{2a}^{w}$, which, other things equal, influences him to consume less leisure as w rises. Similarly, the greater the first-period marginal utility of income (U_{1a}^{Y}), the more likely the worker will be on the upward-sloping section of his labor-supply curve. Finally, it is likely that after controlling for other job and personal characteristics, we will find that employers paying higher wages can more easily replace discharged workers and will therefore be less tolerant of absenteeism, rendering $- P^{Lw}$ negative. Which forces are in fact stronger, the negative or the positive, is an empirical question that will be answered by the statistical analysis below.

Case 2. Status

In the United States "you are what you do." A major component of the nonpecuniary payoff to being employed in any particular occupation derives from the status or respectability of the occupation in the eyes of society at large. When someone accepts a job that pays less money than some alternative opportunity, it is often the case that he is trading income for prestige. It is in the same spirit to hypothesize that people also pay for status through the forfeiture of leisure. An example would be someone who is absent from work less on a higher-status job because he is more concerned about losing the job, and with it his social standing, than he would be on a lower-status job. The notion that status has a positive impact on utility is captured in the model by the assumption that both U_{1a} and U_{2a} are increasing functions of the status associated with the worker's current job.

An additional effect of status is likely to be that the higher the status of the job, the lower the marginal disutility of work. On a more prestigious job workers can be expected to feel better about themselves. They will therefore feel less demeaned while doing the job and may even miss it more when absent. This phenomenon can be embedded in the model through the assumption that the higher the status of the job, the lower the marginal utility of being absent. This can be represented symbolically as $U_{1a}^{LS} < 0$, where S = status.

For some purposes it is useful to think of status as a component of real income. One such instance is when investigating the effect of additional status on the marginal utility of money income. The assumption of a diminishing marginal utility of real income leads to the conclusion that added status reduces the marginal utility of money income Y (at constant prices). Symbolically, this can be written as $U^{YS} < 0$. This conclusion follows as long as status and purchased consumer goods are to some extent substitutes.

It is almost certainly true that there are systematic variations in personnel practices across jobs of differing levels of status and that a dimension of these variations is a difference in the effect of absenteeism on the probability of being fired. In other words, it should be assumed that $P^{LS} \neq 0$. Unfortunately, however, the sign of P^{LS} could plausibly be either positive or negative.

Assuming that $U_{1a}^{LS} < 0$, $U_{2a}^{S} > 0$, $U_{1a}^{YS} < 0$, and $P^{LS} \neq 0$, the following equation expresses the marginal effect of status on optimal leisure (L^*):

(4) $sgn\ L^{*S} = sgn[U_{1a}^{LS} - wU_{1a}^{YS} - P^L U_{2a}^{S} - P^{LS}(U_{2a} - U_{2b})]$.

Although it deserves a place in the formal analysis, U_{1a}^{YS} should be expected to be very small for inner-city black youths and therefore unlikly to be decisive in determining the sign of equation (4). If P^{LS} is positive (or sufficiently small in absolute value if negative), the sign of L^{*S} will be negative, implying that higher status produces lower absenteeism. But if employers providing higher-status jobs are substantially more tolerant of absenteeism (P^{LS} is both negative and of substantial magnitude), L^{*S} may be positive. Thus, the actual effect of job status on absenteeism remains a question for empirical study.

Case 3.   Skills

Consider a variable K that represents the level of industry-specific human capital embodied in a worker. Such capital may be accumulated through on-the-job experience, through organized training, or through both. In general, the more K a worker has, the more costly it is to find someone to replace him. One should therefore expect that firms are less prone to fire people for marginal increases in absenteeism in jobs in which the level of K tends to be high than in jobs in which K tends to be low. In other words, one should expect P^{LK} to be negative for most industries.

If there is any systematic effect of K on job satisfaction, it is likely to be positive, since workers are more likely to enjoy skilled than unskilled work. Other things equal, the marginal utility of being absent is lower when direct enjoyment from work is higher, such that $U_{1a}^{LK} < 0$, and $U_{2a}^{K} > 0$ in equation (5) below. These terms are directly analogous to U_{1a}^{LS} and U_{2a}^{S} in equation (4). In both equations (4) and (5), these terms represent forces pulling absenteeism (leisure) downward.

In equation (5), however, U_{2a}^{K} is more than offset by U_{2b}^{K}, which pulls in the opposite direction. It is reasonable to assume in a model like this, in which the current period is implicitly very short and the menu of opportunities fixed, that the difference $U_{2a} - U_{2b}$ is positive. Nevertheless, $U_{2a} - U_{2b}$ is not the same across all types of people and jobs. People with industry-specific skills will generally have employment alternatives that differ less from their current jobs than the alternatives of most people without such skills. Thus, in most situations the difference $U_{2a} - U_{2b}$ will be a decreasing function of K: $(U_{2a} - U_{2b})^{K} < 0$. Encapsulating the discussion of the last few paragraphs, equation (5) gives the sign of the impact of K on L^*, such that:

$$(5) \qquad sgn \ L^{*K} = sgn \ [U_{1a}^{LK} - P^{LK} \ (U_{2a} - U_{2b}) - P^{L}(U_{2a} - U_{2b})^{K}].$$

To summarize, equation (5) shows that the forces affecting the impact of K on a worker's absenteeism are of three general types: the pleasure of working on a job at which he is skilled; the lower probability of being fired for an incremental increase in absenteeism, since he can less easily be replaced; and the fact that the greater his endowment of specific skills, the better his alternatives relative to his current job, and hence the less he will suffer if he is fired. The first type implies a negative influence of K upon absenteeism, while the second and third imply positive effects. As with the wage rate (w) and status (S), the sign of the influence of K on L cannot be ascertained through theory alone.

The claim that the provision of better jobs will automatically induce better behavior on the part of inner-city black youths is not a conclusion that can be reached directly from microeconomic theory and must, therefore, rest on empirical verification. For the three variables w, S, and K, comparative statics have shown the main forces that might cause absenteeism to increase or decrease with improvement in job quality. The estimated results will distinguish which forces dominate.

7.3 Variable Definitions

The model presented in section 7.2 provides the conceptual foundation of the empirical analysis that follows. A primary goal of the analysis is to establish whether and to what degree the three dimensions of job quality studied above affect absenteeism among members of the NBER data set. To accomplish this, we must hold constant other job characteristics and personality factors that affect absenteeism. The variables employed for this purpose will be defined below. First, however, the three job-quality measures of primary interest—those corresponding to w, S, and K above—will be introduced.

7.3.1 Empirical Measures of Job Quality

Two of the three job characteristics in the model above have close empirical counterparts. A measure of hourly salary ($HRSAL$) on the worker's most recent job has been constructed from the NBER data set by simply dividing weekly before-tax earnings by hours worked for each youth in the sample. To arrive at a measure of job status, three-digit census occupation codes, based on what the respondent said he made or did, have been matched with the Duncan index that ranks occupational codes by socioeconomic status. The Duncan index has been widely employed in the social science literature and is commonly accepted as a measure of how Americans perceive the relative status of occupations. For each young man in the sample the value of the variable $STATUS$ equals the value of the Duncan index for his reported occupation.

Besides $HRSAL$ (w) and $STATUS$ (S), the third job characteristic in the model above is K, which is used to indicate each worker's level of industry-specific skill. Although there is no widely accepted measure of K, there is a relatively new index that comes as close as any we know of to capturing what K represents. Consider the following questions: Why will young people in some occupations remain affiliated with one industry over much of their adult lives, while others will not? What do those who stay within their respective industries have in common, and how do they differ systematically from otherwise similar young people who move around from one industry to another?

Clearly, there are many narrow and specific answers that can be posited to explain behavior in particular industries and occupations. In general, however, besides the possibility that "stable" workers are less desirable workers and hence "locked into" their jobs (an explanation dismissed elsewhere in this paper), there seems to be only one overarching explanation for the systematic patterns we observe: young people in occupations in which industry-specific skills are developed will tend to retain affiliations with the industries in which their skills are most valuable. On the other hand, workers who find it necessary or desirable to move from industry to industry are likely to have less of a comparative advantage in what they are doing for a living at any particular time. They are therefore likely to be easier to replace and to feel less sure of landing jobs as satisfying as the ones they have if they lose them. In other words, they will have higher values of $U_{2a} - U_{2b}$.

This explanation is reinforced by the fact that in certain industries, prospective employers gain valuable information if they know that a job applicant has worked in a job similar to the one for which he is applying. In addition to specific skills, previous experience can be assumed to have provided the applicant with better information about the attributes of the job than is available to other members of the labor force, and therefore to increase the probability that the applicant is better suited to the job than a randomly selected individual. The value of this information will differ systematically across occupations, being higher where the cost of poor worker-to-job matches is higher and where the perception among the general public concerning what the job entails is vague or inaccurate. This effect, together with the development of industry-specific skill, is surely what most often explains the prolonged industry attachment observed for members of certain occupations. They combine to give workers greater security and intra-industry mobility.

Brown (1982) has computed an index from the 1970 Census 1/100 file, using three-digit occupation codes and young men with fewer than ten years of work experience, that ranks each occupation by the probability that a worker in the occupation will be in the same industry at two observations in time five years apart. This index is thus a ranking of occupations by industry retention rates and hence is an appropriate measure to represent the variable K. It is important to realize that these are industry, not firm, retention rates. Indeed, among the young workers analyzed by Brown and in the current study, very few remained with a single employer for anything approaching five years.[8] Brown's index has been matched with our sample, and in the analysis below it will be represented by a variable called *SPECSKILL,* for industry-specific skill. The most common occupations held by members of the

NBER sample, along with the corresponding values of *STATUS*, *SPEC-SKILL,* and mean values of *HRSAL,* are listed in table 7.1.

7.3.2   Other Job Characteristics

The NBER data set permits examination of several other job characteristics besides those discussed above. These include the respondent's perception of whether his boss shows prejudice or favoritism; how long, on average, it takes to learn the job; whether the job is part of a government program (such as CETA); the boss's race; and whether the workplace is unionized. This study tests all of these in various empirical specifications.

The only variable from this list found to bear a significant relationship to absenteeism was the respondent's perception of whether his boss showed "prejudice or favoritism to people on things other than how well they (do/did) on their job." In the results reported below this variable is called *BOSSBIAS*. *BOSSBIAS* equals one for biased bosses and zero for unbiased bosses. Regressions including the other job characteristics listed above (added both collectively and individually to the specifications reported below) show statistically insignificant coefficients and leave the pattern of signs and statistical significance reported below intact. Having been listed here, they therefore will not be further discussed. An interesting aside, however, is that although the race of the boss has little independent effect on absenteeism, it is highly correlated with *BOSSBIAS*. The percentages reporting biased bosses were 15.7 for those with black bosses, 26.0 for those with white bosses, 20.0 for those with Hispanic bosses, and 14.0 for those with bosses of other races. The numbers of respondents reporting bias were 99, 172, 5, and 6 in the four boss's race categories, respectively.

An additional job characteristic is the length of the commute to work in minutes. Clearly, one would expect that the longer or more arduous the journey to work, the more often a person might choose not to go. This is included in the analysis below under the label *COMMUTE*. The mode of commuting was included in a regression not reported here. Its estimated influence was small and statistically insignificant.

7.3.3   The Opportunity Costs of Time at Work

The literature on men in the age bracket under consideration here (16 to 24 years old) tends to emphasize two categories of leisure time activity: illegal activity and "hanging out" with friends. To capture the opportunity cost associated with illegal activity, we included in the regressions a dummy variable called *ILLEGAL*, which takes on a value of one if the respondent reported having received an average of more than one dollar per week of income from illegal sources during the year

Table 7.1 **Most Common Occupations of NBER Survey Respondents**

Occupation Title	1970 Census Code	Sample Size	Duncan Index	Retention Index	Average Hourly Wage (STD.)
Retail Sales Clerks	283	23	41	.5220	$3.22 (1.47)
Shipping Clerks	374	20	24	.5158	4.26 (1.87)
Stock Clerks	381	55	44	.5562	3.76 (2.19)
Teachers' Aids	382	27	63	.6000	3.14 (0.95)
Painters (Construction and Maintenance)	510	40	16	.6623	4.42 (1.91)
Machine Operators (Specified)	690	22	19	.5630	4.16 (1.37)
Delivery Men	705	20	31	.4626	4.51 (3.03)
Construction Laborers	751	52	7	.3924	4.67 (2.49)
Materials Handlers	753	38	9	.5217	4.30 (2.18)
Stock Handlers	762	65	17	.4927	3.68 (1.70)
Cleaners and Charwomen	902	96	8	.4365	3.35 (0.96)
Janitors	903	196	13	.5074	3.53 (1.44)
Cooks	912	72	15	.5172	3.43 (0.79)
Dishwashers	913	35	11	.3846	3.20 (0.49)
Food Service Workers	916	50	11	.3667	3.42 (0.67)
Amusement and Recreation Attendants	932	35	19	.5667	3.07 (0.98)
Child Care Workers	942	34	28	.5455	2.96 (0.53)
Guards and Watchmen	962	54	18	.5944	3.53 (0.73)

Note: Included are all occupations containing 20 or more individuals in the NBER sample. STD = standard deviation.

before the survey. Fourteen percent of the sample fall into the group for whom *ILLEGAL* equals one.

To capture the effect of peer group "street activity," we constructed a variable for the level of employment among close friends. Each respondent was asked whether it was true, somewhat true, or not at all true, that "most of your friends are unemployed." The variable *PEERS* formed from this question had no perceptible relationship to absenteeism. Both simple correlation coefficients and coefficients estimated in multivariate contexts concurred. *PEERS* was therefore omitted from the regressions whose results are reported below. In those in which it was included, it had virtually no impact on the estimated coefficients for the other independent variables.

7.3.4 Personality and Personal Background

An exhaustive array of personality and personal background measures is indispensable in determining whether the coefficients estimated for *HRSAL, STATUS,* and *SPECSKILL* reflect the true effects of job variation rather than the effects of omitted personality measures. Fortunately, the NBER data set contains such an array.

More than 20 personality and personal background measures were tested, both all at once and in a number of different combinations. Except for the small group whose estimates were consistently statistically significant, and which are inlcuded in the results reported below, the inclusion of these additional variables had virtually no effect on the estimated coefficients and t-statistics of *HRSAL, STATUS,* and *SPECSKILL*; these independent variables had small estimated coefficients and produced t-statistics that seldom exceeded 1.0. To check that multicollinearity was not the problem, we tested the variables that typically showed up as insignificant one at a time with the specification for which estimates are reported below. None was statistically significant at or near conventionally accepted levels.

The variables of particular interest that had no significant influence on absenteeism were marital status; the personal importance of religion and the frequency of church attendance; agreement or disagreement with the belief that "if you work hard and get a good education you'll get ahead in America"; peer group employment status; age; and several family background measures, such as whether there was a working adult in the home when the respondent was 14 years old, whether at age 14 he lived with both parents, one parent, or someone else, and whether he lived at home at the time of the NBER interview.

In addition to *ILLEGAL*, which was discussed above, four variables in the personality and personal background category stand apart from those listed in the previous paragraph by having an important impact on absenteeism. They are grades, voter registration status, the respondent's perception of the difficulty of finding another job if he had to, and the number of years of education completed. Apparently, these four variables capture the dominant personality and background traits that are quantitatively important determinants of job attendance. It is highly unlikely that there is some other omitted variable that substantially affects absenteeism and is not highly correlated with at least one of the personality and background variables tested.

As a basis for the variable GRADES, respondents were asked whether in the last year of school completed they earned mostly A's, half A's and half B's, mostly B's, and so on. GRADES thus takes on seven values in our analysis, ranging from 7 for mostly A's to 1 for mostly D's and below. The logical connection of GRADES to absenteeism is straightforward: people who earn high grades are usually more self-disciplined, more conformist, more apt to achieve success through conventional channels, and more eager to please authority figures. Each of these tendencies weighs against the probability of engaging in frivolous absenteeism. GRADES may also indicate more intelligence and therefore individuals who both perceive the consequences of irresponsible behavior and have lower rates of time preference, making them more concerned with the future consequences of current actions.

Being registered as a voter indicates that one has accepted some measure of adult responsibility. A registered voter among youths 24 years of age or under is more likely to be mature and will conduct himself on the job in a fashion consistent with this maturity. VOTE equals one for registered voters, zero for those old enough to vote but not registered, and .52 for those not old enough to be registered (.52 is the fraction of registered voters in the sample among those who are old enough to vote).

Respondents in the NBER survey were asked to rate on a scale of very easy (1), somewhat easy (2), difficult (3), or impossible (4), how hard it would be to find each of six potential jobs: factory laborer, office clerk, check-out clerk in a supermarket, cleaning up neighborhoods, working at a fast-food place, and working at any job at the minimum wage. The question was asked of both employed and unemployed youth. A variable DFINDJ representing the perceived difficulty of finding a job has been constructed as the sum of the numerical answers to these six questions. Thus, the possible range for DFINDJ is from 6, for respondents who answered "very easy" to each job question, to 24, for respondents who answered "impossible" six times. The mean of DFINDJ in the sample is 12.56 with a standard deviation of 3.14. This finding implies that the typical member of the sample did not regard the entry-level labor market as being particularly tight. On the other hand, youths did believe that it was more difficult to find office clerk and factory laborer jobs which they probably regarded as the more attractive possibilities among those listed. Other things equal, we would expect people with low values of *DFINDJ* to be more careless about losing their jobs than people with high values (those who believe jobs are hard to find).

The final personal background variable to be defined is *ED*, which is simply equal to years of schooling completed. *ED* has a mean value in the sample of 10.9 and a standard deviation of 1.5. The sign that should be expected for the relationship between *ED* and absenteeism is not obvious. If the predominant effect of *ED* in the equation is to proxy positive personality traits, then it should be negatively correlated with absenteeism. On the other hand, if people with more education are treated more permissively or have more and better job opportunities than those with less education, then they may be absent more often because they are less afraid of losing their jobs, other factors held constant.

If absenteeism can lead to involuntary dismissal, which our estimates suggest is likely, one might expect a negative relationship between absenteeism and tenure on the job, with the causal link running from absenteeism to tenure. But there is also reason to believe that workers with longer job tenure may be less dispensable and therefore less likely to be fired for any given level of absenteeism. In addition, workers with longer tenure on a job (particularly those who have passed a probationary period) are likely to be governed by more lenient work rules. Both of these factors imply a positive relationship between absenteeism and tenure, and therefore, both *TENURE* and *TENURESQ* have been included in estimated equations.

TENURE is the length of employment on the most recent job and is measured in months. It has a mean of 7.3 and a standard deviation of 10.6. We acknowledge the possibility of simultaneity bias resulting from the effect of absenteeism on involuntary dismissal. Nevertheless, to the extent that the estimated effect of *TENURE* on absenteeism is significant and positive in the results reported below, the negative bias is probably minimal. It is also the case, however, that individuals with very short job tenure may be more likely to answer that they are "never absent" simply because they have not been on the job long enough for their underlying propensities to become evident.

7.4 Determinants of Absenteeism: Estimated Results

7.4.1 Estimation Method

As discussed earlier, the measure of absenteeism used as the dependent variable in this study is derived from answers to the following

question: On your most recent job, "how often would you say you
miss(ed) a day for other reasons besides being sick?" Respondents
were asked to answer: "often," "rarely," "sometimes," or "never."
The young men in our sample are the 71 percent of the NBER sample
who had at least one period of regular employment lasting ten days or
longer during the year preceding the interview. Of that 71 percent, the
number responding with each of the four possible answers is given in
table 7.2. Taking into account that the question excludes sickness as a
reason for skipping work, the distribution of answers seems plausible.

In order for ordinary-least-squares (OLS) regressions to yield best-
linear unbiased estimates, the assumptions of the Gauss-Markov theorem that the error term has an expected value of zero and constant
variance must be satisfied. The theorem fails for qualitative and ordinal
dependent variables that fall into a small number of discrete ordered
categories. Given the assumption that there is some underlying continuous dependent variable that has been partitioned in a monotonic
way and assigned to a small number of discrete categories, OLS regressions will generally produce statistically inconsistent estimates of the
marginal effects of independent variables, appropriately adjusted for
scale. Recognizing this, we have chosen to report both OLS and ordered probit estimates for the effects of the independent variables on
absenteeism.[9]

7.4.2 Estimated Results

Table 7.3 reports the results for the various estimates. The answers
"often," "sometimes," "rarely," and "never" were grouped in three
different combinations for probit estimation. The combination reported
in the second column of table 7.3 takes each of the four as separate
and is called *PROBIT4*. *PROBIT3* pools "often" and "sometimes"
into one category, while keeping "rarely" and "never" separate. The
last column, *PROBIT2*, reports results for a binary probit in which
"rarely" or "never" and "often" or "sometimes" are the two group-

Table 7.2   **Sample Frequencies for Job Behaviors**

	Absenteeism not Due to Illness		Absenteeism Due to Illness		Tardiness	
	Number	Percent	Number	Percent	Number	Percent
Often	29	1.8%	35	2.2%	47	3.0%
Sometimes	138	8.7%	190	12.0%	218	13.8%
Rarely	439	27.7%	547	34.5%	511	32.3%
Never	978	61.7%	812	51.2%	808	51.0%

Note: N = 1584

ings. Because of differences in scaling, the magnitudes of the coefficient estimates are not directly comparable across columns.

Examination of table 7.3 shows that the coefficient estimates are generally twice their standard errors and that, with a couple of interesting and explainable exceptions, the pattern of signs is what would be intuitively expected.

Let us concentrate first on the estimates for the focal job quality measures: *HRSAL, STATUS,* and *SPECSKILL.* These estimates tell an interesting and believable story. In a nutshell, they suggest that youths in the sample value money and status and are better employees the more money and status their jobs afford them, other things equal. At least as far as absenteeism is concerned there is no evidence that the income effect of higher wages dominates the substitution effect.

Table 7.3   Estimated Results for Absenteeism as the Dependent Variable

Independent Variable	OLS	PROBIT4	PROBIT3	PROBIT2
CONSTANT	−.03	−3.20	−2.39	−1.74
	(.18)	(.32)	(.32)	(.50)
HRSAL	−.018	−.033	−.034	−.081
	(.009)	(.020)	(.020)	(.035)
STATUS	−.0034	−.0054	−.0059	−.014
	(.0014)	(.0024)	(.0024)	(.004)
SPECSKILL	.72	1.21	1.24	2.12
	(.22)	(.38)	(.39)	(.60)
BOSSBIAS	.088	.13	.14	.25
	(.048)	(.08)	(.08)	(.12)
COMMUTE	.0020	.0032	.0031	.0042
	(.0008)	(.0013)	(.0013)	(.0019)
ILLEGAL	.15	.25	.27	.24
	(.05)	(.09)	(.09)	(.13)
GRADES	−.032	−.057	−.062	−.060
	(.014)	(.024)	(.024)	(.037)
VOTE	−.10	−.16	−.16	−.24
	(.04)	(.07)	(.07)	(.11)
DFINDJ	−.10	−.015	−.014	−.032
	(.06)	(.010)	(.010)	(.016)
ED	.034	.067	.071	.034
	(.013)	(.023)	(.024)	(.036)
TENURE	.026	.051	.054	.017
	(.007)	(.012)	(.012)	(.017)
TENURESQ	−.00035	−.00086	−.00090	−.00014
	(.0021)	(.00036)	(.00036)	(.00051)

Note: The magnitudes of the estimates are not directly comparable across columns because of scaling. Standard errors are in parentheses.

Similarly, the positive terms in equation (4) showing the effect of status on absenteeism appear empirically to dominate the negative terms. In jobs, however, in which the industry retention rate (and hence *SPEC-SKILL*) is high, young men in the sample were more inclined to be absent than on jobs that, in this dimension, would appear to be less attractive.

Theoretically, the most reasonable alternative interpretation of the results found here is that the estimated coefficients on *HRSAL, STATUS,* and *SPECSKILL* reflect not the impact of job characteristics on employee behavior, but rather the impact of unobserved personality traits. If the market has efficiently sorted the worst workers into the worst jobs and the best workers into the best jobs, and if there exist unmeasured dimensions of worker quality that because of this sorting are highly correlated with job quality, then statistically significant coefficients for the job quality measures might indicate only the effects of these omitted personal characteristics. The weight of evidence, however, is inconsistent with this hypothesis, while being highly consistent with the hypothesis that job characteristics influence worker behavior. Three distinct arguments can be given to support the contention that job quality, not personal characteristics, is responsible for the results.

First, if the estimated results reflect solely an efficient sorting of better and worse employees into more and less attractive jobs, the highly significant coefficient found for *SPECSKILL* has the *wrong* sign. Simple correlations of the characteristics of the respondents with *SPECSKILL* indicate that those youths with high values of *SPEC-SKILL* are the "higher quality" youths. For example, *SPECSKILL* is positively and significantly correlated with grades, employment among the individual's peers, wages, status, the youth's assessment of how satisfied he is with the job, and the tendency to avoid illegal sources of income. Since even the simple correlation between *SPECSKILL* and absenteeism is positive, the estimated impact of *SPECSKILL* on absenteeism should not be a statistical artifact resulting from, for example, some complex form of multicollinearity. Nor does time preference explain this behavior, unless one is willing to make the counterintuitive assumption that workers with the least concern for the future are the most likely to take jobs with high industry retention rates.

Various theoretical explanations for why high levels of industry-specific skills might lead to higher absenteeism were spelled out above in section 7.2.2 (Case 3). The theoretical reasons suggested there were that either the marginal effect of absenteeism on the probability of being punished or involuntarily dismissed from the job is smaller in occupations with high levels of industry-specific skills, or that the average difference between the current job and the next best alternative ($U_{2a} - U_{2b}$) is smaller in those occupations. Employment in a job that requires or teaches an industry-specific skill, or that gives the job holder a credential that leads to long-term association with an industry, also gives the job holder greater general security. Hence, the results found here suggest that greater security may lead to higher rates of absenteeism.

The second argument in support of the interpretation that job quality and not unobserved personal characteristics gives rise to the results found here is that the coefficient estimates for the focal job quality measures are extremely robust to changes in the specification of the estimated equation. If omitting important unobserved or unmeasurable worker traits created seriously biased estimates of the effect of job quality on absenteeism, then these estimates should be very sensitive to the inclusion or exclusion of personality and background variables that would also be correlated with the omitted variables. In fact, the estimated coefficients of *HRSAL, STATUS,* and *SPECSKILL* are very stable. Including in an OLS regression the 20 additional personality and individual background variables that should have been highly correlated with any possible source of omitted-variable bias changed the estimated coefficients for *HRSAL, STATUS,* and *SPECSKILL* from $-.018$, $-.0034$, and $.72$, respectively, to $-.017$, $-.0037$, and $.88$.

The third and perhaps most convincing argument that the estimated relationship between job characteristics and absenteeism is not due to omitted variables comes from analyzing tardiness, absenteeism due to illness, and involuntary dismissals. Of the entire sample of almost 1,600 youths who were employed at the time of the interview or who had been employed at some time during the past year, 90 were not employed at the time of the interview because they had been "discharged or fired" from their last regular job.

The model presented earlier posits that the possibility of being fired is one of the primary disincentives to absenteeism. According to the model, the greater the probability of being fired for a marginal increase in absenteeism, the less the employee will choose to be absent. Similarly, given that absenteeism could cause the employee to face a higher probability of being fired, employees will choose to be absent less often, the greater the relative benefits of remaining employed on the current job.

To confirm that absenteeism does increase the probability of being fired, we conducted a simple binary probit analysis, in which the dependent variable was set equal to zero if the respondent was either employed at the time of the survey or had lost his last job for reasons other than firing or dismissal, and equal to one for those who had been fired or dismissed from their most recent job. Table 7.4 reports the results of this analysis.

Examination of the results shows that, as expected, the probability of being out of work because of dismissal or firing was lower for those

Table 7.4   Binary Probit Results for Dismissed or Fired as the Dependent
                   Variable

Independent Variable	Coefficient	Standard Error
Absenteeism Not Due to Illness	.14	(.05)
Absenteeism Due to Illness	.18	(.05)
Tardiness	.005	(.04)
HRSAL	−.057	(.014)
STATUS	−.0053	(.0024)
SPECSKILL	−.76	(.39)
CONSTANT	.46	(.28)

who were absent less or who had "better" jobs. Tardiness, on the other hand, did not affect the probability of being fired. If the hypothesis that job quality is correlated with absenteeism because of behavioral responses to the probability of being fired (rather than because job quality is capturing the influence of unmeasured personal characteristics) is correct, then tardiness, because it does not affect the probability of being fired, should not be affected by the attractiveness of the job.

Table 7.5 presents four-category ordered probit estimates for absenteeism not due to illness (already seen in table 7.3), absenteeism due to illness, and tardiness, using identical right-hand-side variables. The striking result of this analysis is the difference between the degree of relationship of tardiness to the job quality measures (HRSAL, STATUS, and SPECSKILL) and that of the two forms of absenteeism to these measures. Tardiness is far less closely linked to job quality. The existence of several statistically significant coefficient estimates for other variables in the equation suggests that this lack of statistical significance is not caused by poor data on the dependent variable tardiness. The coefficient estimates for the other variables in the equations indicate that most individual characteristics affect tardiness in much the same way as they affect absenteeism.

If the coefficients for HRSAL, STATUS, and SPECSKILL in the equation for absenteeism not due to illness were capturing hidden effects of personality rather than a behavioral response to job characteristics, the estimated coefficients for these three variables should be much larger and statistically significant in the equation for tardiness, paralleling those in the absenteeism equations. The fact that they are not provides strong support for the interpretation that job quality affects behavior in the manner that the model presented above suggests. Clearly,

Table 7.5 **Estimated Results of Four-Category Ordered Probit for Comparisons of Absenteeism and Tardiness**

	Dependent Variable		
Independent Variable	Absenteeism Not Due to Illness	Absenteeism Due to Illness	Tardiness
CONSTANT	−3.20 (.32)	−2.84 (.30)	−1.73 (.30)
HRSAL	−.033 (.020)	−.009 (.015)	−.008 (.014)
STATUS	−.0054 (.0024)	−.0037 (.0022)	−.0013 (.0022)
SPECSKILL	1.21 (.38)	0.59 (.37)	−0.33 (.33)
BOSSBIAS	.13 (.08)	.045 (.077)	.16 (.08)
COMMUTE	.0032 (.0013)	.0037 (.0012)	.0035 (.0013)
ILLEGAL	.25 (.09)	.10 (.09)	.16 (.08)
GRADES	−.057 (.024)	−.015 (.022)	.008 (.022)
VOTE	−.16 (.07)	−.051 (.069)	−.12 (.07)
DFINDJ	−.015 (.010)	.004 (.009)	−.019 (.010)
ED	.067 (.023)	.006 (.021)	−.003 (.021)
TENURE	.051 (.012)	.080 (.011)	.039 (.011)
TENURESQ	−.00086 (.00036)	−.0014 (.0003)	−.00067 (.00033)

Note: Standard errors are in parentheses.

the interpretation that attributes statistically significant job quality estimates to omitted personal characteristics is inconsistent with the available evidence.

The reasons to expect positive or negative signs on the other variables in the equation for absenteeism were discussed above when these variables were defined. The signs for BOSSBIAS, COMMUTE, ILLEGAL, GRADES, VOTE, and DFINDJ were straightforward to predict and have turned out precisely as expected. The results for BOSSBIAS, COMMUTE, and DFINDJ, like those for HRSAL, STATUS, and SPECSKILL, are further evidence for the influence of incentives on absenteeism. The results for *DFINDJ* are particularly interesting. Apparently, other things equal, workers who think jobs are hard to find do not as often engage in behavior (such as absenteeism) that might cause them to lose the jobs they have.

All four equations presented in table 7.3 show a positive estimate for the impact of increased education on absenteeism. This finding may be symbolic of the fact that workers with more education are more secure in their jobs. It is almost certainly true that they have lower values for $(U_{2a} - U_{2b})$, because education is such an important screening device used by employers. Paradoxically for employers, youths with more education may tend to take advantage of the employer's presumption that they will be more reliable.[10] It is therefore interesting to note that table 7.5 shows no evidence of a link between education and tardiness or absenteeism due to illness. This pattern of results makes perfect sense if employers are less tolerant of absenteeism among those with less education, or if those with less education try harder to avoid being fired because the alternative jobs available to them are less attractive, giving them a higher value of $(U_{2a} - U_{2b})$.[11]

7.5   The Magnitude of the Estimated Effects

The previous section discussed the signs and statistical significance of the coefficients on the variables used to explain absenteeism among the members of the NBER sample. It also presented several reasons for believing that the results reflect actual causal factors rather than statistical artifacts. This section will discuss the magnitude of the effects of job quality and personal factors on absenteeism.

The principal finding is that the effects of job quality and personal characteristics are both substantial and of similar orders of magnitude. The first two tables in this section present a general method of analyzing the magnitude of the effects of the several variables. Both show changes in the probability of different levels of absenteeism that result from changing a single independent variable from one standard deviation below its mean to one standard deviation above its mean, while holding all other independent variables constant at their means. Table 7.6 uses estimates from the *PROBIT4* regression, while table 7.7 uses those from the *PROBIT2* regression.

The numbers in the headings of table 7.6 are the estimated probabilities from *PROBIT4* for each of the four categories, when each of the explanatory variables is equal to its mean value. The means and standard deviations for the explanatory variables are given in the last column. There are three numbers at each independent variable's intersection with each absenteeism category. The top number among the three is the probability of the corresponding absenteeism answer, such

Table 7.6   **The Sensitivity of the Probabilities from the Four-Category Ordered Probit to Changes in the Independent Variables**

Independent Variable	Probability at $x = \bar{x}$, for all x's				
	Often .0166	*Sometimes* .0854	*Rarely* .2952	*Never* .6028	Mean (STD.)
HRSAL	.0139	.0762	.2806	.6293	$ 3.90
	.0197	.0954	.3096	.5753	(2.14)
	−35	−22	−10	9	
STATUS	.0132	.0737	.2763	.6368	23.4
	.0207	.0982	.3136	.5675	(16.1)
	−45	−29	−13	11	
SPECSKILL	.0228	.1023	.3192	.5557	.52
	.0122	.0701	.2697	.6480	(.10)
	64	38	17	−15	
BOSSBIAS	.0188	.0924	.3056	.5832	.21
	.0146	.0798	.2839	.6217	(.38)
	25	15	7	−6	
COMMUTE	.0207	.0982	.3136	.5675	29 min.
	.0132	.0737	.2763	.6368	(23)
	45	29	13	−11	
ILLEGAL	.0207	.0982	.3136	.5675	.14
	.0132	.0737	.2763	.6368	(.35)
	45	29	13	−11	
GRADES	.0139	.0762	.2806	.6293	4
	.0197	.0954	.3096	.5753	(1.4)
	−35	−22	−10	9	
VOTE	.0139	.0762	.2806	.6293	.52
	.0197	.0954	.3096	.5753	(.42)
	−35	−22	−10	9	
DFINDJ	.0146	.0798	.2839	.6217	13
	.0188	.0924	.3056	.5832	(3)
	−25	−15	−7	6	
ED	.0217	.1013	.3174	.5596	10.9 yrs.
	.0125	.0713	.2719	.6443	(1.5)
	55	35	15	−14	

Note: On each line, all independent variables are at their means except for the variable on the line under examination. In each set of three statistics, the first measures the probability of the column's answer (often, sometimes, rarely, or never) when the variable on the line is one standard deviation above its mean; the second measures the probability when the variable is one standard deviation below its mean; and the third measures the difference between the first two, as a percentage of the column probability, when the column probability is calculated with all independent variables at their means.

STD = standard deviation.

as "sometimes", when the variable listed on the respective row, (such as *COMMUTE*), is set at one standard deviation above its mean and all other independent variables are equal to their means. Thus, for example, the estimated probability that the answer "sometimes" would have been given by a respondent who was "average," except for the fact that his commute was one standard deviation longer than the "average" respondent's, is .0982. The second line gives the probability (.0737) that he would have said "sometimes" if, instead, his commute had been one standard deviation below the mean of *COMMUTE*. The number on the third line is formed by subtracting the number on the second line from the one on the first and then dividing by the probability (given at the heading to the column) of the relevant answer ("sometimes") with all variables (including *COMMUTE*) set equal to their means. Thus, the third statistic is a measure of the predicted percentage change in the probability of the corresponding answer for a shift of the independent variable from one standard deviation below its mean to one standard deviation above. For *COMMUTE,* a move from one standard deviation below its mean to one standard deviation above causes the probability of the answer "sometimes" to increase by 29 percent of the probability of this response when evaluated at mean values.

Table 7.7 summarizes the quantitative importance of the changes in the independent variables, using the *PROBIT2* estimates. With all variables at their means, the predicted probability of "sometimes" or "often" from *PROBIT2* is .0885. Each entry in the first column of the table gives the equivalent probability when the other variables remain at their means but the variable on its row is one standard deviation above its mean. The second column provides the related probability for the variable at one standard deviation below its mean. The third column equals the value in the first column minus the value in the second; and the fourth column gives the value in the third as a percentage of the probability at the sample mean, .0885.

Tables 7.6 and 7.7 both show that job and personal characteristics can be quantitatively important in determing the level of absenteeism. Movements from one standard deviation below the mean to one standard deviation above the mean in various characteristics typically change the probability of frequent ("often" or "sometimes") absenteeism by 25 to 75 percent of its value when all variables are at the sample mean. The fundamental point demonstrated is that incentive-related indices (including the job characteristics, as well as *COMMUTE* and *DFINDJ*) have effects on absenteeism that are of a comparable order of magnitude to those of personal characteristics, such as *ILLEGAL, VOTE,* and *GRADES*.

A more intuitive understanding of how the probability of frequent absenteeism varies as a function of changes in the independent variables can be gained from examining tables 7.8 and 7.9.

Table 7.7   **Effects of Changes in the Independent Variables on Frequent Absenteeism, Based on Binary Probit**

Independent Variable	Pr for x̄ + S.D.	Pr for x̄ − S.D.	Difference	Difference as % of Pr for X̄	Mean	(STD)
HRSAL	.0643	.1190	−.0547	62	3.90	(2.14)
STATUS	.0571	.1314	−.0743	83	23.4	(16.1)
SPECSKILL	.1271	.0594	.0677	76	.522	(.009)
BOSSBIAS	.1038	.0749	.0289	33	.207	(.376)
COMMUTE	.1038	.0749	.0289	33	29.2	(22.7)
ILLEGAL	.1020	.0764	.0256	29	.143	(.35)
GRADES	.0764	.1020	−.0256	29	4.04	(1.35)
VOTE	.0735	.1056	−.0321	36	.52	(.42)
DFINDJ	.0735	.1056	−.0321	36	12.6	(3.14)
ED	.0808	.0968	−.0160	18	10.9	(1.52)

Note: Frequent absenteeism equals the responses "often" or "sometimes." The probability for X̄ = .0885. STD = standard deviation.

Table 7.8   Probabilities of Frequent Absenteeism, Based on Binary Probit, for Selected Job and Worker Characteristics

Independent Variable	Job or Worker Characteristic			
	(1)	(2)	(3)	(4)
HRSAL	$3.00 .1003	$4.00 .0869	$5.00 .0749	$6.00 .0643
HRSAL (w)	Dishwashers $3.20 .0985	Painters $4.42 .0823	Guards/Watchmen $3.53 .0934	Stock Clerks $3.76 .0901
STATUS (S)	Dishwashers 11 .1210	Painters 16 .1075	Guards/Watchmen 18 .1020	Stock Clerks 44 .0505
SPECSKILL (K)	Dishwashers .38 .0495	Painters .66 .1446	Guards/Watchmen .59 .1151	Stock Clerks .56 .1038
w,S,K	Dishwashers .0778	Painters .1611	Guards/Watchmen .1401	Stock Clerks .0604
COMMUTE	35 Minutes .0912	25 Minutes .0853	15 Minutes .0793	5 Minutes .0735
BOSSBIAS	Yes .1251	Yes .1251	No .0808	No .0808
ILLEGAL	Yes .1271	Yes .1271	No .0838	No .0838
GRADES	Mostly D .1210	Mostly C .0985	Mostly B .0793	Mostly A .0630
VOTE	No .0912	No .0912	Yes .0721	Yes .0721
DFINDJ	Impossible .0444	Difficult .0643	Somewhat easy .0918	Very easy .1271
ED	9 Years .0793	10 Years .0838	11 Years .0885	12 Years .0951
Column Probability	.1335	.2776	.0655	.0028

Note: Frequent absenteeism equals the responses "sometimes" or "often."
For variables in each row, variables in the other rows are set at the sample mean.
Column probabilities are evaluated using all values in the column except that for *HRSAL* (w) from the second row; the value for *HRSAL* is taken from the first row. Values in this table may not be representative of variation within the sample.

Each row of table 7.8 presents four selected values of the associated independent variable. Beneath each value is the probability of frequent absenteeism (derived from the *PROBIT2* equation), evaluated at the given value of the independent variable and the sample mean for all the other independent variables. The fifth row, labeled "*w, S, K,*" shows the probabilities of frequent absenteeism when all three of the variables *HRSAL*, *STATUS*, and *SPECSKILL* are given the value that holds for the occupation given in the column and when all other independent variables are given the sample mean value. The last row of the table, labeled "column probability," indicates the probability of frequent absenteeism for a composite "person" formed by combining all of the characteristics in the column (including the value of *HRSAL* given in the first row). These composites are meant to give an insight into the sensitivity of the analysis; any resemblance to an actual individual is purely coincidental.

Table 7.9 is probably the easiest to understand and the most interesting of the four tables in this section. Using "composite people," it provides a direct comparison of the relative effectiveness of changing job or personal characteristics in attempting to induce less absenteeism among young black men. Five occupations—janitors, dishwashers, retail sales clerks, delivery men, and a hypothetical "good job" with both *HRSAL* and *STATUS* one standard deviation above their sample means—are combined with three hypothetical young men: one attractive young man who is registered to vote, earns no illegal income, and was a "B" student; one who is not registered, earns no illegal icome, and was a "C" student; and one who is not registered, does earn illegal income, and was a "C" student. Values of the other variables for these composite young men (*COMMUTE, BOSSBIAS, DFINDJ,* and *ED*) are set at sample means.

Inspection of table 7.9 shows again that the occupational and personal factors are of similar quantitative importance. The youth with the worst personal characteristics (youth C) holding the job that most encourages absenteeism (janitor) would have a .2119 probability of reporting frequent absenteeism. Changing this youth to the one with the best characteristics (youth A) would reduce the predicted probability of frequent absenteeism to .0901. Similarly, giving youth C an attractive job (delivery man) reduces his predicted probability of frequent absenteeism to .1075.

A phenomenon discussed earlier and readily apparent in tables 7.8 and 7.9 is that simply improving job quality may not lead to lower absenteeism. In particular, if specific skill (which may proxy job security) is increased along with wages and status, there may be offsetting effects, and the direction of the impact of improved job quality on absenteeism is of ambiguous sign. Notice that although dishwasher is

Table 7.9   **Probabilities of Frequent Absenteeism for Three Hypothetical Youths in Five Alternative Occupations**

	Occupation				
Job Characteristics	Janitor	Dishwasher	Retail Sales	Delivery Man	Hypothetical High Wage and Status
Mean HRSAL	$3.53	$3.20	$3.22	$4.51	$6.04 ($\bar{w}$ + STD)
STATUS	13	11	41	31	40 ($\bar{S}$ + STD)
SPECSKILL	.51	.38	.52	.46	.52 ($\bar{K}$)
Probability of Frequent Absenteeism:					
Youth C	.2119	.1539	.1251	.1075	.0869
Youth B	.1492	.1038	.0833	.0694	.0548
Youth A	.0901	.0594	.0455	.0375	.0329

Note: Frequent absenteeism equals the responses "sometimes" or "often."
Youth C is not registered to vote, earns illegal income, and was a "mostly C" student. Youth B is not registered to vote, does not earn illegal income, and was a "mostly C" student. Youth A is registered to vote, does not earn illegal income, and was a "mostly B" student. The other variables have been set equal to the sample means. STD = one standard deviation.

the least attractive job in table 7.9, it does not have the highest probability of frequent absenteeism. The positive effects of increasing the wages and status of a dishwasher when he moves to being a janitor are more than offset by the negative impact of higher *SPECSKILL.*

7.6 Summary and Conclusions

Few readers, if any, will be surprised at the extent to which personal factors have been shown by this study to affect absenteeism. The study's findings simply confirm widely held beliefs about this problem. The main finding that may challenge the usual assumptions is that the labor market behavior of black youths is significantly affected by job-related incentives, including aspects of job quality. These effects are complex, and whether improving job quality leads to more or less absenteeism depends on the specific manner in which quality is improved.

The empirical findings of the study strongly support the view that inner-city black youths behave rationally and that they can, therefore, be induced to modify their behavior by appropriately designed and targeted incentives, both "carrots" and "sticks". The main "stick" in the labor market under analysis is the possibility of being involuntarily dismissed (fired) for unsatisfactory behavior. Absenteeism was found to increase the probability of being fired, while tardiness has essentially no impact on the probability of being fired. Hence, although tardiness may not go unnoticed, it does not carry nearly as heavy a potential penalty as absenteeism. Accordingly, youths with higher-status, higher-wage jobs that they should want to keep are absent less often than those on poorer jobs, but they are tardy just as frequently.

An interesting and important finding is that in one aspect of job quality, improvement apparently diminishes a youth's fear of being fired and therefore leads to more absenteeism. This is the aspect measured by *SPECSKILL,* which represents the probability that the worker will be in the same industry five years in the future. The increased level of industry attachment associated with higher values of *SPECSKILL* is presumed to reflect industry-specific skills and credentials that both increase the value of the worker to his current employer (reducing the likelihood of firing for some worker behaviors) and facilitate mobility from firm to firm within the industry. Other things equal, a worker with higher *SPECSKILL* not only should be less likely to be fired for a given level of absenteeism, but also should experience shorter durations of involuntary unemployment and, if discharged, be more likely to find a job of similar quality to that of the job he lost. Thus, it is perfectly rational for workers in what are essentially *less* dead-end jobs to be absent *more* often than their counterparts in jobs that teach fewer skills and confer less valuable credentials.

Just as the fear of being fired seems to be less effective in discouraging absenteeism among youths who have more industry-specific skills and who presumably would have less trouble acquiring new employment, the fear of job loss appears to be a more effective deterrent the more difficult the individual thinks it will be to find alternative employment. The variable *DFINDJ* (which measures this expected difficulty) is estimated to have a significant effect on whether the youth is frequently absent. Simple correlations show that *DFINDJ* is greater among youths with low scores on background and personal indices, who in turn should be less attractive to employers. In the same vein, years of education, which is often viewed as a sign of worker quality, has a small but significant positive impact on absenteeism; however, this relationship may reflect a sample-selection problem inherent in the NBER data.

Because incentives seem to work so powerfully, the design and targeting of inducements to greater worker reliability is a tricky process. Program operators may be disappointed to find that unless carefully structured, supposedly better opportunities may actually lead to less desirable behavior. What is needed, then, are policy approaches that offer attractive opportunities along with strict mechanisms to hold youths accountable for their performance. This might involve a well-coordinated evaluation and referral system through which past performance could have a direct link to future opportunities.

There are other important issues that we, as economists, less typically discuss but that are centrally related to the topic under analysis. These involve the relationship between the inner-city black youth and his employer. As previously mentioned, the variable in the estimated equations called *BOSSBIAS* measured whether the youth believed his supervisor showed bias against individuals on some basis other than how well they performed their jobs. Twenty percent of the youths in the sample believed that their bosses showed such a bias. *BOSSBIAS* was estimated to have a significant impact on absenteeism, with a youth who believed his boss to be biased having had a 50 percent greater probability of being frequently absent than one who did not hold such a belief (see table 7.8). The relationship of this variable to tardiness was even stronger (see table 7.5). Some of this effect may, of course, be the result of youths with poor behavior eliciting strong responses from their supervisors, thereby causing the youths to feel that they are being "picked on." Whichever the dominant direction of causality in this relationship, given strong preconceptions on both sides, there may be a large element of a self-fulfilling prophesy at work here. In any event, these findings strongly suggest that the employer-employee relationship should be a fruitful topic for both further research and employer and community action.

The estimated results showed several direct relationships between personal characteristics and absenteeism, each with the expected sign. Youths with over $50 of illegal income in the past year were estimated to be one and one-half times more likely to be absent frequently than those who did not have such income (see table 7.8). Although this finding may, in part, represent the opportunity costs of time spent at work, it is more likely to be a proxy for the type of individual and his value system. Grades and voter registration were other personal characteristics that strongly predicted employee dependability. The results of this study suggest that grades may be a more reliable criterion by which to screen job applicants than the more commonly used criterion of the level of education attained.

Finally, we turn to the issue of unemployment. Lowering the extent of absenteeism among inner-city black youths may ultimately lead to a substantial reduction in their level of unemployment. It is unlikely, however, that a change in the frequency of involuntary dismissals will be an important contributing factor. Although the probability of being fired is significantly related to absenteeism, dismissals in the NBER sample accounted for a relatively small percentage (less than 15 percent) of separations. Further, if the probability of having been "fired from the last job" for youths in the sample who were absent "often" or "sometimes" had been equal to the lower probability experienced by those who were absent "rarely" or "never," the fraction of the sample that was not employed at the time of the interview would have been only 0.6 percent lower. This effect is clearly negligible in light of the fact that 60 percent of those who had worked at some point in the past year were not employed (either unemployed or not desirous of employment) at the time of the survey.

If a change in the level of absenteeism, or in behavior more generally, is to affect the level of unemployment among these youths, it will be by improving their attractiveness to *potential* employers and thereby their position in the hiring queue. If stronger incentives for good behavior are developed and maintained, and good referral mechanisms are implemented so that those who have been dependable employees can be easily identified by potential employers, our research indicates that inner-city black youths will respond to these incentives by becoming more reliable employees. And if they become more reliable, employers will be encouraged to hire them for better jobs, thereby setting in motion a potential upward spiral in these youths' employment opportunities.

Notes

1. Crude measures of absenteeism can be computed from Current Population Survey (CPS) data. Specifically, those individuals who usually worked 35 or more hours a week at a job but who, in the survey week, worked fewer than 35 hours were asked the reason for this discrepancy. In the May 1979 CPS extract (for a time period roughly coincident with that in the NBER survey), 1.5 percent of adult white men, 1.9 percent of adult black men, 2.0 percent of young white men, and 3.0 percent of young black men reported working a short week for personal, nonillness reasons. Given the sample sizes involved, these percentages represent a differentially high absenteeism rate for young black men that is highly statistically significant. The CPS data are not sufficiently well measured to support a statistical study of the causes of these intergroup differences.

2. Simultaneity bias resulting from causation running from current absenteeism to job characteristics is not a problem, since the observed absenteeism occurred after the job was acquired, while tenure in the sample was typically so short that it is unlikely that many respondents had either received or failed to receive wage increases or promotions based on their current job performance (including their absenteeism record).

3. Previous studies include Allen (1981a and 1981b), Ehrenberg (1970), Reza (1975), Thomas (1980), and Winkler (1980). Most studies of absenteeism have been done by psychologists or management scientists, who generally attribute absenteeism to job dissatisfaction and the inadequacy of specific personnel policies (see Steers and Rhodes 1978). Although the theoretical approaches in these studies provide useful insights, they leave many of the questions that economists ask unanswered.

4. For an analysis of absenteeism that also relys on the rigidity of contracted wages and conditions of employment, see Reza (1975).

5. Obviously, this value represents a combination of the expected values from the best available alternative job and unemployment along with the probabilities of these two states.

6. The prevalence in such jobs of inconsistent and arbitrary personnel practices is frequently also mentioned. Although we will not discuss this aspect of menial jobs in the formal model, it is at least partially captured in the empirical analysis that follows by a variable measuring perceived bias on the part of the worker's supervisor.

7. It should be acknowledged here that the "environment" of a "good" job and the hope and self-respect such a job may engender in the worker might cause tastes to change. If this is the case, the tools of economic analysis, including the comparative statics that follow, may fall short of achieving their purpose.

8. It should be noted that higher industry retention rates do not necessarily imply longer tenure with any given employer.

9. Readers unfamiliar with the ordered probit estimation technique are referred to McKelvey and Zaroina (1975).

10. Nonetheless, we can offer no good reason why employers should hold onto such a presumption in the face of experience to the contrary.

11. An alternative explanation, discussed by others working with the NBER sample (see Bound 1983) is that education in the sample is highly correlated with age and that "good," older workers have moved out of the sample areas (the poverty tracts) because they have succeeded, leaving only the "poorer," older youths (and younger teenagers of all qualities) remaining behind to be included in the sample.

References

Allen, S. G. 1981a. Compensation, safety, and absenteeism: Evidence from the paper industry. *Industrial and Labor Relations Review* 34: 207–18.

Allen, S. G. 1981b. An empirical model of work attendance. *Review of Economics and Statistics* 63: 77–87.

Anderson, E. 1980. Some observation on black youth employment. In *Youth Employment and Public Policy*, ed. B. Anderson and I. Sawhill. Englewood Cliffs, N.J.: Prentice-Hall.

Banfield, E. 1974. *The unheavenly city revisited*. Boston: Little, Brown.

Bound, J. 1983. *NBER minority youth survey undercount*. Unpublished memorandum. Cambridge, Mass.: NBER.

Brown, C. 1982. Dead-end jobs and youth unemployment. In *The youth labor market problem*, ed. R. Freeman and D. Wise. Chicago: University of Chicago Press.

Clark, K., and L. Summers. 1982. The dynamics of youth employment. In *The youth labor market problem*, ed. R. Freeman and D. Wise. Chicago: University of Chicago Press.

Ehrenberg, R. G. 1970. Absenteeism and the Overtime Decision. *American Economic Review* 60: 352–57.

Freeman, R., and D. Wise. 1982. The youth labor market problem: Its nature, causes, and consequences. In *The youth labor market problem*, ed. R. Freeman and D. Wise. Chicago: University of Chicago Press.

McKelvey, R., and W. Zaroina. 1975. A statistical model for the analysis of ordinal level dependent variables. *Journal of Mathematical Sociology* 4: 103–20.

Reza, A. 1975. Labor supply and demand, absenteeism, and union behavior. *Review of Economic Studies* 42: 237–47.

Steers, R., and S. Rhodes. 1978. Major influences on employee attendance: A process model. *Journal of Applied Psychology* 63: 51–61.

Thomas, R.B. 1980. Wages, sickness benefits, and absenteeism. *Journal of Economic Studies* 7: 51–61.

Winkler, D. 1980. The effects of sick-leave policy on teacher absenteeism. *Industrial and Labor Relations Review* 33: 232–40.

Comment   Charles Brown

Conclusive research on the effects of job characteristics on labor market outcomes has often proven difficult, both because the relevant job characteristics are difficult to measure and because the issue of omitted worker characteristics keeps arising. Ferguson and Filer's conclusions about the effects of job characteristics on absenteeism are therefore likely to be controversial. Their analysis of the effects of measured worker characteristics is less controversial, but no less interesting.

Charles Brown is associate professor of economics, University of Maryland, and research associate, National Bureau of Economic Research.

The theoretical section of the paper investigates the comparative static effects of changes in a job's wage, status, and level of industry-specific human capital (K) on absenteeism. This investigation requires some armchair psychology, since cross-partial derivatives of the utility function are usually required. But since the theme of this section is the ambiguity of the theoretical results and since that theme is amply justified for wages and status, one's reservations here (does additional status really reduce the marginal utility of money income?) are not very important. The effect of increasing industry-specific human capital seems to me more controversial.

The sign of this effect depends on three effects of K. It depends positively on U^{LK}, the effect of K on the marginal utility of leisure; negatively on P^{LK}, the effect of K on the marginal impact of leisure (that is, absenteeism) on the probability of discharge; and negatively on $(U_{2a} - U_{2b})^K$, the effect of K on the utility difference between holding the current job and finding another job in the next period. Ferguson and Filer argue that more-skilled jobs are more pleasant, so U^{LK} is negative; that employers lose more from firing skilled workers, so P^{LK} is negative; and that K gives the worker the ability to move to other jobs in the same industry, so (holding the current wage constant) $(U_{2a} - U_{2b})^K$ is negative.

I find the last two arguments, and particularly their juxtaposition, somewhat puzzling. If the skills in question are readily transferrable within an industry, workers should pay the full cost of training, and there is no extra cost to the firm from firing absentee workers. Alternatively, if discharging an absentee worker would be costly to the firm, it should pay a wage somewhat above the alternative wage to discourage absenteeism and reduce discharges. I suspect that the solution to the puzzle lies in what is happening when we compare workers with different levels of industry-specific human capital but equal wages. If the worker with less industry-specific human capital has better luck rather than more general capital, Ferguson and Filer's view may be correct: K would have an element of firm specificity, which explains the reluctance to discharge a worker who has it, and an element of transferability, which luck presumably lacks.

Even then, the reluctance-to-discharge argument may be weak. Suppose one plots P, the probability of discharge, against L, the extent of absenteeism. Such a curve would be upward sloping. Now compare the two curves, for different levels of K. The assertion that P^{LK} is negative says that the $P(L)$ curve will be flatter with more K. But $P(L)$ should be zero at low levels of L, and equal to one at very high levels of L, for any value of K. If the two $P(L)$ curves coincide at zero absenteeism and at extreme absenteeism, it is impossible for one curve to be uniformly flatter than the other. If one interprets P as the probability of discharge for all causes, then $P(L)$ is probably lower for those with specific human capital at low levels of L but roughly the same (that is, one) at high levels of L. In this case, $P(L)$ could be uniformly lower for the worker with more K, but again could not be uniformly flatter (indeed, it could be uniformly steeper).

My skepticism about the authors' analysis on this point should not be overstated. I read their discussion to say that, on a priori grounds, greater industry-specific human capital could quite plausibly increase absenteeism. My own prior is that such a response is perhaps possible, but certainly not likely.

In the transition from theory to evidence, the measurement of the variables used becomes important. The NBER survey data contain some very interesting information here; it is used well and supplemented by two indices based on the respondents' occupation, the Duncan socioeconomic status score and the industry retention rate of the occupation. The authors interpret the latter as a measure of industry- rather than firm-specific skill. I am not certain that this interpretation is warranted, especially since in the NLS youth sample over 80 percent of the industry stayers were firm stayers (Brown 1982, 44, n. 13).

The empirical results are very interesting. The virtues of a special-purpose survey are evident in the wide range of variables not available to previous researchers. One very striking result is the list of variables that proved unrelated to absenteeism. Perhaps the most surprising of these are age and marital status, because both are regarded by employers as signs of dependability.

Among the variables that do matter, the results for personal attributes are strikingly in line with expectations, except for education (and I find Ferguson and Filer's explanation more plausible than any alternative I can invent). Among the job characteristics, wage and status reduce absenteeism, while the perception that one's boss is biased and commuting distance increase it. All these findings are in line with one's expectations, though the findings for wage and status could not be proven in a formal sense. Increasing the industry-specific human capital measure increases the absenteeism rate. As I have indicated above, I am not comfortable with this result. To be fair, I cannot think of a plausible after-the-fact rationalization of it.

Are the job characteristics really job characteristics? I agree with the authors that the omitted-variables story does not explain the negative effect of the industry-specific human capital measure on absenteeism. I find the robustness of the results to the addition of many other personal characteristics reassuring, although I wish the survey provided information on the extent of absenteeism on the previous job for use as a control variable.

I am less convinced by the final argument the authors offer on the issue of absenteeism. They observe that personal reliability should be reflected in a lack of absenteeism and a lack of tardiness. On the other hand, if the probability of losing one's job because of unreliability is the key (unobserved) job characteristic, measured job characteristics will be related to absenteeism and tardiness only to the extent that absenteeism and tardiness are in turn related to the probability of discharge. Ferguson and Filer find that although their job characteristics predict absenteeism, they do not bear much relationship to tardiness; moreover, though absenteeism is related to the probability of discharge, tardiness is not. This says that "better late than never" is truer than we realized, but that "better timely than tardy" is not. Even if tardiness is unrelated to discharge, one still wonders why the difficulty of finding another job should be negatively related to tardiness (table 7.5). Thus, I find the tardiness results more a puzzle than a proof that the job characteristics are in fact measuring just job characteristics.

However one labels them, the job characteristics and personal attributes used in the final model do have effects on absenteeism that are fairly characterized as large. But since discharges are a small share of separations in this sample, and the effect of absenteeism on discharges is positive but not enormous, the effect of absenteeism on unemployment caused by discharges is "small." Of course, absenteeism can affect unemployment in other ways: by making new jobs harder to find; by making the new job lower paying and hence less worth keeping; or by creating tensions with one's employer that lead to "quits." Thus, Ferguson and Filer's results do prove to be a worthwhile contribution to the literature on black youth unemployment.

Taken as a whole, their study isolates quite a few important predictors of absenteeism and finds that several others do not matter. An interesting possibility for future research would be to compare factors considered by employers to predict absenteeism with their actual results. My own impression is that age, education, and marital status are widely used as indicators of reliability, while grades are rarely and voter registration never used. Such a negative relationship between employer practice and the findings of this study would suggest that there is much yet to be done to understand the economics of absenteeism.

References

Brown, Charles. 1982. Dead-end jobs and youth unemployment. In *The youth labor market problem,* ed. R. Freeman and D. Wise. Chicago: University of Chicago Press.

IV   Causes: Supply

8 Market Incentives for Criminal Behavior

W. Kip Viscusi

8.1 Introduction

Since the seminal article by Becker (1974), the economic analysis of criminal behavior has focused on the economic incentives to engage in illegal actions. These incentives are the integral components of a model of the rational choice to engage in criminal acts. According to this model, if the expected rewards from criminal behavior exceed the net benefits of alternative pursuits, the individual will choose to engage in crime.[1] Crime is not fundamentally different from legitimate occupational pursuits. The expected losses from sanctions against crime enter the criminal choice decision in much the same way as, for example, the nonpecuniary aspects of a job would in the choice of employment.

Consider a theoretical framework in which there are three components to the individual's choice: the expected financial gains from crime, the expected legal sanctions against crime, and the expected job income if the individual chooses not to engage in crime. It should be emphasized that the expected values of these three factors are based on the individual's subjective assessment of the probabilities involved; one need not assume that the individual has full knowledge of the true probabilities affecting the decision. For simplicity let the time allocation decision be a discrete choice between crime and noncriminal employment. Then, the individual will become a criminal if:

$$
\begin{bmatrix} \text{expected} \\ \text{gains from} \\ \text{crime} \end{bmatrix} - \begin{bmatrix} \text{expected} \\ \text{legal} \\ \text{sanctions} \end{bmatrix} > \begin{bmatrix} \text{expected} \\ \text{job} \\ \text{income} \end{bmatrix},
$$

W. Kip Viscusi is professor of economics, Northwestern University, and research associate at the National Bureau of Economic Research.

which can be rewritten as

$$(1) \quad \begin{bmatrix} \text{expected} \\ \text{gains from} \\ \text{crime} \end{bmatrix} - \begin{bmatrix} \text{expected} \\ \text{job} \\ \text{income} \end{bmatrix} \equiv EXYGAP > \begin{bmatrix} \text{expected} \\ \text{legal} \\ \text{sanctions} \end{bmatrix}.$$

Using data from the NBER Survey of Inner-City Black Youth, I will construct an explicit measure of *EXYGAP* for each of the respondents in the sample based on his assessment of his criminal and legitimate earnings prospects. Also included in the analysis will be information on whether the respondent believed that crime offers greater rewards than employment does. These measures therefore offer the opportunity for a very explicit test of the role of economic incentives in determining criminal behavior. In that regard, this study is distinctive from all previous analyses.

The focus of the existing empirical literature on crime is quite different from that in this study. With one principal exception, recent studies such as Ehrlich (1973, 1975) have focused on aggregative data by location, using either a cross-sectional or a time-series approach. Some studies reviewed in Freeman (1983) take the form of social experiments, thereby raising additional problems of interpretation. For example, was an ex-offender more responsive to the "supported work" experiment than he would have been to market incentives?

The most successful vein of research has been on the deterrent effect of legal sanctions.[2] The legal sanction variables in the aggregative studies include such measures as the average length of prison terms, the arrest rate per crime, the conviction rate per crime, and the imprisonment rate per crime for a particular city or state. In Witte's (1980) study of the criminal behavior of released prisoners, the individual's frequency of arrests and convictions before his prison term was used as the deterrence proxy. Although many of these studies have provoked considerable controversy, the overall thrust of their results is that criminal deterrence clearly decreases criminal activity.

A second line of research has been to examine the linkage between crime and the labor market, principally the relationship between unemployment and crime. In terms of the criminal incentives discussed above, higher unemployment rates should lower the expected-job-income component of *EXYGAP*, thus enhancing the attractiveness of crime. Diminished job prospects also reduce the opportunity costs of incarceration, since the forgone earnings will be less, thereby reinforcing the job-income effect. Although there are many who strongly believe that these relationships hold, there has never been any strong empirical support for the crime–labor market linkage. The empirical impact of the unemployment variable is typically not as strong as that of the deterrence variables. As Freeman (1983, 106) notes in a recent critical survey of the crime literature, "The bulk of the studies examined here show some connection between unemployment (and other labor market variables) and crime, but they fail to show a well-defined, clearly quantifiable linkage."

The source of the ambiguity varies according to the type of study. Of the ten time-series analyses reviewed by Freeman, nine revealed a crime–labor market linkage, but this effect was not as strong as the deterrence variable in the three studies that examined both effects. In a regression of crime rates on unemployment and a time trend, Freeman (1983, 96–98) found a positive crime-unemployment relationship that fell just short of that required to pass the usual tests of statistical significance. A major inherent drawback of these time-series studies is the extreme collinearity of the aggregative data. Moreover, even if there is an observed effect, one cannot ascertain whether unemployment fluctuations influence the level of crime or simply its timing. Individuals may simply postpone their criminal pursuits until they have more free time during the periods of temporary unemployment.

The implications of the 15 cross-section studies also reviewed by Freeman are more mixed. Unemployment and income measures (such as the percentage of the population in poverty) had no strong effects in the correct direction in more than one-third of the studies, whereas the deterrence variables exhibited predictive strength in two-thirds of the studies.

This impression of the weak performance of the labor market variables persists in studies of individual data and social experiments. In her study of 641 prisoners released in North Carolina, Witte (1980) obtained conflicting results with the wage variable (statistically significant effects with differing signs and some insignificant effects) and an unexpected negative effect of unemployment on crime.

Taking these results at face value, one could conclude that the "stick" is clearly more effective than the "carrot" in discouraging criminal behavior. Indeed, one might question whether there is any solid evidence that improved economic opportunities will exert any substantial effect on crime.

Before dismissing the role of the labor market, however, one should recognize the imbalance in the research questions posed by these studies. In terms of the components of equation (1), the empirical studies have provided a comprehensive analysis of the various legal sanction components that contribute to the losses expected from criminal activities. But no study has provided a comprehensive variable pertaining to *EXYGAP*. The most that has been done is to establish proxies for expected job income (such as the national unemployment rate),[3] while the expected-crime-income component has been ignored.

If *EXYGAP* is subject to random measurement error, the importance of the labormarket will be underestimated. In practice, it is likely that the error will not be entirely random, since the expected gains from crime will also be correlated with the expected-job-income proxy. And if opportunities for property crime, for example, decline with increases in unemployment, one cannot even be confident that *EXYGAP* is a positive function of the unemployment rate.

Rather than dismiss the importance of the labor market on the basis of fragmentary and potentially biased evidence, we should conduct a fairer test of the economic motivation hypothesis to assess whether a more refined measure of *EXYGAP* also fails to suggest a significant relationship. This test is the primary focus of this paper.

The nature of the NBER sample makes its data base on crime pertinent to many more issues than simply the professional controversy over the significance of *EXYGAP* or, more generally, the role of economic incentives to commit crime. Youths in the age bracket represented in the NBER sample account for well over half of all criminal arrests, and minority youths account for a disproportionate share of that amount. The sample consequently permits the analysis of a major segment of the urban crime problem.

In addition, minority youths comprise a particularly distressed segment of the labor force, to which their attachment has been notoriously low.[4] A fundamental issue of social policy is the nature of the activity of youths who are not employed or in school. Does this group resort to criminal activity as a means of support? If so, we may be less concerned with their welfare in terms of their income status, but we will be more concerned with the adverse impact of their criminal acts on the rest of society.

Section 8.2 provides a description of the sample and the variables employed in the analysis, with particular attention to the overall relationship between criminal activity and the principal variables of interest. The impact of the various substantive variables, such as *EXYGAP*, on individual decisions to engage in crime is the subject of section 8.3. A closely related issue, how the explanatory variables influence the total level of crime income an individual receives, is the focus of section 8.4. These causal influences differ depending on the type of crime. Section 8.5 offers a detailed analysis of the categories of criminal activity, their interrelationships, and the role of the causal variables in each case. In section 8.6 I consider the behavior of three different subsamples of the population: those in school, those who are employed, and those who are neither in school nor at a job. The role of economic incentives and the patterns of criminal behavior will be shown to be quite different across these groups.

The most important implication of this study is that economic incentives do exert a powerful influence on criminal behavior. Both current employment status and the relative economic rewards from crime are instrumental in both the decision to participate in crime and the intensity of criminal activity.

8.2   The Sample and the Variables

The NBER Survey of Inner-City Black Youth provides detailed information on the respondents' personal characteristics and activities, including criminal behavior. The criminal activity questions, which are of primary interest here, provide a comprehensive perspective on the nature of the youths' illegal activities, their earnings from crime, and their perceptions regarding the attractiveness of criminal pursuits. For ease of reference, table 8.1 provides a glossary of the variables used in this study.

The characteristics of the sample are summarized in table 8.2. Means and standard deviations are provided for the entire sample of 2,358 youths and for the two crime subsamples, the 349 individuals (15 percent) who reported having committed a crime in the past month and the 439 youths (19 percent) who reported having committed a crime in the past year.

Through its focus on the criminal behavior of black youths, the NBER sample addresses a substantial part of the overall crime problem, as youths 15 to 24 years of age account for almost 60 percent of all city arrests. Given this concentration of crime among the young, there must necessarily be a drop in criminal activity as one ages. The peak crime years for the types of activities surveyed by NBER occur in the 15–24 age bracket. Specifically, arrests for robbery, drug law violations, and forgery peak between the ages of 17 and 21, while arrests for auto theft, burglary, and larceny peak among youths 15 to 16 years old.[5]

Within the age span covered by the NBER sample, there is a very small relationship between age and crime. The mean age of those who had engaged in crime is somewhat higher than those who had not (see table 8.2). The year-by-year crime breakdowns in table 8.3 suggest that participation in crime appears to increase somewhat with age, with ages 22 and 24 the peak years. The amount of income earned by those who had committed crimes also tends to follow a similar pattern, as monthly crime income peaks for those aged 20 and 22 while yearly crime income is greatest for those aged 22 and 23.

These data do not indicate any age-related decline in crime. The overall trend is relatively flat, with some evidence of an age-related increase. This pattern will be borne out by all of the subsequent statistical analysis, as will most of the other patterns in table 8.2. Age does not play a major role as an independent, statistically significant

Table 8.1   **Glossary of Variables**

Variable Symbol	Definition
AGE	Age in years
EDUC	Years of schooling
MARRIED	Marital status dummy variable (d.v.); MARRIED = 1 if respondent is married, 0 otherwise.
DRINK	Drinking d.v.; DRINK = 1 if respondent ever drinks beer, or wine, or hard liquor; 0 otherwise.
DRUGS	Drug use d.v.; DRUGS = 1 if respondent ever uses drugs such as cocaine, heroin, barbituates, amphetamines, or LSD; 0 otherwise.
POT	Marijuana use d.v.; POT = 1 if respondent currently uses marijuana, 0 otherwise.
RELIGION	Religion d.v.; RELIGION = 1 if respondent attends religious services at least once a month, 0 otherwise.
JOB	Employed d.v.; JOB = 1 if respondent was working most of the last week, 0 otherwise.
SCHOOL	School d.v.; SCHOOL = 1 if respondent was going to school most of the last week, 0 otherwise.
NOJOBSCHOOL	Neither employed nor in school d.v.; NOJOBSCHOOL = 1 if respondent was neither employed nor in school most of the last week, 0 otherwise.
PROBT	Number of months on probation during the time-line period.
JAILT	Number of months in jail during the time-line period.
GANG	Gang membership d.v.; GANG = 1 if respondent was a member of a gang or had friends in a gang, 0 otherwise.
CNBD	Crime in neighborhood d.v.; CNBD = 1 if respondent believed that crime and violence in the neighborhood was a serious problem, 0 otherwise.
CRIME-MO	Crime d.v.; CRIME-MO = 1 if respondent committed criminal acts in the past four weeks, 0 otherwise.
CRIME-YR	Crime d.v.; CRIME-YR = 1 if respondent committed criminal acts in the past year, 0 otherwise.
EXYGAP	Expected income gap, namely, (adjusted) expected annualized earnings from crime minus expected job income.
YSTREET	Relative rewards d.v.; YSTREET = 1 if respondent believes he could make more on the street than on a legitimate job, 0 otherwise.
CHANCE1	Criminal opportunities d.v.; CHANCE1 = 1 if respondent has opportunities to make money illegally a few times a day.
CHANCE2	Criminal opportunities d.v.; CHANCE2 = 1 if respondent has no chance at all to make money illegally.
BOS	Region d.v.; BOS = 1 if respondent lives in Boston, 0 otherwise.
CHI	Region d.v.; CHI = 1 if respondent lives in Chicago, 0 otherwise.
PHILA	Region d.v.; PHILA = 1 if respondent lives in Philadelphia, 0 otherwise.

Table 8.2   **NBER Sample Characteristics: Means and Standard Deviations within Sample Groups (standard deviations in parentheses)**

Independent Variable	Full Sample	Committed Crime in Past Month	Committed Crime in Past Year
Personal Characteristics			
AGE	19.1	19.8	19.6
	(2.6)	(2.6)	(2.6)
EDUC	10.8	10.8	10.7
	(1.6)	(1.4)	(1.4)
MARRIED	.036	.043	.043
	—*	—*	—*
DRINK	.59	.82	.82
	—*	—*	—*
DRUGS	.03	.16	.14
	—*	—*	—*
POT	.36	.71	.68
	—*	—*	—*
RELIGION	.33	.22	.23
	—*	—*	—*
Labor Market Status			
JOB	.26	.24	.25
	—*	—*	—*
SCHOOL	.40	.22	.25
	—*	—*	—*
NOJOBSCHOOL	.34	.55	.50
	—*	—*	—*
Earnings (month)	$394.80^a	$381.66^a	$379.10^a
	(339.65)	(342.78)	(337.97)
Expected Earnings (year)	$4,366.44	$3,834.15	$4,013.47
	(4,265.12)	(4,646.74)	(4,837.57)
Total Income	$2,837.31^a	$3,961.61^a	$3,832.55^a
	(3,762.57)	(4,809.74)	(4,612.21)
Crime-Related Background			
Probation Dummy Variable	.07	.20	.21
	—*	—*	—*
Probation Months (Conditional)	6.7	7.1	6.9
	(4.4)	(4.2)	(4.3)
PROBT	.04	1.5	1.4
	(2.0)	(3.4)	(3.4)
Jail Dummy Variable	.03	.09	.08
	—*	—*	—*
Jail Months (Conditional)	4.2	4.2	4.0
	(3.5)	(3.3)	(3.1)
JAILT	.01	.03	.03
	(.84)	(1.5)	(1.4)

Table 8.2 (continued)

Independent Variable	Full Sample	Committed Crime in Past Month	Committed Crime in Past Year
GANG	.08 —*	.17 —*	.16 —*
CNBD	.39 —*	.52 —*	.52 —*
Criminal Activity:			
CRIME-MO (past month)	.15 —*	1.0 —*	.97 —*
Number of Crimes (past month)	.24 (.70)	1.6 (1.1)	1.2 (1.7)
Crime Income (past month)	$35.34[a] (219.93)	$254.98[a] (540.76)	$259.34[a] (546.55)
CRIME-YR (past year)	.19 —*	.77 —*	1.0 —*
Number of Crimes (past year)	.33 (.91)	1.9 (1.4)	1.2 (1.7)
Crime Income (past year)	$252.17 (1,551.04)	$1,568.77 (3,715.61)	$1,354.52 (3,383.69)
Expected Crime Income (week)	$441.25[a] (793.55)	$593.94[a] (939.39)	$601.43[a] (903.41)
EXYGAP	$−1,899.25[b] (5,773.49)	$−601.25[b] (6,992.86)	$−754.69[b] (6,927.00)
YSTREET	.28 —*	.48 —*	.48 —*
CHANCE1	.20 —*	.41 —*	.40 —*
CHANCE2	.43 —*	.09 —*	.11 —*
Location			
BOS	.32 —*	.30 —*	.32 —*
CHI	.34 —*	.29 —*	.28 —*
PHILA	.34 —*	.41 —*	.40 —*
Sample Size	2,358	349	439

[a]Nonresponses were set as missing values and not used in calculating means, that is, the sample size differs from that stated.

[b]Nonresponses to the expected crime income question were set equal to zero.

*Standard deviations of 0-1 dummy variables were omitted because they could be calculated from their fraction m in the sample, where the standard deviation is $(m − m^2)^{0.5}$.

Table 8.3   **Criminal Activity in the NBER Sample, by Age**

Age, in Years	CRIME-MO	Average Monthly Crime Income ($)[a] (Conditional)	CRIME-YR	Average Yearly Crime Income ($)[a] (Conditional)
15[b]	0	0	0	0
16	.079	249.38	.124	761.84
17	.128	267.66	.173	1083.74
18	.155	182.96	.185	880.25
19	.152	250.29	.184	2173.76
20	.173	335.24	.206	1601.33
21	.144	190.09	.191	840.03
22	.227	369.51	.271	2285.62
23	.158	181.88	.194	2324.31
24	.223	212.89	.250	1351.20

[a]The crime income figures are conditional on committing crime in the particular time period.

[b]Figures for this age group are not reliable because there was only one 15-year-old in the sample.

influence. This result does not imply that age is not an important determinant of crime, only that age variations within the narrow age range of this sample do not play a pivotal role.

Such a finding is not unprecedented in the crime literature. In a recent study of arrests rates that adjusted for a number of factors, such as differing sizes of offender populations, Blumstein and Cohen (1979) reached a similar conclusion. Although their sample of arrestees was not a random sample from the population, it is not clear a priori how their analysis of the criminal histories of these individuals biased the age-crime results. Blumstein and Cohen found that arrest rates for robbery, aggravated assault, larceny, auto theft, and weapons offenses exhibited no trends, but that arrest rates for burglary, narcotics, and the residual "all other" offense category actually rose with age.

The NBER sample results may provide a more accurate picture of the age-crime linkage than do the aggregative arrest statistics. Moreover, the NBER crime mix is quite different from that in the FBI Uniform Crime Reports. The bulk of the reported crimes in the NBER sample are for numbers and gambling and for drug sales. Since these offenses do not drop off as sharply with age as do, for example, car thefts, it is not surprising that the conventional age effects do not hold.

Two other personal background factors, total years of schooling (EDUC) and marital status (MARRIED), also display no substantial differences across the entire NBER sample and the crime subsamples in table 8.2. The young men surveyed averaged just under an eleventh grade education, and few of them were married, irrespective of their crime status. The variable EDUC shows little variation across the sample, as one would expect in view of legal constraints on schooling.

A series of personal characteristic variables were included as proxies for crime-related personal attributes.[6] There was a higher concentration of crime among those who drank (*DRINK*) or who smoked marijuana (*POT*), but the greatest relative disparity was in the use of more serious drugs (*DRUGS*), which was about five times as frequent among criminals as among the entire sample. Church attendance (*RELIGION*) also was negatively related to illegal activity.

The incentive to engage in crime depends in part on the individual's overall labor market status. An individual can choose to participate in crime as his principal pursuit, to augment schooling or a job with crime, or to engage in no criminal acts. Labor market status is consequently an endogenous part of the crime decision; but given any particular status (such as being in school), that status will also affect the incentives to engage in crime. The results show that a respondent who engaged in crime was almost as likely to be employed (*JOB*) as one who did not. Much more variation is displayed based on whether the respondent was in school (*SCHOOL*) or neither employed nor in school (*NOJOBSCHOOL*).

These general relationships suggest that it is school attendance rather than the level of schooling that is the more salient determinant of criminal behavior among young black men. Employment does not appear to play a key direct role in reducing crime; it does, however, play an indirect role by moving one out of the high crime category of youths who were neither employed nor in school.

It should be emphasized, particularly with respect to the *SCHOOL* variable, that these variables capture not only the influence of educational activities on crime, but also the fact that respondents who chose to attend school had quite distinct personal characteristics that were highly correlated with their decision to self-select into the in-school group. The subsequent empirical results will therefore overstate the likely crime reduction to be obtained by increasing school attendance.

The labor market earnings for all groups in the sample who responded to the wage questions were roughly the same, about $400 per month. Since the group of nonrespondents (those who did not answer the questions) included many individuals without a job, this figure overstates the average earnings across the entire sample. The total expected earnings figure assigns to each respondent his actual wage (calculated on an annual basis using hours data). Those without a job were assigned their expected wage rate.[7] This variable is intended to measure labor market opportunities. In general, there is only a minor difference in criminal status by the level of expected market earnings, which were about 10 percent less among criminals than among the full sample.

The total income figure represents actual income from all sources rather than prospective income. Since many who did not engage in crime were in school, the total income for the full sample was substantially below their expected earnings. Respondents who engaged in crime had higher overall earnings (crime income plus legitimate earnings) than noncriminals, with a gap of roughly $1,000, or about one-third of the average income of the full sample. The criminals thus were not the most impoverished members of the sample but instead appear to have been among those who displayed the greatest initiative with respect to earning income in a variety of ways.

The next set of variables in table 8.2 measures factors quite closely linked to criminal experience. The probation dummy variable represents the fraction in the sample who had been on probation during the past year. This group constituted roughly one-fifth of those who had committed crime. Conditional on being on probation during the time-line period (13 months), the average probation time was seven months. The probation variable used in the statistical analysis is the actual probation time (*PROBT*), which assumes a value of zero if the respondent was not on probation during the period covered by the time line.

The jail variables are defined similarly and are also designed to measure the degree of recidivism in the sample. Whereas 3 percent of the entire sample had been in jail during the past year, the criminal sub-samples contained almost triple this percentage. Among those who had been in jail, the average amount of time spent in jail during the time-line period was about four months. The jail-time (*JAILT*) variable that will be used in the empirical work is the unconditional version of the variable, that is, it assumes a value of zero for respondents who had not been in jail.

The final two crime-related variables may partly reflect the respondent's current decision to engage in crime. First, *GANG* is a dummy variable for whether or not the respondent was a gang member or had friends in a gang. Those who had committed crime were more than twice as likely to meet this criterion as the sample members as a whole. *GANG* is not completely exogenous to the crime decision. An individual may associate with gang members or join a gang to enhance his criminal opportunities. Any prior commitment to engage in criminal acts increased the endogeneity of this variable.

Second, the degree to which the respondent regarded crime in the neighborhood as a serious problem (*CNBD*) was also strongly linked to criminal behavior. This variable may capture greater criminal opportunities and lax criminal enforcement, each of which should boost crime rates. It is also possible that those who committed crime blamed their acts on the alleged prevalence of crime in their neighborhood. To allow for this possibility, the empirical analysis will treat this variable as if it were at least partially endogenous, as in the case of the *GANG* variable.

The variables in the next section of table 8.2 pertain to the degree of criminal activity. They play a central role throughout the analysis. The first issue, which also serves as the basis for the crime subsample stratification, is whether or not the individual engaged in crime. These rates are determined on the basis of self-reported criminal activity. The respondents were asked whether they had participated in any of ten specified criminal activities (such as having "sold or fenced stolen goods"), one of which was "any other illegal activities," The crime participation variables (*CRIME-MO* and *CRIME-YR*) have a value of one if the individual had participated in any of the types of crime during the past month or the past year, respectively. The crime participation rates observed were .15 for *CRIME-MO* and .19 for *CRIME-YR*. The similarity of these figures suggests that crime is a persistent activity of a small group of the sample rather than a random event; if a random event, the past-year crime rate would have been .86.

A different possibility is that the same individuals who were willing to admit to crimes committed in the past month were those willing to discuss their criminal activities over the past year. Suppose, for example, that half of the sample had given a negative response to all of the crime questions, regardless of their actual criminal activities. The observed .15 crime participation in the past month would have been generated if 30 percent of the group willing to discuss crimes had admitted to the crimes, and the .19 annual figure would have been generated if 38 percent of that group had committed crime in the past year. As in the reported data, 79 percent of those who had committed crime in the past month committed crime in the past year. A potential bias arises only if the group unwilling to discuss criminal involvement includes a disproportionately different share of persistent criminals.

Ideally, the use of self-reported data should provide a more refined measure of criminal behavior than is obtained by using, for example, aggregative crime statistics for geographic areas. Particularly in the case of blacks, however, there is a severe underreporting problem. Hindelang, Hirschi, and Weis (1981) estimated that the degree of underreporting by blacks ranges from a factor of 2 to 4. Rather than only one-fifth of the NBER sample participating in crime, the actual amount therefore probably ranges from two-fifths to four-fifths.

This underreporting could potentially create difficulties for the subsequent empirical analysis. The study by Hindelang, Hirschi, and Weis suggests, however, that the behavioral equations for within-group behavior are not distorted; the principal effect of the biased reporting is to shift the constant term rather than the slope in the regressions.[8] Since the NBER sample includes only black youths, the problems that arise in cross-population analyses do not arise here.

When attempting to assess the overall level of criminal behavior, one should nevertheless be cognizant of the likely understatement of criminal activity. Adjustments other than the factor of 2 to 4 yield similar results. Wolfgang, Figlio, and Sellin (1972) estimated that among their sample of nonwhites the rate of juvenile delinquency (namely, police contact at some point in one's youth) was 50 percent. If the true crime rate for the NBER sample is 50 percent rather than the reported annual rate of 19 percent, the reporting bias factor is 2.6, which is just below the midpoint of the earlier range.

A final approach to estimating the actual crime rate of the sample is to use information on the frequency of jail terms for those sampled and to estimate the number of crimes that are likely to be associated with these levels of incarceration. To do this, I employed information for the Washington, D.C. area reported by Blumstein and Cohen (1979), particularly the crime categories in their analysis that were most similar to the NBER groupings. Each crime committed was estimated to have a probability .58 of being reported; if reported, a .15 chance of leading to an arrest; and if arrested, a .16 chance of a conviction that leads to serving time in jail.[9] For every jail term, the number of crimes can be roughly estimated as equalling 74. Three percent of the NBER sample, or 71 respondents, had done time in jail in the past year, implying that the entire sample committed an estimated 5,254 crimes.

If this estimate is valid, the number of crimes was 2.22 times the total sample size. To obtain an estimate of the total number of criminals, one must make some assumptions about the degree of repeated criminal activity. Each respondent who had committed a crime in the past month participated in an average of 1.9 crime categories. If there were no repeated crimes within a crime category during the past month, the underreporting factor would be 6. If crimes in each of these categories were committed twice monthly, an estimate of the total criminal population is three times as large as the reported number. This estimate is consistent with the earlier bias estimates, but is probably more speculative.

The implications of the reporting bias for the relative role of criminal activity is summarized in table 8.4. Based on reported results, crime income accounted for 9 percent of the sample's average income. With an underreporting factor of 3, which I will adopt as the best estimate, crime accounted for 23 percent of the sample's total income. These adjustments take into account only the bias in the frequency of self-reported crime. If the amount of criminal income is also understated, the role of crime income will be even greater.

The number of crime categories in which the respondent had committed crimes tends to be quite low, under two on both the past-month and past-year basis. Since the evidence presented in section 8.5 below

Table 8.4   Reporting Bias and the Role of Crime as an Income Source

Reporting Bias Factor	Average Crime Income ($)	Average Total Income ($)	Crime Income as Fraction of Total Income
1	252.17	2,837.31	.09
2	504.34	3,089.48	.16
3	756.51	3,341.65	.23
4	1,008.68	3,593.82	.28
6	1,513.02	4,350.33	.35

indicates that the respondents were not particularly specialized in their criminal pursuits, a likely explanation for this low number is that the respondents listed only their major criminal activities. One indication that they were selective in their listing is that the list of activities for the past year often did not include all the crime categories in which they individually had participated in the past month.

The two variables governing the relative attractiveness of crime are YSTREET and EXYGAP. The YSTREET variable takes on a value of one if the respondent believed that he could make more on the street than on a legitimate job, and a value of zero otherwise. This variable therefore provides a direct measure of the relative economic attractiveness of crime. Almost half of the criminal subsample had YSTREET values of one, whereas just over one-fourth of the full sample had those values. As anticipated, those who expected to make more from crime were more likely to commit crime. These responses may be biased, however, if those who committed crime were seeking to justify their behavior by claiming that crime was a more lucrative activity.[10] As discussed in section 8.4 below these responses are nevertheless broadly consistent with the respondents' crime income expectations.

The variable EXYGAP is intended to measure the extent of this discrepancy between actual and expected income. This variable is constructed by subtracting expected earnings in the labor market from expected crime income. The crime income component of the variable represents expectations over a week, which were converted to an annual basis. Criminal pursuits might offer substantial rewards over such a short period, since a person could pursue only his most attractive options. Crime income over the year will be much lower; and as anticipated, the expected crime income amounts exceeded the actual crime income levels for respondents who had recently engaged in crime. For example, those who had committed crime in the past month had an expected weekly crime income of $600 (or yearly income of $31,200), a figure much lower than their observed yearly crime income under $1,600.

For those who had committed crime in the past year, actual crime earnings exceeded expected earnings for a comparable period by a factor of 9.3. To adjust for the likely reduction in actual criminal opportunities over the year as compared with what the respondent might hope to reap in a single week, the expected crime income figures were divided by 9.3 before subtracting expected annual labor market earnings to obtain *EXYGAP*. Even with this adjustment, expected crime income was not too dissimilar from expected labor market earnings. The net effect was that *EXYGAP* had a value of about −1,900 for the entire sample and a much smaller gap for the criminal subsamples, as one might expect. Because of this adjustment, *YSTREET* is a more reliable measure than *EXYGAP* of the relative economic attractiveness of crime.

The economic incentive variables *YSTREET* and *EXYGAP* are strongly correlated with criminal opportunities. The two opportunity variables I will use pertain to whether the respondent had several opportunities a day to make money illegally (*CHANCE1*) and whether he had no such opportunities (*CHANCE2*). The intermediate responses are not included in these two variables.

Over half of all respondents had some criminal opportunities. These opportunities were strongly related to reported criminal activity, as two-fifths of those who had committed crime had several such chances a day. Since the opportunities could be generated by the respondent himself by, for example, cruising the streets or associating with criminals, *CHANCE1* and *CHANCE2* are very endogenous to the criminal participation decision. In the analysis below they will be treated as variants of a crime participation variable. When included as independent variables in the crime equations, *CHANCE1* and *CHANCE2* play a dominant role.

The final set of variables measures the distribution of the sample across the three locations: Boston (*BOS*), Chicago (*CHI*), and Philadelphia (*PHILA*). There were stark differences in reported offense rates across these cities. In 1981 criminal offenses per 100,000 inhabitants were 14,000 in Boston and 6,000 in Chicago and Philadelphia.[11] Boston had a much lower murder rate than the other two cities but a far higher rate of property crime, such as auto theft. These differences are not apparent in the NBER sample, whose Philadelphia respondents exhibited the greatest criminal propensity. If Boston's higher crime rate is due to a greater proportion of crimes committed by whites, the overall crime statistics may be consistent with the pattern in the sample.

8.3 The Crime Participation Decision

An individual will choose to engage in criminal behavior if the expected net rewards from doing so (that is, *EXYGAP*) are positive.

One component of this calculation is the legal penalties likely to be incurred as a result of criminal acts. Although the NBER survey did not ask all respondents what they perceived would be the legal sanctions for their criminal behavior, it did solicit detailed information on the perceptions of those who actually engaged in crime.

The prevailing view of the respondents coincided with the general findings of the crime deterrence literature. Quite simply, there is very little threat of legal sanctions for crime. Only one of the 320 individuals who responded to the enforcement questions viewed the chances of arrest, conviction, and going to prison as being high. In contrast, 60 percent of this subsample viewed each of these possible outcomes as being low.

Table 8.5 summarizes the legal sanction results. Almost three-fourths of the sample viewed the chance of arrest as being low. Conditional on being arrested, an even greater proportion viewed the chance of conviction as being low. And even if convicted, few respondents believed that there was much chance that they would go to prison. The strongest perceived consequence posed by the criminal justice system was the conviction-prison relationship, but even this linkage was quite weak.

The implications of legal sanctions for the respondents' daily lives was also not great. The final three columns in table 8.5 present different possible events following arrest or conviction, such as losing one's job. These questions were worded to generate hypothetical responses from individuals who had no job. The perceived chance of losing one's job was somewhat higher than any of the other risks in the table. The chance of losing one's wife or girlfriend if sent to prison were lower than the chance of losing one's job. By far the lowest risk was that of losing one's friends. Going to prison appears to have a negligible stigmatizing effect among the respondents' peers.

One would expect the law enforcement perceptions of the noncriminal subsample to be somewhat greater, since those who perceive substantial risks will select themselves into the noncriminal group. Nevertheless, unless there is a strong difference in perceptions, it is unlikely that expected legal penalties will be very large. This does not mean that law enforcement is irrelevant to the crime participation decision. Since most values of *EXYGAP* were close to zero, small variations in expected sanctions for crime may alter the decision.

The focus of this section will be on the determinants of respondents' decisions to commit crime during the past month or the past year. In each case, the probability of participating in crime is a function of a set of explanatory variables. Since the dependent variables are dichotomous, the equation to be estimated will not be a linear regression but a logit equation estimated by maximum-likelihood techniques.

Table 8.5 Perceptions of Law Enforcement

Perceived Enforcement Level	Chance of Arrest	Conditional Chance of Conviction	Conditional Chance of Prison	Conditional Chance of Losing Job If Arrested	Conditional Chance of Losing Wife or Girlfriend If Sent to Prison	Conditional Chance of Losing Friends If Sent to Prison
Low	.73	.79	.73	.70	.79	.92
Medium	.21	.13	.15	.15	.10	.04
High	.06	.08	.12	.15	.10	.03

Each equation includes a set of personal characteristics, crime-related background variables, and criminal incentive variables. In addition, the equations are run both with and without a set of four variables that are at least partially endogenous to the crime decision: *JOB, SCHOOL, GANG,* and *CNBD.* The semi–reduced form estimates that exclude these intervening linkages consequently capture the full direct and indirect effects of the explanatory variables. Including these variables allows an analysis of the influence of factors such as gang membership; but to the extent that gang membership is simply a mechanism by which the respondent chooses to engage in crime, it will lead to a reduction in the influence of the other variables.

Table 8.6 summarizes the logistic estimates for the *CRIME-MO* equations, and table 8.7 provides the *CRIME-YR* results. What is most striking about these results is the similarity in the two time periods, both in terms of the nature of the effects and their magnitude.

In each case, the three personal characteristic variables (*AGE, EDUC,* and *MARRIED*) had no statistically significant impact. In the case of *EDUC* and *MARRIED*, this pattern seems attributable to the lack of much variability in the sample. Most respondents had the same level of schooling and were unmarried. The age range considered may not be sufficiently broad to capture the dramatic drop in criminal activity during the twenties.

The next four variables, which measure crime-related characteristics, all had the expected effects. The most powerful influence was the use of hard drugs (*DRUGS*).[12] The variable that ranked next in importance was use of marijuana; the *POT* variable had roughly half the impact on crime as did *DRUGS*. Next in importance was the use of alcohol (*DRINK*), which had approximately three-fifths of the impact of *POT*. The least consequential variable was attendance at religious services (*RELIGION*), which had under half the impact of the *DRINK* variable. In each case the variable may be capturing not only the impact of the particular background factor but also omitted factors correlated with it.

The probation time (*PROBT*) and jail time (*JAILT*) variables both have comparable, positive effects on the propensity to commit crime. These effects do not imply that legal sanctions have no deterrent effect, nor do they necessarily suggest that prison experience leads to further crime activity. The high recidivism rate occurs in part because some respondents were, no doubt, hard-core criminals. The *PROBT* and *JAILT* variables may simply serve as a proxy for the crime-related variables that have not been included in the equation.

The two city dummy variables *CHI* and *BOS* are consistently negative, which suggests that the third city, Philadelphia, is more likely to generate crime, holding constant the other variables in the equation.

Table 8.6   **Logistic Parameter Estimates for Past-Month Crime Participation Equations (asymptotic standard errors in parentheses)**

Independent Variable	(1)	(2)	(3)	(4)
Intercept	−2.637	−2.491	−2.148	−2.174
	(.599)	(.608)	(.709)	(.703)
AGE	.012	.014	−.016	−.007
	(.030)	(.030)	(.034)	(.033)
EDUC	−.039	−.035	−.021	−.018
	(.047)	(.047)	(.049)	(.049)
MARRIED	−.079	−.158	.003	−.076
	(.034)	(.336)	(.345)	(.340)
DRINK	.617	.630	.532	.546
	(.170)	(.169)	(.172)	(.172)
DRUGS	1.946	1.976	1.908	1.947
	(.279)	(.276)	(.284)	(.281)
POT	1.178	1.210	1.132	1.167
	(.146)	(.144)	(.148)	(.146)
RELIGION	−.304	−.296	−.279	−.272
	(.155)	(.154)	(.158)	(.157)
PROBT	.013	.013	.012	.012
	(.003)	(.002)	(.003)	(.002)
JAILT	.012	.011	.009	.008
	(.006)	(.006)	(.006)	(.006)
CHI	−.276	−.332	−.288	−.339
	(.160)	(.158)	(.163)	(.161)
BOS	−.623	−.543	−.482	−.404
	(.160)	(.157)	(.167)	(.164)
YSTREET	.620	—	.577	—
	(.138)		(.140)	
EXYGAP	—	$25E-6$	—	$20E-6$
		$(10E-6)$		$(11E-6)$
JOB	—	—	−.574	−.578
			(.168)	(.167)
SCHOOL	—	—	−.619	−.569
			(.184)	(.186)
GANG	—	—	.904	.968
			(.199)	(.198)
CNBD	—	—	.385	.366
			(.134)	(.133)
−2 Log Likelihood	1,583.01	1,612.02	1,535.15	1,562.75

Table 8.7   **Logistic Parameter Estimates for Past-Year Crime Participation Equations (asymptotic standard errors in parentheses)**

Independent Variable	(1)	(2)	(3)	(4)
Intercept	−1.578	−1.481	−1.212	−1.297
	(.550)	(.557)	(.659)	(.650)
AGE	−.017	−.012	−.038	−.026
	(.028)	(.028)	(.032)	(.031)
EDUC	−.063	−.057	−.053	−.046
	(.044)	(.043)	(.045)	(.044)
MARRIED	.087	−.037	.148	.026
	(.317)	(.312)	(.321)	(.317)
DRINK	.683	.721	.610	.651
	(.153)	(.152)	(.155)	(.154)
DRUGS	2.091	2.100	2.058	2.069
	(.301)	(.298)	(.305)	(.302)
POT	1.094	1.120	1.053	1.080
	(.132)	(.130)	(.134)	(.32)
RELIGION	−.287	−.253	−.269	−.233
	(.140)	(.138)	(.144)	(.141)
PROBT	.016	.016	.015	.015
	(.003)	(.003)	(.003)	(.003)
JAILT	.011	.012	.009	.010
	(.006)	(.006)	(.006)	(.006)
CHI	−.318	−.376	−.336	−.387
	(.150)	(.147)	(.152)	(.150)
BOS	−.545	−.418	−.433	−.303
	(.146)	(.143)	(.152)	(.149)
YSTREET	.743	—	.704	—
	(.128)		(.130)	
EXYGAP	—	$26E−6$	—	$21E−6$
		$(10E−6)$		$(10E−6)$
JOB	—	—	−.431	−.460
			(.157)	(.155)
SCHOOL	—	—	−.478	−.432
			(.169)	(.170)
GANG	—	—	.939	.999
			(.190)	(.188)
CNBD	—	—	.368	.358
			(.124)	(.122)
−2 Log Likelihood	1,797.22	1,848.01	1,750.19	1,797.71

The size of these effects is relatively modest, roughly on the same order as that of *RELIGION* and *DRINK*.

The key variables of interest are *YSTREET* and *EXYGAP*. Each of these economic incentive variables exerts the expected positive effect on criminal behavior. The size of the influence is roughly the same in all cases, though the past-year effects are a bit larger than the past-month effects. The inclusion of the four partially endogenous variables reduces the role of these economic incentive variables somewhat, in part because the crime decision affects such intervening variables as the decision to work. In terms of the size of the coefficients, the influence of *YSTREET* is comparable to that of *DRINK*, but is much less important than, for example, drug use.

This comparison is somewhat misleading, since *YSTREET* has a mean value of .28, whereas *DRUGS* has a mean value of .03. A better measure of a variable's contribution to the crime probability is its mean value multiplied by the size of the coefficient. By that measure, *YSTREET* is of greater consequence than *DRUGS*. The relative importance of the other variables changes as well, with the ranking of the impact of the personal background factors being, in descending order of importance *POT, DRINK, RELIGION,* and *DRUGS*. The impact of *YSTREET* lies between that of *DRINK* and *RELIGION*. The *EXYGAP* coefficient multiplied by the mean *EXYGAP* difference between the criminal and noncriminal subsamples reflects a much smaller impact, in part because of the greater measurement error associated with this variable.

The differential earnings from crime and legitimate occupations are a significant, but by no means dominant determinant of criminal behavior. Using the results for *CRIME-YR* in equation (1), one can calculate the overall crime propensity, if the expected crime income was below the expected labor market income, as being .16. Consequently, .03 of the .19 rate of criminal activity is accounted for by *YSTREET*. Although *YSTREET* accounts for only one-sixth of crime participation, the intensity of crime may be affected by *YSTREET* as well. This possibility will be explored in section 8.4 below. Another indicator of the impact of *YSTREET* on crime is that a *YSTREET* value of one instead of zero boosts the probability of engaging in crime from .16 to .29, or almost double. Among respondents who believed the economic rewards from crime were greater than those from a job, economic incentives played a powerful role in their decision to engage in crime.

Although relative earnings from legitimate and illegitimate pursuits did have a significant effect on criminal behavior, the total level of other income sources (such as welfare payments and an allowance from family) never had a statistically significant effect in any of the crime equations and was therefore not included in the final versions of the equations. In this sample it is not poverty *per se* that drives criminal behavior but the relative economic rewards from crime.

The final set of variables embodies influences that will capture in part the mechanism for the crime participation decision. As one might expect, respondents were less likely to engage in crime if currently employed (*JOB*), thus reinforcing the earnings influence in *YSTREET* and *EXYGAP*. The joint influence of *YSTREET* and *JOB* was roughly one and one-half times the influence of *YSTREET* alone, indicating that relative economic incentives had a more powerful effect than did current employment. Educational level did not affect crime, but being in school did, since *SCHOOL* had roughly the same coefficient as *JOB*. At least in terms of the crime participation decision, what matters most is whether one is gainfully occupied either in school or at a job. A respondent's status in one or the other of these two groups was not of great consequence.

Respondents' peers and criminal environment also played a major role. Gang membership or having friends in a gang was especially important. In terms of their effect on criminal propensity, *GANG* and *POT* had roughly comparable coefficients. The prevalence of a serious problem of crime in the neighborhood (*CNBD*) had a much smaller coefficient than did *GANG*; but since neighborhood crime was much more common than gang membership, the overall contribution of *CNBD* to observed crime levels was greater.

8.4 Crime Income

Since the central economic issue in this discussion is the relationship between the relative rewards from crime and criminal behavior, a fundamental relationship to be investigated here is the nature of the factors that affect both actual and expected rewards from crime. Total crime income is also a fundamental concern, because it reflects both the frequency and intensity of criminal behavior.

The first of these issues I will consider is the determinants of *YSTREET, EXYGAP, CHANCE1*, and *CHANCE2*. What personal characteristics are most likely to lead an individual to believe that criminal pursuits are more lucrative than a legitimate job and thus to seek out criminal opportunities? The equations reported in table 8.8 address this issue.

The two personal characteristics *AGE* and *EDUC* should boost expected market earnings, since these are the principal human capital variables. *AGE* increases expected crime earnings by greater amount than *EDUC* does, since the coefficients in the *EXYGAP* and *YSTREET* equations are always positive. *EDUC* somewhat surprisingly does not have a negative effect on relative criminal and legitimate earnings. The

Table 8.8   **Determinants of the Economic Incentives to Commit Crime (standard errors in parentheses)**

Independent Variable	YSTREET	EXYGAP	CHANCE1	CHANCE2	YSTREET
Intercept	−3.176	−5468.10	−1.564	−.988	−3.421
	(.512)	(1180.90)	(.562)	(.476)	(.535)
AGE	.053	151.90	.033	.064	.079
	(.025)	(59.00)	(.028)	(.024)	(.027)
EDUC	.060	2.39	.056	−.011	.057
	(.037)	(82.15)	(.04)	(.032)	(.040)
DRINK	.473	669.94	.369	−.631	.330
	(.116)	(248.36)	(.131)	(.100)	(.120)
DRUGS	.701	1781.42	.652	−.459	.493
	(.243)	(496.20)	(.240)	(.255)	(.247)
POT	.535	432.29	.485	−.571	.357
	(.104)	(233.36)	(.117)	(.098)	(.106)
CHI	−.770	−458.17	−.579	.499	−.648
	(.128)	(271.12)	(.139)	(.107)	(.134)
BOS	.340	242.52	.032	−.220	.335
	(.116)	(280.52)	(.130)	(.113)	(.121)
PROBT	.003	7.15	.004	.005	.002
	(.002)	(5.78)	(.002)	(.003)	(.002)
JAILT	.005	13.11	.012	−.012	.001
	(.005)	(13.63)	(.005)	(.008)	(.005)
GANG	.554	570.26	.257	−.551	.471
	(.174)	(426.05)	(.188)	(.183)	(.181)
CNBD	.137	410.78	.360	−.267	.040
	(.100)	(230.80)	(.110)	(.092)	(.105)
JOB	.122	1224.14	−.399	.241	.249
	(.125)	(298.03)	(.138)	(.120)	(.131)
SCHOOL	−.103	−3185.23	−.634	.397	.063
	(.139)	(311.96)	(.151)	(.126)	(.144)
CHANCE1	—	—	—	—	.833
					(.125)
CHANCE2	—	—	—	—	−.938
					(.125)
−2 Log Likelihood	2519.35	NA	2163.30	2933.30	2354.54
R̄²	NA	.17	NA	NA	NA

same types of skills that enhance productivity in a legitimate job may reap criminal rewards as well.

Having been in jail or on probation does not have a consistently strong effect, but the crime-related characteristics *DRINK*, *DRUGS*, and *POT* do. These variables capture in part the role of personal characteristics correlated with the particular activity. Drinking does not make a better criminal and will usually worsen the drinker's labor market prospects. All three activities were positively related to criminal opportunities. The youths who drank or took drugs were generally more apt to engage in illegitimate pursuits and more likely to be exposed to illegitimate earnings opportunities.

The criminal environment is also of consequence. For *YSTREET*, being a gang member or knowing people in a gang (*GANG*) has a strong effect on the expected criminal earnings. The existence of a severe problem of crime in the neighborhood (*CNBD*) also has a significant influence for both *YSTREET* and *EXYGAP*.

These criminal environment and crime-related background results are to be expected. The more surprising finding is that the same variables (*AGE* and *EDUC*) that are usually linked most strongly to labor market earnings also boost expected criminal earnings by at least the same amount. This is not to say that older and better-educated youths will, on balance, be more prone to crime. Other variables correlated with those human capital variables, such as whether those youths currently hold a job, also enter. The net direct effect in the crime participation equations in section 8.3 was not significant, but these variables exert a significant positive indirect influence on crime through *YSTREET* and *EXYGAP*.

The most striking difference in the *EXYGAP* and *YSTREET* equations is the effect of the *JOB* and *SCHOOL* variables. These status variables have no effect on *YSTREET* but exert a powerful influence on *EXYGAP*. Respondents who were employed were more likely to have positive *EXYGAP* values, whereas those in school were more likely to have strongly negative *EXYGAP* values. Although the schooling result is not unexpected, the positive employment effect may reflect overoptimistic crime income estimates, particularly in light of the weaker *JOB* effect on *YSTREET*.

The determinants of the frequency of criminal opportunities, *CHANCE1* and *CHANCE2*, are not unlike the relative income results. What is most striking is that many of the effects are quite strong. Frequent criminal opportunities (*CHANCE1*) are strongly and positively related to *DRINK, DRUGS, POT,* and *CNBD,* and negatively related to living in Chicago and being in a job or at school. All of these variables have the opposite effect for the variable measuring no illegal earnings opportunities (*CHANCE2*). The performance of the two opportunity variables gives at least as strong a result in the expected direction as do the crime participation equations. These findings alone suggest that criminal opportunities are at least partially endogenous.

In the final *YSTREET* equation in table 8.8, *CHANCE1* and *CHANCE2* are included to indicate the extent of the interrelationships. The positive effect of *CHANCE1* and the negative effect of *CHANCE2* are dominant variables in the equation; the coefficients of these variables dwarf those of all other dummy variables included in the equation. The criminal opportunity variables appear to represent a mixture of the crime participation and relative crime income variables. Although the determinants of *CHANCE1* and *CHANCE2* are of interest, these variables do not appear as well suited to serve as explanatory variables in a crime activity equation.

The determinants of actual levels of crime income follow a pattern not unlike the determinants of expected income. For the purposes of this analysis, the dependent variable is the natural logarithm of crime income for all respondents in the sample.[13] This variable thus captures both the decision to commit crime and the extent of criminal activity. This comprehensiveness is a mixed blessing: although it offers a broad perspective on crime income, it raises the potential problem of selectivity bias. Since crime income will be received only by those who choose to engage in crime, the equation can be viewed as suffering from specification error, such that the missing variable pertains to the sample-selection process governing crime participation.

To adjust for these problems, I include a selectivity variable (inverse Mills ratio) based on a probit estimate of the crime participation equation for the past year.[14] The past-month participation equation is not used because of convergence problems. The crime participation equations, analogous to equation (1) in tables 8.6 and 8.7, are estimated using a weighted nonlinear least-squares probit method. These results are then used to construct the distribution function for respondent i's crime participation (CP_i), where $F(CP_i)$ is the cumulative distribution of a standard normal variable and $f(CP_i)$ is the corresponding density function. The selectivity variable is $-f(CP_i)/F(CP_i)$ for those who engaged in crime and $f(CP_i)/[1 - F(CP_i)]$ for those who did not.

Table 8.9 presents the regression results for both time periods. The regressions including the selectivity variables are equations (4) and (8). The other equations differ according to the inclusion of partially endogenous variables and the relative crime versus legitimate earnings variables. Most of the principal effects are consistent across all of the equations.

The series of crime-related personal characteristics has a positive effect on crime income. Respondents who drank, smoked marijuana, or took drugs tended to have more crime income, with the effect of drugs being particularly strong. These variables reflect not only the youth's proclivity toward crime but also his opportunities for crime. Those who took drugs were more likely to have the opportunity to sell drugs and earn criminal income. Similarly, those who attended religious services (*RELIGION*) were less likely to have criminal contacts and may have had the kind of family background that led them to place a

Table 8.9 Regression Equations for Natural Logarithm of Crime Income (standard errors in parentheses)

Independent Variable	Past-Month Income Equations				Past-Year Income Equations			
	(1)	(2)	(3)	(4)	(5)	(6)	(7)	(8)
Intercept	-5.98	-5.67	-4.91	-5.27	-5.78	-5.33	-4.81	-5.35
	(.64)	(.65)	(.77)	(.67)	(.80)	(.83)	(.96)	(.71)
AGE	.03	.02	-.03	-.01	.02	.01	-.03	-.01
	(.03)	(.03)	(.04)	(.03)	(.04)	(.04)	(.05)	(.04)
EDUC	-.09	-.08	-.05	-.02	-.07	-.05	-.03	.02
	(.05)	(.05)	(.05)	(.04)	(.06)	(.07)	(.06)	(.05)
MARRIED	-.90	-.98	-.77	-.75	-.41	-.51	-.26	-.20
	(.40)	(.40)	(.39)	(.34)	(.50)	(.50)	(.49)	(.36)
DRINK	.32	.37	.22	.13	.61	.67	.47	.28
	(.16)	(.16)	(.16)	(.13)	(.20)	(.20)	(.20)	(.15)
DRUGS	2.45	2.50	2.45	2.61	3.38	3.44	3.37	3.69
	(.32)	(.32)	(.31)	(.27)	(.40)	(.40)	(.39)	(.29)
POT	1.20	1.29	1.14	.77	1.47	1.58	1.39	.77
	(.15)	(.15)	(.15)	(.13)	(.19)	(.19)	(.19)	(.14)
RELIGION	-.46	-.44	-.36	-.43	-.54	-.52	-.44	-.56
	(.15)	(.16)	(.15)	(.13)	(.19)	(.20)	(.19)	(.14)
PROBT	.03	.03	.03	.03	.04	.04	.04	.04
	(4E-3)	(4E-3)	(4E-3)	(3E-3)	(4E-3)	(5E-3)	(5E-3)	(3E-3)
JAILT	.02	.03	.02	.02	.02	.03	.02	.02
	(9E-3)	(9E-3)	(9E-3)	(8E-3)	(.01)	(.01)	(.01)	(8E-3)

	(1)	(2)	(3)	(4)	(5)	(6)	(7)	(8)
CHI	.15 (.18)	.03 (.17)	.12 (.17)	.09 (.15)	$-9E-3$ (.22)	$-.16$ (.22)	$-.03$ (.22)	$-.07$ (.16)
BOS	$-.43$ (.18)	$-.36$ (.18)	$-.21$ (.18)	$-.22$ (.16)	$-.32$ (.22)	$-.23$ (.22)	$-.06$ (.22)	$-.08$ (.17)
YSTREET	1.11 (.17)	—	1.05 (.17)	1.18 (.14)	1.45 (.21)	—	1.34 (.21)	1.58 (.15)
EXYGAP	—	$4E-5$ $(1E-5)$	—	—	—	$5E-5$ $(2E-5)$	—	—
JOB	—	—	-1.00 (.19)	-1.17 (.16)	—	—	-1.10 (.24)	-1.38 (.18)
SCHOOL	—	—	$-.95$ (.20)	$-.93$ (.17)	—	—	-1.02 (.25)	$-.99$ (.18)
GANG	—	—	1.20 (.27)	1.10 (.23)	—	—	1.89 (.34)	1.77 (.25)
CNBD	—	—	.32 (.15)	.37 (.13)	—	—	.46 (.18)	.52 (.14)
Selectivity Variable	—	—	—	-1.32 (.05)	—	—	—	-2.22 (.05)
$\bar{R}^2$	.17	.15	.19	.39	.18	.17	.21	.56

higher value on legal sanctions, thus decreasing their proclivity toward crime.

Past criminal experiences also exert a positive influence on crime income. Both time on probation and time spent in jail over the past year are positively related to current crime income. The stronger of the two effects is probation time, as each month of probation time has roughly double the impact of jail time. These variables are probably serving as proxies for crime-related personal characteristics omitted from the equation.

The two relative crime-versus legitimate income variables have the expected positive effect on criminal behavior. Respondents who expected to make more from crime than from a legal pursuit tended to have more crime income. These economic incentive effects are a fundamental determinant of crime income levels. A youth who viewed crime income as more lucrative than job income had an expected crime income level $78 larger than the expected monthly crime income amount of $26 for the youth who did not believe that crime income was more lucrative. On an annual basis, the perception that crime income was more profitable led to a crime income level of $714, whereas the opposite perception led to a $167 crime income level.[15]

In terms of the mean effects of *YSTREET*, the perception of the economic attractiveness of crime accounted for 26 percent of past-month crime income and 34 percent of past-year crime income. These effects are roughly twice as large as the influences on the crime participation rate. This differential impact suggests that the economic incentives for criminal behavior affect both the crime participation decision and the intensity of criminal behavior, but the larger of these two effects is on intensity.

Since many youths in the sample had minor criminal involvement (such as in numbers and illegal gambling), the crime participation results include many crimes that were not as strongly driven by the income opportunities they offered. Gambling, for example, may provide substantial recreational value. When crime intensity is measured by using a crime income variable, the economic incentives to commit crime play a more dominant role.

The partially endogenous variables also continue to be instrumental in generating crime income. Being employed and being in school have statistically indistinguishable effects. The size of these coefficients is about the same for *YSTREET*. The contribution of *JOB* in explaining crime income is about the same as the contribution of *YSTREET*, whereas the mean effect of *SCHOOL* is much greater. The most important way that any particular youth can reduce his crime income is for him to avoid the crime-prone state of being out of school without a job. Gang associations also have a positive impact on criminal behavior, as does the comparatively weaker influence of crime problems in the neighborhood.

Equation (9) reports the results of exploratory regressions including *CHANCE1* and *CHANCE2*. Crime income bears a strongly positive relationship to frequent opportunities to make money illegally and a negative relationship to not having such opportunities. These variables are dominant in part because they not only affect the youths' crime decisions but are also influenced by these decisions. Inclusion of these variables eliminates roughly half of the impact of *YSTREET* because of the substantial overlap between *YSTREET* and the crime opportunity variables. For example, only 5 percent of respondents who believed they could make more money on the street believed that they had no opportunities to make money illegally (*CHANCE2*). Since *CHANCE1* and *CHANCE2* are highly endogenous to the crime decision, they are not included in the subsequent equations.

Equations (4) and (8) report results including the selectivity variable (adjusted for heteroscedasticity). Because of convergence problems with the past-month crime participation equation, the selectivity variable included pertains to past-year crime participation. In each case, the effect of the variable on the other coefficients is very modest. The principal coefficient of interest, *YSTREET*, is unchanged in the past-month income equation and raised by almost 20 percent in the past-year income equation. The latter estimate implies that the mean effect of *YSTREET* accounts for 40 percent of all annual crime income.

8.5 A Profile of Criminal Behavior

The crime participation variables that have been analyzed thus far were based on a series of survey questions that addressed the nature of the respondents' criminal involvement. These self-reported measures are of interest because they indicate to what extent official statistics, such as arrest rates, provide an accurate view of the extent of criminal behavior among black youths. Moreover, in conjunction with the data on earnings from crime, we can construct measures of the levels of income that arise from different types of criminal activity.

Table 8.10 summarizes the pertinent national arrest statistics for 1981. The second column lists the distribution of city arrests of youths 15 to 24 years old. The chief arrest category is larceny-thefts, which accounts for two-fifths of all arrests. Drug violations and burglary each account for almost one-fifth of all arrests, with the remainder spread over the other nine crime categories.

The third column presents a somewhat different perspective on youth crime, indicating the fraction of all city arrests accounted for by arrests of youths aged 15 to 24. For many crime categories—larceny-theft,

Table 8.10   National Data on City Arrests for Selected Offenses, 1981

Offense Category	Fraction of Arrests of 15- to 24-Year-Olds	15- to 24-Year-Olds as Fraction of Arrests In Offense Category
Larceny and Theft	.39	.59
Drug Violations	.18	.62
Burglary	.17	.72
Aggravated Assault	.06	.44
Robbery	.05	.64
Motor Vehicle Theft	.04	.67
Fencing Stolen Property	.04	.59
Fraud	.03	.35
Forgery and Counterfeiting	.02	.47
Gambling	.10	.23
Forcible Rape	.10	.49
Murder	.00	.44
Total	1.0	.58

Source: U.S. Department of Justice, Federal Bureau of Investigation, *Uniform Crime Reports, Crime in the United States* (Washington: GPO, 1982), 186–187, 191.

motor vehicle theft, burglary, robbery, stolen property, and drug violations—arrests of youths in that age range account for well over half of all arrests for that particular crime. Indeed, only in gambling and fraud does this age cohort fail to account for at least 44 percent of all arrests.

The extent of crime in the NBER sample of black youth is quite different, in large part because of differing rates of arrest across crime categories. Tables 8.11 and 8.12 present the distributions for past-month and past-year criminal activity. The second columns in the tables list the fraction of the entire sample in each category. Since crime was a pursuit of under one-fifth of the sample, none of these categories is particularly large. Only numbers (and other illegal gambling) is pursued by at least 10 percent of the sample.

More instructive are the third columns of the tables, which give the crime distribution conditional upon the individual engaging in criminal acts. Once again, numbers and illegal gambling play a dominant role, as about two-thirds of all who committed crimes were guilty of these two offenses. Since gambling accounted for only one percent of all city arrests of all youths aged 15 to 24 in 1981 (see table 8.10), the arrest rate for this activity must be extremely small.

About a third of the criminal subsample admitted to having been a drug dealer (that is, they sold marijuana or other drugs). This activity was about equally important on both a monthly and an annual basis. Many of the more serious crime categories were of greater consequence

Table 8.11   **Past-Month Criminal Activity**

Crime Category	Fraction of Sample Who Committed in Past Year	Behavior Conditional on Crime Activity		
		Fraction Who Committed Category	Average Total Crime Income ($)	Weighted Average Crime Income ($)
Numbers	.10	.67	187.70	103.01
Fencing Stolen Goods	.03	.17	541.82	191.78
Drug Dealing	.05	.32	412.14	189.42
Burglary	.01	.05	478.24	134.56
Mugging	1E − 3	.02	365.71	94.61
Shoplifting	.01	.09	596.67	149.03
Forgery	1E − 3	.02	940.00	120.95
Con Games	.02	.16	427.34	133.84
Robbery	.01	.04	737.69	242.78
Other	.01	.05	1,110.00	443.51

Table 8.12   **Past-Year Criminal Activity**

Crime Category	Fraction of Sample Who Committed in Past Year	Behavior Conditional on Crime Activity		
		Fraction Who Committed Category	Average Total Crime Income ($)	Weighted Average Crime Income ($)
Numbers	.12	.63	1,116.16	565.14
Fencing Stolen Goods	.03	.19	2,670.41	720.85
Drug Dealing	.07	.37	2,181.42	994.54
Burglary	.02	.11	2,708.23	760.78
Mugging	.03	.13	2,989.28	744.36
Shoplifting	.01	.03	1,869.23	373.17
Forgery	.01	.07	3,991.30	891.48
Con Games	.01	.03	1,318.18	337.67
Robbery	.03	.16	1,707.89	624.39
Other	.01	.07	4,900.58	1,928.98

on an annual basis than on a monthly basis. Burglary (burglary and entry, larceny, and auto theft), muggings (and purse snatching), forgery (cashed or forged stolen checks), and robbery (robberies, holdups, and stickups) were much more common on an annual basis, which suggests that participation in these crime categories is a more occasional activity. By a similar token, the share for less-severe crimes was lower on an annual basis. Shoplifting (or stealing from cars and trucks) and con games exhibited the steepest declines.

The final two columns of tables 8.11 and 8.12 report the crime income levels associated with each crime category. The information reported in the NBER survey was for the youth's total crime income rather than his crime income from each type of criminal act. The crime income figures in the fourth columns are unweighted; each crime category is credited with the youth's total crime income. This measure overstates the actual crime income from each form of crime. To adjust for this double-counting problem, the weighted income figures divide all crime income from several activities on a proportional basis (that is, total crime income divided by the number of criminal activities), leading to much lower crime income levels.

By far the most lucrative crime category was "other crimes" (namely, any other illegal activities), which yielded about $2,000 annually. Youths who were reluctant to admit to a specific crime were likely to fall into this category. To the extent that these youths committed more than one type of crime, the figures will overstate the earnings from any specific class of criminal acts. Nevertheless, since even the unweighted crime income figures for the "other crimes" category are higher than those for the specific crime categories, it is likely that many of the high-income criminals refused to admit to their specific crimes, despite the fact that they did disclose their crime income.

For the remaining crime categories the leading sources of income varied depending on the time period considered. For the past-month data, the five principal income-generating crimes were robbery, fencing stolen goods, drug dealing, shoplifting, and burglary. Only three of these categories appeared among the five leading past-year crime income sources: drug dealing, forgery, burglary, muggings, and fencing goods. The most prevalent criminal pursuit, numbers and other illegal gambling, was among the lowest income generators. This activity is popular because it not only is recreational but also poses a very low risk, as there are few gambling arrests among youths. The severity of the punishment for gambling is also low.

Since the respondents generally engaged in several criminal activities, one would expect to observe some interdependencies across activities. Youths who engaged in robbery, for example, might also have fenced stolen goods. For each crime category, tables 8.13 and 8.14 present the linkages between the activities within each time period.

Table 8.13   **Interrelationships Among Past-Month Criminal Activities**

		Other Crimes in Which the Respondent Was Involved:								
Crime Category	Numbers	Fencing	Drug Dealing	Burglary	Mugging	Shoplifting	Forgery	Con Games	Robbery	Other
Numbers	1.0	.09	.20	.03	—*	.05	.02	.11	.02	.01
Fencing	.38	1.0	.40	.22	.05	.31	.09	.36	.14	.09
Drug Dealing	.42	.20	1.0	.08	.03	.11	.03	.22	.07	.05
Burglary	.42	.68	.47	1.0	.16	.37	.05	.42	.21	.10
Mugging	.12	.38	.38	.38	1.0	.38	.12	.50	.62	.25
Shoplifting	.36	.58	.39	.23	.10	1.0	.10	.32	.16	.12
Forgery	.57	.71	.43	.14	.14	.43	1.0	.29	.14	.14
Con Games	.46	.38	.45	.14	.07	.18	.04	1.0	.12	.07
Robbery	.27	.53	.53	.27	.33	.33	.07	.47	1.0	.13
Other	.12	.31	.38	.12	.12	.25	.06	.25	.12	1.0

*Fewer than one percent of respondents.

Table 8.14 **Interrelationships Among Past-Year Criminal Activities**

Crime Category	Other Crimes in Which the Respondent Was Involved:									
	Numbers	Fencing	Drug Dealing	Burglary	Mugging	Shoplifting	Forgery	Con Games	Robbery	Other
Numbers	1.0	.15	.27	.06	.09	.02	.04	.02	.13	.05
Fencing	.51	1.0	.57	.37	.38	.12	.22	.07	.32	.09
Drug Dealing	.46	.28	1.0	.15	.18	.06	.12	.04	.22	.07
Burglary	.34	.60	.50	1.0	.40	.14	.26	.04	.30	.10
Mugging	.45	.53	.52	.34	1.0	.19	.22	.09	.31	.14
Shoplifting	.47	.67	.67	.47	.73	1.0	.73	.13	.67	.13
Forgery	.33	.60	.67	.43	.43	.37	1.0	.20	.47	.13
Con Games	.54	.46	.54	.15	.38	.15	.46	1.0	.31	.23
Robbery	.50	.37	.50	.21	.26	.14	.20	.06	1.0	.14
Other	.45	.26	.38	.17	.28	.07	.14	.10	.34	1.0

Respondents who engaged in numbers and other illegal gambling had little propensity toward any other criminal activity, with the possible exception of dealing in drugs, which was a pursuit of roughly one-fourth of this group. Fencing stolen goods had much stronger linkages to drug dealing and to complementary crimes, such as mugging, shoplifting, burglary, and robbery. Drug dealers exhibited a fairly narrow crime pattern; they engaged in numbers and illegal gambling but otherwise did not exhibit high levels of concentration in the other crime categories.

The majority of burglars also fenced stolen goods. Drug dealing, numbers, muggings, and con games were also frequent pursuits of burglars. Most respondents who reported mugging were also fences and drug dealers. Particularly for the past-year data, shoplifting displays strong interdependencies, as at least two-thirds of all shiplifters were represented in each of five other crime categories. Those who committed forgery were very likely to fence stolen goods or deal in drugs, and the majority of those who were involved in con games or robberies also dealt in drugs and played numbers or engaged in illegal gambling (past-year data).

The picture that emerges is one of widespread criminal involvement among black inner-city youths. The criminal subsample was not engaged in highly specialized forms of crime. Illegal gambling and drug dealing, for example, were highly popular means for augmenting crime income from other sources. Rather than specialize in particular types of crime, the modus operandi appears to be that of taking advantage of a diversity of criminal opportunities as they arise. These opportunities are not random; otherwise the off-diagonal elements in the rows in tables 8.13 and 8.14 would be identical. Many of the discrepancies that appear in these supplementary criminal activities appear to be due to some specialization in terms of the nature of criminal behavior, as, for example, fencing stolen goods was very common among those who engaged in burglary, shoplifting, and mugging.

A comparison of criminal activities during the past month and during the past year is also feasible using the data on the NBER sample. This breakdown, provided in table 8.15, is instructive for two reasons. First, it provides a check on the consistency of individual responses. Second, it indicates which longer-term criminal pursuits are associated with the more continuous pursuits reflected in the past-month data.

The most extreme example of inconsistency in responses is that ten youths who reported having committed particular crimes in the past month did not admit to any criminal activity in the past month. Since seven of these ten aberrant responses were made by youths whose crime was playing numbers, this pattern reflects the more questionable criminality of minor gambling offenses.

Table 8.15 **Relationship Between Past-Month and Past-Year Crime Categories**

Past-Month Crime Categories	Conditional Fractions in Past-Year Crime Categories										
	Numbers	Fencing	Drug Dealing	Burglary	Mugging	Shoplifting	Forgery	Con Games	Robbery	Other	No Crime
Numbers	.96	.13	.25	.06	.07	.02	.04	.03	.12	.03	*
Fencing	.48	.97	.52	.34	.38	.10	.24	.09	.36	.09	0
Drug Dealing	.50	.28	.99	.15	.16	.08	.15	.05	.20	.02	0
Burglary	.42	.84	.47	1.0	.47	.16	.37	.05	.42	.10	0
Mugging	.12	.38	.38	.38	.62	.62	.75	.25	.38	.12	0
Shoplifting	.42	.68	.52	.42	.90	.19	.26	.10	.32	.13	*
Forgery	.71	.71	.57	.14	.43	.14	.57	.86	.14	.14	0
Con Games	.54	.39	.54	.25	.27	.14	.21	.71	.86	.07	*
Robbery	.27	.53	.53	.47	.47	.53	1.0	.07	.47	.07	0
Other	.31	.38	.38	.12	.31	.12	.12	.06	.25	.81	0
No Crime	.02	*	.02	*	*	*	*	*	*	.04	.95

*Fewer than one percent of respondents.

The diagonal elements in table 8.15 reflect the fraction of people in each past-month crime category who committed a particular crime in the past year. Since the "last four weeks" is included within the "past 12 months," presumably these figures should all be 1.0. Nevertheless, only one crime category—burglary—meets this test, and only half of the categories have at least 90 percent overlap. In the most extreme case, shoplifting, only 19 percent of those who admitted to this crime during the past month admitted to it in the past year. One possible explanation for these discrepancies is that respondents may have reported only their principal criminal activities during the time period in question.

In some cases, there are no strong interdependencies. Youths who played numbers or gambled illegally in the past month had no strong criminal tendencies during the past year. The majority of fences were also drug dealers, but the reverse was not true; drug dealers mostly engaged in numbers and gambling. Fencing stolen goods was also a dominant pursuit of those who engaged in burglary, shoplifting, or forgery in the past year. Among the strongest cross-crime linkages were that 90 percent of all who shoplifted in the past month participated in muggings in the past year and that 86 percent of all forgers were involved in con games in the past year, while a comparable percentage of those who were involved in con games also committed robberies in the past year.

The last line of table 8.15 lists all the respondents' who reported having committed no crimes in the past month. Ninety-five percent of this group committed no crime in the past year. The three crime categories over which the remaining 5 percent were distributed were numbers, drug dealing, and "other crimes." These categories tend to represent less violent crimes than those of robbery and mugging, for example. In addition, there are not as many strong criminal interdependencies for these categories as there are for the other crime groups.

There consequently appear to be three principal groups. First, a majority of the sample reported no criminal activity. Second, there is a small criminal element involved in comparatively nonviolent crimes, such as drug dealing and numbers, on a periodic basis. Finally, most youth crime stems from a hard-core criminal group for whom crime is a persistent activity.

Because of the small sample size of many of the crime categories, it was not possible to perform a comprehensive statistical analysis of the determinants of all criminal pursuits. It is feasible, however, to present an analysis of the larger crime categories. Table 8.16 displays the logit results for four crime participation equations. Variables that played an insignificant role[16] in the preliminary analysis were omitted to ensure convergence in the maximum-likelihood procedure.

Table 8.16   **Maximum Likelihood Estimates of the Determinants of**
Participation in Crime Categories
(asymptotic standard errors in parentheses)

Independent Variable	Numbers Games (Year)	Numbers Games (Month)	Fencing (Year)	Drug Dealing (Year)
Intercept	−2.658	−2.904	−1.239	−4.327
	(.176)	(.190)	(1.01)	(.275)
AGE	—	—	−.207	—
			(.055)	
DRINK	.701	.599	.558	—
	(.175)	(.188)	(.361)	
DRUGS	1.063	.800	2.368	2.308
	(.261)	(.272)	(.315)	(.274)
POT	.769	.848	1.645	2.223
	(.150)	(.163)	(.327)	(.254)
RELIGION	−.396	−.341	—	−.318
	(.163)	(.174)		(.230)
PROBT	.010	.001	—	.009
	(.002)	(.002)		(.003)
CHI	−.440	−.325	—	−.333
	(.163)	(.173)		(.237)
BOS	−.958	−.894	—	−.491
	(.174)	(.184)		(.217)
YSTREET	.570	.607	.456	.902
	(.144)	(.153)	(.251)	(.188)
−2 Log Likelihood	1,486.87	1,339.00	565.94	856.69

The estimates for the two equations for participation in numbers games are quite similar. The variables *DRINK, DRUGS*, and *POT* all have the expected positive effect on participation in this crime. What is most striking is that the coefficients are all of similar magnitude, unlike the overall crime results. For such a minor and prevalent offense, the nature of one's crime-related personal characteristics does not play a major role. The positive impact of the economic incentives variable *YSTREET* is comparable to that in the aggregative crime equations.

The more serious crimes of fencing stolen goods and dealing in drugs are much more strongly linked to *DRUGS* and *POT*. The role of economic incentives appears to be particularly great in the case of drug dealing, where the *YSTREET* coefficient is about 50 percent larger than in most of the earlier results. This finding is consistent with the crime income results, which suggests that *YSTREET* is a more powerful determinant of intense criminal activity than of crime participation, such as numbers.

8.6 Behavior Conditional on Status

The findings for crime participation and crime income suggested that being in school or holding a job discouraged criminal behavior with roughly similar effects. The primary distinction was whether the respondent was in the relatively idle *NOJOBSCHOOL* state. Although the possibility that respondents' status shifted the intercept of the crime equations was considered, the nature of behavior as reflected in the coefficients may change as well. In this section I will address these differences in behavior in greater detail.

Table 8.17 summarizes the source of income and degree of crime participation conditional on the respondents' status. Those with a job had the highest annual earnings, over $5,000. Nevertheless, about a fifth of those who were employed also committed crime, but the magnitude of criminal earnings had little effect on the average income of those who worked. Because of the very large variance in crime income, however, some employed respondents obviously realized a substantial income supplement from crime. Those in school had very low labor market earnings or illegitimate earnings, and only one-eighth of this group participated in crime during the past year. Among those not then employed or in school, annual income was equally divided between crime income and job earnings. Approximately half of this group participated in crime during the past year.

Tables 8.18 and 8.19 present the *CRIME-MO* and *CRIME-YR* logit equation estimates. Because of the thinness of the subsamples, some variables were omitted from the equations because of convergence problems. For example, since only eight of the in-school population took drugs, the *DRUGS* coefficient could not be estimated for this subsample. The greatest difference from the previous findings is the performance of *YSTREET*. Both in terms of the magnitude of the coef-

Table 8.17   **Means of Income Sources, by Status (standard deviations in parentheses)**

Status	Annual Earnings ($)	Annual Crime Income ($)	CRIME-YR
JOB	5,328.89	177.45	.18
	(4,350.33)	(1,163.64)	—*
SCHOOL	609.88	79.49	.12
	(1,497.31)	(563.09)	—*
NOJOBSCHOOL	487.03	505.35	.51
	(2,002.66)	(2,341.14)	—*

*Standard deviations of 0–1 dummy variables were omitted because they could be calculated from their fraction m in the sample, where the standard deviation is $(m - m^2)^{0.5}$.

ficient and its statistical significance, *YSTREET* plays no apparent role for those in the *JOB* or *SCHOOL* states. The behavior of these groups is driven by variables such as *DRINK, DRUGS, POT,* and *GANG* (for the in-school group).

These variables are of consequence for the *NOJOBSCHOOL* population as well. But here *YSTREET* plays a much more powerful role, with effects up to twice as large as those estimated previously. The thinness of the criminal population among the *JOB* and *SCHOOL* groups should lead one to be cautious in drawing conclusions from these re-

Table 8.18   ***CRIME-MO* Logistic Parameter Estimates, by Status (asymptotic standard errors in parentheses)**

Independent Variable	JOB	SCHOOL	NOJOBSCHOOL
Intercept	−1.006	−4.107	−2.418
	(1.416)	(1.447)	(1.020)
AGE	−.062	.112	−.030
	(.065)	(.088)	(.044)
EDUC	−.037	−.170	.031
	(.105)	(.079)	(.074)
MARRIED	.429	—	−.145
	(.482)		(.491)
DRINK	.550	.808	.366
	(.356)	(.354)	(.246)
DRUGS	1.684	—	1.812
	(.470)		(.401)
POT	.880	1.495	.961
	(.275)	(.325)	(.213)
CHI	−.409	−.163	−.174
	(.332)	(.375)	(.224)
BOS	−.719	−.439	−.343
	(.309)	(.328)	(.260)
RELIGION	−.284	−.145	−.402
	(.292)	(.311)	(.249)
PROBT	.001	.030	.012
	(.006)	(.007)	(.003)
JAILT	.006	.031	.006
	(.014)	(.044)	(.006)
GANG	.381	1.626	.872
	(.381)	(.389)	(.305)
CNBD	.501	.157	.446
	(.259)	(.287)	(.198)
YSTREET	.032	.436	.982
	(.270)	(.308)	(.200)
−2 Log Likelihood	428.42	438.92	693.28

Table 8.19   ***CRIME-YR*** **Logistic Parameter Estimates, by Status (asymptotic standard errors in parentheses)**

Independent Variable	JOB	SCHOOL	NOJOBSCHOOL
Intercept	− .485	− 2.851	− 1.359
	(1,271)	(1,230)	(.981)
AGE	− .096	.066	− .04
	(.059)	(.079)	(.043)
EDUC	.005	− .145	− .034
	(.094)	(.073)	(.070)
MARRIED	.415	—	.033
	(.455)		(.463)
DRINK	.549	1.010	.347
	(.315)	(.293)	(.232)
DRUGS	2.408	—	1.644
	(.498)		(.416)
POT	.963	1.067	.959
	(.247)	(.261)	(.203)
CHI	− .338	− .463	− .169
	(.303)	(.330)	(.217)
BOS	− .578	− .190	− .276
	(.279)	(.272)	(.252)
RELIGION	− .120	− .377	− .298
	(.258)	(.262)	(.235)
PROBT	.007	.036	.015
	(.005)	(.008)	(.003)
JAILT	.001	.019	.009
	(.017)	(.040)	(.007)
GANG	.432	1.715	.937
	(.350)	(.354)	(.303)
CNBD	—	—	.362
			(.191)
YSTREET	.116	.292	1.214
	(.244)	(.263)	(.194)
− 2 Log Likelihood	569.61	498.66	729.45

sults. Nevertheless, the relative importance of economic incentives for criminal behavior is clearly greater for those in the *NOJOBSCHOOL* state.

This result is what one should expect. Those working at a job have less of an economic motivation to commit crime, since they have their labor market income. Moreover, the decision to accept a job reflects their greater satisfaction with the level of wages offered in the market than that of youths who have no job. Similarly, youths in school tend to be supported by their parents. It is the out-of-school group without gainful employment who have the greatest economic incentive to engage in criminal acts.

8.7 Conclusion: Crime as an Alternative Income Source

Youth crime has been the subject of a number of analyses because of its central role in the overall crime problem. For the black youths in the NBER sample, crime serves an economic function by providing many with a substantial income source. After adjusting for the likely underreporting of crime, I estimate that roughly one-fourth of all income of those in the sample was from criminal pursuits.

The black youth crime problem is, however, not pervasive among the entire demographic group. Roughly one-fifth of the sample reported criminal activity, but up to three-fifths of the sample may have engaged in crime (after adjusting for self-reporting bias). Those who reported criminal activity were a fairly hard-core criminal group. There was very little entry into and exit from this criminal population, which remained quite stable over the year. Those engaged in crime undertook multiple criminal activities, some of which were related (for example, mugging and burglary), but there also seemed to be an opportunistic effort to take advantage of various criminal activities as they arose.

Those predisposed toward crime also possessed characteristics not conducive to success in legitimate forms of work, and they had greater contact with criminal opportunities. Drinking, drug use, gang membership, past criminal activity (as indicated by probation or jail time), and problems of crime in the neighborhood all were strongly correlated with criminal behavior. In short, the types of youths who commit crime differ quite starkly and systematically from those who do not.

A fundamental influence on criminal behavior is the role of economic factors, such as labor market status. Respondents who were in school or employed were much less likely to engage in crime. What was most important was being out of the *NOJOBSCHOOL* category rather than being in the *JOB* or *SCHOOL* group. Although the respondent's status reflects in part an endogenous decision to allocate time to criminal behavior, the criminal behavior of these groups was quite different. Respondents who were not employed or in school were much more strongly driven by the economic incentives to commit crime.

The role of economic incentives to commit crime received particularly strong support in the *NOJOBSCHOOL* group and was statistically significant overall. If youths can make more money from crime than from labor market earnings, they will be more likely to engage in crime. Although these effects were statistically significant, making the gains from employment larger than the gains from crime would directly eliminate only one-sixth of the crime participation by black youths.

Economic incentives are more consequential for higher-income crimes, such as drug dealing, than for minor crimes, such as numbers. When one takes into account the intensity of criminal behavior, as measured by crime income, the comparative economic rewards for crime account for one-third of all crime. This impact is roughly double the influence on crime participation. Even this amount probably understates the potential long-term effectiveness of economic incentives because of a stabilizing effect of employment. Including the effect of having a job roughly doubles the impact of the labor market; the labor market variables may therefore account for as much as two-thirds of all crime income. Economic incentives are instrumental for a relatively small portion of the criminal population, but this segment accounts for a disproportionate share of all crime income.

In terms of the relative efficacy of the "carrot" of improved economic opportunities and the "stick" of stricter criminal enforcement, there is strong evidence that the "carrot" is more effective. The magnitude of this influence is not so dominant, however, that society should abandon its criminal enforcement efforts. On the other hand, this is not to say that improved economic opportunities are unimportant. The fringe crime group is particularly likely to be affected by more employment opportunities. Although minor changes in the economic environment may not dramatically alter the overall youth crime problem, the criminality among those who are not in school or employed is very sensitive to economic incentives. Since members of this group are responsible for most of youth crime, they comprise a major, economically responsive component of the criminal population.

Notes

1. More rigorously, the expected utility from crime must exceed the expected utility from legitimate activities. In the case of risk-neutral criminals, expected rewards and expected utility are equivalent. In addition to the early articles by Becker (1974), Ehrlich (1973, 1975), and Block and Heineke (1975), see the survey by Heineke (1978) of the theoretical literature on crime. The job-risk counterpart to this problem is the focus of the analysis in Viscusi (1979).

2. Among the many surveys that review this literature are those by Cook (1977, 1980), Taylor (1978), and Wilson and Boland (1976). See Freeman (1983) for a comparison of the deterrence and unemployment literatures.

3. Witte's (1980) study uses the wage received on the first job as the income measure, but even this is not an ideal index of a person's present opportunities.

4. The recent conference volume edited by Freemen and Wise (1982) addresses these issues in great depth.

5. These age-related trends are discussed in Greenberg (forthcoming).

6. Two background variables that might be expected to be linked to crime—being registered to vote and income other than from earnings (such as from food stamps)—

never had a significant influence on criminal behavior and are not included in the results reported here.

7. Respondents who had no job and who had no expected wage were assigned a wage value equal to the mean expected wage of those who were not employed.

8. See, in particular, the authors' discussion on pages 173–76 and 213. They concluded, "We did learn from the data supporting the optimistic conclusion that the self-report method can produce reliable and valid results within the population to which it is generally applied" (p. 213).

9. The crime categories for these calculations were as follows: reporting rate (burglary, larceny, and auto theft); conditional arrest rate (robbery, burglary, larceny, and auto theft); and conditional rates of serving time in jail (robbery, burglary, larceny, auto theft, narcotics, and others). The variation in the crime categories is the result of both differences in data availability and the unreliability of some data. For example, arrest rates for narcotics violations were very high because these violations usually go unreported, except when discovered by the police.

10. I am indebted to James Q. Wilson for this observation.

11. These numbers were derived from population figures and offense reports given in U.S. Department of Justice (1982, 39, 68, 75 and 98).

12. This result is not unexpected. See Moore (1983) for a discussion of the importance of drug use and related "criminogenic" traits.

13. Since some individuals had no crime income, the zero values had to be coded in a manner that would permit the use of natural logarithms. For purposes of estimation the natural logarithm of zero was set equal to -6.9.

14. More specifically, I used the weighted nonlinear least-squares program supplied to me by Gregory M. Duncan. For an excellent discussion of the sample-selectivity correction, see Duncan (1981). A recent application of this correction to labor economics issues appears in Duncan and Leigh (1980).

15. These estimates were obtained using equations (1) and (5) in table 8.9.

16. No variables with t-statistics above 1.0 in the OLS counterpart of these logit equations were dropped. Most excluded variables had t-statistics on the order of 0.1.

References

Becker, G. S. 1974. Crime and punishment: An economic approach. In *Essays in the economics of crime and punishment*, ed. G. Becker and W. Landes, 1–54. New York: Columbia University Press.

Block, M., and J. Heineke. 1975. A labor theoretic analysis of the criminal choice. *American Economic Review* 65: 314–25.

Blumstein, A., and J. Cohen. 1979. Estimation of individual crime rates from arrest records. *Journal of Criminal Law and Criminology* 70: 561–85.

Cook, P. J. 1977. Punishment and crime: A critique of current findings concerning the preventive effects of punishment. *Law and Contemporary Problems* 40: 164–204.

———. 1980. Research in criminal deterrence: Laying the groundwork for the second decade. In *Crime and Justice: An Annual Review of Research*, ed. N. Morris and M. Tony. Chicago: University of Chicago Press.

Duncan, G. M. 1981. Sample selectivity as a proxy variable problem: On the use and misuse of gaussian selectivity corrections. Washington State University Working Paper no. 1181-1. Pullman, Wash.: WSU.

Duncan, G. M., and D. Leigh. 1980. Wage determination in the union and nonunion sectors: A sample selectivity approach. *Industrial and Labor Relations Review* 34: 24–34.

Ehrlich, I. 1973. Participation in illegitimate activities: A theoretical and empirical investigation. *Journal of Political Economy* 81: 521–65.

———. 1975. The deterrent effect of capital punishment: A question of life and death. *American Economic Review* 65: 397–417.

Freeman, R. B. 1983. Crime and the labor market. In *Crime and public policy*, ed. J. Q. Wilson, 89–106. San Francisco: Institute for Contemporary Studies.

Freeman, R. B., and D. Wise, eds. 1982. *The youth labor market problem: Its nature, causes, and consequences.* Chicago: University of Chicago Press.

Greenberg, D. n.d. Age and crime. In *Encyclopedia of crime and justice*, ed. S. Kadish. New York: Macmillan. Forthcoming.

Heineke, J. M. 1978. Economic models of criminal behavior: An overview. In *Economic models of criminal behavior*, ed. J. M. Heineke, 1–33. Amsterdam: North-Holland.

Hindelang, M. J., T. Hirschi, and J. Weis. 1981. *Measuring delinquency.* Beverly Hills, Calif.: Sage.

Moore, M. 1983. Controlling criminogenic commodities. In *Crime and public policy*, ed. J. Q. Wilson, 125–44. San Francisco: Institute of Contemporary Studies.

Taylor, J. B. 1978. Econometric models of criminal behavior: A review. In *Economic Models of Criminal Behavior*, ed. J. M. Heineke, 35–81. Amsterdam: North-Holland.

U.S. Department of Justice, Federal Bureau of Investigation. 1982. *Uniform crime reports: Crime in the United States.* Washington, D.C.: GPO.

Viscusi, W. K. 1979. *Employment hazards: An investigation of market performance.* Cambridge: Harvard University Press.

Wilson, J. Q., ed. 1983. *Crime and public policy.* San Francisco: Institute for Contemporary Studies.

Wilson, J. Q., and Boland, B. 1976. Crime. In *The Urban Predicament*, ed. W. Gorham and N. Glazer. Washington, D.C.: The Urban Institute.

Witte, A. D. 1980. Estimating the economic model of crime with individual data. *Quarterly Journal of Economics* 94: 57–84.

Wolfgang, M., R. Figlio, and T. Sellin. 1972. *Delinquency in a birth cohort.* Chicago: University of Chicago Press.

Comment   James W. Thompson and James Cataldo

In this paper, one of the first individual-level employment and crime analyses of a sample *not* drawn from an offender population, Viscusi concludes that "roughly one-fourth of all income of those in the sample was from criminal pursuits." If this finding can be upheld (and we believe that it is generally correct), then it carries far-reaching implications for future research on the inner-city youth labor market. At last we can replace armchair speculations from aggregate data on economic incentives and crime deterrence with close examination of the full spectrum of income generation, ranging from legitimate employment in well-established firms to off-the-books and underground economic activities, and from these to street crimes such as muggings, burglaries, and drug selling. If Viscusi's work succeeds in establishing a commitment to this broader focus, his contribution will remain important.

But accepting that crime occupies an important place in the income-generating activities of inner-city youths does not automatically advance our understanding of the problem. Here, Viscusi's example is instructive, sometimes for its success in addressing thorny issues, and sometimes for its failures. The strength of Viscusi's approach is that he has developed a clear conception of the nature of economic incentives to engage in crime, namely, the difference between illegal and legal earnings expectations (*EXYGAP* and *YSTREET*); and he has adhered to this conception in estimating the determinants of crime participation and of crime income levels. The flaws in his analysis arise in his implementation, and they include the manner in which he specifies *EXYGAP* and his exclusive use of self-reported measures of crime participation.

EXYGAP and Relative Earnings from Work and Crime

In his model of employment and crime, Viscusi claims to adopt a framework of "discrete choice between crime and noncriminal employment." Such a model, though possible, is at variance with Viscusi's own data showing that 24 percent of youths (aged 16 to 24) admitting to crime in the past month *also* held jobs. Indeed, employment and crime studies have typically found a large amount of concurrent crime and employment. For example, the Vera Institute's survey of 902 Brooklyn male arrestees in the summer of 1979 found that roughly 40 percent of the young (aged 16 to 24) blacks in the sample also held

James W. Thompson and James Cataldo are, respectively, director and research associate in the Employment and Crime Project of the Vera Institute of Justice.

jobs. This evident mixing of legal with illegal sources of income is also implicitly acknowledged by Viscusi when he develops his logistic regressions. In some of these, *JOB* and *SCHOOL* are introduced as explanatory variables into equations that have crime participation as a dependent variable. This procedure would be meaningless if a "discrete choice between crime and noncriminal employment" were in fact at issue. If crime and work are alternative activities, then the introduction of one as an independent variable would be equivalent to introducing the logical complement of the dependent variable as an explanatory variable.

On the other hand, if the choice framework is not binary, it would appear that the variables *EXYGAP* and *YSTREET* are not entirely appropriate for modeling crime participation, since they measure total potential income rather than differences in earnings at the margin. For example, a working youth is likely to encounter at least a few opportunities for crime that offer marginal returns much higher than those from legitimate work. Nevertheless, such a youth's total potential income from work would likely be much greater than his total income obtainable from crime, since, as Viscusi observes, the quality of his criminal opportunities would deteriorate rapidly as he began to "use up" his best crime options. Even so, some youths would be expected to continue to engage in those occasional criminal activities whose marginal returns equalled or exceeded their wage rates.

Adding to the difficulty associated with the binary choice framework are other perplexities associated with the key variable *EXYGAP* itself. *EXYGAP* is the difference between expected illegal and expected legal earnings. It thus has two distinct components, and problems are inherent in each one.

First consider expected illegal income. A point that Viscusi too little emphasizes is that expected illegal earnings are extraordinarily high; they are $22,945 on an annualized basis for the sample as a whole and they rise to $31,200 for those respondents who reported crime during the past month. Such levels are hardly comparable to either expected legal earnings ($3,800 for the crime-committing subgroup), nor are they at all comparable to *actual* annual crime income ($1,570).

What is going on here? Viscusi suggests, as we already noted, that expectations of illegal income opportunities are overly influenced by a few relatively good opportunities close at hand and by the fact that the youths do not adequately discount their longer-term crime prospects once these short-term options are used up. This phenomenon is familiar to anyone who has tried to sell scout cookies by working outward from his or her immediate family, but one that sharply distinguishes income-producing crimes from legal work.

How expectations about crime income are formed and what factors determine them are at the heart of the crime decision. Viscusi implicitly assumes that everyone exaggerates crime opportunities in the same way, and in fact he develops a single discount factor (9.3) by comparing *offenders'* expected (annualized) crime returns to their actual crime income. But the extent to which youths anchor their crime income potential on their best opportunities implies that the tendency to exaggerate would decline with greater levels of participation in crime. Those who commit no or only a few crimes would be more prone to extrapolate from a few good opportunities not yet explored, while experienced offenders would be more likely to make realistic, long-term appraisals. This hypothesis might be tested by comparing different discount factors, such as between those with low and high actual crime incomes or among different subgroups defined in terms of age and school and job status.

Next consider legal earnings expectations. Just as it is likely that illegal income expectations depend partly on the level of crime experience, it is plausible to suppose that legal income expectations also derive from experience in the labor market. But in a sample of inner-city youths, such experience is very unevenly distributed. In the NBER sample, only about a quarter (26 percent) were at work, two-fifths were in school, and a third (34 percent) were neither at work nor in school. These groups surely form expectations of legal earnings in very different ways. Those in jobs may have realistic (lower?) expectations concerning legal income prospects, since they are already in the market; those in school, by contrast, have less direct knowledge about prevailing legal opportunities, and their expectations may be largely based on their current self-investment activities; and finally, those neither in jobs nor in school may well have the lowest expectations. As with illegal income, Viscusi once again combines actual and expected earnings, using the former for those in jobs and the latter for the remainder.

Such blending of actual with expected legal income, combined with the previously described assumptions underlying the discounting of expected illegal gains, makes *EXYGAP* an odd hybrid with hidden complexity, rather than the seemingly simple motor driving crime decision making that is initially introduced in the paper. There is in fact still one more source of difficulty: The likely dependence of legal and illegal income expectations on the individual's level of participation in these activities raises the same issue of endogeneity that Viscusi notes with respect to several other variables in the study—chances to engage in crime, gang affiliation, and perceived crime in the neighborhood. Clearly, the path of future research should be to develop additional independent measures of legal and illegal opportunities and to employ longitudinal designs that are capable of unraveling complex causal relationships.

Self-reports and the Prevalence of Criminal Activity

It is from exclusive reliance upon self-reported measures that a second set of difficulties arises. Although Viscusi at various places discusses problems with the self-reported measure of criminal activity (and, indeed, ultimately concludes that there was *three times* as much crime in the sample as sample members themselves reported), he is insufficiently cautious in approaching several pieces of internal evidence that cast doubt on the measure: the surprising lack of an age-crime association, the apparently skewed distribution of types of crimes in the sample, and the nearly complete absence of movement between crime and noncrime states.

In table 8.3 Viscusi finds no association between age and the prevalence of self-reported crime. He correctly observes that the truncated age distribution in his sample (16 to 24 years) would lessen the otherwise very sharp dropout effects that would appear with broader age groupings; but his argument that the failure to see any of this pattern is a result of the virtual absence of muggings, burglaries, and robberies in the self-reports of his sample (crimes that show especially sharp declines with age) begs the question. Only be accepting the veracity of the self-reports can we believe that these street crimes (which are particularly prevalent among younger inhabitants of inner-city minority neighborhoods) are absent from his sample. If they were present, we would expect an age-related decline in crime even in the age range from 16 to 24 years. The absence of this decline suggests that members of one subgroup, active in relatively violent and risky crimes, are not talking about their activities.[1]

Viscusi cites a study by Blumstein and Cohen (1979) to suggest that this lack of an age-crime pattern is "not unprecedented." But the Blumstein-Cohen study addressed an entirely different facet of the age-crime relationship: the intensity of criminal activity among a subgroup of active offenders, rather than rates of participation in crime at different ages.

The Blumstein-Cohen study found that the intensity of illegal activity among people still active in their criminal careers did not vary significantly by age; the well-established sharp decline in aggregate arrests per capita among older age groups in the general population therefore results from the fact that some people "drop out" from crime, rather than from a smooth tapering off of criminal activity as active offenders age.

More concern over the failure to find an expected age-crime association or self-reports of crimes such as muggings and burglaries might have led to more caution concerning a third issue, the near absence of an increase in crime in the sample between the past-month and past-year time periods. The fact that self-reported crime rose only from 15 to 19 percent of the sample between these two periods leads Viscusi to infer, as he puts it in his concluding section, "Those who reported criminal activity were a fairly hard-core criminal group. There was very little entry into and exit from this criminal population, which remained quite stable over the year."

This image of a "hard core" group hardly jibes with Viscusi's own acceptance of an underreporting factor of 3 (which implies that 57 percent of his sample engaged in crime over the past year), or with the close similarity in employment rates between the entire sample (26 percent) and those who admitted to crime (24 to 25 percent). If it is a hard-core criminal group, it is at least an *employed* hard-core group.

Although self-reported measures are valuable in this type of study, they should be complemented with official arrest data. If this is not possible, one should refrain from poorly supported conjectures about a "hard core" of criminal youth. The best current estimate, developed by Blumstein and Grady from a combined study of longitudinal and cross-sectional data, is that black men living in large (not "inner") U.S. cities experience a cumulative lifetime probability of one or more *felony* arrests of 51 percent, whereas white men in the same cities have a cumulative probability of 14 percent.[2] Most of this arrest risk occurs by the middle twenties. This estimate is one of many indications of widespread crime among poor, minority youths, and it further suggests that in some "high risk" inner-city (as against large-city) areas, participation in crime for income gains is a predominant pattern, not at all confined to a hard-core group.

Only if others follow the lead of the NBER study, and only if we overcome the sterile isolation of crime research from the study of broader labor market phenomena, will we be able to come to grips with the full implications of the fact that income-generating street crime is both widespread within poor populations and, within the individual life cycle, relatively short-lived.

Notes

1. Bias might also have arisen in other, indirect ways. For example, perhaps interviewers concerned about their own safety selected meeting times and places or types of respondents that led to the relative exclusion of this group. The study methodology is not described, a serious problem in studies such as this of hard-to-reach populations.

2. Alfred Blumstein and Elizabeth Grady, "Prevalence and Recidivism in Index Arrests: A Feedback Model," *Law and Society Review* 16, no. 2 (1981–82).

9

Who Escapes? The Relation of Churchgoing and Other Background Factors to the Socioeconomic Performance of Black Male Youths from Inner-City Tracts

Richard B. Freeman

9.1 Introduction

The 1970s witnessed severe economic plight among inner-city black youths that went beyond the worst predictions of even pessimistic social scientists. Rates of unemployment among young black men rose to unprecedented levels; their labor-force participation rates fell; and as a consequence their ratio of employment to population plummetted to extraordinarily low levels. In 1980, even before the major recession of 1982–83, the unemployment rate stood at 39 percent for black men 16 to 19 years of age and at 24 percent for black men 20 to 24; the comparable rates for young white men in the same age groups were 16 percent and 11 percent, respectively. Civilian labor-force participation rates in the same year were 32, 56, and 79 percent, respectively, for black men aged 16 to 17, 18 to 19, and 20 to 24; they were 54, 74, and 87 percent, respectively, for white men in the same age brackets.[1] Throughout the 1970s, crime rates rose among black youths and problems of drug addiction and alcoholism worsened. Many observers, in both the academic community and the black community, expressed serious concern about the potential loss to the labor force and to the broader society of a large part of an entire generation of youths in the inner city.

Although the number of youths who lacked jobs was unprecedented, a significant number still managed to surmount the socioeconomic problems facing them to advance in the society. Some did well in high school and went on to college. Some obtained work and held down regular, well-paying jobs in the mainstream economy. Some escaped the often pathological environment of inner-city slums.

Richard B. Freeman is director of the Labor Studies program at the National Bureau of Economic Research and professor of economics at Harvard University.

What were the characteristics of these youths? How important were personal and family factors in their overcoming the burden of being raised in the worst slums in the country? What determines "who escapes"?

This paper examines these questions with data from the 1979–80 NBER-Mathematica Survey of Inner-City Black Youth, and from the 1979–81 National Longitudinal Surveys of young men (NLS). The NBER survey had the advantage of gathering information on youths' allocation of time in a day and on socially deviant behavior (such as crime and drug use), in addition to standard school and work questions. The NLS data, on the other hand, permit comparisons of young blacks and whites not possible with the NBER data.

The primary finding of this study is that the measured backgrounds of inner-city youths, in particular their churchgoing behavior and the welfare status of their families, provide remarkably good predictions about "who escapes." There is also some indication that at least part of the relationship between background and achievement among young black men represents a "true" causal link rather than a sorting of youths between "good" and "bad" kids.

This paper is divided into four sections. Section 9.2 describes the outcome and background variables analyzed, in particular the NBER survey data on the allocation of time of inner-city black youths. Section 9.3 presents the results of least-squares regressions linking the outcome variables to various measures of the youths' background including churchgoing. Section 9.4 probes the possible ways in which churchgoing influences behavior, particularly, whether churchgoing operates through (or stands for) religious (and other) attitudes and general market factors. Section 9.5 discusses the possible causal significance of the estimated links, that is, whether the estimates reflect the "true" impact of the independent variables or whether they reflect sorting or selectivity of youths by background and outcome; and the last section summarizes the results of the study and presents some conclusions.

9.2 Outcome and Background Variables

The first step in evaluating the socioeconomic success of inner-city black and other youths is to develop a set of outcome variables relevant to their position in life. Commonly used variables, such as school and work activity questions in the Current Population Survey (CPS), though useful, are far from adequate in judging the status of youth. Classifications like "out of the labor force" or "unemployed" provide little information on the actual activities of youth: they tell us what youths are not doing with their time, rather than what they are doing.[2] Even when youths report themselves employed at a given wage, the information is potentially less valuable than comparable information for adults because of the high mobility and frequent changes in status early in the work life.

Accordingly, this paper will examine several unconventional measures of what youths do—namely, two measures of their allocation of time and several measures of socially deviant activity—as well as some standard outcome variables.

9.2.1   Time Allocation

Since, in principle, the allocation of a youths' time provides the most complete measure of his behavior, particular attention will be paid to the daily activity and monthly time-line questions in the NBER survey. The daily activity module of the questionnaire asked youths what their *main* and *other* activities were in a 24-hour weekday.[3] Responses to this question provide us with our best picture of what out-of-school nonemployed youths are doing with themselves. In the monthly time-line question the principal activity of youths in each month over the past year was organized on a monthly basis.[4] Responses to this question provide us with our best picture of the changing activities of youth over time.

Figure 9.1 summarizes the responses to the two time allocation questions for all youths, for youths out of school at the time of the survey, and for nonemployed out-of-school youths. Taking the average allocation of months first, parts 1 of panels A, B, and C show the division of main activities among employment, school, looking for work, and other activities for the sample as a whole. One-third of the months were spent at work, just about a third were spent in school or in training programs, and just over a third were spent in other activities, primarily looking for work. For the out-of-school youths (panel B) only 42 percent of months were spent at work and 9 percent at school or in training, leaving half of their time in other activities. Most disturbing of all, those out of school and not employed at the time of the survey (panel C) spent only 20 percent of their months in the past year at work and 35 percent in a fruitless search for work.

The daily time allocation questions asked youths their main activity during a 24-hour weekday and, also, as noted, other activities they did at the same time. There are several ways in which one might analyze the dual use of time. For descriptive purposes I have simply recorded allocation of time across main activities and supplementary activities in parts 2 of the panels and allocation of time across main activities only in parts 3 of the panels. Both sets of figures show that, on a daily basis, proportionately less time is spent on earning or learning or on searching for a job than was indicated in the monthly time line. This is because these activities, although they may be the major activity in

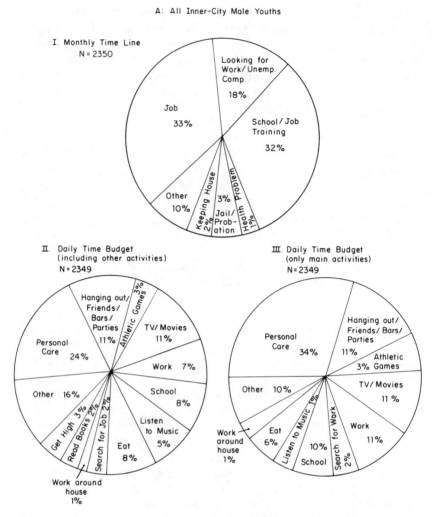

A: All Inner-City Male Youths

I. Monthly Time Line
N = 2350

Job 33%

Looking for Work/Unemp. Comp. 18%

School/Job Training 32%

Other 10%

Keeping House 2%

Jail/Probation 3%

Health Problem 1%

II. Daily Time Budget (including other activities) N = 2349

Personal Care 24%

Hanging out/ Friends/ Bars/ Parties 11%

Athletic Games 3%

TV/Movies 11%

Work 7%

School 8%

Listen to Music 5%

Eat 8%

Search for Job 2%

Read Books 2%

Get High 3%

Other 16%

Work around house 1%

III. Daily Time Budget (only main activities) N = 2349

Personal Care 34%

Hanging out/ Friends/ Bars/ Parties 11%

Athletic Games 3%

TV/Movies 11%

Work 11%

Search for Work 2%

School 10%

Listen to Music 1%

Eat 6%

Work around house 1%

Other 10%

Fig. 9.1   The Activities of Inner-City Black Male Youths in a Typical Day

a month, do not take up all of the youths' time. For the out-of-school, nonemployed youths, no more than two hours a day can be classified as likely to be socially productive. The major activities, outside of "personal care," are "hanging out/talking with friends" and "watching TV/movies." Although from one perspective these are consumption activities, the youth are not the idle rich. They are in the part of their life cycle where investments in human capital, either in school or on the job, are traditionally made for long-term economic advancement.

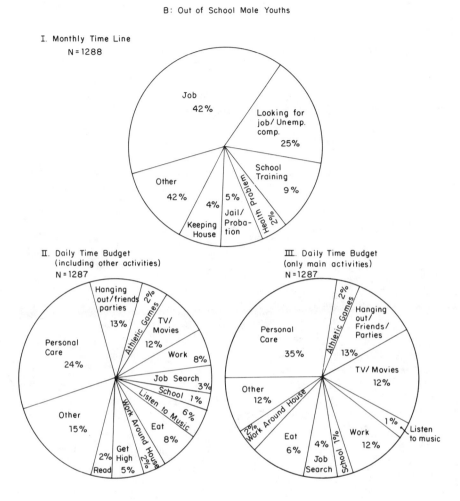

B: Out of School Male Youths

I. Monthly Time Line
   N = 1288

II. Daily Time Budget
(including other activities)
N = 1287

III. Daily Time Budget
(only main activities)
N = 1287

Fig. 9.1 (continued)

9.2.2 Other Outcome Measures

Table 9.1 records the mean values of some standard measures of socioeconomic outcomes, such as unemployment and wages, and of selected measures of socially deviant behavior, notably criminal activity and drug and excessive alcohol usage, in the NBER data on inner-city black male youths and, where available, in the NLS data on black and white young men nationwide.

The data on labor-force status show, as one might expect, that the NBER youths are in a markedly worse position in the job market than both all black youths and all white youths. Thirty-eight percent of the

C: Out of School and Not Employed Male Youths

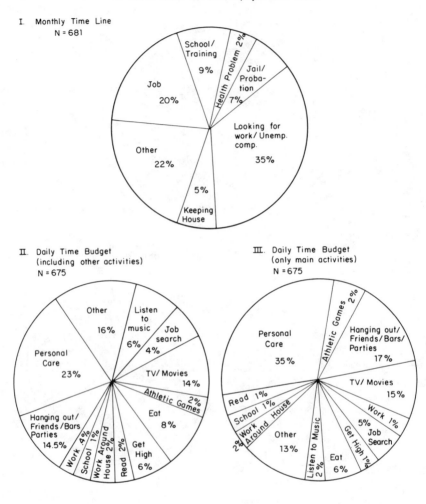

Fig. 9.1 (continued)

NBER sample were employed in the survey week, and only 48 percent of the out-of-school subsample were employed. Consistent with studies based on CPS data (for example, Freeman and Medoff 1982), the NBER data show that the low percentage of inner-city black youths who work is due as much to low labor-force participation as to high unemployment. By contrast, the wage figures for 1979–80 indicate that their wages differed only modestly from the wages paid other youths in 1980, with much of the observed difference due to the difference in periods

Table 9.1   The Standard Socioeconomic Measures of Youth Activity

Activity	All Youths			Out-of-School Youths			Out-of-School, Nonemployed Youths		
	NBER Blacks	NLS Blacks	NLS Whites	NBER Blacks	NLS Blacks	NLS Whites	NBER Blacks	NLS Blacks	NLS Whites
Labor-force/ school status									
1. Percentage in school	.451	.186	.155	—	—	—	—	—	—
2. Percentage in labor force	.669	.735	.797	.804	.903	.942	.627	.749	.763
3. Percentage of labor force unemployed	.430	.320	.196	.410	.320	.196	—	—	—
4. Percentage of total employed	.382	.500	.640	.479	.614	.758	—	—	—
5. Wage rate	$3.97	$4.22	$4.45	$4.26	$4.29	$4.53	$4.14	$3.94	$4.04

Table 9.1 (continued)

Activity	All Youths			Out-of-School Youths			Out-of-School, Nonemployed Youths		
	NBER Blacks	NLS Blacks	NLS Whites	NBER Blacks	NLS Blacks	NLS Whites	NBER Blacks	NLS Blacks	NLS Whites
Social Deviance									
6. Involved in any crimes in the past 12 months (NBER)[a]	12%	21%	16%	29%	23%	18%	32%	32%	
7. Drugs	27%	14%	21%	26%	16%	23%	27%	15%	25%
8. Drink alcohol every day or almost every day (NBER)[b]	16%	11%	28%	20%	12%	31%	22%	11%	30%
Annual Activity									
9. Weeks worked[c]	21	26	34	26	29	37	13	15	22
10. Annual Income	$4,025	$3,014	$4,973	$5,374	$3,591	$5,657	$3,409	$1,265	$2,521
11. Weekly Consumption Expenditures	$85	—	—	$110	—	—	$86	—	—

Source: The NBER survey and the NLS.

Note: Sample sizes varied, depending on the activity and subsample examined. Sample sizes ranged as follows: (1) *all youths*, NBER, 1,161–2,358; NLS blacks, 872–1,332; NLS whites, 2,410–3,629; (2) *out-of-school*, NBER, 928–1,295; NLS blacks, 824–1,084; NLS whites, 2,262–3,067; and (3) *out-of-school, nonemployed*, NBER, 362–681; NLS blacks, 210–331; NLS whites, 427–596.

[a] NLS figures are based on the survey question, "Amount of total income in past year from illegal activities?"

[b] NLS data were available only for those younger than age 18. Also, the figures include those who drank at least once a week, as opposed to at least once a day, as in the NBER survey.

[c] NBER figures were calculated by taking the months worked multiplied by 4.

covered (late 1979 to early 1980 in the NBER sample versus late 1980 in the NLS sample).

Perhaps the most surprising statistics in the table are those on socially deviant behavior. Although the youths in the NBER survey show considerably high levels of illegal activity, drug use, and drinking, both black and white youths in the NLS exhibit levels just as high or even higher.[5] Some of this similarity is explicable (whites have more money to spend on drugs) but other differences are hard to understand and may reflect inexplicable self-reporting biases. Some studies of self-reporting of socially deviant activities find an underestimate by black youths (Hindelang, Hirschi, and Weis 1981), which might explain the results for the NBER sample but not the high proportions of crime reported by the NLS sample.

Finally, the evidence on income and work over the year shows some differences and similarities among the groups. For all youths, annual incomes are relatively similar, and the incomes are close to the weekly consumption expenditures reported in the NBER survey ($4025 $\approx$ 85 $\times$ 52). For all youths out of school and not employed, the main difference is between blacks and whites in the NLS, while the blacks in the NBER survey have earnings comparable to those of the NLS whites. For all youths out of school, the lack of employment among blacks in both the NBER survey and the NLS produces lower incomes than those of white youths in the NLS.

In judging the earnings and consumption data it is important to remember that the vast majority of the black youths in the NBER sample were living with their parent(s), so that their housing and at least some of their food and clothing costs were presumably paid for by the parent. From this perspective, the incomes and spending are of a magnitude comparable to that of college students (ignoring tuition charges). The problem of black youths is therefore less one of low income as one of unproductive allocation of time, as indicated earlier in figure 9.1

9.2.3   Measures of Background

Most studies of the impact of background factors on socioeconomic achievement focus on the education or occupation of the individuals' parents and on whether they grew up in a one-parent (female-headed) or two-parent family. Some look at family income. Others look at related measures of the position of the family: whether the family is on welfare or resides in a public housing project.[6] The NBER survey supplements these standard variables with information on two other background characteristics that may be particularly influential in the lives of poor inner-city youths: whether other members of the family are engaged in productive activity, notably working;[7] and whether the youth is involved with potentially supportive social institutions, in par-

ticular, organized religion in the form of the church. Churchgoing differs
from the usual measures of family background because it reflects the
individual's relation to a broader social institution.[8] For this reason,
and because of the importance of the black church in the black community,[9] I will pay particular attention in this study to the impact of
church going on the achievement of black youths.

Table 9.2 records the mean levels of the various background variables
of interest in the NBER and NLS samples. By virtually all of the
measures, the ordering of the groups of youths is the same: The inner-
city black youths have the most disadvantaged background; the black
youths in the NLS are at a somewhat lesser disadvantage; and the
white youths in the NLS have the most advantaged background. For
example, only 43 percent of the youths in the inner-city sample reported
living with both parents at age 14, whereas the comparable figure for
black youths in the NLS is 58 percent, and for white youths in the
NLS, 84 percent. Nearly a third of the NBER group resided in public
housing projects, whereas only 10 percent of all black youths and only
1 percent of all white youths in the NLS lived in public housing. Churchgoing follows a similar pattern, with proportionately more inner-city
youths never attending church and fewer attending once a week or
more than other youths. In short, there is no doubt that by these
measures of background, the inner-city youths in the NBER survey
were the most disadvantaged, and far more so than the average black
youth.

The next question is: Do the background variables, particularly
churchgoing, affect the outcomes described earlier?

9.3   The Impact of Background

To determine whether or not background factors are important determinants of which young inner-city blacks escape from the pathol-
ogies endemic to inner-city slums, I estimated least-squares regressions
linking the outcome variables to the background variables. It is important to recognize that such regressions do not tell us whether background factors cause outcomes or whether good (bad) background and
good (bad) outcomes go together for other reasons, such as by sorting
heterogeneous persons and families. In other words, the regression
results do not imply that changes in a background variable will cause
changes in an outcome. To draw such an inference requires both a
structural model of causality and a treatment of possible sorting and
other noncausal interpretations of the data. Least-squares regressions
are, however, an essential first step toward accomplishing a more sophisticated analysis of the data.

Table 9.2   **The Proportions of Youths with Various Background**
                 Characteristics in the NBER and NLS Samples

| Background | NBER | NLS | |
Characteristic	Blacks	Blacks	Whites
Both Parents Present at Age 14	.43	.58	.84
Men in Household	.28	.51	.69
Household Members Working or in School	.41	.56	.71
Family on Welfare	.45	—	—
Family in Public Housing Project	.32	.10	.01
Attendance at Church			
not at all	.40	.19	.24
several times a year	.27	.23	.29
once a month	.09	.11	.09
2 or 3 times a month	.09	.17	.10
once a week	.11	.21	.20
more than once a week	.05	.09	.08
Part of Church Group	.18	—	—

Note: Sample sizes differ depending on the number of respondents who answered the question. In the NBER survey, the sample sizes ranged from 2,170 to 2,358; in the NLS, the sample sizes ranged from 3,213 to 3,629 for whites and from 1,174 to 1,332 for blacks.

Because none of the background variables is categorical, the technique for measuring the responses can affect the results (see Grether 1974). If the variable is placed on a numeric scale (6 = highest response, 1 = lowest, and so on), monotonic transformations can, under some circumstances, alter regression results significantly. If the variable is entered as a set of dummy variables taking a value of one if the response is in the category and zero otherwise, the regression may yield a number of confusing coefficients. What I have done is to transform the categorical variables into Z-scores, on the assumption that they reflect an underlying normal distribution.[10] I use these Z-scores for the churchgoing variable in this section and for churchgoing and several other variables in section 9.4.

9.3.1   Time Allocation

Table 9.3 summarizes the results of regressions linking the percentage of daily time and the percentage of months spent on "socially productive" as opposed to "socially nonproductive" activities. In the daily calculations "productive time" includes the following activities: working, searching for work, traveling to work, going to school, doing housework, and reading. "Nonproductive time" includes "hanging out, playing games, watching TV/movies, going to parties, listening to music, and getting high." In the monthly calculations, productive time includes months spent on a job, in training, or in school, and nonproductive time includes months spent in jail, unemployed, and so forth.

The calculations reveal powerful and statistically significant effects of two of the background variables on youths' allocation of time. On the positive side, churchgoing invariably raises the amount of time a youth spends on productive activity, while on the negative side, coming from a family on welfare invariably reduces the amount of time spent on productive activity. The other background variables have more mixed influences on youths' time allocation, with the proportion of men in the household generally having a negative impact on time allocation, while the proportion of household members who work has in several cases a positive effect, due (as we shall see) in large measure to its impact on work activity.

Differences in time allocation between productive and nonproductive activities reflect specific outcomes, such as committing illegal acts, going to school, working, and so forth. By examining the effect of churchgoing and of other variables on specific outcomes, we will have a better picture of the routes by which the variables operate and some insight into their possible causal significance. Accordingly, I estimated the relationship between the various background variables and socially deviant activities, school-going, and, for out-of-school youths, labor market activity.

Table 9.4 presents the estimated coefficients, standard errors, and percentage effects of churchgoing on the various outcomes. The most salient result is that churchgoing has a powerful negative impact on socially deviant activity and a positive impact on school attendance, but only a modest positive impact on employment or time worked and relatively little impact on wage rates or annual income. The pattern of results is sufficiently comparable across the NBER and NLS samples to give us considerable confidence in these results. It suggests that the major effect of churchgoing is to influence or reinforce the youth's decision to allot his time to activities having a potential future reward without affecting his immediate labor market position. By increasing the time youths spend in school, churchgoing will ultimately raise their earnings and employment levels; but it does not have a strong effect on the employment and earnings of youths currently out of school.

Table 9.5 summarizes the estimated effects of the other background variables in terms of plus or minus signs for whether the variable has or does not have a reasonably significant impact ($t > 1.5$) on the outcome measure. The pattern of signs reveals some interesting relationships. First, and most important, *the various background factors have differential effects on different variables.* Some, such as being a gang member, have a strong effect on deviant activity and may indeed be

Table 9.3 Determinants of Time Allocation by Inner-City Black Youths

Independent Variable	All Youths		Out-of-School Youths		Out-of-School Nonemployed Youths	
	Productive Hours	Productive Months	Productive Hours	Productive Months	Productive Hours	Productive Months
	All Hours	All Months	All Hours	All Months	All Hours	All Months
Intercept	.56 (.42)	.25 (.66)	−.19 (.45)	−.13 (.52)	−.09 (.19)	.32 (.30)
Both Parents Present at Age 14	−.00 (.16)	.02 (1.50)	.01 (.45)	−.04 (1.84)	−.01 (.54)	.06 (2.66)
Proportion of Men in Household	−.02 (.73)	−.04 (1.44)	−.07 (1.92)	−.06 (1.47)	−.03 (.69)	−.04 (.81)
Age	−.02 (5.96)	−.05 (15.39)	.01 (3.38)	−.06 (1.72)	.01 (2.67)	−.02 (3.92)
Married (1 = Yes)	.12 (3.53)	.13 (3.51)	.07 (2.00)	.11 (2.53)	.02 (.39)	.02 (.39)
Boston (1 = Yes)	−.02 (1.31)	.01 (.47)	.04 (2.10)	.01 (.85)	.01 (.29)	.07 (2.79)
Chicago (1 = Yes)	.08 (5.18)	.12 (7.13)	.03 (1.37)	.13 (5.00)	−.04 (1.27)	.17 (5.11)
Number of Persons in Household	−.002 (.68)	.005 (1.68)	−.003 (.72)	.006 (1.43)	−.01 (2.92)	−.004 (.89)
Public Housing (1 = Yes)	−.01 (.99)	−.03 (2.29)	−.02 (1.09)	−.04 (1.96)	.02 (.77)	−.00 (.11)
Proportion of Household Working	.02 (.60)	.08 (2.85)	.02 (.47)	.13 (3.25)	−.09 (2.27)	.03 (.66)
Household on Welfare (1 = Yes)	−.07 (4.09)	−.06 (4.14)	−.11 (5.51)	−.11 (4.64)	−.05 (2.33)	−.04 (1.49)
Gang Member (1 = Yes)	−.07 (1.64)	−.03 (.69)	−.10 (1.49)	−.04 (.56)	−.03 (.37)	.05 (.54)
Churchgoing (Z-score)	.04 (5.21)	.04 (4.80)	.03 (2.74)	.04 (3.33)	.01 (1.25)	.03 (2.47)
Years of School Completed	.02 (4.35)	.06 (11.06)	.03 (4.24)	.06 (8.06)	.01 (1.83)	.04 (4.32)
	$N = 2,119$	$N = 2,047$	$N = 1,145$	$N = 1,166$	$N = 609$	$N = 620$
	$R^2 = .09$	$R^2 = .19$	$R^2 = .12$	$R^2 = .17$	$R^2 = .06$	$R^2 = .13$

Note: t-statistics in parentheses. *Productive hours* defined as work, search for job, work travel, in school, study/do homework, watch children/keep house, read books/magazines/etc. *Productive months* defined as regular work, casual work, training, and school. (*Hours* includes secondary activity hours.)

Table 9.4   The Effect of Churchgoing on Socioeconomic Outcomes

	NBER Blacks		NLS Blacks		NLS Whites	
Outcome	Coefficient (t)	% Impact	Coefficient (t)	% Impact	Coefficient (t)	% Impact
All Youths						
Illegal Activities[a]	-.024 (3.10)	-20	-.029 (1.98)	-10	-.039 (5.10)	-19
Drug Use	-.050 (5.21)	-23	-.038 (3.54)	-27	-.07 (9.84)	-33
Alcohol Use[b]	-.022 (1.90)	-15	-.035 (2.18)	-31	-.046 (3.55)	-17
In School	.042 (4.41)	9	-.002 (.17)	-1	.019 (3.00)	12
Grades in School	.117 (3.52)	—	—		—	
Consumption	-5.73 (1.85)	-7	—		—	
Out-of-School Youths						
Employment	.028 (1.75)	6	.025 (1.62)	4	.023 (2.89)	3
Wage	.098 (.80)	2	.04 (.96)	1	-.131 (1.23)	-3
Months Worked/ Weeks Worked	.26 (1.49)	4	.50 (.79)	2	1.23 (3.73)	3
Annual Income	164 (1.20)	4	-57 (.41)	-2	63 (.68)	1

Note: Sample sizes ranged as follows: NBER, 836–2,358; NLS Blacks, 773–1,332; and NLS Whites, 2,191–3,428.
[a]NLS figures are based on the survey question, "Amount of total income in past year for illegal activities?"
[b]NLS data were available only for those younger than age 18. Also, the figures include those who drank at least once a week, as opposed to at least once a day, as in the NBER survey. Sample sizes were 501 for NLS blacks and 1,231 for NLS whites.

regarded as part and parcel of that activity, while others, notably the proportion of adults in the household who work, have rather mixed effects, increasing deviant activity while also improving the labor market position of the youths. Even the variable with the most consistent pattern, coming from a household on welfare, does not affect the wage rate. What these differential patterns suggest is that the results do *not* reflect a single background factor ("good" versus "bad" family background) but rather that the various background factors operate in distinct and sensible ways. For instance, a family with a high proportion of adults working is likely to provide less supervision of youth, permitting the increased socially deviant activity found here; but at the same time, that family is likely to provide the labor market contacts that help the youth in the job market (see Rees and Gray 1982).

In sum, the evidence shows that churchgoing and other background factors have generally substantial and plausible effects on the socioeconomic outcomes but that these effects are not uniform across outcome variables. Instead their effects are concentrated in some outcomes, giving plausibility to more complex causal analyses of the determinants of "who escapes."

9.4   What Are the Routes of Impact?

Finding strong linkages between background variables and who escapes is just the first step in analyzing the impact of background on socioeconomic outcomes. An important issue that will help us interpret the findings is the routes by which the background factors affect behavior. Do they operate by influencing attitudes, as social psychologists suggest, or do they operate by altering market opportunities, through contacts, references, and the like? In this section I examine these questions by employing a simple intervening-variables path model. I introduce into the regressions of tables 9.3 and 9.4 two types of intervening variables: variables measuring attitudes or motivation (which can be interpreted as reflecting the utility function of economics); and variables measuring labor market opportunities. I then examine the changes in the coefficients of churchgoing and the other background factors. If these new variables are significant intervening variables, the coefficients on churchgoing and on the other factors will decline. Alternatively, however, it could be argued that declines in the coefficients imply that the previous regressions yielded spurious results, namely, the attitude and market variables were omitted factors that belonged in the equation in the first place. At the very least, entering a variety of attitude and market variables into the equation provides a further test of the conclusion that churchgoing and some of the other background factors have important connections to socioeconomic outcomes.

Table 9.5   Effects of Background Variables in Regressions for Diverse Outcomes

Background Variable	Illegal Activity	Drugs	Alcohol	School Grades	School Attendance	Employment	Wage	Months/Weeks Working
NBER Blacks								
1. Proportion of Adults Working								
2. Welfare Home	+	+	+	+	+	+	+	+
3. Public Housing			+	−	−	−	−	−
4. Proportion of Men in Household	−		−		−	−	−	−
5. Gang Member	+	+	+					
6. Parents Present at Age 14	+	−	+					
7. Household Size	−							
8. Churchgoing	−	−	−	+	+	+		+
NLS Blacks								
1. Proportion of Adults Working	+	+	+		−	+		+
2. Public Housing		−	−					
3. Proportion of Men in Household						−		−
4. Parents Present at Age 14	+				−	+		
5. Household Size								+
6. Churchgoing								
NLS Whites								
1. Proportion of Adults Working								+
2. Public Housing	+	+	+		−			
3. Proportion of Men in Household								
4. Parents Present at Age 14						−		
5. Household Size		−			+	−		−
6. Churchgoing	−	−	−			+		−

Note: + or − indicates variable had a t-statistic of ≥ 1.5.

To measure attitudes I have taken eight questions from the NBER survey.[11] The most important question is "How strong a role does religion play in your life?" because it represents a related but alternative variable to churchgoing. To the extent that churchgoing either operates through religious attitudes or is itself dependent on them, religious attitudes should enter significantly and greatly reduce the impact of churchgoing. To the extent that churchgoing reflects other forces, such as community connections or reinforcement of certain kinds of behavior, it should remain an important factor.

Measuring market opportunities is difficult because, exclusive of the city of residence (already in the calculations), the only information available in the NBER survey and the NLS is data on the individual's views of the market; it is therefore necessary to assume that these views reflect the actual market rather than some mix of attitudes and reality. The two most important questions I use here are "How often do you have a chance to make money illegally?" which I have coded one if the respondent answered a few times a day or a few times a week and zero otherwise, and "What do you think are your chances of getting a job at this time?" which I have coded as a Z-score variable. In addition, I included three other measures of the market in the calculations.[12]

The effect of introducing the vectors of the intervening attitude and market variables on the estimated impact of churchgoing is shown in table 9.6, which records the coefficients of churchgoing with and without the intervening variables in the regressions and the coefficients of religious attitudes and the two major market variables. The regressions include all the other variables used in tables 9.3 and 9.4 and the full set of attitude and market variables indicated in the table note.

There are three notable findings. First is the general continued effect of churchgoing on outcomes in the presence of the additional variables. Except for illegal activities and months employed, both of which were reduced largely by the introduction of the market variables, the inclusion of additional variables barely affected the churchgoing coefficients. Similarly, the effect of other background variables was at most modestly reduced by the addition of the attitude and market variables, suggesting that the various sets of factors operate essentially orthogonally. The second finding is the general insignificance of religious attitudes in the equations, a result consistent with Datcher-Loury and Loury's results (in this volume). It is the act of churchgoing, not religious attitudes, that affects behavior. This finding suggests that it is the role of the church as a social institution that underlies the statistical findings. Third, the market variables have extremely significant and powerful effects on the outcomes. Youths who have many chances to make money illegally spend fewer hours and months on socially pro-

Table 9.6   Effects of Adding Attitude and Market Variables on Churchgoing in NBER Regressions

Outcome	Churchgoing		Religious Attitude[a]	Market: Can Find Job[a] Easily	Market: Chance to Make Money Illegally[b]
	Before	After			
Productive, All Hours	.04 (5.21)	.04 (4.45)	-.01 (.93)	.04 (5.19)	-.06 (4.61)
Productive, All Months	.04 (4.80)	.03 (3.71)	-.00 (.26)	.06 (7.79)	-.06 (4.45)
Committed Illegal Act (Yes = 1)	-.024 (3.10)	-.016 (1.88)	-.00 (.16)	.00 (.60)	.12 (8.34)
Takes Drugs (Yes = 1)	-.050 (5.21)	-.045 (4.25)	-.00 (.41)	.00 (.09)	.11 (6.09)
Alcohol Use	-.022 (1.90)	-.025 (2.06)	.01 (1.23)	.02 (2.21)	.06 (2.92)
Attends School	.042 (4.41)	.041 (3.95)	-.02 (1.53)	.01 (1.16)	-.07 (3.91)
Employed	.030 (1.75)	.030 (1.77)	-.02 (1.41)	.08 (5.34)	-.10 (3.39)
Months Employed	.26 (1.49)	.08 (.41)	.09 (.57)	.88 (5.72)	-.41 (1.30)

Note: Regressions include all other variables contained in table 9.3 and seven other attitude and three other market variables, as listed in notes 11 and 12. t-statistics in parentheses.

[a]As a Z-score.

[b]1 = a few times daily or weekly.

332

ductive activities, engage in more socially deviant activities, and work less, whereas youths who think jobs are easy to find spend more hours on productive activities, notably, working.

The continued impact of churchgoing and the other background variables after having added the intervening variables is in some ways encouraging and in other ways discouraging. Their consistent impact means the relationships persist despite changes in specification. But it also means we have not been able to pin down the routes by which the various background factors affect behavior.

9.5 Possible Causal Significance of the Estimated Links

Those regressions impress me. Now I know what to do to improve the economic position of inner-city black youths. Force them to go to church. Kick their families off welfare. Get jobs for their family members.—Simple Activist

Those regressions tell us nothing about what to do. All they show is that there are good families and good kids and bad families and bad kids in the inner city. The good ones go to church. The bad ones live on welfare. The good ones will be good no matter what; the bad ones will be bad no matter what. Put a bad kid in church and he'll disrupt everything. There's nothing in the analysis that says what to do. —Simple Do-Nothingist

We must now ask to what extent, if at all, the estimated effects of the background variables reflect true causal influences as opposed to a sorting of individuals and their families by unobservable "good" and "bad" characteristics. To answer this question requires a genuine experiment in which one changes the relevant background variables and observes the ensuing behavior. For instance, one could provide money to black churches to expand their membership and see whether the youths attracted to the churches altered their behavior. In the absence of such experiments, it is difficult to draw more than tentative inferences about causality. Even longitudinal data, which are widely used to control for fixed unobservables, may not suffice because of the possible endogeneity of changes: a family that on its own accord leaves welfare, a youth who on his own accord starts going to church, are likely to behave differently from the randomly selected experimental family or youth in the ideal experiment. Difficult though the causal issue may be, it is incumbent upon us to address it, if only to highlight the shortcomings of causal inferences from survey data of the types used here.

In this section I probe, albeit tentatively, some aspects of the relationships among churchgoing and the other variables to see if it is possible "to wrest some intelligence from less than ideal information and to cope with intrinsically refractory problems of conceptualization and model specification" (Duncan and Featherman 1973, 230).

One potential alternative to the analyses of churchgoing in sections 9.3 and 9.4 is to look at it as a dependent variable, causally determined by other background factors. If churchgoing is highly dependent on other factors in a manner similar to that of the outcome variables, one might prefer to view it as endogenous rather than exogenous. If there were plausible instrumental variables in the data set (which I do not believe there are), one might further seek to instrument churchgoing on those factors.

Table 9.7 presents the results of some calculations that relate churchgoing to various explanatory factors in the data sets. Although there are some definite links between churchgoing and other factors, the pattern of coefficients on the independent variables is different from that found in regressions of other "outcomes" on those variables. Having both parents present at age 14, for example, greatly raises churchgoing but has no significant effect on outcomes; living in a public housing project reduces churchgoing but has a generally negligible effect on outcomes. In the NBER survey, religious attitudes, which affected virtually no outcome, is, of course, closely related to churchgoing. These patterns of effects are not definitive, but they do illustrate once more that background factors have drastically different effects on different outcomes, including their effects on churchgoing as an outcome.

9.6 Summary and Conclusions

All told, although we cannot reject the possibility that the effects of churchgoing are noncausal, the patterns of regression coefficients are clearly inconsistent with relatively simple single-factor "omitted heterogeneity" explanations of its impact. At the very least, more complex factor models are needed; and here, as elsewhere, reliance on increasing numbers of omitted factors to explain results calls into question the noncausal explanation.

Even if one rejects the causal interpretation of the relationships found in this paper, however, it is important to recognize that the analysis has identified an important set of variables that separate successful from unsuccessful young men in the inner city. More specifically, the empirical analysis shows, first, that the principal variable on which the paper focuses, churchgoing, is associated with substantial differences in the behavior of youths, and thus in their chances to "escape" from inner-city poverty. Churchgoing affects allocation of time, school attendance, work activity, and the frequency of socially deviant activity. Although it is difficult to determine the causal links by which churchgoing affects behavior—in particular, whether churchgoing is simply

Table 9.7   **Estimates of the Effects of Background and Other Factors on Churchgoing**

Independent Variables	NBER Blacks		NLS Blacks	NLS Whites
	(1)	(2)		
Intercept	1.06	1.11	1.45	.41
Both Parents Present at Age 14	.21 (5.09)	.17 (4.54)	.19 (3.65)	.16 (3.63)
Proportion of Men in Household	.02 (.19)	−.02 (.24)	−.24 (1.76)	.14 (2.10)
Percent Adults Working	−.01 (.12)	−.01 (.08)	.14 (1.37)	−.08 (.91)
Age	−.08 (8.88)	−.07 (7.90)	−.11 (8.04)	−.11 (11.86)
Marital Status	.26 (2.45)	.25 (2.50)	.17 (1.08)	.09 (1.36)
Household Size	−.01 (1.19)	−.01 (.85)	−.04 (3.39)	.06 (5.39)
Public Housing	−.19 (4.36)	−.19 (4.65)	−.21 (2.55)	−.28 (2.07)
Welfare	−.09 (2.13)	−.07 (1.81)		
Gang	−.06 (.47)	−.05 (.45)		
Education Completed	.05 (3.15)	.03 (1.56)	.06 (3.71)	.11 (10.47)
Boston	.07 (1.41)	.09 (1.97)		
Chicago	.02 (.39)	.06 (1.30)		
South			.26 (4.93)	
Urban			.04 (.58)	.18 (5.03)
Attitude Variables				−.04 (1.16)
Religious		.38 (19.84)		
Other Attitude		√		
Market Variables		√		
R^2	.07	.23	.09	.08

Note: t-statistics in parentheses.

an indication that youths are "good kids" or whether it truly alters behavior—the pattern of statistical results suggests that at least some part of the churchgoing effect is the result of an actual causal impact. At the least, the effect of churchgoing is not the result of churchgoing youths having "good attitudes" or having better market opportunities than others.

Second, the diverse background factors examined in this study do *not* have comparable effects on the various outcomes. Some significantly influence certain outcomes and not others, thereby rejecting the possibility that the background factors measure simply a single, unobserved, family-person heterogeneity factor. Indeed, the differential effects of the background factors suggest true causal impacts, with, for example, the proportion of a youth's family who work having positive effects on his labor market activity but not on his other activities.

Third, in addition to churchgoing, the background factors that most influence "who escapes" are whether other members of the family work and whether the family is on welfare. By contrast, youths from homes in which both parents were present at age 14 do only marginally better than those from homes in which only one parent was present at that age, implying that, by itself, the female-headed home is not a major deterrent to socioeconomic success. In addition, having some men in the household who are *not* employed appears to have negative effects on some outcomes.

Finally, youths' allocation of time and other activities are significantly influenced by market opportunities (or the youths' perceptions thereof), with those who believe it would be easy to find a job if they had to find one more likely to engage in socially productive activities than others, and youths who see many opportunities to make illegal money less likely to engage in socially productive activities than other youths.

Notes

1. These data are from U.S. Department of Labor (1981, table A-5).
2. In addition, there are substantial "errors of measurement" when adults report about the activity of their children in the standard government surveys. See Freeman and Medoff 1982a.
3. For the specifics, see Mathematica Policy Research, Inc.
4. See Mathematica Policy Research, Inc. (1979).
5. In fact, the socially deviant behaviors reported in the NLS are even more serious than those elicited by the NBER questionnaire. If one takes all the reported acts of crime by NLS youth (some of which are minor), it turns out that upward of 50% of all youths in the NLS reported committing at least one.
6. See Duncan, Featherman, and Duncan (1972).
7. This variable has been found to be important in whether youths work in Rees and Gray (1982).
8. Churchgoing has not been studied in previous research. To my knowledge the most comparable work is that of Duncan and Featherman (1973) on the effect of religion on achievement.
9. There is an extensive literature on the black church in America, beginning with the early work of Franklin Frazier (1963).
10. In this technique each regression is given a different numeric value approximately equal to its standard deviation in a normal distribution with zero mean and unit standard deviation.
11. These questions are:
[Are the following statements] true, somewhat true, or not at all true?
(a) "Knowing the right people is the key to finding a job."
(b) "If you work hard and get a good education you'll get ahead in America."
(c) "Having a good education is very important, somewhat important, not at all important to you in your life right now."
(d) "Working at a job is very important, somewhat important, not at all important to you in your life right now."
Would you say [each of the following statements] depends a lot, somewhat, a little, or not at all on your having a job?
(e) "Your being respected by other people."
(f) "Your being able to afford the things you want."
(g) "How strong a role does religion play in your life?"

12. The questions used for the variable described in the text are:
(a) "Say that for some reason you had to get (a job/another job) righu now. Keeping in mind your past experiences, your education and your training . . . what do you think are your chances of getting that kind of job (best job you think you can get) at this time?"
(b) "Suppose you were really desperate for money. How easy would you say it would be for you to find a job working at any job at the minimum wage?"
The other three measures are:
(a) "If a friend comes to you and says he desperately needs to make some money, what would you tell him to do?" A dummy variable equals zero if the respondent suggested an illegal job or giving up and one if he suggested a legal job.
(b) "How often do you have a chance to make money illegally?" Two dummy variables: one for a few times a week or a few times a day; and the second for less than a few times a week or no chance at all.
(c) "How much do you think you could make on the street doing something illegal compared to on a straight job you could get?" A dummy variable equals one if more on the street or about same on each and zero if more on a job.

References

Blau, P. M., and O. D. Duncan. 1967. *The American occupational structure.* New York: John Wiley & Sons.

Duncan, O. D. 1968. Inheritance of poverty or inheritance of race? In *On understanding poverty,* ed. D. P. Moynihan, 85–110. New York: Basic Books.

Duncan, O. D., and D. Featherman. 1973. Psychological and cultural factors in the process of occupational achievement. In *Structural models in social science,* ed. O. D. Duncan and A. Goldberger, 229–53. New York: Seminar Press.

Duncan, O. D., L. Featherman, and B. Duncan. 1972. *Socioeconomic background and achievement.* New York: Seminar Press.

Frazier, E. F. 1963. *The negro church in America.* New York: Schocken Books.

Freeman, R. B. 1981. Black economic progress after 1964: Who has gained and why? In *Studies in Labor Markets,* ed. S. Rosen. Chicago: University of Chicago Press.

Freeman, R. B. 1977. *Black elite: The new market for highly qualified black Americans.* New York: McGraw-Hill.

Freeman, R. B. and S. Medoff. 1982a. Why does the rate of youth labor force activity differ across surveys? In *The youth labor market problem,* ed. R. B. Freeman and D. A. Wise. Chicago: University of Chicago Press.

Freeman, R. B., and J. Medoff. 1982b The youth labor market problem in the U.S.: An overview. In *The youth labor market problem: Its nature, causes, and consequences,* ed. R. B. Freeman and D. A. Wise. Chicago: University of Chicago Press.

Grether, D. 1974. Correlations with ordinal data. *Journal of Econometrics* 2: 241–46.

Hindelang, M. J., T. Hirschi, and J. Weis. 1981. *Measuring delinquency,* vol. 123, Sage Library of Social Research. Beverly Hills, Calif.: Sage.

Mathematica Policy Research, Inc. 1979. *Young black men employment study.* Princeton, N.J.: Mathematica Policy Research. (October 9.)

Rees, A., and W. Gray. 1982. Family effects in youth employment. In *The youth labor market problem: Its nature, causes, and consequences,* R. B., Freeman and D. A., Wise. Chicago: University of Chicago Press.

U.S. Department of Labor. 1981. *Employment and training report of the President.* Washington, D.C.: GPO.

10   The Effects of Attitudes and Aspirations on the Labor Supply of Young Men

Linda Datcher-Loury and Glenn Loury

10.1   Introduction

Any discussion of the causes of earnings inequality inevitably raises the question of the extent to which earnings differences reflect differences in the opportunities available to individuals versus differences in the behavior of individuals faced with similar opportunities. On one hand, conservatives invariably call attention to the fact that different people with the same objective opportunities will not generally choose to act in such a way that their earnings are equal. Liberals, on the other hand, tend to stress the importance of divergent opportunities as an explanation of earnings disparities. Liberals further argue that since values, attitudes, and beliefs may themselves partially reflect an individual's previous labor market experiences (namely, past opportunities), their contemporaneous correlation with individual earnings is not sufficient evidence to establish the direction of the causality implicitly assumed by the conservative argument.

This divergence of views about the importance of subjective versus objective factors in individual earnings determination takes on particular significance in the discussion of racial economic inequality. The practice of racial discrimination in employment has made it quite natural to seek an explanation of the still substantial gap in earnings between blacks and whites in the presumably different opportunity structures they face. But many observers of American society have called attention to cultural differences between blacks and whites that may have economic consequences (Myrdal 1946; Moynihan 1965; Liebow

Linda Datcher-Loury is assistant professor of economics at Tufts University. Glenn C. Loury is professor of political economy at Harvard University, J. F. Kennedy School of Government.

1967; Banfield 1974). This notion achieves its clearest expression in the "culture of poverty" argument, which posits that the persistence of poverty over generations is partly the consequence of the inculcation in poor children of cultural norms inconsistent with the attainment of material success.

Despite the importance of these considerations for understanding the roots of inequality, there has not been a great deal of empirical work in the economics literature that measures the impact of subjective attitudes, values, and beliefs on earnings and employment. This state of affairs no doubt reflects the difficulty of quantitatively measuring an individual's subjective state of mind. It is also a consequence of the conceptual problem facing economists who attempt to integrate the ideas and findings of the other social sciences into our choice-theoretic model of individual behavior. Because we economists have so little to say about how preferences are formed, we tend to eschew explanations of economic differences that rely in an essential way upon variations in attitudes, values, and beliefs (see, for example, Becker and Stigler 1977).

This paper describes the results of an empirical investigation of the relationship between a variety of subjective factors, on the one hand, and the labor supply behavior of young black and white men, on the other. While controlling for an array of economic factors ordinarily thought to determine labor supply, we seek to estimate what effect our subjective variables have on the work effort of these young men. Our findings suggest that some measures of attitudes, values, and beliefs are, holding constant economics factors, important determinants of labor supply for the individuals in our samples. We also find that this relationship between subjective factors and work effort is quite different for black and white young men.

10.2   Theoretical Framework

In this section, where that ubiquitous device of economists—the model—ordinarily appears, we attempt to provide a plausible, illustrative scenario for why attitudes and aspirations might affect work hours and to discuss some relevant theory in the literature. This scenario is suggested by the recent application of psychological cognitive dissonance theory to the study of economic behavior by Akerlof and Dickens (1982).

Imagine a dynamic model of labor supply in which the real wage varies randomly over time, following a stationary stochastic process with an unknown parameter. Suppose further that hours worked may not be instantly or costlessly adjusted from period to period, so that optimal labor supply at any particular time depends on the worker's estimate of this parameter, hereafter referred to as the *permanent wage*. Plausibly, optimal hours could be taken as an increasing function of the estimated permanent-wage rate. For example, if the worker remains on the same job, he supplies more hours when expected wage growth is higher given the current wage. In the case in which the worker is unemployed for some period, he exerts more effort in his job search when he anticipates a greater expected payoff.

Now suppose that beliefs about the expected value of the permanent wage are not simply a matter of statistical inference based on objective conditions and past experience, but are also affected by the worker's preconceptions about himself and the labor market. Following Akerlof and Dickens, we postulate that the worker chooses those beliefs, given his preconceptions, to maximize his utility. Utility is, on one hand, enhanced by adopting a posterior parameter estimate of the permanent wage in keeping with subjective preconceptions and is, on the other hand, reduced by adopting a posterior estimate inconsistent with the objective statistical data. The result of this trade-off is the adoption of posterior estimates of the expected value of the permanent wage biased away from the "correct" statistically efficient estimate in the direction of the parameter values most consistent with the worker's preconceived notions about himself and the labor market, that is, *cognitive dissonance*. This means that a worker who is optimistic about his chances for success in the labor market will anticipate a higher permanent wage and, as a result, work more hours than an otherwise identical worker who is relatively pessimistic.[1]

The main problem associated with estimating the size of this hypothesized effect is the measurement of beliefs. In this study of young men in their late teens and early twenties, we proxied these beliefs mainly by the youths' occupational aspirations at age 30. There are a number of ways of interpreting their responses to this question. They may reflect the youths' subjective assessment of their own abilities, or alternatively, of the opportunities they expect to face. A teenager aspiring to a managerial or crafts job at age 30 could plausibly be regarded as having a higher subjective evaluation of his capabilities than a contemporary who hopes to be a laborer when he grows up. This correlation between expected labor market success and occupational aspirations is weakened to the extent that youths choose occupations that they know they have little hope of attaining. The importance of this slippage is investigated in one of the data sets used here, which not only reports aspirations but also distinguishes among youths who think their chances are excellent, good, fair, or poor.

Another possibility is that low occupational aspirations for a given youth reflect his belief that it is pointless to hope for a higher-level occupation because such opportunities are not available for "people like him.'' Alternatively, reported occupational aspirations may reflect the normative judgment of the prospective worker as to what he "ought" to want for himself when older. The expectations of his family and friends would then presumably influence his reported aspirations.

It is not possible to know with certainty which of these speculations is correct. Nonetheless, in our analysis of the labor supply of these young men, we make an effort to control for the objective worker characteristics likely to influence future opportunities and for the family background characteristics and attitudes of "significant others" likely to affect the young worker's normative judgment.

Although occupational aspirations serve as the principal proxy for beliefs, they are supplemented by survey items measuring attitudes toward work, education, and religious commitment. We assume that expectations about labor market success are positively correlated with beliefs about the efficacy of job search and the importance attached to work and schooling. The extent of religious commitment is the least obvious of the proxies for labor market success. It is employed here to identify youths whose level of religious commitment was far lower than that of their peer group; it therefore may serve as a general measure of alienation.

Although the effect of attitudes and aspirations on labor market behavior has not received a great deal of attention in the economics literature, a few empirical studies have tested for its impact on labor market outcomes. Using a sample of young and middle-aged men taken from the National Longitudinal Surveys of Labor Market Experience (NLS), Andrisani (1977) investigated whether the perceived relationship between initiative and success affected labor market experience. He measured this relationship by the respondent's score on an abbreviated version of Rotter's Internal-External Scale. Andrisani's analysis strongly suggested that attitudes and initiative are important factors explaining differences in earnings, earnings growth, occupation, and occupational advancement for blacks and whites as well as for the young and the middle-aged sample members. Furthermore, his results indicated the payoffs from these factors are as high for blacks as for whites.

Duncan and Morgan (1981) attempted to replicate Andrisani's findings of the effects of attitudinal efficacy on subsequent changes in economic status using a sample of men aged 18 to 36 taken from the University of Michigan Panel Study of Income Dynamics. They found that their measures of efficacy had no significant effect on hourly earnings two years hence for either blacks or whites. But the estimated impact for a four-year change was about three times as large as the two-year effect and, in the case of whites, significantly different from zero.

The analysis performed here expands on this earlier work in three main ways. First, it identifies whether occupational aspirations and other attitudinal factors not examined by Adrisani or Duncan and Morgan have an impact on labor market experience. Second, it examines the effect of these variables on labor supply rather than on earnings or on occupational status. Third, the analysis includes a large sample of low-income black youths, a group with particularly intractable labor market problems.

10.3 Data

The data used here to test hypotheses about the effects of aspirations and attitudes on labor supply come from (1) a sample of men aged 16 to 24 years taken from the 1979 NBER Survey of Inner-City Black Youth in Boston, Chicago, and Philadelphia and (2) a sample of men aged 14 to 19 in 1966 taken from the National Longitudinal Survey of Young Men.

Table 10.1 presents the mean values of the important variables in the analysis. The labor-supply, income, and work-experience variables for the NLS sample were constructed from responses to the 1973 interviews and were measured as of 1972. Occupational aspirations were measured at ages 17–19, that is, in 1966 for the older group and in 1969 for the younger subsample. All other items were measured as of 1971, since no interview was conducted in 1972. We restricted the sample to youths with positive work hours and earnings in 1972 who were last enrolled in school in 1971 or earlier. We also limited it to youths living in SMSAs, for comparability with the NBER data. The NBER labor-supply and income variables refer to the 12 months preceding the interview, while the other items were measured as of the survey date. As in the case of the NLS, the NBER sample was restricted to those with positive work hours and earnings and no schooling in the past year.

The distribution of attitudes and occupational aspirations is of special interest for our purposes. The attitudes measured in the NBER survey are represented by dummy variables, with a respondent coded as a one for attitudes 1 and 2, respectively, if he answered "true" to the statements "Most of your friends are unemployed" and "The people you know who are unemployed could find work if they really wanted to." A respondent coded as a one for attitudes 3 and 4, respectively, if he answered "very important" to the question whether having a good education and working at a job were "very important, somewhat important, or not at all important in life right now." Finally, sample members are coded as a one for attitude 5 if they answered that the role of religion was "very strong, strong, or somewhat strong" in their lives.

Table 10.1   Means of Selected Variables from NBER and NLS Samples

Variable	NBER Blacks		NLS 14–16		NLS 17–19	
	16–19	20–24	Blacks	Whites	Blacks	Whites
Annual Hours of Work	1,083.0	1,455.9	—	—	—	—
Weeks Worked	29.6	37.6	44.9	47.6	48.0	47.7
Hours Worked per Week	35.5	39.1	—	—	—	—
ln Hourly Earnings	.77	1.05	—	—	—	—
ln Weekly Earnings	4.27	4.69	4.70	4.97	4.84	5.14
Years of Schooling	10.5	11.4	11.5	12.2	11.7	12.9
Work Experience	1.7	4.5	3.4	2.8	6.1	4.9
Age	18.2	21.9	15.0	15.1	17.9	17.9
ln Nonlabor Income	2.43	1.96	4.74	5.24	4.90	4.75
Household Head	.07	.20	.36	.48	.57	.70
Lives in South	—	—	.60	.26	.53	.23
Lives in Philadelphia	.29	.34	—	—	—	—
Lives in Chicago	.41	.35	—	—	—	—
Lives in Boston	.30	.31	—	—	—	—
Union at Workplace	.20	.29	.27	.26	.32	.30
Professional or Managerial Worker	.02	.05	.06	.14	.12	.22
Clerical or Sales Worker	.13	.13	.09	.13	.14	.20
Craftsman	.15	.15	.11	.20	.12	.21
Operative	.18	.23	.37	.29	.37	.23
Laborer, Service Worker, or Other	.52	.44	.37	.24	.14	.25

Percentage of Weeks Worked, 1967–71	—	—	43.2	49.3	77.7	66.7
Attitude 1: Most Friends Are Unemployed	.37	.28	—	—	—	—
Attitude 2: Unemployed Could Find Work If They Wanted to	.54	.46	—	—	—	—
Attitude 3: Having a Good Education Is Very Important	.73	.73	—	—	—	—
Attitude 4: Working at a Job is Very Important	.88	.88	—	—	—	—
Attitude 5: Religion Plays Strong Role	.65	.71	—	—	—	—
Professional or Managerial Worker at Age 30	.37	.47	.34	.39	.34	.48
Sales or Clerical Worker at Age 30	.07	.09	.08	.04	.10	.03
White-Collar at Age 30, Excellent Chance	.09	.11	—	—	—	—
White-Collar at Age 30, All Others	.35	.45	—	—	—	—
Craftsman at Age 30	.31	.19	.21	.18	.20	.20
Craftsman at Age 30, Excellent Chance	.09	.05	—	—	—	—
Craftsman at Age 30, All Others	.22	.14	—	—	—	—
Operative at Age 30	.12	.11	.08	.06	.12	.06
Laborer, Service Worker, or Other at Age 30	.13	.13	.29	.33	.24	.23

In both the NLS and NBER surveys the occupational aspiration measures are derived from responses to the question "What type of job or occupation would you like to have when you are 30 years old?" In addition, the NBER survey codes distinguish between respondents who thought their chances of attaining that job or occupation were "excellent" and those who thought their chances were only "good, fair, poor, or don't know."

Table 10.1 shows that there are only small differences in attitudes between the older and younger NBER subsamples. The overwhelming majority of both groups reported that religion played a strong role in their lives and that having a good education and working at a job was very important to them at that time. In addition, although approximately one-third of each group believed that most of their friends were unemployed, about half of each group thought that the unemployed could find work if they wanted to.

Table 10.1 also indicates that occupational aspirations were relatively uniform across races and age groups. For all samples, occupational aspirations were concentrated in the professional-managerial category, with one-third to one-half of young men falling into this group. The crafts category generally made up about one-fifth of both the black and white samples, but blacks were somewhat more prevalent in the operative and sales-clerical groups.

Table 10.2 shows the relationship between adult occupation and occupational aspirations. As indicated earlier, aspirations were measured at ages 17–19 for both NLS samples, while actual occupation was measured as of ages 20–22 for the younger group and ages 23–25 for the older group. Because the NBER study does not include a longitudinal component, both actual occupation and occupational aspirations were taken from the 1979 interviews. The underlined figures in table 10.2 give the fraction of the sample with occupational aspirations in the specified category and the subgroups give the actual occupational distribution within each aspirational level. For example, 37 percent of NBER men aged 16 to 19 aspired to be professional or managerial workers. Only 3 percent of this group, however, actually held professional or managerial jobs.

Table 10.2 suggests that, especially in the case of white-collar and crafts jobs, blacks were much less likely to obtain jobs within their desired occupational category. Forty-five percent of NLS blacks aged 17 to 19 who in 1966 aspired to be professional or managerial workers ultimately held operative, service, or laborer jobs by 1971, compared to only 27 percent of the whites. Similarly, 65 percent of the blacks aged 17 to 19 who aspired to be craftsmen held jobs in the operative or service-laborer categories; the portion of comparable whites was only 45 percent. The congruence between the current occupation and

Table 10.2   **Distribution of Actual Adult Occupation by Occupational Aspiration**

Occupation Aspiration	NBER Blacks		NLS 14–16		NLS 17–19	
	16–19	20–24	Blacks	Whites	Blacks	Whites
Professional or Managerial Aspiration	37.2	47.7	33.6	38.9	33.7	48.5
Professional or Managerial	2.7	8.9	2.6	23.3	24.2	30.6
Clerical or Sales	21.9	18.2	13.2	14.3	21.2	24.3
Crafts	11.0	11.7	10.5	16.5	9.1	17.9
Operative	11.0	20.2	36.8	21.8	24.2	13.2
Other	53.4	41.1	38.8	24.1	21.2	13.9
Clerical or Sales Aspiration	6.6	8.9	8.0	3.8	10.2	3.1
Professional or Managerial	0	2.2	0	15.4	10.0	9.1
Clerical or Sales	30.8	28.3	11.1	30.8	0	54.6
Crafts	15.4	8.7	0	15.4	10.0	18.2
Operative	23.1	28.3	55.6	15.4	40.0	9.1
Other	30.8	32.6	33.3	23.1	40.0	9.1
Craftsman Aspiration	30.1	19.8	21.2	17.8	20.4	19.9
Professional or Managerial	1.7	1.0	8.3	4.9	5.0	9.9
Clerical or Sales	6.8	4.9	12.5	3.3	10.0	9.9
Crafts	22.0	30.1	20.8	39.3	20.0	35.2
Operative	15.3	24.3	33.3	31.2	50.0	32.4
Other	54.2	39.8	25.0	21.3	15.0	12.7
Operative Aspiration	12.2	11.4	8.0	5.9	12.2	5.9
Professional or Managerial	0	3.4	0	0	0	4.8
Clerical or Sales	4.2	5.1	0	10.0	8.3	4.4
Crafts	16.7	6.8	0	20.0	16.7	28.6
Operative	29.2	39.0	66.7	65.0	50.0	52.4
Other	50.0	45.8	33.3	5.0	25.0	9.5
Other Aspiration	13.8	12.3	29.2	33.6	23.5	22.7
Professional or Managerial	3.7	3.1	12.1	10.4	8.7	19.8
Clerical or Sales	7.4	6.3	3.0	15.7	17.4	19.8
Crafts	7.4	14.1	9.1	13.9	8.7	12.7
Operative	29.6	17.2	27.3	32.2	26.1	28.4
Other	51.9	59.4	48.5	27.8	39.1	19.8
Total	100.0	100.0	100.0	100.0	100.0	100.0

occupational aspirations is smallest for the NBER 16–19 group. With the exception of the small part of the sample that had clerical or sales aspirations, at least half of these workers tended to fall into the service-laborer category, regardless of their desired occupation at age 30. Nevertheless, this finding is largely an artifact of measuring both occupational aspirations and actual occupation as of ages 16–19. As these individuals mature, their profile may become closer to that of the older NBER group.

10.4   Estimates of the Effects of Attitudes and Aspirations

Findings for the effects of attitudes and aspirations on labor supply are listed in table 10.3 for the NBER samples and in table 10.4 for the NLS samples. Treating the log wages as endogenous, the first two columns of table 10.3 report the two-stage least-squares coefficient estimates for annual work hours.[2] Examination of the variables other than attitudes and aspirations shows that, for both age groups, the labor supply slopes upward; nonlabor income reduces annual work hours; and being a household head significantly raises the amount of labor supplied.[3] The impact of these variables, however, is measured much more precisely for the 20–24 age group than for the 16–19 cohort. In the case of the latter, only the coefficient of household head is even marginally significant. The findings for both age categories also indicate that, with the exception of professional and managerial workers, the current occupation has no significant impact on work hours.

The results for the attitudinal variables for the 20–24 cohort show that they are generally significant and have the expected signs. Respondents who believed that having a good education was very important, who believed that the unemployed could find work if they wanted, and who did not report that most of their friends were unemployed averaged almost 150 more hours of work per year than the remaining respondents. Similarly, those who stated that religion did not play a strong role in their lives worked significantly fewer hours.

The effect of attitudes on work hours for the 16- to 19-year-old sample appears to be much more limited. Only "having a good education" is significant at the 5 percent level. Furthermore, its sign is the opposite of what was expected. The occupational aspiration items also fail to have any major impact on the labor supply of that age cohort. In general, it appears that the variation in labor supply for this group is not very systematically related to the variables included in this analysis. This finding may largely result from the youthfulness of this sample. Since the respondents were at the beginning of their working lives, job instability caused by the amount of time devoted to job search and gathering

Table 10.3 **Estimated Coefficients from Labor-Supply Regressions for NBER Men with Nonzero Work Hours and No Schooling in Previous Year**

	Annual Work Hours Coefficients		Supplementary Analysis for Ages 20–24	
	Ages 20–24	Ages 16–19	Weeks Worked	Hours per Week
Intercept	−72.6	−835.0	−24.94	27.069
	(502.4)	(1349.4)	(18.92)	(6.488)
ln Wages	484.4 **	21.8	10.01**	−1.040
(predicted)	(193.6)	(512.8)	(4.57)	(2.500)
ln Nonlabor Income	−49.9 ***	−20.8	−1.48***	.156
	(13.2)	(27.4)	(.32)	(.170)
Age	24.6	88.7	.24	.428
	(23.9)	(81.7)	(.61)	(.308)
Household Head	233.2 ***	370.7 *	6.48***	.817
	(78.6)	(221.1)	(1.91)	(1.015)
Professional or	285.8 *	756.9	3.52	2.860
Managerial Worker	(147.0)	(520.3)	(3.59)	(1.898)
Clerical Worker	6.4	−0.9	−2.12	1.911
	(99.8)	(183.1)	(2.44)	(1.289)
Craftsman	10.1	67.2	.54	−.077
	(100.0)	(187.3)	(2.44)	(1.291)
Operative	20.3	2.5	−1.10	1.849*
	(82.2)	(155.3)	(2.02)	(1.062)
Laborer, Service Worker, or Other	—	—	—	—
Attitude 1: Most Friends Are Unemployed	−153.7 **	47.5	−3.85**	−.197
	(71.8)	(160.1)	(1.74)	(.927)
Attitude 2: Unemployed Could Find Work If They Wanted to	130.6 **	198.2	2.40	−.281
	(65.3)	(120.9)	(1.59)	(.843)
Attitude 3: Having a Good Education Is Very Important	145.5*	−325.8 **	3.27*	1.227
	(78.7)	(143.6)	(1.89)	(1.016)
Attitude 4: Working at a Job Is Very Important	39.7	384.9 *	.47	1.080
	(102.9)	(234.3)	(2.52)	(1.329)
Attitude 5: Religion Plays Strong role	183.77**	−27.0	5.64***	.020
	(69.4)	(121.2)	(1.69)	(.896)
White-Collar at Age 30, Excellent Chance	351.8 ***	77.0	8.85***	1.098
	(134.1)	(262.3)	(3.29)	(1.731)
White-Collar at Age 30, All Others	233.0 **	103.6	6.32**	.396
	(102.7)	(178.3)	(2.50)	(1.327)

Table 10.3 (continued)

	Annual Work Hours Coefficients		Supplementary Analysis for Ages 20–24	
	Ages 20–24	Ages 16–19	Weeks Worked	Hours per Week
Craftsman at Age 30, Excellent Chance	347.3 ** (163.4)	261.9 (264.6)	5.09* (2.79)	2.143 (2.110)
Craftsman at Age 30, All Others	140.2 (122.6)	86.0 (192.3)	5.09* (2.79)	−.885 (1.583)
Operative at Age 30	284.1 ** (130.1)	−44.8 (213.7)	3.35 (3.23)	3.809** (1.680)
Service Worker, Laborer, or Other at Age 30	—	—	—	—
N	507	194	507	507
R²	.17	.11	.17	.04

Note: Asymptotic standard errors are in parentheses. The symbol *** denotes significance at the one percent level, ** denotes significance at the 5 percent level, and * denotes significance at the 10 percent level, all in two-tailed tests.

information about the job market may have hidden systematic differences between workers.

The largest effect of occupational aspirations on work hours comes from the 20- to 24-year-old subsample. Respondents who aspired to be white-collar workers or craftsmen by age 30 and who thought their chances of doing so were excellent worked 350 more hours per year than those who wanted to be service workers or laborers. Note, in addition, that at least 120 annual hours of work separate white-collar and crafts aspirants who believed their chances were excellent from those who did not. This suggests that the confidence with which the aspiration is held is a major factor determining the extent of its impact on work hours. Respondents who aspired to be operatives worked more hours, *ceteris paribus,* than those who had higher crafts and white-collar aspirations but who were relatively uncertain about their chances for success. Initially, separate coefficients for the effects of professional-managerial and clerical-sales aspirations were estimated; but since they were virtually identical, they were constrained to be the same here. The coefficients for aspiring to be an operative with an excellent chance and aspiring to be an operative without an excellent chance were constrained to be equal for the same reason.

In order to determine whether the impact of the attitudinal and aspirational items occurred because of more weeks worked per year or because of more hours worked per week, we ran separate regressions using these dependent variables. With the exception of "operative at age 30," weeks worked appears to account for most of the effect of both attitudes and aspirations, since their respective hours-per-week coefficients are uniformly insignificant and are generally quite small. Furthermore, if the attitude and aspiration coefficients in the third column of table 10.3 are multiplied by 39—the average number of hours worked per week in the sample—the resulting figures are close to the estimated effect on annual work hours in the first column.

Thus, the evidence presented so far is consistent with the hypothesis that occupational aspirations and attitudes affect labor supply independent of objective individual or labor market characteristics. The evidence is not conclusive, however, because the attitude and aspiration variables may be endogenous for either of two reasons. First, they could be simply acting as proxies for other attributes that may affect an individual's ability to find work, such as family background and unmeasured productivity characteristics. Suppose, for example, a sample member believes that his chances of becoming a manager are high because his father owns his own firm and plans to pass it on to his son at retirement. In this case, the causal relationship lies between parental characteristics and hours worked rather than between aspirations and hours worked. Independent of the connection through the father, managerial aspirations may have little, if any, impact on labor supply.

Second, attitudes and aspirations may be endogenous because past and current labor market experience have altered current views and expectations. Workers who have had trouble finding or keeping jobs in the past may, as a result, have both a lower current labor supply and less optimistic expectations about their future occupations. It is quite possible that attitudes and aspirations may be completely dependent on past labor market experience and not exert an independent effect. In either case the estimated coefficients may be biased because the included attitudes and aspirations are correlated with the error term in the labor-supply regressions.

In order to control as much as possible for the first endogeneity problem, we included in preliminary regressions (not reported here) a wide array of parental background characteristics and neighborhood and other influences on attitudes about work and jobs. Among these were parental education and occupation, whether the respondent lived in a broken family at age 14, and the extent to which family members, friends, teachers, community leaders, and others affected his beliefs about jobs and job search. None of these supplementary influences had any significant impact on labor supply, nor did they noticeably alter the effect of the included attitude and aspiration variables. Furthermore, regressions of the attitude and aspiration items on these supplementary factors indicated that they explain very little of the observed variation in aspirations and attitudes. It is therefore unlikely that aspirations and attitudes are merely acting as proxies for background measures in the labor-supply equations estimated here.

It is also unlikely that the attitude and aspiration variables are proxies for unmeasured productivity characteristics. Such characteristics can be expected to affect wages as well as labor supply. The earnings regressions in the appendix show, however, that none of the attitude and aspiration variables is significant at the 5 percent level.

The most straightforward approach to control for the possibility that past labor supply affects attitudes and aspirations would be to include measures of these items prior to any significant labor market experience. Since all the NBER data were obtained from the single 1979 interview, this unfortunately was not possible. An alternative would be to develop an empirical model of the determination of attitudes and aspirations and then eliminate the contaminating impact of endogeneity by using instrumental variables. Unfortunately, extensive searching failed to produce variables that would be correlated with attitudes and aspirations but uncorrelated with the error terms in the labor-supply equations. Thus, using the NBER data alone, it is not possible to determine the extent of the endogeneity of attitudes and aspirations.

In order to address this issue as well as to determine whether attitudes and aspirations have the hypothesized impact for a sample of youths broader than the relatively restricted NBER group, we also analyzed a sample of black and white men aged 14 to 19 in 1966 taken from the NLS. Because the NLS data are longitudinal, it is possible to determine whether aspirations as of ages 17 to 19, prior to any significant labor market experience, affected subsequent labor supply three to six years later. As suggested earlier, the endogeneity problem with the NBER data largely derives from the fact that occupational aspirations and labor supply are measured as of the same date.

The results from the NLS labor-supply analysis are reported in table 10.4. Among blacks aged 17 to 19 in 1966, their occupational aspirations in 1966 had a significant effect on their weeks worked in 1972.[4] This finding is unchanged by the inclusion of the percentage of postschooling weeks worked between 1967 and 1971, even though this variable would help to control for endogeneity by aspirations acting as a proxy for other variables.

The NLS sample of black men 17 to 19 years old differs considerably from the NBER 20–24 cohort because the latter is restricted to individuals living in low-income, inner-city areas of three large northeastern and midwestern SMSAs, whereas the former is a nationally representative sample of all youths of the relevant age group living in any SMSA. Furthermore, labor supply for the NLS group was measured as of 1972, whereas for the NBER sample it was 1979. Yet the magnitudes of the

Table 10.4   **Estimated Coefficients from 1972 Weeks-Worked Regressions for NLS Men with Nonzero Work Hours**

	Ages 17–19		Ages 14–16	
	Blacks	Whites	Blacks	Whites
Intercept	17.57	27.52	−68.16**	32.43**
	(26.70)	(19.25)	(28.80)	(16.02)
ln Wages	−2.59	3.40	17.58**	3.56
(predicted)	(5.73)	(3.39)	(5.80)	(2.93)
ln Non labor Income	−.18	−.27**	−.08	.02
	(.25)	(.13)	(.26)	(.12)
Age	2.02	.19	1.94	−.43
	(1.48)	(.69)	(1.65)	(.66)
Household Head	−1.35	1.33	−.04	.97
	(1.90)	(1.27)	(2.32)	(1.05)
Professional or	−1.76	−1.92	3.01	2.91**
Managerial Worker	(4.19)	(1.94)	(4.62)	(1.70)
Clerical or	−1.29	−1.93	−4.31	2.12
Sales Worker	(3.78)	(2.09)	(3.93)	(1.72)
Craftsman	−4.34	−.83	−7.40**	1.31
	(3.32)	(1.96)	(3.62)	(1.57)
Operative	−1.47	−2.36	−4.92*	.07
	(2.52)	(1.87)	(2.95)	(1.41)
Laborer, Service Worker, or Other	—	—	—	—
Percentage of Weeks	.07**	.03*	.002	.01
Worked, 1967–71	(.03)	(.01)	(.027)	(.01)
Professional or Managerial Worker at Age 30	5.49**	−1.17	5.92**	1.55
	(2.55)	(1.40)	(2.93)	(1.20)
Sales or Clerical	8.04**	4.49	7.95*	5.02*
Worker at Age 30	(3.60)	(3.33)	(4.24)	(2.77)
Craftsman at Age	6.48**	−2.43	4.15	3.91**
30	(2.89)	(1.79)	(3.85)	(1.52)
Operative at	.64	1.64	10.77**	2.23
Age 30	(3.37)	(2.54)	(4.17)	(2.27)
Laborer, Service Worker, or Other at Age 30	—	—	—	—
N	98	357	113	342
R^2	.20	.06	.29	.06

Note: Asymptotic standard errors are in parentheses. The symbol ** denotes significance at the 5 percent level and * denotes significance at the 10 percent level, all in a two-tailed test.

aspiration effects in the two samples are very similar. For example, the size of the NLS coefficient for sales or clerical aspirations (8.0 additional weeks per year) is comparable to that for the "white collar–excellent chance" variable in the NBER data (8.9 additional weeks per year). Moreover, the size of the NLS coefficient for craftsmen is within 25 percent of its NBER counterpart, and the impact of operative aspirations on weeks worked is insignificant in both the NBER and the NLS data.

The estimated aspiration coefficients for the younger black NLS sample generally support the findings for the older group and for the NBER sample. For example, professional-managerial and sales-clerical aspirations are significant at the 5 percent level and raise labor supply by five and nine weeks, respectively. Nevertheless, the pattern of coefficient sizes does not completely conform to the earlier results, indicating a relatively small impact of crafts aspiration and a relatively large impact of operative aspiration.

Racial differences in the effects of aspirations on labor supply are noteworthy. In the case of NLS white men aged 17 to 19 in 1966, the estimated coefficients are uniformly insignificant and, in some cases, not even of the expected sign. In the case of NLS white men aged 14 to 16 in 1966, only the crafts-aspiration coefficient is significant at the 5 percent level.

The insignificant coefficients of the aspiration variables in the NBER wage regressions provided evidence that occupational aspirations were not simply proxies for unmeasured productivity characteristics. The NLS wage regressions listed in the appendix replicate this finding. Furthermore, because the NLS data are longitudinal, an additional test of the extent to which aspirations are proxies for unmeasured opportunities can be made based on estimates of the objective probability of attaining the desired occupation. The NLS reports the respondents' actual occupations in 1980, when the members of the older subsample were aged 31 to 33. Thus, using logit analysis, we can estimate the objective probability of obtaining the desired occupation or a better one. If the coefficients of the aspiration variables fall substantially with the inclusion of these estimates in the labor-supply equation, then the aspiration items can be interpreted as proxies for objective factors. If, on the other hand, the impact of the aspiration items is unaffected by such an addition, the case for aspirations measuring subjective phenomena rather than actual opportunities is strengthened.

The logit analysis to predict the actual occupation in 1980 is presented in the appendix.[5] Table 10.5, however, reports the labor-supply results when the explanatory variables include the estimated probability of achieving the desired or a better occupation, based on the logit coefficients listed in the appendix and the respondent's characteristics. The table shows that not only are the predicted values uniformly insignificant, but also they fail to alter significantly the aspiration coefficients estimated in table 10.4. This finding is not affected by changing the occupational attainment variable to an estimate based on a linear-probability equation instead of logit analysis or to a dummy variable for whether or not the respondent achieved the desired or a better occupation in 1980.

Besides questions measuring occupational aspirations, the NLS also includes items measuring the sense of efficacy similar to some of those in the NBER analysis referred to earlier. The estimated impact of these variables on labor supply is not reported here because these items did not exert any significant effect.

All of the results given above are subject to the qualification that there may be sample-selection bias present because each sample includes only respondents with positive work hours. This bias would result from confounding the effects of respondents' attitudes and aspirations on whether they worked and on the amount of time they worked. This bias is likely to be quite small in the case of the NLS 17–19 cohorts, since over 90 percent of each sample worked at least one week during the year. Attempts to correct the bias for this group using the Heckman sample-selection technique were unsuccessful because the parameters of the probit equations could not be precisely estimated. This is evidence that the included variables were relatively uncorrelated with whether the respondents worked. Attempts to correct the problem for the other groups were unsuccessful because of collinearity between the items included in tables 10.3 and 10.4 and the Heckman lambda term. Collinearity occurred when lambda was approximately equal to a linear combination of the included variables over the sample range, suggesting that nonlinearity of the inverse Mill's ratio alone is insufficient to identify the selection bias in these data.

10.5 Summary

Most previous studies of the labor-supply behavior of young men have attempted to account for the observed variation in work hours by examining differences in labor market conditions or differences in individuals' productivity characteristics. The results obtained in this analysis indicate that a young man's subjective attitudes and occupational aspirations have a large, significant effect on the hours they work, independent of such variations in objective factors. These effects are much stronger among black men than among white men and in the case of the former are relatively constant across widely varying data samples. Supplementary evidence from the NLS further suggests that observed effects of occupational aspirations are not merely a reflection of some spurious correlation but rather are causal factors altering labor supply.

Table 10.5   **Estimated Coefficients from 1972 Weeks-Worked Regressions for NLS Men with Nonzero Work Hours (Regressions Include Objective Probability of Achieving Desired Occupation)**

	Ages 17–19		Ages 14–16	
	Blacks	Whites	Blacks	Whites
Intercept	20.93	26.66	−57.28*	33.84**
	(26.93)	(19.30)	(30.17)	(16.03)
In Wages (predicted)	−3.07	3.40	15.74***	3.19
	(5.61)	(3.30)	(5.82)	(2.96)
In Nonlabor Income	−.17	−.27*	−.07	.02
	(.25)	(.14)	(.26)	(.13)
Age	1.96	.26	1.58	−.53
	(1.65)	(.70)	(1.71)	(.67)
Household Head	−1.20	1.57	−.05	.03
	(1.92)	(1.51)	(2.34)	(1.33)
Professional or Managerial Worker	−1.19	−1.90	3.48	3.00*
	(4.53)	(1.96)	(4.64)	(1.72)
Clerical or Sales Worker	−.79	−1.93	−4.66	2.24
	(3.62)	(2.09)	(3.97)	(1.73)
Craftsman	−4.18	−.88	−8.10	1.55
	(3.46)	(1.97)	(3.70)	(1.57)
Operative	−1.36	−2.40	−4.14	.18
	(2.59)	(1.89)	(2.99)	(1.42)
Laborer, Service Worker, or Other	—	—	—	—
Percentage of Weeks Worked, 1967–71	.07**	.03*	.01	.02
	(.03)	(.02)	(.03)	(.01)
Professional or Managerial Worker at Age 30	5.53**	−1.15	5.97**	1.41
	(2.59)	(1.43)	(2.94)	(1.21)
Sales or Clerical Worker at Age 30	8.22**	4.54	7.85**	5.07*
	(3.68)	(3.35)	(4.28)	(2.77)
Craftsman at Age 30	6.51**	−2.40	5.06	3.79**
	(2.87)	(1.82)	(3.54)	(1.53)
Operative at Age 30	1.09	1.77	10.88	2.01
	(3.54)	(2.63)	(4.19)	(2.28)
Laborer, Service Worker, or Other at Age 30	—	—	—	—
Probability of Achieving Desired Occupation at Age 30	−1.06	−1.13	7.91	5.90
	(6.16)	(5.90)	(7.80)	(5.28)
N	98	357	113	342
R²	.20	.06	.30	.07

Note: Asymptotic standard errors are in parentheses. The symbol *** denotes significance at the one percent level, ** denotes significance at the 5 percent level, and * denotes significance at the 10 percent level, all in two-tailed tests.

Appendix

Table 10.A.1   **Estimated Coefficients from Earnings Regressions for NBER Men with Nonzero Work Hours and No Schooling in Past Year**

Independent Variable	ln Hourly Earnings		ln Weekly Earnings	
	Ages 20–24	Ages 16–19	Ages 20–24	Ages 16–19
Intercept	−.068	−.488	2.725***	2.627***
	(.427)	(.916)	(.444)	(.949)
Years of Schooling	.133***	.111	.140***	.138*
	(.030)	(.078)	(.032)	(.080)
Work Experience	.041***	.098	.055***	.092
	(.020)	(.082)	(.021)	(.085)
Lives in Chicago	−.003	−.173	.001	−.232
	(.076)	(.147)	(.079)	(.153)
Lives in Philadelphia	.022	−.029	.060	−.092
	(.075)	(.154)	(.078)	(.159)
Lives in Boston	—	—	—	—
Union at Workplace	.248***	−.179	.277***	−.085
	(.066)	(.154)	(.069)	(.160)
Professional or Managerial Worker	.153	−.394	.180	−.193
	(.137)	(.479)	(.142)	(.496)
Clerical or Sales Worker	.044	−.103	.097	−.228
	(.095)	(.181)	(.098)	(.188)
Craftsman	.186**	.099	.183**	.241
	(.090)	(.177)	(.093)	(.184)
Operative	.055	.079	.082	.194
	(.076)	(.160)	(.079)	(.166)
Laborer, Service Worker, or Other	—	—	—	—
Attitude 1: Most Friends Are Unemployed	−.044	−.215*	−.047	−.245*
	(.067)	(.126)	(.069)	(.130)
Attitude 2: Unemployed Could Find Work If They Wanted to	.001	−.095	.001	−.017
	(.063)	(.121)	(.065)	(.125)
Attitude 3: Having a Good Education Is Very Important	−.099	−.075	−.065	−.154
	(.074)	(.146)	(.077)	(.151)
Attitude 4: Working at a Job Is Very Important	.049	.215	.076	.281
	(.096)	(.200)	(.100)	(.208)
Attitude 5: Religion Plays Strong Role	−.035	.047	−.054	.034
	(.065)	(.125)	(.008)	(.130)
White-Collar at Age 30, Excellent Chance	.031	−.188	.057	−.049
	(.124)	(.249)	(.129)	(.258)
White-Collar at Age 30, All Others	−.065	−.051	−.055	.045
	(.098)	(.185)	(.102)	(.191)

Table 10.A.1 (continued)

Independent Variable	ln Hourly Earnings		ln Weekly Earnings	
	Ages 20–24	Ages 16–19	Ages 20–24	Ages 16–19
Crafts at Age 30, Excellent Chance	.071 (.152)	.218 (.258)	.147 (.158)	.245 (.267)
Crafts at Age 30, All Others	−.100 (.115)	−.032 (.202)	−.138 (.119)	.094 (.209)
Operative at age 30	.006 (.121)	.049 (.225)	.087 (.126)	.205 (.233)
Service Worker, Laborer, or Other at at 30	—	—	—	—
N	507	194	507	194
R²	.09	.10	.10	.13

Note: Asymptotic standard errors are in parentheses. The symbol *** denotes significance at the one percent level, ** denotes significance at the 5 percent level, and * denotes significance at the 10 percent level, all in a two-tailed test.

Table 10.A.2   **Estimated Coefficients from ln Weekly Earnings Regressions for NLS Men with Nonzero Work Hours**

Independent Variable	Ages 17–19		Ages 14–16	
	Blacks	Whites	Blacks	Whites
Intercept	3.249*** (.831)	3.769*** (.646)	2.406*** (.643)	4.329*** (.399)
Years of Schooling	.072 (.048)	.085** (.087)	.158*** (.044)	.032 (.027)
Work Experience	.110* (.059)	.029 (.040	.043 (.054)	.017 (.033)
Lives in South	−.236** (.112)	−.155* (.095)	−.009 (.084)	−.023 (.058)
Union at Workplace	.159 (.129)	.167** (.082)	.090 (.100)	.393*** (.061)
Professional or Managerial Worker	.463** (.207)	.122 (.125)	.130 (.177)	.115 (.088)
Clerical or Sales Worker	.292** (.174)	−.253** (.124)	.089 (.150)	.015 (.088)
Craftsman	.162 (.176)	.192 (.124)	−.194 (.144)	.117 (.078)
Operative	.035 (.137)	.102 (.121)	.282*** (.098)	.002 (.071)

Table 10.A.2 (continued)

	Ages 17–19		Ages 14–16	
Independent Variable	Blacks	Whites	Blacks	Whites
Laborer, Service Worker, or Other	—	—	—	—
Percentage of Weeks Worked, 1967–71	− .001 (.002)	.003*** (.001)	.002* (.001)	.002** (.001)
Professional or Managerial Worker at Age 30	.040 (.141)	− .138 (.092)	.147 (.112)	− .005 (.061)
Sales or Clerical Worker at Age 30	.246 (.190)	− .097 (.217)	− .077 (.171)	− .161 (.136)
Craftsman at Age 30	.055 (.160)	− .162 (.111)	.288** (.122)	.048 (.077)
Operative at Age 30	.013 (.181)	− .131 (.167)	.165 (.165)	− .183 (.116)
Laborer, Service Worker, or Other at Age 30	—	—	—	—
N	98	357	113	342
R²	.23	.12	.32	.16

Note: Asymptotic standard errors are in parentheses. The symbol *** denotes significance at the one percent level, ** denotes significance at the 5 percent level, and * denotes significance at the 10 percent level, all in a two-tailed test.

Table 10.A.3   **Logit Estimates of Probability of Achieving the Desired or a Better Occupation by 1980 for NLS Men Ages 17–19 in 1966**

Independent Variable	Blacks	Whites
Intercept	− 7.911 (5.868)	− 1.979 (2.328)
Years of Schooling	.170 (.125)	.156*** (.047)
Age	.265 (.309)	(.031 (.124)
Household Head in 1971	− .050 (.496)	.561** (.216)
Father's Occupation: White-Collar	− .106 (1.199)	− .017 (.303)
Father's Occupation: Craftsman or Operative	− 1.232** (.502)	.501* (.283)

Table 10.A.3 (continued)

Independent Variable	Blacks	Whites
Father's Occupation: Laborer, Service worker, or Other	—	—
Mother's Occupation: White-Collar Worker	1.214 (1.031)	.036 (.226)
Mother's Occupation: Crafts or Operative	.645 (.837)	.045 (.347)
Mother's Occupation: Laborer, Service worker, or Other	—	—
Father's Years of Schooling	.087 (.105)	−.052 (.043)
Mother's Years of Schooling	−.019 (.124)	−.026 (.047)
Don't Know Father's Education	.425 (1.005)	−.509 (.531)
Don't Know Mother's Education	.492 (1.296)	.404 (.652)
Score on Rotter Internal-External Scale	.092 (.125)	−.064 (.046)
Rotter Score Missing	.260 (1.227)	−.598 (.423)
N	88	442

Note: Asymptotic standard errors are in parentheses. The symbol *** denotes significance at the one percent level, ** denotes significance at the 5 percent level, and * denotes significance at the 10 percent level, all in a two-tailed test.

Notes

1. This is not the only "story" one could tell to rationalize the inclusion of aspirational or attitudinal measures in a labor-supply function. We could instead hypothesize that workers act as Bayesian statisticians, continually updating their estimates of the permanent wage, but starting with different priors for each estimate. It is not clear how one could observationally distinguish the cognitive dissonance hypothesis from the Bayesian one.

2. The labor-supply equations are identified by the inclusion of schooling, union at the workplace, and city of residence in the wage regressions and their exclusion here. The wage regressions are listed in the appendix.

3. Other studies of the labor supply of young men (for example, Boskin 1973; Ellwood 1982) also find a negative effect of nonlabor income but a negative or insignificant uncompensated wage effect.

4. As in the case of the NBER sample, the 1966 NLS interviews ascertained whether the respondent thought his chances of attaining his desired occupation were excellent, good, fair, or poor. Nevertheless, because of the relatively small number of blacks aged

17 to 19 in 1966, it is not possible to obtain separate coefficient estimates of the effects of aspirations by this expected likelihood.

5. The dependent variable for the logit analysis was coded as one if (1) the desired occupation was professional or managerial and the attained occupation was professional or managerial; (2) the desired occupation was crafts or clerical and the attained occupation was professional, managerial, clerical, or crafts; or (3) the desired occupation was operative and the attained occupation was professional, managerial, clerical, crafts, or operative. The dependent variable was coded as zero otherwise.

References

Andrisani, Paul. 1977. Internal-external attitudes, personal initiative, and the labor market experience of black and white men. *Journal of Human Resources* 12: 308–38.

Akerlof, George, and William T. Dickens. 1982. The economic consequences of cognitive dissonance. *American Economic Review* 72: 307–19.

Banfield, Edward. 1974. *The unheavenly city revisited.* Boston: Little, Brown.

Becker, Gary, and George Stigler. 1977. De gustibus non est disputandum. *American Economic Review* 67: 76–90.

Boskin, Michael. 1973. The economics of labor supply. In *Income Maintenance and Labor Supply,* ed. Glenn Cain and Harold Watts. Chicago: Markham.

Duncan, Greg, and James Morgan. 1981. Sense of efficacy and subsequent change in earnings—A Replication. *Journal of Human Resources* 16: 649–57.

Ellwood, David. 1982. Teenage unemployment: Permanent scars or temporary blemishes? In *The youth labor market problem: Its nature, causes, and consequences,* ed. Richard B. Freeman and David A. Wise. Chicago: University of Chicago Press.

Liebow, Elliott. 1967. *Tally's corner.* Boston: Little, Brown.

Moynihan, Daniel P. 1965. *The negro family: The case for national action.* Washington, D.C.: Office of Policy Planning and Research, U.S. Department of Labor.

Myrdal, Gunnar. 1946. *An American dilemma.* New York: Harper.

Comment   Michael J. Piore

This paper constitutes an attempt to expand the conventional behavioral model used in labor economics to include attitudes and aspirations.

Michael J. Piore is professor of economics, Massachusetts Institute of Technology.

The empirical literature on this topic is thin; the authors cite only two previous papers. The theoretical literature is more extensive but extremely diffuse, spread out over a number of different disciplines. Moreover, its relationship to the conceptual categories we use in economics is ambiguous and confused. The paper is therefore welcome, but like most pioneering efforts, it raises more questions than it answers. I will focus on four of these.

First, it is important to note the exact character of the data. The most extensive data on attitudes and aspirations are drawn from the NBER sample of inner-city black youth. The survey of that sample was conducted at only one time; therefore, labor market behavior was measured at the same time as the attitude and aspiration variables. The supplementary data from the NLS are measures of behavior six years after the aspiration variable was measured, but they contain no attitudinal information. The NLS does, however, include both black and white men.

Second, the authors emphasize that both the attitude and aspiration variables yield significant results, but the findings they report but do not emphasize are a little different and a good deal more interesting. The attitude and aspiration variables are significant in explaining weeks worked. But they do not appear to explain either wages or work hours per week. The two sets of variables therefore seem to measure mainly how hard the youths looked for jobs and how successful they were at keeping the jobs once they found them. Also interestingly, the aspiration variables affect black behavior but apparently not white behavior (we do not have information on white attitudes).

Third, exactly what aspiration and attitude variables measure is unclear. The variables themselves are not drawn from any specific theoretical literature and have a rather ad hoc character about them. The authors perform some tests and find the variables uncorrelated with family background characteristics or the attitudes of neighbors, teachers, and others. In the longitudinal sample, the aspirations seem to have little to do with subsequent success and thus appear to be subjective not objective. The authors make reference early in the paper to cognitive dissonance theory, but that theory seems, at least to me, to be essentially tautological.

The inability to interpret the variables is no small problem in examining a topic of study so important to public policy: One cannot say whether or not it would aid the economic performance of these youths to inculcate in them "good" aspirations and attitudes or, if so, how one might go about doing so. The authors make no such effort to do so, and their reticence on this score is an indication of their integrity as scholars.

Finally, I tend to believe that the labor market behavior of black youths reflects a fear that they will be trapped for life in the menial jobs that are generally open to youth in the U.S. labor market but that whites have historically left behind as they matured and blacks have not. The data seem consistent with this view: Black youths who think of themselves as moving on to higher-level jobs accept and hold the jobs that are available to them as youths, whereas black youths who think they will remain in those jobs permanently have a much weaker attachment to them. White youths exhibit behavior that is little influenced by aspirations.

11   Do Welfare Programs Affect the Schooling and Work Patterns of Young Black Men?

Robert I. Lerman

11.1 Introduction

Youths from poor and near-poor households have traditionally contributed to their families by working and sharing their earnings, even if that meant leaving school at an early age. Given their financial needs, one might expect that low-income youths work as much as or more than youths from moderate- and high-income families. The reality is that poor and near-poor youths experience extremely high rates of joblessness. Moreover, their subpar employment and high unemployment are not entirely associated with the job-finding problems of black youths (who tend to live in low-income households). Low-income white youths also have high unemployment rates and low employment-population ratios.[1]

The job market problems of low-income youth may result from location barriers, inadequate education, lack of family connections to jobs, a decline in agricultural and other unskilled jobs, little or no knowledge of the job market and how to search for jobs, poor work attitudes, and employment discrimination against black and Hispanic youth. Other papers in this volume analyze several of these possible causes.

This paper instead looks at the role of income-transfer programs in explaining the employment problems of low-income black youth. It is natural to consider the impact of welfare benefits because they reduce both the urgency of the need to work and the potential gain from work.

The scope of welfare effects on income and racial differentials is substantial. In 1980, 68 percent of children in low-income families lived

Robert I. Lerman is senior research associate at the Heller Graduate School for Advanced Studies in Social Welfare and director of research at the Center for Human Resources, both at Brandeis University.

in female-headed households, and 53 percent of black children aged 14 to 17 lived in families with no father present. It is among these single-parent families that welfare and other income-support benefits account for a large share of income and could affect labor market outcomes. Moreover, the rise in black youth unemployment took place over the years of rapid growth in the welfare rolls. Although the latter increase slowed during the mid-1970s, young black women since then have been having children with no father present at rates high enough to insure the continuation of high rates of participation in the welfare system.[2]

In spite of the widespread interest in racial differentials in youth unemployment and the importance of welfare to the black population, no one to my knowledge has systematically analyzed the impact of welfare and other income transfers on youth employment and un-employment. In the last major NBER volume on the youth employment problem, only one chapter (Freeman 1982) gave the welfare-employment issue more than passing attention.[3] Although Freeman found no effect on youth employment patterns in SMSAs caused by variations in area Aid to Families with Dependent Children (AFDC)/population ratios, his individual-level regressions showed that living in a family receiving welfare, food stamps, and public housing exerted significant (though not always negative) effects on the work patterns of young men. These results are of interest, but they indicate little about how welfare affects schooling and work or about potential racial differentials in such effects.

High unemployment among youths from families on welfare could result from several causes. One is that youth labor supply may decline in response to the high benefit-reduction rates that lower net wage rates and to the benefit levels that raise family income. Such effects may be especially pronounced among youths whose families receive benefits from a combination of programs. In addition to discouraging youths from accepting low-wage jobs, welfare incentives may lead them to take informal or illicit jobs that are easy to misreport.

Some economists have closely investigated the employment and schooling effects of benefit reduction rates and income guarantees provided through experimental negative income tax payments. As we will see below, however, the rules for actual income-support programs differ markedly from those used in the income-maintenance experiments.

West (1978) and Venti (1983), in analyses of youths' work responses to similar incentives provided through a negative income tax (NIT), found that NIT plans did tend to reduce employment.[4] To some extent, positive NIT effects on schooling offset these negative employment effects. The two analyses yielded somewhat differing results, however, on the size of the offsetting effects on schooling. Venti's overall estimate of NIT effects on whether 16- to 21-year-olds attended school or worked was near zero, whereas West's results for 19- to 24-year-olds indicated the NIT increased the share neither at work nor at school.

An alternative to the welfare incentives explanation is the cultural-environmental view. According to this view, the same factors accounting for the family's poverty and welfare status also weaken the youth's chances in the labor market. Examples of such factors are high unemployment, racial discrimination, poor schooling, and few contacts with relatives who hire or have access to other jobs. The absence of the youth's father no doubt contributes to poverty and welfare status, and possibly to youth unemployment as well.

A third possibility is that young women who become mothers and family heads at an early age do not complete their education or gain experience in entry-level jobs because of their child care responsibilities. Welfare might even affect young men not receiving any transfers. If welfare were to encourage childbearing among young, unmarried women, young men responsible for child support payments may avoid making them in part by looking for jobs that are hard to track. Finally, on the positive side, welfare income may encourage young people to complete their schooling and to participate in government employment and training programs.

The purpose of this paper is to explore the role of these factors and assess their importance in determining the school and labor market outcomes of young black men. Because this study is one of the first to concentrate on the welfare-employment relationship, its emphasis is on presenting several results from two large bodies of data, rather than on insuring the most refined models and estimation techniques.

The next section examines the potential dimensions of the effects by estimating the numbers of all youths and of black youths who receive some form of income transfer. Given the underreporting in the census surveys and the turnover on the AFDC rolls, this task is far from straightforward. The third section examines in more detail the ways in which welfare programs may influence youth labor market outcomes. In particular, it reviews the rules concerning the treatment of youth earnings under AFDC and other income-transfer programs.

The fourth section outlines a research methodology and derives estimates of welfare and family effects on young black men. Finally, the fifth section gives some brief concluding remarks about the findings and their implications for racial differentials in employment.

11.2 Numbers and Characteristics of Youths in Welfare Families

Learning about youths in welfare families is difficult largely because of the underreporting or nonreporting of welfare income in household surveys. The Current Population Survey (CPS), the standard source of labor-force data on the U.S. population, has in recent years included questions on in-kind as well as cash-transfer programs. Yet underreporting and nonreporting of transfer income are substantial. In 1980 recipients reported only 66 percent of benefits paid.[5] The extent of nonreporting is unclear because the CPS measures receipt of AFDC at any time over the year, while administrative sources record only AFDC receipts in a particular month.

The biannual AFDC surveys are one source of data on the numbers of youths in AFDC families. According to the March 1979 AFDC survey, 3.4 million families were recipients in that month. Over two million youths in the 16–24 age group lived in those families. About one million youths aged 16 to 20 were AFDC mothers. Nearly all the AFDC youths were either in school or mothers of young children. Perhaps this is one reason why employment levels reported on the AFDC survey are incredibly low. Of the 680,000 youths aged 16 to 20 who were part of the AFDC unit, only 5 percent had earnings reported on the survey.[6]

The best way to determine the numbers and characteristics of youths in families receiving welfare and other income transfers is to turn to surveys of youths. This paper employs the 1979 through 1981 waves of the National Longitudinal Surveys of Labor Market Experience (NLS) when focusing on youth as a whole and the NBER Survey of Inner-City Black Youth when analyzing young black men living in black communities in Boston, Chicago, and Philadelphia. Together the two surveys offer a rich body of information on income transfers. Both provide data on own and household AFDC benefits. Data on food stamp benefits received by the young respondents are available in both surveys, but the NLS does not record food stamps received by other household members. Although housing benefits in the form of public housing appear in both surveys, only the NLS includes data on rent subsidies.

Table 11.1 draws on the NLS data to display the characteristics of the nation's youth population in 1979, by receipt of AFDC and by age, schooling, and race. The share of minority youths in AFDC units is substantial, especially among high school students and high school dropouts. As expected, young women show up on welfare in larger numbers than young men, except among 16- to 17-year-olds.

The strong relationship between family status, race, and the presence of children emerges in tables 11.2 and 11.3. Black and Hispanic young men often find themselves in welfare families because of the absence of the father and because one-parent minority families rarely achieve moderate income levels. More interesting are the differences between black and Hispanic young men and between all blacks and ghetto blacks. Young Hispanic men move away from the parental home sooner than do black men; when they do live away from their parents, Hispanics

Table 11.1 Welfare Status by Age, Race, Gender, and School Status, 1979 (numbers [in thousands] and percent in welfare families)

Age, School Status	Female				Male			
	Hispanics	Blacks	Whites	Total	Hispanics	Blacks	Whites	Total
Age								
14–15								
Number	60	147	176	383	58	122	153	333
Percent	26	30	6	11	23	23	5	9
16–17								
Number	38	150	143	331	61	186	147	394
Percent	16	27	4	8	23	33	4	10
18–19								
Number	54	168	149	371	39	127	124	290
Percent	21	29	5	9	16	23	4	7
20–21								
Number	56	164	130	350	30	100	58	188
Percent	21	29	4	9	13	21	2	5
Total								
Number	209	630	599	1,438	188	535	482	1,205
Percent	21	28	5	9	18	25	4	8
School Status								
High School Student								
Number	104	314	282	700	119	313	270	702
Percent	22	28	5	10	22	26	4	8
Student, Post–High School								
Number	17	42	17	76	4	29	17	50
Percent	15	15	1	4	3	15	1	2
Dropout								
Number	74	170	121	365	48	138	121	307
Percent	29	52	9	19	22	35	9	16
High School Graduate								
Number	17	104	78	199	15	48	78	141
Percent	10	21	3	6	11	13	3	5

Source: Unpublished tabulations from the NLS.

are unlikely to remain in welfare families. As expected, blacks in the low-income areas of the three cities show much higher welfare rates than do blacks in the nation as a whole. Their higher involvement in welfare comes largely from the substantial welfare rates of ghetto two-parent families.

A surprisingly large share of black young men continue residing at home even through their early twenties. In the NBER sample, only 17 percent of 20- to 21-year-olds live away from their parents or another responsible relative. Even at ages 22 to 24, about 60 percent still reside with parents or other responsible relatives. At the national level, young black men do move away from their parental home at a higher rate than they do in low-income areas. Nevertheless, the tendency to remain in a parental home is still substantially higher among young black men than among young Hispanic or young white men. In 1979 over 70 percent of blacks 20 to 21 years old lived at home, whereas only 55 percent of young Hispanics and 53 percent of young whites did so.

Racial differentials in the family characteristics of youths are especially significant among young women. Note in table 11.3 that among

Table 11.2   **Family Head and Welfare Status of 16- to 21-Year-Old Men, by Race: The Nation and Blacks in Three Poor Urban Areas**

Family and Welfare Status	National Sample (NLS)			Inner-City Sample (NBER)
	Hispanics	Whites	Blacks	Blacks
Living with Both Parents				
Total Number[†]	295	4,979	533	464
Percent of Total in Any Family Status	51	66	44	28
Percent in Family with Welfare Income	9	2	8	34
Living with One Parent				
Total Number[†]	120	955	437	932
Percent of Total in Any Family Status	21	13	36	56
Percent in Family with Welfare Income	41	9	41	55
Living with Neither Parent				
Total Number[†]	162	1,577	243	277
Percent of Total in Any Family Status	28	21	20	16
Percent in Family with Welfare Income	10	3	28	44

[†]The numbers are in thousands from the NLS and in actual numbers from the NBER survey. The NBER survey includes only those who reported knowledge of whether the family received any welfare income.

Source: Unpublished tabulations from the NLS and NBER survey.

Table 11.3   **Welfare and Marital Status of 16- to 21-Year-Old Women With and Without Children, by Age and Race, 1979**

Age, Marital and Welfare Status	Hispanics		Blacks		Whites	
	With Children	Without Children	With Children	Without Children	With Children	Without Children
16–17						
Percent of Total	11.1	88.9	13.5	86.5	2.8	97.2
Percent Married	37.2	33.8	10.6	0.0	45.1	2.7
Percent in Families with Welfare Income	42.7	13.1	49.4	22.9	41.1	3.4
18–19						
Percent of Total	24.7	75.3	31.8	68.2	11.2	88.8
Percent Married	64.7	35.3	15.7	3.0	75.9	9.2
Percent in Families with Welfare Income	22.2	19.7	52.1	17.5	15.6	3.0
20–21						
Percent of Total	37.2	62.8	51.0	49.0	22.2	77.8
Percent Married	65.8	34.2	23.7	8.9	77.6	21.5
Percent in Families with Welfare Income	36.6	12.6	45.7	11.6	13.5	1.1
16–21						
Percent of Total	27.3	72.7	35.9	64.1	13.9	86.1
Percent Married	64.3	12.8	19.9	4.0	75.7	12.1
Percent in Families with Welfare Income	30.7	15.7	48.6	17.1	15.3	2.4

Source: Tabulations from NLS.

16- to 21-year-olds, the share of black women with a child is three times the share of white women in the same age group. The racial differentials among young, unmarried mothers are even more dramatic. Nearly three of every ten black women aged 16 to 21 are unmarried mothers, as compared to only three of 100 whites and about one of ten Hispanics. These differences in family characteristics account for almost all the racial and ethnic differentials in the receipt of welfare income.

The contact with income transfers for youths and their families goes beyond receipt of cash welfare. It may include food stamp, medicaid, and housing benefits. Table 11.4 displays the combinations of benefits going to youths and their families in the three-city, low-income sample and, on a less detailed basis, to youths throughout the nation. About half of the NBER sample with usable data reported benefits going either to themselves or to another member of the household. Most households receiving benefits obtained aid from more than one program. One in four of the families receiving transfers lived in public housing and had neither welfare nor food stamp income. On the other hand, over half were on welfare and in at least one other program.

The NLS data point to a relatively small overlap between housing and welfare benefits. Although the percentage of minority youths living in families that receive benefits from welfare and housing is many times that of white youths, the percentage receiving combined welfare and housing benefits is small for all groups.

11.3 Welfare Rules and Potential Employment Effects

Any serious effort to assess how welfare benefits affect youth employment must begin with a specification of the financial parameters relevant to labor market outcomes. A large body of work on the effects of NIT plans provides a conceptual basis for relating budget constraints to empirical analyses. Still, there is no substitute for a systematic review of specific program rules.

Understanding the benefit structures of income-support programs can prove helpful in distinguishing the financial incentive explanation from the cultural-environmental view. In general, assessing the contribution of each aspect of those structures is difficult because the poorest families will have access to the highest benefits, while also being the least able to undertake acts that enhance youth job opportunities, such as providing jobs, job-related skills, and role models.

11.3.1 Welfare Coverage, Benefit Structures, and Work Incentives

Researchers and policy analysts have provided detailed examinations of the financial work incentives built into the welfare system.[7] The

Table 11.4   **Combinations of Benefits Received by Households of Black Youths, NBER and NLS Samples, 1979**

	Inner-City Sample (NBER)			
	Benefits Received by Other Household Members			Benefits Received by Youth
	Family Head			
Combinations of Benefits	Mother and Father	One Parent	Other Adult Relative	Youth Head of Household
Percent Missing	24.4	36.1	28.1	1.4
Percent of Those with Complete Data				
None	70.0	37.9	46.2	64.9
Food Stamps Only	1.9	3.7	3.1	0.4
Welfare Only or with Food Stamps	11.3	20.4	20.3	12.4
Public Housing or with Food Stamps	11.5	16.9	15.2	16.3
Welfare and Public Housing or Welfare, Food Stamps, and Public Housing	5.3	21.1	15.2	5.8

	National Sample (NLS)					
	Hispanic		Black		White	
	Men	Women	Men	Women	Men	Women
Percent with Welfare or Housing Benefits	24.8	25.4	34.6	37.3	4.2	6.3
Percent with Public Housing or Rent Subsidies Only	2.9	2.9	8.5	9.4	0.8	1.6
Percent with Both Welfare and Housing Benefits	4.5	2.4	7.4	6.6	0.5	0.4

Source: Tabulations from NBER survey and NLS.

discussion usually begins by describing the AFDC treatment of earnings and then moves on to show the combined impact on net earnings from benefit reductions associated with food stamps, medicaid, and subsidized housing programs. Prior to changes mandated in 1981, AFDC earnings beyond $30 per month were subject to a marginal benefit-reduction rate of 66⅔ percent, though recipients gained credits for all work expenses. Because of the liberal treatment of work expenses, AFDC recipients often apparently faced low average tax rates on earnings. The 1981 Omnibus Budget Reconciliation Act tightened the rules in order to restrict the earnings welfare recipients could retain without any loss of AFDC benefits. In addition, it limited income eligibility for AFDC to 150 percent of the state's standard of need, a change that has removed large numbers of recipients from the AFDC rolls.

In general, the food stamp program requires reductions in benefits with added earnings, at a marginal rate of about 24 to 25 percent. Housing programs providing subsidized rents call for the rental payment of the recipient to rise by about 25 cents for each dollar increase in earnings.

These aspects of how income support programs treat recipient earnings are relatively well known, but rules on youth earnings are less so. It turns out that AFDC benefits do not decline at all with the earnings of dependent children who are full-time or part-time students not holding a full-time job. This important fact means that each dollar of the youth's net earnings does far more to raise spendable family income than each dollar earned by others in the family. It also implies that in-school youths face no AFDC tax rate to reduce the gain from working.

For youths who are not in school, AFDC's treatment of earnings is tied into its definition of the family AFDC unit. Under AFDC the unit eligible for benefits and subject to benefit reductions need not correspond to the nuclear family (or census family unit of people living together related by blood, marriage, or adoption). Until the 1981 Budget Reconciliation Act, about three-quarters of states classified children ages 18–21 as in the unit only if they were attending a school or training program.[8] Thus, the only children whose benefits were subject to AFDC benefit reductions were out-of-school 16- to 17-year-olds. Yet even for this group the potential reductions in family benefits from their earnings cannot be large, since families can choose to exclude the youths from the increase in the family's grant available for an additional person. The increment to the grant level varies across states and sometimes with the size of the family. In Massachusetts, for example, each additional person beyond the first raised the maximum grant by about $65 per month in 1983. Other states granted incremental amounts that varied from about $30 per month in Mississippi to over $100 per month in California. Assuming an effective benefit-reduction rate on earnings of 50 percent, families whose out-of-school children earned $100 per week would maximize their income by excluding children from the family's grant.

Youth work disincentives probably are also small under food stamps. As in AFDC, the food stamp program disregards student earnings through age 18. Earnings of children older than 18 reduce the grant at a marginal rate of 24 percent, net of allowable work expenses. But, again, the family can simply report the youth as outside the household if he or she finds a well-paying job. The family's loss would then be the food stamps of one household member, or about $65 per month in 1983.

The earnings of youths in public housing or rent-subsidized units are subject to benefit reductions that come in the form of increased rental payments. Since the regulations do not exclude the earnings of children, the family may face an increased rental payment of 25 percent of the child's net earnings. Of course, enforcement of these kinds of provisions is slack in most areas.

The interaction among program rules is what determines the budget constraint facing youths from families participating in several programs. In general, combinations of programs tend to level differences in constraints based on individual programs. If tax rates from cash welfare are high, the tax rates from in-kind programs add little to the cumulative rate. But if youth earnings are subject to a zero tax rate under the cash program, the effects of food stamp and housing benefit reductions may raise the level of cumulative tax rates to nearly 50 percent.

This review suggests, first, that benefit reductions associated with AFDC rarely apply to children under age 21. Second, the work disincentives that affect children result largely from the combined effects of AFDC, food stamp, and housing programs. Third, until 1982 AFDC and food stamp rules encouraged youths to remain in school at least through age 18 and in some states through age 21. Fourth, income and tax rate effects vary by school status and age, with AFDC rules excluding student earnings through age 21, but in some states paying a higher grant level for students 18 to 21 than for nonstudents 18 to 21. Finally, AFDC and other income-transfer programs have lessened the cost of teenage parenting to young women; this, in turn, brings the work disincentive features of welfare programs to substantial numbers of young potential workers.

11.3.2 Potential Employment Effects

The program rules discussed above suggest that welfare's work disincentive effects often do not apply to youths in welfare families. How, then, might we expect welfare programs to influence youth employment patterns? One possibility is that by providing benefits that raise family incomes, welfare programs lessen the need for young people to work and thus reduce their labor-force participation. A second way they may affect youth employment is to stimulate longer schooling, which in turn would reduce youth labor-force participation. On the basis of the incentives embedded in the program rules, we would expect that income-support benefits will both exert a larger negative effect on nonstudents than on students and encourage youths to remain in school, especially in those states that pay benefits on behalf of students 18 to 21 years old.

A third and significant potential role played by welfare programs is their effect on childbearing by young women, especially unmarried young women. If welfare programs do increase childbearing, the effect would almost certainly have negative consequences for the employment and earnings of young women. And it is also possible that this negative employment outcome will extend to young absent fathers. If these young men have to make child-support payments to the state that rise with their earnings, these obligations will act as a tax on earnings, except in the case of the worker finding an off-the-books job.

A fourth issue is welfare's indirect impact on youth employment resulting from the negative effect on work by the youth's parent. In other work, I found that parents' nonemployment exerted a negative impact on their children's employment, holding the children's characteristics constant.[9]

A fifth potential work disincentive may arise from the experience on welfare. Gaining familiarity with the use of public income support may exert an impact that is distinct from the pure financial incentives of welfare. This is one reason why we might expect welfare programs to exert different effects from those of an experimental NIT.

We should distinguish between welfare as a cause of poor labor market outcomes for youths and merely its association with those outcomes. Youths in welfare families are likely to have lower than average education, work experience, and other employment-related abilities, for reasons that have little to do with the family's receipt of a welfare benefit. Some of these differences are difficult to measure, especially the differences in motivation that may explain why some families who are eligible for benefits do not actually take them. To the extent that unmeasured attitudinal and motivational factors determine the welfare status of the family, one might find negative program effects that actually represent differences among family background factors. Nonetheless, the association between welfare status and weak employment outcomes is of policy interest even if causation does not run from welfare to unemployment. Establishing strong associations can help in the targeting of benefits at reducing youth unemployment and in considering what program features affect unemployed youth and could affect efforts to lower youth unemployment. For this reason, this paper will analyze the direct connection between welfare programs and unemployment among low income and black youth.

In examining welfare's causal role in reducing youth employment, the remainder of the paper will focus on three major questions:

1. How do welfare programs alter the current employment of low-income and black young men?

2. How does the mix of family and program characteristics associated with income-transfer programs affect school enrollment, employment, and unemployment among low-income and black youths?

3. To the extent that any welfare-induced effects occur, do they account for any of the racial differences in youth employment outcomes?

11.4 Welfare and Family Effects among Young Men

Welfare rules and youth behavior suggest that responses to transfer programs and family characteristics will vary sharply between young men and young women. Young men in a welfare family generally will be living with one or both parents or another adult relative. In contrast, young women often become unmarried mothers and draw benefits on their own. Among the other differences are the more extensive involvement of young men in illicit income-generating activities and the different occupational interests and opportunities of young men and women. Finally, the NBER survey dealt exclusively with young men. For all these reasons, the analysis examines the labor market experience of young men only.

The first task is to offer descriptive information on the school and work behavior of young men. Tables 11.5 and 11.6 display an exclusive and exhaustive breakdown of activities by age, race, and welfare status for young men in the NBER and NLS samples, respectively. In both samples, young men in families receiving welfare are more likely than other youth to fall into the two least desirable activities—not in school and unemployed or outside the labor force. Among the younger groups, though the share in jobs and not in school differs only moderately by welfare status, those not in welfare families are much more likely to attend school than those in welfare families. The differences in activity status are especially striking among 19- to 24-year-old black men in the low-income urban areas. Moreover, the ranking across groups by benefit category shows that youth outcomes worsen as one moves from public housing only to welfare only and then to the combination of welfare and public housing. The combined benefit group has astoundingly poor labor market outcomes, with out-of-school unemployment rates of 76 percent.

Table 11.5   School and Work Activities of Young Black Men in Low-Income Areas of Boston, Chicago, and Philadelphia, 1979

Age, Benefit Group	Percentage Not in School			Percentage Enrolled in School		
	Employed	Unemployed	Not in Labor Force	Employed	Unemployed	Not in Labor Force
16–18						
None	7.7	9.5	4.3	22.1	22.5	34.0
Welfare No Public Housing	5.8	13.1	4.6	18.9	26.3	31.3
Public Housing, No Welfare	6.9	16.4	3.4	14.4	28.1	30.8
Welfare and Public Housing	5.4	17.9	8.1	12.1	29.2	27.4
Total, All Categories	6.6	13.1	5.0	18.2	25.6	31.5
19–24						
None	41.1	28.0	11.1	8.9	3.9	7.0
Welfare, No Public Housing	28.6	43.8	15.9	2.5	5.0	7.0
Public Housing, No Welfare	35.0	34.3	16.8	5.1	3.7	5.1
Welfare and Public Housing	15.6	52.0	18.5	5.2	5.8	2.9
Total, All Categories	33.5	36.3	14.1	6.3	4.4	5.5

Source: Tabulations from NBER survey.

Table 11.6   School and Work Activites of a National Sample of Young Men, by Race, Spring 1979

Race, Welfare Status, Age	Percentage Not in School			Percentage Enrolled in School		
	Employed	Unemployed	Not in Labor Force	Employed	Unemployed	Not in Labor Force
Blacks						
Welfare						
16–17	12.5	8.4	6.2	30.9	24.2	17.7
18–19	27.4	14.2	9.7	11.7	9.8	27.2
20–21	52.3	20.7	8.8	8.2	1.7	8.3
16–21	31.0	14.6	8.5	16.2	11.5	18.5
No Welfare						
16–17	4.8	2.1	4.4	26.3	24.5	37.9
18–19	29.0	10.9	8.6	20.7	14.0	16.8
20–21	57.4	12.3	4.4	10.2	4.0	11.7
16–21	33.9	9.5	6.3	18.1	12.6	19.4
Whites, Not Hispanic						
Welfare						
16–17	13.6	18.2	4.6	16.6	19.3	30.8
18–19	31.7	19.0	8.0	28.8	6.6	5.9
20–21	51.4	17.1	15.9	5.9	7.5	2.3
16–21	30.6	18.4	7.7	20.5	10.4	12.4
No Welfare						
16–17	5.2	1.6	0.8	50.0	10.0	32.5
18–19	40.8	5.3	2.9	27.7	3.6	19.8
20–21	52.5	5.4	2.6	23.6	1.9	14.0
16–21	38.2	4.5	2.4	30.6	4.2	19.9
Hispanics, 16–21						
Welfare	30.1	20.5	10.4	13.4	9.7	16.0
No Welfare	33.9	9.5	6.3	18.1	12.6	19.4

Source: Tabulations from NLS data.

The time allocation across activities over the year is another indicator of how young men may differ by welfare status. Data on months spent by young men in school and labor-force activities appear in table 11.7 for the NBER sample. Again, the family's welfare status is associated with the school and labor-force patterns of youths ages 19 to 24. Those in multibenefit families performed far more poorly than did other young men. They spent well over half (7.6 months) of the 13-month period neither working nor in school. Those in families receiving no income transfers averaged only one-third of the period in the no work, no school situation. In comparison to the nonwelfare group, those in multibenefit families showed much lower employment-population ratios (.34 versus .58) and much higher unemployment rates (49 versus 27 percent).

11.4.1   A Methodological Overview

Families that must resort to welfare programs may transmit to young men the same weaknesses that led to the earnings problems experienced by the parents. Thus, tabulations showing a welfare-employment connection may actually measure social class differences rather than program effects. We must guard against ignoring all but program effects, since social class differences are themselves partly the result of or closely associated with the effects of the income-transfer programs. Before describing any specific empirical analysis, I will begin with a broad review of the approaches used to distinguish among competing explanations concerning the welfare-employment connection.

To begin, consider the following four sets of variables:

Set Y = the variables measuring youths' work and school status. Examples are earnings and time allocated to work, school, looking for work, and leisure.

Set A = welfare program variables and other geographic area characteristics that are exogenous to the family and youth behavior. Examples are the area's AFDC plus food stamp income guarantee, local availability of public housing slots, and local unemployment rates.

Set C = family variables measuring race and social class factors that affect the family's probability of receiving income transfers and that are directly linked to youths' activity patterns or are likely to be transmitted to youths within the family. Examples are personal connections to jobs, attitudes about work, native ability, and presence of parents in the home.

Set W = variables measuring the actual receipt of income transfers by the youth or the youth's family.

Set F = family variables that affect the probability of welfare status but that are less likely than set C to exert a direct influence on the youth's school or work status. Examples are family and household size.

Table 11.7 NBER Sample's Months in Alternative Labor-Force States, by Age and by School and Welfare Status of Families, 1979

| | Over Past 13 Months, Mean Number of Months: | | | | | |
| | Not in School | | | Enrolled in School | | |
Age/ Welfare Status	Employed	Unemployed	Not in Labor Force	Employed	Unemployed	Not in Labor Force
16–18						
None	1.9	0.9	1.7	2.1	1.0	5.4
Welfare, No Public Housing	1.9	1.1	1.9	2.1	0.9	5.2
Public Housing, No Welfare	2.1	1.1	1.8	1.6	1.0	5.3
Welfare and Public Housing	1.9	1.3	2.2	1.4	0.8	5.3
Total, All Categories	1.9	1.0	1.9	1.8	0.9	5.4
19–24						
None	6.6	2.3	2.0	1.0	0.1	1.1
Welfare, No Public Housing	5.6	2.8	3.2	0.6	0.2	0.7
Public Housing, No Welfare	5.7	2.8	2.7	0.8	0.1	0.8
Welfare and Public Housing	3.9	4.3	3.3	0.6	0.1	0.8
Total, All Categories	5.8	2.8	2.6	0.8	0.1	0.9

Source: NBER survey.

Set I = variables that measure youth-specific characteristics that may have some impact on youths' work and school outcomes. Examples are grades in school, involvement in criminal behavior. and reservation wages.

The mix of youth outcomes, Y, may be causally dependent on variables from any or all of sets A, C, W, F, and I. But, the relationships among the sets are complex. The C variables help determine W status, which in turn affects such C variables as the work of the family head. The C variables may also influence the I variables. The F and A variables partly explain variations in W status. Because of the program rules and actual program administrative practices (described above in section 11.3), we expect the youth outcomes to exert little impact on W. The absence of simultaneity between W and Y allows a direct estimate of how W variables affect Y. Nevertheless, several issues arise in developing such estimates.

Consider the following two equations:

(1) $$W_i = g\,(A_i,\, C_i,\, F_i) + e_i$$

(2) $$Y_i = f\,(A_i,\, C_i,\, W_i,\, I_i) + u_i,$$

where u and e are error terms. One approach to the question of how welfare affects youth outcomes is to examine W's effect on Y. True, W is partly determined by social class and family status, but including both W and C variables in the multivariate models should yield estimates of independent effects. Still, isolating W's effect from the C variables could be difficult because of multicollinearity between the two sets of variables. Including both could understate the full impact of welfare, since if experience on welfare is partly responsible for the youth's living in a one-parent family with no workers, then the negative effects on youth outcomes from such C variables should be partly attributed to the impact of welfare. The main effect of multicollinearity would be to make the coefficients unstable. For the most important instances of multicollinearity, I provide estimates with W and C variables and with W variables alone.

Another potential problem arises because the *unmeasured* attitudinal and other factors that cause families to take up welfare might well exert an impact on youths' school and employment outcomes. Families with job attitudes or capacities that are poorer than what is captured by measured characteristics are more likely to receive benefits as well as have children who do not perform well in the labor market. This implies an omitted-variable problem, since the error term in equation (2) would be correlated with W. To remove the bias in W's impact on Y requires one to predict W as a function of the C, F, and A variables and then to use the predicted W values to explain youth outcomes. Yet this procedure to purge the influence of unmeasured attitudinal effects may well create an errors-in-variables problem. Suppose, for example, that experience on welfare helped shape poor job attitudes. Then, the predicted welfare variable would not capture the full impact of welfare. If those with a high probability of receiving welfare (based on measured characteristics) but whose families never received welfare did well in the labor market, it would not imply the absence of an impact from welfare. Rather, the error in measuring the concept underlying the independent variable would tend to bias downward the estimate of the welfare effect.

Thus, the use of actual welfare status may either understate or overstate the overall role of welfare in influencing youth outcomes. To bound the probable range of welfare effects, I developed estimates based on actual as well as predicted values of W and estimates that did and did not include indirect effects of welfare through various family variables. When using the NLS sample, one can take advantage of the natural variability in state welfare levels when estimating the predicted welfare status of the youth's family. The availability in the NLS data of this important, exogenous predictor raises the credibility of effects based on predicted values.

This general discussion is not intended to suggest that no econometric problems remain in the following analysis. But as stated above, the emphasis in this paper is to examine what relatively basic techniques applied to two relatively unmined data sources can tell us about the relationship between welfare and youth employment. The next subsection analyzes, with several techniques, the impact of the welfare variables on young black men living in three low-income urban areas. Section 11.4.3 develops a similar analysis of the welfare effects on the nationally representative sample of young black men in the NLS.

11.4.2   Effects of Transfer Programs and Family Factors on the School and Work Activities of Young Black Men in Three Low-Income Urban Areas

The NBER sample comprises young black men ranging from ages 16 to 24. These ages capture two very different periods of life. Young people in the 16–18 period are normally in high school and living at home. By age 19, virtually everyone has either completed or dropped out of high school. At this point, the school and work experiences of young people diverge substantially. Some go to college, others find full-time jobs, some go into a training program, and still others find themselves without work or any other constructive activity. The ages 19 to 24 are also a time when many youths move away from their parents' home.

For these and other reasons, the sample is divided by age in order to undertake the analysis of welfare and family effects. The empirical work consists of probit equations determining the family's receipt of welfare benefits; regressions on youth earnings; regressions on the months youths spend working, attending school, and doing neither; and multinomial logit equations on the youths' current work, job-search, and schooling patterns.

Determinants of the Family's Benefit Status

The tabulations reported above indicated sharp differences between youths in families with and without income transfers and between youths in single-benefit and multibenefit families. Given these expectations two sets of probits were estimated, one on determinants of any transfers and a second on whether or not a family receiving a transfer participated in welfare and public housing programs.

The discussion here will concentrate on the estimates developed on "any transfers," since these showed a closer fit than the ones on multibenefit participation. The results of the probit equations for the families of youths aged 16 to 18 and 19 to 24 appear in table 11.8. One might have expected the determinants of "any transfers" to vary by the age of the youths, but little difference emerged in the results.

Family and Welfare Effects on the Current Work and School Status of Youth

The close interaction between work and school complicates the analysis of the current activity status. Since the mix of labor-force and school activities are often the outcome of a joint time-allocation decision, it is appropriate to estimate the effects of the family and welfare variables on the probability of taking part in one activity relative to the other. The statistical technique for accomplishing this task is multinomial logit.[10] The procedure yields estimates of the impact of the welfare variables on the mix of school, work, and job-search activities. The activities used as dependent variables vary by age. The breakdown for youths aged 16 to 18 is (1) neither work nor school; (2) work only; (3) school only; and (4) both work and school. The breakdown for the 19- to 24-year-olds is (1) school (whatever the labor-force status); (2) work (not school); (3) unemployed (not school); and (4) neither in school nor in the labor force.

Several specifications provided estimates of the role of the welfare and family variables. The welfare variable appeared in three forms: (1) the family's receipt of any income transfer, (2) the *predicted* probability of the family's receiving any transfer benefit, and (3) two dummy variables representing whether the family received any cash welfare, any other transfer (but no welfare), or no transfer at all. Given the concern about multicollinearity the equations were run with and without the presence of other workers in the family and with and without the youth's reservation wage.

Table 11.8   **Determinants of the Welfare Status of Families of Black Young Men in the NBER Sample**

	Probability of Welfare at the Mean of the Other Explanatory Variables		Impact of a Change in the Explanatory Variable on Probability of Receiving Welfare		t-Value	
	16–18 Group	19–24 Group	16–18 Group	19–24 Group	16–18 Group	19–24 Group
Overall Mean	.69	.63				
Explanatory Variables						
Both Parents Present	.58	.53	−.16	−.14	−2.60	−2.35
One Parent Present	.72	.68	.07	.11	1.32	2.22
One Working Adult (not youth)	.50	.46	−.29	−.25	−6.78	−5.51
Two Working Adults (not youth)	.32	.34	−.48	−.40	−10.21	−8.01
Household Size	.78	.77	.08	.14	5.16	7.31
Chicago	.70	.67	.01	.07	0.29	1.57
Philadelphia	.72	.68	.04	.08	1.06	1.77
Attends Church Very Often	.60	.49	−.13	−.16	−3.20	−3.27
Attends Church Moderately	.66	.59	−.05	−.06	−1.38	−1.39
Age 18	.68		−.02		−0.61	
Ages 22–24		.61		−.03		−0.83

Note: The changes in the probabilities noted in the middle two columns represent the impact of going from zero to one in the dichotomous variables and of a rise of one standard deviation in the continuous variables.

Source: NBER survey.

The pattern and sign of the welfare effects are similar across specifications, but the significance levels vary sharply. Tables 11.9 and 11.10 display the estimated effects from the equations using the family's receipt of a transfer as the welfare variable and controlling for other workers and for the youth's reservation wage. Additional explanatory variables were residence (Chicago, Philadelphia, or Boston); presence of the youth's father, mother, and/or adult worker when the youth was age 14; and the youth's grades, illicit income, age, education, and church attendance.

According to these results, welfare did matter. In three of six cases, the family's receipt of an income transfer exerted significant effects that were independent of the current work status of other family members. It is worth noting that several other variables also induced substantial effects on a group that one might have thought was otherwise relatively homogeneous. Welfare's primary influence was to raise the probability of being neither in school nor at work, by seven percentage points for the 16–18 age group and by 26 points for the 19–24 age group.

Welfare effects on other outcomes also varied by age. In the 16–18 group, the transfer variable had an insignificant impact on those working but not in school (by two percentage points) and on those attending school but not working (by six points). This would imply that many fewer youths from welfare families were both working and attending school than were youths from families receiving no income transfer. It is interesting that the combining of school and work is precisely the activity that welfare rules would tend to encourage by counting the earnings of nonstudents 16 to 18 years old while excluding student earnings. Apparently, welfare incentives had little impact on this group of young men.

Receipt of transfers by the families of the 19- to 24-year-olds exerted substantially larger negative effects. Transfers lowered by 14 points those youths' probability of being in school and by 13 points their probability of working and being out of school. The result was a shift toward staying outside the labor force rather than toward looking for work (and thus counted as unemployed).

Youths who regularly attended church, whatever their other individual or family characteristics, had significantly more positive outcomes than those with no religious involvement. This variable probably reflects attitudes of the family as well as of the youths. As shown above, the family's involvement with transfers was negatively related to frequent churchgoing. Yet church attendance was positively associated with improved school and work outcomes, whatever the family's involvement with income transfers.

A number of area and individual variables also yield significant and interesting results. Youths in Chicago and Philadelphia had weaker labor market outcomes than youths in Boston. The grades youths reported receiving in their last year of school were significant indicators of the youths' outcomes. Youths with high grades in school generally remained in school at much higher rates than other youths. On the other hand, youths reporting illegal income showed significantly poorer outcomes than other youth. Illegal income among the 16–18 group

Table 11.9   **Determinants of School, Work, and Job-Search Behavior of Black Men 16 to 18 Years Old in the NBER Sample: Results of Multinomial Logit Equations**

Explanatory Variables	Effects on No Work, No School		Effects on Work, No School		Effects on School, No Work	
	Derivative	t-Value	Derivative	t-Value	Derivative	t-Value
Constant	.214	1.85	-.028	-.56	.670	4.11
Any Transfer	.076	1.99	.023	1.29	.061	1.14
1 Worker in Family	-.121	-2.47	-.060	-2.56	-.159	-2.08
2 Workers in Family	-.117	-2.12	-.027	-1.12	-.119	-1.42
Illegal Income	.009	2.13	.002	.98	-.004	-.45
Chicago	.163	3.83	.049	2.59	.188	3.31
Philadelphia	.196	4.04	.057	2.58	.242	3.44
2 Parents Present Youth at 14	.005	.07	.006	.18	.071	.62
1 Parent Present, Youth at 14	.013	.18	.006	.19	.027	.25
1 or More Worker, Youth at 14	-.024	-.54	.027	1.24	-.088	-1.31
Attends Church Very Often	-.159	-3.32	-.087	-3.59	-.115	-1.76
Attends Church Moderately	-.091	-2.19	-.056	-2.98	-.156	-2.44
Age 18	.120	3.08	.052	2.95	-.105	-1.76
HS Graduate	.201	2.99	.086	3.23	.037	.30
Mostly A's and B's	-.111	-2.34	-.054	-2.49	-.097	-1.37
Half B's and C's	-.120	-2.71	-.058	-2.92	-.153	-2.28
Reservation Wage	-.063	-2.97	-.002	-.40	-.064	-2.57

Number of Observations: 1,114

Source: Equations performed on NBER survey data.

Table 11.10 Determinants of School, Work, and Job-Search Behavior of Black Men 19 to 24 Years Old in the NBER Sample: Results of Multinomial Logit Equations

Explanatory Variables	Effects on School, Any Labor-Force Status		Effects on Work and No School		Effects on Job Search of Nonemployed	
	Derivative	t-Value	Derivative	t-Value	Derivative	t-Value
Constant	.049	.36	.017	.09	.392	2.18
Any Transfer	-.142	-2.89	-.134	-2.03	.018	.26
1 Worker in Family	-.019	-.32	.096	1.17	-.013	-.17
2 Workers in Family	-.029	-.48	.154	1.83	-.057	-.68
Illegal Income	-.004	-1.64	-.005	-2.15	-.003	-1.91
Chicago	-.119	-2.05	-.159	-1.92	.058	.66
Philadelphia	-.236	-3.87	-.182	-2.22	-.071	-.81
2 Parents Present, Youth at 14	.134	1.30	-.078	-.62	-.014	-.12
1 Parent Present, Youth at 14	.084	.85	-.093	-.79	-.013	-.11
1 or More Worker, Youth at 14	.026	.44	.118	1.49	.127	1.64
Attends Church Very Often	.071	1.12	.092	1.05	.090	1.02
Attends Church Moderately	.115	2.21	.137	1.94	.060	.83
Ages 22–24	-.096	-1.91	.048	.75	.089	1.34
HS Graduate	.132	2.75	.240	3.65	.102	1.53
Mostly A's and B's	.087	1.49	-.054	-.70	-.070	-.88
Half B's and C's	.094	1.58	.069	.89	.053	.69
Reservation Wage	-.015	-.81	.018	.74	-.084	-2.84

Number of Observations: 927

Source: Equations performed on NBER survey data.

meant less schooling; in the 19–24 group, those with illegal income were much more frequently out of the labor force and less frequently in school, in a job, or looking for a job.

Sensitivity of the Estimates to Different Specifications

A variety of interpretations could be consistent with the estimates of significant welfare effects observed in tables 11.9 and 11.10. Among the possibilities noted above were, first, that the estimates attribute too much to welfare, since unmeasured family attitudes may be causing both receipt of transfers and the low work achievement of youth and, second, that the estimates attribute too little to welfare, since welfare, by causing adults to reduce work effort and youths to raise reservation wages, has indirect as well as direct negative effects on youth outcomes.

Estimates derived from other specifications, shown in table 11.11, shed some light on the issue. The specifications using *predicted* receipt of transfers include one that holds constant the youth's reservation wage but not the presence of other workers and a second that holds constant the presence of other workers in the family but not reservation wages. The predicted values come from the results shown in table 11.8, in which the absence of workers in the family is a determinant of the receipt of transfers. Both estimates based on actual transfers are independent of the presence of other workers in the family; the only difference is that one includes and one excludes the youth's reservation wage.

The pattern of results is similar across specifications, but the size and significance of effects are not. By far the largest effects are in the specification using the predicted receipt of transfer payments and excluding the presence of other family workers in the youth outcome regression. This specification does avoid attributing welfare effects to unmeasured family attitudes, but by excluding the presence of other workers it may overstate the role of transfers. On the one hand, the specification allows the welfare variable to capture fully the *indirect* impact of other workers on youth outcomes that occurs through its effect on the family's receipt of welfare. On the other hand, this approach attributes some *direct* effects of the presence of other workers on youth outcomes to the welfare variable. There is no easy way out here, since including the presence of the workers with predicted transfers leads to multicollinearity.

The importance of this multicollinearity is clear from the dramatic drop in estimated welfare effects that occurs when one includes the presence of other workers in the family alongside actual or predicted receipt of welfare. Without a full modeling of work-welfare and welfare-family characteristics interactions—a job beyond the scope of this paper and probably not achievable with this data set—one cannot pre-

Table 11.11 Estimates of Welfare Effects Based on Alternative Specifications (t-values in parentheses)

Effects on 16–19 Group	No Work, No School	Work Only	School Only	Both School and Work
No Controls for Other Workers Present in Family				
Predicted Transfers	.502	.167	.315	−.984
	(5.09)	(3.58)	(2.19)	
Controls for Presence of Other Workers in Family				
Any Transfers	.076	.023	.061	−.160
	(1.99)	(1.29)	(1.14)	
No Controls for Reservation Wage				
Predicted Transfers	.048	.011	.060	−.119
	(1.05)	(0.59)	(0.90)	
Any Transfers	.073	.009	.032	−.114
	(2.00)	(0.55)	(0.67)	

		Not in School		
Effects on 19–24 Group	In School, Any Labor-Force Status	Working	Unemployed	Not in Labor Force
No Controls for Other Workers Present in Family				
Predicted Transfers	−.695	−.167	.338	.524
	(−5.80)	(−0.90)	(1.85)	
Controls for Presence of Other Workers in Family				
Any Transfers	−.142	−.134	.018	.258
	(−2.89)	(−2.03)	(0.26)	
No Controls for Reservation Wage				

	In School	Work	Unemployed/ Not in Labor Force
Predicted Transfers	−.080	−.044	.124
	(−2.47)	(−1.08)	
Any Transfers	−.116	−.107	.223
	(−3.66)	(−2.68)	

Source: Multinomial logit equations performed on NBER survey data.

cisely distinguish the effects of the family's receipt of transfers from the presence of other workers. Nevertheless, although the strong link between the two variables is well known, their major importance in determining youth outcomes is a striking result that adds to our understanding of the employment problems of young black men.

It is also noteworthy that in spite of the variation in the observed effects of a family's receipt of transfers, even the lowest estimates indicate a negative influence of welfare on youth outcomes.

Family and Welfare Effects on Earnings and on School and Work Activities over the Year

In examining how family and welfare variables influenced the youths' earnings and school and work activities over the year prior to the interview, one confronts a similar set of specification problems. This section adopts the same strategy as in the preceding section for estimating the effects of predicted and actual welfare status, including and not including the presence of other workers in the family and reservation wages.

A summary of the results of ordinary-least-squares (OLS) equations on earnings and on school and work activities appears in tables 11.12 and 11.13. These estimates are broadly similar to the earlier estimates of the effects on the youth's current status. In some specifications of the continuous variables, however, the family's receipt of transfers had *no* negative effects on the school and work outcomes of the 16–18 group. In contrast, transfers were consistently associated with a worse mix of current activities.

Still, the similarities are pronounced. High probabilities of receiving transfers induced much larger and more consistently negative effects on the 19–24 age group than on the 16–18 group. The important role of family variables associated with welfare shows up in the analysis of school and work outcomes over the year as a negative influence on youth outcomes, as it did in the analysis of current activities. Youths who lived with two or more family members who held a job tended to do considerably better than youths in families without any workers. The role of other workers was significant for both age groups.

11.4.3   Family and Welfare Effects on a National Sample of Young Black Men

Conclusions derived from the NBER inner-city sample of Boston, Chicago, and Philadelphia youths may or may not hold for a national sample of young black men. It is worth noting that differences may arise either because of genuine variations in relationships across geographic areas, because of differences in the data collected, or because of differences in the characteristics of youths in the two samples.

Table 11.12   **Family and Welfare Influences on 16- to 18-Year-Olds: Work and Earnings Patterns During the 13 Months Before the NBER Interview**

Explanatory Variables	Months Neither Working Nor in School		In Earnings	
	(1)	(2)	(1)	(2)
Intercept	1.94***	3.05***	6.09***	4.52***
Predicted Receipt of Transfers	1.00**	−.16	−.1.05*	.49*
1 Person in Family Worked		−.28		.55**
2 or More Persons in Family Worked		−.72		1.00***
Chicago	.76***	.76***	−.89***	−.88***
Philadelphia	1.08***	1.10***	−1.99***	−2.02***
Attend Church Very Often	−.66***	−.81***	.06	.25
Attend Church Moderately	−.63***	−.69***	.56**	.62**
Age 18	1.37***	1.34***	.91***	.96***
Illegal Income, in Dollars	.07***	.07***	−.00	−.00
HS Graduate	.58	.60	.43	.43
Still in School			−.97*	−.96***
Mostly A's and B's	−.87***	−.88***	.63**	.67**
Half B's and C's	−.56***	−.59***	.35	.39
Mean	2.88	2.88	4.66	4.66
N	1,094	1,094	972	972
R²	.12	.12	.09	.10

Note: Superscripts, ***, **, and * represent significance at the one, 5, and 10 percent levels, respectively. The regressions also included three variables that were insignificant in all regressions: the presence of both parents when the youth was age 14; the presence of only one parent when the youth was age 14; and the presence of a worker in the family when the youth was age 14.

Source: Computed from NBER survey data.

The NLS data did have some advantages for this analysis. Area differences in welfare guarantees, labor market conditions, and the extent of urbanization all helped in isolating the role of income transfers. The three years of data allowed an accounting of prior labor market activities and welfare histories in the estimates of current outcomes.

Determinants of the Family's Welfare Status

How area welfare levels and other welfare variables affect the family's receipt of benefits not only is of interest in itself, it also has special importance for assessing the effect of income transfers on young men. Consider two families, A and B, that are similar to each other except

Table 11.13   **Family and Welfare Influences on 19- to 24-Year-Olds: Work and Earnings Patterns During the 13 Months Before the NBER Interview**

Explanatory Variables	Months Neither Working Nor in School		ln Earnings	
	(1)	(2)	(1)	(2)
Intercept	4.41***	4.43***	6.89***	5.77***
Predicted Receipt of Transfers	2.49***	1.81	−1.26**	.07
1 Person in Family Worked		.34		.05
2 or More Persons in Family Worked		−.63		1.05***
Chicago	1.81***	1.82***	−1.11***	−1.14***
Philadelphia	1.85***	1.87***	−1.69***	−1.74***
Attend Church Very Often	−.47	−.56	.13	.32
Attend Church Moderately	−.77**	−.80**	.33	.38
Ages 22–24	.24	.21	.14	.18
Illegal Income in Dollars	.03***	.03***	−.01**	−.01**
HS Graduate	−2.16***	−2.19***	.96***	.99***
Still in School			−.35	−.33
Mostly A's, B's	−.61	−.62	−.19	−.15
Half B's, C's	−.81**	−.80**	.39	.39
Mean	5.37	5.37	6.34	6.34
N	897	897	876	876
R^2	.16	.17	.10	.11

Note: Superscripts *** and ** represent significance levels at the one and 5 percent levels, respectively. The regressions also included the three insignificant variables noted in Table 11.12.

Source: Computed from NBER survey data.

for state of residence. Assume family A lives in a high-payment state, while family B lives in a low- or moderate-payment state. One would expect that family A would be more likely to receive welfare than family B simply because of the income threshold in its state. Suppose these higher guarantees do, indeed, lead to more families receiving payments in one state than similar families in other states. Then, we would have an ideal situation for identifying independent effects of welfare. One merely has to examine how youths in families that receive welfare because of the state's higher income threshold perform relative to youths in similar families not on welfare because of low state benefit levels.

The first step is to analyze whether state benefit levels and other area variables have any impact on the welfare status of the families of young black men. Table 11.14 displays solid evidence from probit equations showing that state benefit levels raised sharply the chances that a youth lived in a family receiving welfare. The state's income guarantee from AFDC and food stamps exerted large and statistically significant effects on the presence of welfare income in 1978, 1979, and 1980. In 1978, for example, a youth in a family with the mean area and family characteristics had a .20 probability of living in a welfare family. The results of the probit equations indicate that an increase of one standard deviation in the AFDC plus food stamp guarantee level (holding other characteristics constant) induced an increase of 8.5 percentage points in this probability.

The other area and family variables generally had the expected influences on the family's receipt of welfare benefits. One exception

Table 11.14   **Effects of Selected Variables on the Probability of Young Black Men Living in a Family Receiving Welfare: Probit Equations for 1979, 1980, and 1981 (t-values in parentheses)**

Explanatory Variables	Effects on Receiving Welfare in:		
	1978	1979	1980
Probability at the Mean of the Independent Variables	.202	.165	.167
AFDC Food Stamp Guarantee (in 100s)	.089 (4.19)	.061 (3.87)	.055 (3.48)
Big City Residence	−.149 (−2.68)	−.074 (−1.60)	−.128 (−2.61)
Central City Residence	−.046 (−1.12)	.012 (0.32)	.024 (0.70)
Big City × Central City	.146 (2.13)	.081 (1.38)	.120 (1.96)
Unemployment High in Area	−.029 (−0.94)	−.011 (−0.44)	−.048 (−1.89)
Father Present in 1979	−.311 (−10.85)		
Father Present in 1980		−.214 (−8.48)	−.188 (−7.51)
Mother Present in 1979	−.044 (−1.08)		
Mother Present in 1980		.115 (3.55)	.089 (2.76)
Family size	.031 (4.73)	.024 (4.32)	.015 (2.73)
N	1,114	1,173	1,166

Source: Equations performed on NLS data for 1979, 1980, and 1981.

was the negative (but usually insignificant) effect of living in a high-unemployment area. The pattern of city effects was interesting. Neither the pure big city or inner-city effect was positive; instead, what sharply and significantly raised the probability of welfare receipt was the combined effect of living in the inner part of a large city.

Alternative Estimates of Welfare and Family Effects on Earnings and on the School and Work Status of the Nation's Young Black Men

Use of a national sample of black young men yields results that have general relevance and avoids the potential problem in the NBER data of bias due to outmigration of successful members of welfare families from the low-income urban areas. In addition, by drawing on three years of NLS data, one can assess how past welfare experience affects current employment and earnings as well as whether the estimated welfare effects are similar from one year to another. This section reports on several empirical efforts to test for welfare and family effects. The specific estimates reported here, however, by no means exhaust the potential uses of NLS data to determine the impact of welfare variables.

The alternative estimates of the family and welfare variables appear in table 11.15. As in the analysis of the NBER inner-city sample, welfare effects on the national sample were generally larger and more significant among the older group (those 10 to 23 in 1980) than among teenagers (16 to 19 in 1980). Note that the impact of living in a family receiving cash welfare was to lower the expected 1980 earnings of the 20–23 age group by a whopping 100 percent. This effect was independent of the youth's 1978 earnings. Living in a welfare family in 1980 was closely associated with negative school and work outcomes in 1981, especially among the 20- to 23-year-olds. A change in welfare status raised the share neither working nor in school by 21 percentage points for the older group (a 100 percent increase), but by only four points for the younger group.

These estimates of welfare effects may be partly capturing the impact of attitudinal or other factors that cause both the family's receipt of welfare and poor outcomes among youths. To avoid this problem, I conducted a two-stage procedure in which the predicted receipt of welfare (based on the probit equations shown in table 11.13) substituted for actual welfare as an explanatory variable in the youth outcome equations. This adjustment should lessen or eliminate bias resulting not only from unmeasured factors causing both welfare and youth outcomes, but also from the consequent separate-errors-in-variables problem. If the experience of young black men on welfare causes poor outcomes, then substituting predicted values will not fully take account of welfare's impact on youth employment. Predicted welfare status did turn out to exert negative effects on school and work outcomes. Al-

Table 11.15   Effects of Welfare and Family Variables on 1980 Earnings and on
                     1981 School and Work Status of Black Men 16–19 and 20–23 in
                     1980

Explanatory Variables	ln 1980 Earnings		Probability of Neither Work Nor School, 1981	
	Parameter	t-Value	Derivative	t-value
Ages 16–23 in 1980:				
Lived in Welfare Family in 1980	−.553	−2.29	−.105	3.59
Predicted Welfare in 1980	.022	0.08	.061	1.80
Ages 16–19 in 1980:				
Lived in Welfare Family in 1980	−.171	−0.53	.044	1.35
ln 1978 Earnings	.220	5.14	−.007	−1.51
Predicted Welfare in 1980	−.170	−0.46	.071	1.78
ln 1978 Earnings	.211	4.95	−.004	−0.92
Welfare in 1978 Only	−.457	−1.03	.043	0.94
Welfare in 1979 Only	−1.043	−2.01	.130	2.51
Welfare in 1978 and 1979	−.219	−0.58	.041	1.02
ln 1978 Earnings	.213	4.90	−.006	−1.21
Ages 20–23 in 1980:				
Lived in Welfare Family in 1980	−.997	−2.70	.201	3.73
ln 1978 Earnings	.294	6.94	−.018	−2.88
Predicted Welfare in 1980	.261	0.70	.041	0.70
ln 1978 Earnings	.289	6.87	−.019	−3.03
Welfare in 1978 Only	−.941	−2.33	.082	1.32
Welfare in 1979 Only	−2.254	−4.17	.197	2.46
Welfare in 1978 and 1979	−.156	−0.31	.088	1.18
ln 1978 Earnings	.263	6.23	−.017	−2.64

Source: Regression and probit equations derived from NLS data.

though the impact on earnings was not statistically significant, the effect
on the share neither working nor in school was. In decompositions by
age, the significant effect on school and work status was concentrated
in the 16–19 group. On average, 17 percent of this group were in the
no work, no school category. Moving from zero to one in predicted
welfare raised that probability by over seven percentage points.

These results yield somewhat conservative estimates of welfare effects, since they hold constant the youth's earnings in 1978. If welfare status weakened past as well as current labor market outcomes, including the prior earnings could well understate the overall welfare effects. It did turn out that the size and significance of the welfare variable's influence on 1980 and 1981 outcomes rose when the youth's 1978 earnings did not appear as a control variable.

A final test of the welfare variables was to calculate whether youth outcomes were sensitive to the timing or recent years of welfare participation. Youths were classified into one of four statuses: (1) no welfare in the family during 1978 or 1979; (2) welfare received by the family in 1978 but not 1979; (3) welfare received in 1979 but not 1978; (4) welfare received in both years.

The results were not entirely consistent with the expectation that longer welfare durations lead to worse outcomes. Oddly, those in families receiving welfare both in 1978 and 1979 had more positive outcomes than did those whose families received welfare only in 1979. Moreover, the young men in families with two years of welfare did no worse in 1980–81 than those whose families received welfare only in 1978.

11.4.4   Summary of the Welfare Effects on the Employment Patterns of Young Black Men

The array of results above provides powerful evidence for the importance of welfare programs, and family characteristics closely associated with welfare programs, in leading young black men to experience serious school and labor market problems. In tests relating the family's receipt of welfare benefits to a variety of youth outcomes in both the inner-city, low-income sample and the national sample, welfare variables consistently yielded significant and negative effects. Although the tests did not disentangle entirely the family influences leading to welfare from welfare incentive effects leading to the welfare experience, the significance of the welfare variable survived a variety of specifications.

In the analysis of the NBER data set, it became clear that what complicates the interpretation is not the problem of accounting for unmeasured family characteristics but rather the problem of isolating the impact of welfare from that of the presence of other workers in the family.

The analysis did reveal larger and more consistently negative effects on the older (19–24) than on the younger (16–18) subgroups. One possible reason for these effects is that youth outcomes vary more as young men move beyond high school. A second possibility is that the more successful older members of welfare families leave home, while the more successful younger members of welfare families remain with their parent or parents. This could reconcile the findings, but casting doubt on this view is the fact that only a small share of young men within the relevant age groups lived away from home.

11.5 Conclusions and the Implications of Racial Differentials

Racial differentials in the share of youths living with a family on welfare are enormous. With 25 to 30 percent of black youths and only 5 percent of white youths receiving benefits from the welfare system, any welfare effects on youth employment may account for a significant part of the large racial differentials in youth employment levels.

This paper takes some first steps in the process of moving from speculating about welfare's role to estimating the actual size of its role. Before developing empirical estimates, I pointed out that the standard welfare disincentive effects often do not apply to youth. Nevertheless, other mechanisms could be at work to link the youth's welfare status with his poor school and work outcomes. Among them are the experience on welfare and the lack of connections to jobs that come about when parents are either not present or not working.

No doubt several of the mechanisms may interact in ways not easy to measure in quantitative analyses of grouped data. Whatever the precise elements going into the observed effects, we can draw some conclusions about welfare's role in explaining black youth employment problems.

First, among black male youths living in inner-city ghetto areas, poor school and work outcomes were closely associated with welfare status. Although the presence of other workers in the family appeared of most significance, a family's receipt of income-transfer benefits exerted a role independent of the presence of workers in the family. And second, among black male youths in the nation as a whole, welfare status also exerted negative effects on school and work outcomes. Black youths were more likely to be neither working nor in school if they lived in welfare families. Moreover, even having simply a higher probability of falling into a welfare family, perhaps because of residence in a high-benefit state, seemed to worsen school and work outcomes.

Nothing in these conclusions suggests that it is wise to alter the shape or generosity of the current welfare system. The findings do make clear the importance of the linkages between family characteristics, welfare programs, and the employment outcomes of young black men. Understanding how these interactions operate is essential for devising policies that can make a difference for black youth. It may be, for example, that family-centered policies—that raise job holding and family stability among black adults—are the best approach for improving the employment chances of black youth.

Notes

1. For example, among white men 18 to 19 years old, the unemployment rate in spring 1979 was 24 percent among those in low-income families and 11 percent among those in middle- and high-income families.
2. These figures come from the U.S. Bureau of the Census (1982).
3. Layard (1982) and Wachter and Kim (1982) both gave cursory treatment to the role of welfare in explaining youth employment outcomes.
4. Both analyzed youth outcomes on the basis of data generated from the Seattle-Denver income maintenance experiment.
5. See U.S. Bureau of the Census (1981, 220–23).
6. See U.S. Department of Health and Human Services (1982, p. 41, table 23).
7. See, for example, Lerman (1973).
8. Under the 1981 amendments, states as of fiscal year 1982 could not receive federal reimbursement for covering any 18- to 21-year-olds, except those 18 about to finish school. Limited evidence is available on the impact of this change. A report by the Children's Defense Fund (1983) claimed that 29 percent of the substantial fiscal year 1982 reduction in Ohio AFDC outlays came about as a result of eliminating students in that age bracket.
9. See Lerman (1970).
10. Pindyck and Rubinfeld (1981, 287–312) provide a discussion of this procedure.

References

Barnow, Burt, Glen Cain, and Arthur Goldberger. 1980. Issues in the analysis of selectivity bias. In *Evaluation of studies review annual*, vol. 5, ed. George Farkas and Ernst Stomsdorfer, Beverly Hills, Calif.: Sage.

Children's Defense Fund. 1983. *A children's defense budget*. Washington, D.C.: Children's Defense Fund.

Freeman, Richard B. 1982. Economic determinants of geographic and individual variation in the labor market position. In *The youth labor market problem: Its nature, causes, and consequences*, ed. Richard B. Freeman and David A. Wise. Chicago: University of Chicago Press.

Layard, Richard. 1982. Youth unemployment in Britain and the United States compared. In *The youth labor market problem: Its nature, causes, and consequences*, ed. R. B. Freeman and D. A. Wise. Chicago: University of Chicago Press.

Lerman, Robert. 1970. An analysis of youth labor force participation, school activity, and employment rates. Ph.D. thesis. Cambridge: Massachusetts Institute of Technology.

Lerman, Robert. 1973. Incentive effects in public income transfer programs. Paper No. 4, *Studies in public welfare*, Subcommittee on Fiscal Policy, Joint Economic Committee, U.S. Congress. Washington, D.C.: GPO.

Pindyck, Robert, and Daniel Rubinfeld. 1981. *Econometric models in economic forecasts*, 2d ed. New York: McGraw-Hill.

U.S. Bureau of the Census. 1982. Current population reports, series P-20, no. 371. In *Household and Family Characteristics: March 1981*. Washington, D.C.: GPO.

U.S. Bureau of the Census. 1981. Current population reports, series P-60, no 132. In *Money incomes of households, families, and persons in the United States: 1980*. Washington, D.C.: GPO.

U.S. Department of Health and Human Services. 1982. Aid to Families with Dependent Children 1979 Recipient Characteristics Study. Washington, D.C.: GPO.

Venti, Steve. 1983. The effects of income maintenance on work, schooling, and non-market activities of youth. Photocopy. Dartmouth College, Hanover, N.H.

Wachter, Michael, and Choongsoo Kim. 1982. Time series changes in youth joblessness. In *The Youth Labor Market Problem: Its Nature, Causes, and Consequences*, ed. R. B. Freeman and D. A. Wise. Chicago: University of Chicago Press.

West, Richard. 1978. The effects of the Seattle and Denver income maintenance experiments on the labor supply of young nonheads. Palo Alto: Stanford Research Institute. Photocopy.

Comment   Samuel L. Myers, Jr.

Lerman's empirical analysis seeks to address three questions concerning the interaction of welfare, work, and education. All are of potential policy significance.

His first question is: Do welfare programs alter the current employment of young black men? His answer, derived from *single equation* estimates of labor-force choices and earnings is "yes," especially for black men over age 18. In the NBER data set, Lerman finds a negative relationship between coming from a family that received welfare benefits and various measures of favorable employment outcomes.

His second question is: Does the mix of family characteristics and income-transfer program characteristics affect school enrollment, employment, and unemployment among young black men? Apparently, Lerman's answer here is also "yes," although it is not clear whether the question was or can be adequately addressed using the NBER data. Dummy variables for number of wage earners in the family and city

Samuel L. Myers, Jr., is associate professor of economics at the Graduate School of Public and International Affairs, University of Pittsburgh.

were included in multinomial logit regressions for schooling and labor-force decisions among NBER black men. The purpose was to isolate family and welfare program effects from welfare participation effects. Arguably, the city dummies, which provide strikingly large coefficient estimates and t-values in the multinomial logit regressions—and which are curiously omitted from the earnings equations—are less than satisfactory proxies for welfare program characteristics. In the NLS regressions, however, state AFDC and food stamp guarantees are used to capture program effects. There, the results that Lerman reports show mixed responses. Statistically significant effects of AFDC and food stamp guarantees on the welfare recipiency equations are found among the NLS black men. But when the predicted welfare receipt value is included as a variable in the employment equations, that variable is not found to be highly significant.

Finally, Lerman asks: To the extent that any welfare-induced effects occur, do they account for any of the racial differences in youth employment outcomes? This question is left unanswered, although it is perhaps the most interesting of all.

The single-equation framework that Lerman employs in addressing each of the questions is clearly inconsistent with his own implicit model of jointly endogenous schooling, work, and welfare decisions. Lerman, of course, notes the limitations of his estimation procedure and takes great pains to reason around the simultaneity problem. One of the efforts in the paper to account for simultaneity points up the problem here. In table 11.15 Lerman estimates earnings and unemployment equations. When he includes actual welfare participation, its estimated impact is highly significant; when he includes *predicted* welfare, it is insignificant at the one percent level. It seems quite likely that welfare participation is endogenous and that the OLS estimates on the actual welfare variable are biased.

The really interesting question looming in this paper, however, is whether welfare explains any of the racial gap in earnings. The results of Darity and Myers (1980a; 1980b) provide insights that may help address this question. Using 1968 and 1978 CPS samples, they estimated log-earnings and labor-force participation equations for blacks and whites, for both positive income earners and the "potential labor force." Zero-earners in the last mentioned group were assigned the wage of those in their age, race, gender, and region cohort.

These equations are simultaneous because earnings depend on labor-force participation and labor-force participation depends on (potential) earnings. Labor-force participation also depends on welfare income. Thus, it is possible to estimate from the Darity-Myers results the effect of welfare income on black-white earnings inequality. Focusing on the positive income samples, we find that welfare income lowered blacks' weeks worked and raised their weeks unemployed in 1978, but it had no statistically significant impact on the labor-force participation of blacks in 1968 or whites in 1968 or 1978. Moreover, increased labor-force participation reduced racial earnings inequality in the positive-income sample. Thus, increased welfare participation can be expected to increase racial earnings inequality, at least when estimates are based on those who are employed.

When the potential labor force is the base for estimates, however, the answer is reversed. In this expanded sample, increased welfare participation actually reduces earnings inequality; welfare reduces both black and white labor-force participation, although more so for whites than for blacks.

Still, whether one uses the positive-income sample or the potential labor force, the *magnitude* of the effect of welfare income recipiency is minuscule. My estimates, based on the Darity-Myers regressions, reveal percentage changes in the 1978 black-white earnings ratio due to an increase in welfare recipiency ranging from $+.0008$ to $-.017$. These extremely inelastic results in both directions dim any hopes of finding major new explanations for wage inequality in the phenomenon of welfare participation. In principle, one could perform the same exercise using the NBER or NLS data. From Lerman's results alone, I suspect that his estimates of the effects of welfare on inequity would be much larger.[1]

Lerman argues that there is an association between welfare and the schooling and labor market experiences of young black men and women. I agree. He suggests that there is a causal relationship running from welfare experiences to employment. His evidence is insufficiently persuasive to warrant acceptance of this simple unidirectional perspective. My own view, influenced by the compelling historical record of the continuing and pervasive dependency of the black underclass in the United States, is that welfare recipiency, dropping out of school, and poor employment are inextricably intertwined in a much more complex manner than is admitted in Lerman's simple model.

Furthermore, the results showing an effect of family welfare status on employment and schooling may be suspect for reasons beyond the simultaneous-equations bias. I am struck by the large number of men in the NBER sample who reported themselves to be living at home. Could it be that the probability of being in the sample is higher for those living at home, whatever their employment and welfare status? Could it be that those with low earnings or high unemployment have higher probabilities of living at home when the family receives welfare income? Lerman's observed effect of welfare on employment may be a simple occurrence of this sample-selection effect.

In sum, this paper raises a number of interesting policy questions that certainly deserve additional investigation.

Note

1. In earlier versions of the paper Lerman estimated that 20 to 90 percent of the racial gap was explained by welfare. Whether this was due to the suspicious nature of his estimates or the age composition of his sample stands to be shown.

References

Darity, William A., Jr., and Samuel L. Myers, Jr. 1980a. Black economic progress: A case against the dramatic improvement hypothesis. Institute for Research on Poverty Discussion Paper no. 613–80. Madison: University of Wisconsin.

————. 1980b. Changes in black-white income inequality, 1968–1978: A decade of progress? *Review of Black Political Economy.*

Appendix:
NBER-Mathematica Survey of Inner-City Black Youth: An Analysis of the Undercount of Older Youths

John Bound

The NBER-Mathematica Survey of Inner-City Black Youth was intended to be a random sample of youths from low-income, predominantly black areas of three cities.[1] Yet older youths are poorly represented in the survey, with half as many in their twenties as in their teens. Comparisons of population counts between the NBER and 1980 census data for targeted areas suggest that this difference is the result of the NBER survey having undercounted older youths. This appendix examines why the undercount may have occurred and evaluates its possible biasing of the results presented in this volume.

The Undercount

Table A.1 reports population counts from the NBER survey and from the 1980 Census for Boston, Chicago, and Philadelphia. The census data include counts for both the central cities and for the particular poverty tracts targeted by NBER. There are noticeable differences between the NBER and the census data on the age distribution, with the NBER having six to seven percentage point greater numbers of younger youths and commensurately fewer older youths. This apparent undercount of older youths naturally raises doubts about the representativeness of the survey, particularly regarding the older youths.

We should not be too surprised that the NBER survey undercounted older youths. Typically, the Census has had the most trouble enumerating working-aged black men. The Census estimates its own undercount of 20- to 24-year-old black men to have been over 12 percent in 1960 and 1970 and over 7 percent in 1980.[2] The Census does not

John Bound is a graduate student in economics at Harvard University.

Table A.1 Comparison of Age Distributions of Young Black Men: in the NBER Survey and the 1980 Census, by City and Age

	Chicago			Boston			Philadelphia		
		Census			Census			Census	
Age	NBER	Poverty Tracts[a]	City[b]	NBER	Poverty Tracts[a]	City[b]	NBER	Poverty Tracts[a]	City[b]
16–17	36.9	30.2	25.6	35.1	25.8	.246	32.5	25.9	35.0
18–19	23.9	23.6	23.3	26.8	24.9	.246	24.0	26.1	19.9
20–21	16.6	21.1	21.8	17.3	20.8	.215	19.6	22.7	18.3
22–24	22.6	25.1	29.3	20.7	28.5	.323	24.0	25.3	26.7
N	800	12,710	105,245	757	4,530	11,873	801	8,740	59,927

[a]Population counts for black men in predominantly black poverty tracts in the city. For Boston, census tracts that had at least 20 percent of families below the poverty line and that were at least 60 percent black in the 1970 Census. For Chicago and Philadelphia, census tracts that had at least 30 percent of families below the poverty line and that were at least 70 percent black in the 1970 Census.

[b]Population counts for black men in various cities. 1980 Census, *General characteristics of the population.*

Sources: 1979 NBER Survey of Inner-City Black Youth Survey and 1980 Census.

report undercount percentages for inner-city youths, but the common presumption is that they are even higher.

The Census traces its undercount of black men to a number of sources. Because the count is based on dwellings, the census surveyors miss people who live in places not recognized as dwelling units, who live alone and are rarely at home, or who tend to move from one place to another. Those who refuse to respond to the surveyor because of their lack of awareness, lack of interest, or distrust are also not counted. Census analysts determine the basic demographic breakdown of the undercount by comparing birth and death statistics; and to obtain a more detailed picture, they use a variety of supplementary surveys designed to identify individuals missed by the Census itself. These supplemental surveys tend to indicate that the undercount is caused by a lack of family attachments, but they otherwise show nothing to suggest that the undercount is not random.[3]

The NBER survey, like the Census, used a dwelling-based sampling scheme. Eligible youths were identified through household screening. Once an eligible youth was identified the NBER interviewer had to find the youth and convince him to be interviewed. The Census, on the other hand, uses one respondent to report on all members of the household. This strategy ensures the highest possible response rate (which is what Census analysts want), but given both the kind and quality of information that the NBER researchers were trying to collect, they decided this strategy was out of the question.

NBER interviewers made many follow-up calls, searched local hangouts, and left word with potential respondents of means by which they could contact the interviewer. Despite all these efforts, 15 percent of those originally identified were never successfully interviewed, either because they refused (3.7 percent) or because they were never located (11.5 percent).[4] If, as seems plausible, the 15 percent were concentrated among older youths (since older youths would be less likely to be at home, their parents would be less likely to know their whereabouts, and they would be less likely to find the $5 compensation for the interview sufficient), they could account for the entire discrepancy between the NBER and the census samples.

The Problem: Potential Biases

The real question is not so much why the undercount may have occurred but whether it was random with respect to the variables of interest in the research studies in this volume. On a priori grounds, one can argue that the undercount may have biased the estimated economic and social activities of the older youths in either a positive or negative direction. It is possible, for example, that it was the most troubled youths who were the hardest to find and to interview. If so, we might expect that the NBER survey would, for example, overestimate employment rates and underestimate rates of criminal activity. Alternatively, however, it may have been that the most active youth, those most consistently away from home, were the ones NBER interviewers had the most trouble finding. If this was the case we might expect that the survey underestimated both criminal activity and employment.

It is important to recognize, however, that a biased estimate of the level of a variable does not necessarily imply a biased regression coefficient on the effect of the variable on outcomes. If, for example, the NBER survey tended to miss a certain number of the employed, estimates of employment rates would be biased, but estimates of the impact of a high school diploma on employment would be biased only if the undercount was concentrated among either high school graduates or dropouts. Constant response biases affect estimates of proportions and means but not estimates of slope coefficients. Response biases that affect the variances of the dependent variable affect the magnitudes of coefficients, but they tend to do so proportionately. The gravest problems occur not in sampling the dependent variable but in a sampling that is jointly dependent on the dependent and independent variables.[5]

Analysis of the Undercount

Is the undercount in the NBER survey random with respect to the jointness of the variables? In the remainder of this piece I review the available evidence on the randomness of the NBER undercount. We already know that it was concentrated among older youth. My focus will be on whether sampling was random with respect to various outcomes: enrollment, educational attainment, employment, and wages. These outcomes are certainly central to any assessment of the socioeconomic status of inner-city black youths, but they are also outcomes about which we already have some evidence.[6] I will make three kinds of comparisons. First, for characteristics reported in enough detail in the 1980 Census, I compare the NBER and census tabulations. Second, I use activities reported in the NBER time line to compare youths' reports of their current activities to their reports of those of a year earlier. Lastly, following the techniques popularized by Heckman,[7] I test whether standard sample-selection corrections affect the NBER estimates.

The Census-NBER comparison is straightforward, but here we need to keep in mind the differences in survey instruments. The Census relies primarily on questionnaires filled out by a member of the household and returned by mail. The NBER survey relied on direct interviews with the youths themselves. There is ample evidence that such differences in survey instruments can have substantial effects on the data collected.[8] What is more, the evidence suggests that the discrepancies are wider among young black men than among members of other groups.

The idea behind the time-line comparison is also quite simple. Retrospective responses by older youths give us another reading on youths a year younger. The discrepancies in responses suggest sampling biases. Here again, alternative explanations of any particular discrepancy will always be possible. If, for example, the retrospective responses are systematically biased with respect to the current responses or if the economic environment is not stable, we may find discrepancies that have little to do with the sampling. At the same time, with sampling biases of the same magnitude on both cross-sectional and longitudinal data, differences will not be evident.[9]

Consider the following explication of an outcome that varies with age and year:[10]

$$Y_{ijt} = \alpha_i + \beta_i T + \epsilon_{ijt},$$

where i indexes individuals; j, time periods; and t, years in the labor force; and Y is the outcome; T measures length of time in the labor force; and α and β are individual-specific constants and growth rates. For simplicity's sake consider only two ages ($t = 0,1$) and two time periods ($j = 0,1$).[11]

As long as the sample is random it will yield unbiased estimates of $\bar{\alpha}$ and $\bar{\beta}$, using cross-sections from either year, and of β, using longitudinal comparisons. The different estimates should agree as to sampling error. Disparities will suggest sampling biases. Thus, for example, if the NBER had tended to miss those worse off, only $\bar{\alpha}$ might be biased; but if attrition also rose with age, cross-sectional biases on $\bar{\beta}$ might also be the case. In either case, however, comparisons over time would correctly estimate $\bar{\beta}$, since selection is on the permanent component that is differenced out of the equation. Alternatively, suppose that those missed by the survey were missed partly because they were away from home. This would suggest that the NBER survey tended to miss those currently employed, in legal or illegal activity. Here, cross-sectional comparisons will tend to underestimate $\bar{\alpha}$. How estimates of $\bar{\beta}$ are affected depends on how sampling varies with age. The longitudinal estimates $\bar{\beta}$ will potentially be the most seriously affected, since the sampling is based on current rather than past status.

More formally, imagine that inclusion in the survey depends on this selection rule: A member of the target population is sampled only if a unit-variance variable, Z,[12] is below a threshold level, $Z < \bar{Z}_t$. Z is a function of the components of Y, such that:

$$Z_{ijt} = \lambda_1 \alpha_i + \lambda_2 \beta_i T + \lambda_3 \epsilon_{ijt} + \nu_{ijt}.$$

Selection into the sample depends on age directly through Z and indirectly through Z's dependence on $\beta_i T$. Now, in the population as a whole:

$$E(Y \mid j,t) = \alpha_i + \beta_i T = Y \cdot jt,$$

but in the sampled population:[13]

$$E(Y \mid j,t,Z < \tilde{Z}_t) = Y \cdot jt + \sigma_{yz} \times E(Z/Z < \tilde{Z}_t) =$$

$$Y \cdot jt + \kappa \{\lambda_1 \sigma_\alpha^2 + \lambda_2 \sigma_\beta T + (\lambda_1 + \lambda_2) \sigma_{\alpha\beta} T + \lambda_3 \sigma_\epsilon^2\}.$$

A cross-sectional estimate of β would simply be $Y \cdot j1 - Y \cdot j0$ with a bias.

$$(\lambda_1 \sigma_\alpha^2 + \lambda_3 \sigma_\epsilon^2)\Delta\kappa + \{\lambda_2 \sigma_\beta^2 (\lambda_1 + \lambda_2)\sigma_{\alpha\beta}\}\kappa.$$

A longitudinal estimate of β would be Y.11 $-$ Y.00 with a bias.

$$\sigma_\epsilon^2 \kappa + \{_2 \sigma_\beta^2 + (\lambda_1 + \lambda_2)\sigma_{\alpha\beta}\}\kappa.$$

We see that, in general, the biases will not be the same in the two estimates. If selection is primarily on the permanent component, that is, if λ_1 dominates Z, then the cross-sectional estimates will be more biased. On the other hand, if selection depends only weakly on age and depends strongly on the transitory components of outcomes, we would expect biases to be larger for the longitudinal comparisons.

This formulation clearly shows that nonrandom sampling is likely to bias cross-sectional and longitudinal estimates differently. Still, without some prior interpretation, we cannot judge the precise difference between the two. Moreover, in many cases the biases will run in the same direction and will be quantitatively close, so that we will not notice any significant discrepancies.[14]

Finally, the fact that the undercount seems to have been more severe in Boston than in Philadelphia or Chicago suggests another simple check on sampling biases: We would expect any biases to be larger in Boston. Thus, differences across cities might suggest sampling biases. We do not want to exclude the possibility that employment or wage rates might have been higher in one city than in another, but we may be more willing to expect regression coefficients to be comparable.

In essence, examining the sample-selection techniques, at least as a specification test, is simply one version of this kind of comparison. One looks for exogenous influences on the probability of being sampled that do not affect the outcome in question. If the estimates vary systematically with the probability of being sampled, the discrepancies can be interpreted as evidence of nonrandom sampling. In the case of the NBER sample, we can use the apparent city differences in sampling, and also the apparent undercount of those living on their own,[15] to estimate the true underlying age by the household status distributions of the targeted populations. From this we can impute selection rules to use in testing for selection biases. Because we do not want to exclude either the city or family status effects from the primary equations, we will have to capture these sampling effects from the interaction terms and the nonlinearity implicit in the selection correction.

The problems with the sample-selection procedure are well known. In particular, the technique is sensitive to misspecification in either the original or the auxiliary equation.

Each of these three comparisons—between the NBER and the census data, between the current and retrospective data, and among the data collected in the three cities—carries its own problems of interpretation. Differences in the data may be the result of sampling biases but could also arise for many other reasons. The focus here will therefore be on a search for common patterns.

Census-NBER Comparisons

Table A.2 compares the census to the NBER tabulations on enrollment, employment, and educational attainment for each of the two cities for which census data were available at the time of writing. The samples are large enough that differences of even a few percentage points are significant. The first thing to notice is the broad agreement between the two tabulations. Both report proportionately more youths in school, in school past the twelfth grade, and employed in Boston than in Chicago. A more detailed comparison shows some differences, however. The Census reports a higher proportion of youths in school, a higher proportion with more education than a high school diploma, and in three out of four cases, a lower proportion employed than the NBER reports.

Taking the Census numbers at face value, we would conclude that the NBER survey undersampled the enrolled-in-school and the unemployed youths. Yet this pattern fits no simple selection explanation. The NBER survey does not seem to have missed the more active or the most disadvantaged youths. Of course, we can imagine other sampling schemes that would have given these contrasts. Still, there is another explanation. We know that there is some tendency for self-reported surveys to show higher employment and lower school enrollment rates than do surveys that rely on proxies. For example, Freeman and Medoff (1982) reported discrepancies for black youths of around 2 percent for enrollment rates and from 5 to 10 percent for employment rates between the National Longitudinal Surveys (self-reported) and the Current Population Survey (proxies). The closeness with which these differences match the discrepancies in table A.2 is striking.

Table A.2   Comparison of School Enrollment and Employment Rates in the NBER Survey and the 1980 Census, by City and Age

	School Enrollment Rates			Employment Rates		
	Census			Census		
Age	City	Poverty Tracts	NBER	City	Poverty Tracts	NBER
			Boston			
16–17	.898	.937	.857	.285	.271	.373
18–19	.656	.651	.567			
20–21	.407	.350	.229	.620	.619	.723
22–24	.268	.173	.166			
Proportion with Fewer Than 12 Years of Education				Proportion with More Than 12 Years of Education		
18–24	.357	.456	.511	.276	.180	.121
			Chicago			
16–17	.863	.845	.831	.184	.060	.204
18–19	.504	.463	.393			
20–21	.230	.203	.158	.478	.365	.322
22–24	.146	.132	.066			
Proportion with Fewer Than 12 Years of Education				Proportion with More Than 12 Years of Education		
18–24	.449	.556	.552	.209	.147	.109

Note: Universe defined as in table A.1. For the Census, samples are one of six out of the population. For the NBER Survey, they are the same as in table A.1.

The undercount was more severe in Boston than in Chicago by 30 percent, suggesting that if the NBER differences can be explained in terms of sampling biases in the data, we should see the larger differences in Boston. There is little evidence of this effect for either school enrollment or educational attainment. Employment presents a bit more complicated pattern. Among older youths the discrepancy in employment rates is larger for Boston. Among teens the discrepancy is largest for Chicago, but here the census number is almost unbelievably low. A possible interpretation of these disparate numbers is that there is, in fact, a sampling bias for the older youths in Boston, but for teens, the undercount of whom is not severe, the differences caused by differences in the two survey instruments represent the crucial element. The plausibility of this interpretation awaits other corroborating evidence.

Time-Line Comparisons

Table A.3 tabulates currently and retrospectively reported school enrollment rates from the time line of the NBER survey and compares them to similar data for black youths from the National Longitudinal Surveys (NLS). In the NBER data, the currently reported enrollment rates are consistently higher than the retrospectively reported ones. No similar pattern is evident in the NLS data. Retrospective 17-year-old enrollment rates represent the proportion of 18-year-olds who reported that they were enrolled in school the previous year. Serving as summary statistics are the weighted average differences between the two cross-sections and chi-squared tests on the homogeneity of the aging effect across the two years. The differences between the current and retrospective data are clearly significant, with a slight indication that the pattern of aging differs between the two cross-sections.

Does the contrast between the current and retrospective responses suggest sampling biases? Perhaps the NBER tended to miss youths currently out of school. The problem with this interpretation is that the sampling bias runs in the opposite direction to the one found in the NBER-Census comparisons. An alternative interpretation is to explain the discrepancy in terms of differences between what we can expect from current and retrospective reports. We can, in fact, easily imagine a variety of reasons why currently reported enrollment rates would be

Table A.3   **Comparison of Current and Retrospective School Enrollment Rates in the NLS and NBER Survey, by Age**

Age	Total lag	Total cur	Chicago lag	Chicago cur	Boston lag	Boston cur	Philadelphia lag	Philadelphia cur	NLS 1979	NLS 1980
16	81.1	92.8	73.9	92.1	84.3	90.7	84.6	96.1	94.6	93.4
17	64.0	74.7	50.9	69.8	81.7	80.3	57.6	73.9	90.7	92.9
18	39.2	52.1	34.6	45.5	62.7	67.5	20.9	41.5	51.0	81.4
19	26.6	28.0	24.7	30.9	36.8	40.9	19.8	12.8	44.8	24.5
20	16.8	16.9	17.3	17.3	21.8	23.7	12.1	11.0	16.2	27.6
21	14.4	14.5	10.0	13.5	20.8	21.8	13.7	9.1	12.1	13.5
22	10.9	14.9	3.8	13.1	22.0	16.7	5.7	15.1	14.3	9.1
23	4.9	12.1	4.4	5.7	4.0	22.0	6.1	7.6		
N	1,913	2,173	624	732	618	707	671	734	254	308
Weighted Mean Differential	6.9		8.5		4.4		5.7		−7.4	
Standard Error	(1.2)		(2.0)		(2.1)		(1.8)		(1.9)	
χ^2 Test of Homogeneity	18.71		9.54		7.94		18.07		15.02	
Degrees of Freedom	7		7		7		7		6	

higher than the retrospectively reported ones. For example, youths who were only marginally attached to school a year ago might be less likely to report themselves as having been enrolled.

Table A.4 compares current and retrospective employment rates in the NBER and NLS data. We see virtually no indication of any differences between the two cross-sections. It is customary to report employment rates separately for those enrolled in school, but for our purposes this would be a mistake. The enrolled are a self-selected population whose composition changes over time. If we were to make employment status conditional on enrollment status, we would confound these compositional effects with the sampling biases we are looking for.

Table A.5 compares current and retrospective wage rates in the two samples. These data are more difficult to interpret for a number of reasons. Perforce, we must make wages conditional on employment both at the time of the survey and a year earlier. Moreover, the NBER Survey reports only one wage per job, thereby capturing only between-job not within-job wage growth. The table shows that wages were higher in the NBER current data, but even more so in the NLS data, in which average hourly compensation rose over the period by about 10 percent per year. This fully accounts for the differences between the two NLS series. The NBER numbers actually show less wage growth than we would expect given the growth in compensation, but this could easily be due to the lack of within-job wage growth. The linear age terms summarize the cross-sectional aging effect for each survey. No great differences stand out.

Finally, although the NBER survey did not ask retrospective questions about educational attainment, the time line shows whether the rising attainment is consistent with the enrollment rates. Table A.6 reports current attainment by age and the predicted future attainment based on current enrollment and educational attainment. If there was no sampling bias, the predicted rates should be slightly higher than the actual rates. Not everyone finished the year and not everyone was promoted. The table fits exactly this pattern.

To summarize, we have found little indication of sampling biases. The exception was with enrollment data, but here the pattern went in the opposite direction from that found in the Census-NBER comparison. It is therefore easier to explain both the discrepancies in terms of the differences in survey instruments rather than in terms of sampling biases.

Cross-City Comparisons

Wage and employment equations with age, education, and enrollment status as explanatory variables were run separately for each

Table A.4   Comparison of Current and Restrospective Employment Rates in the NLS and NBER Survey, by Age

Age	NLS 1979	NLS 1980	Total lag	Total cur	Chicago lag	Chicago cur	Boston lag	Boston cur	Philadelphia lag	Philadelphia cur
16	19.6	27.9	19.4	21.6	16.0	20.5	31.5	29.5	10.8	14.7
17	48.8	25.0	31.3	32.5	26.4	23.5	45.8	48.0	19.8	25.4
18	42.9	58.1	37.6	39.0	37.0	37.3	48.2	51.7	27.9	26.4
19	65.5	59.2	45.6	45.2	34.6	37.0	63.2	60.2	40.7	38.4
20	67.6	72.4	55.5	49.6	51.9	35.8	65.5	61.8	50.0	51.7
21	84.9	67.6	56.4	50.3	55.0	38.5	68.8	70.9	49.3	42.4
22	71.4	84.9	56.4	55.3	54.7	41.7	66.1	83.3	47.2	48.0
23			57.1	57.6	50.0	50.9	80.0	66.1	47.0	54.7
N	254	308	1,913	2,173	624	732	618	707	671	734
Weighted Mean Differential		−2.0		−.10		−2.2		0.3		2.0
Standard Error		(3.9)		(1.5)		(2.5)		(2.6)		(2.3)
χ^2 Test of Homogeneity		12.83 (.05)		3.56		8.05		7.36		3.17
Degrees of Freedom		6		7		7		7		7

Table A.5   Comparison of Current and Retrospective Average Wage Rates in NLS and NBER Survey, by Age and City

	NLS		Total		Chicago		Boston		Philadelphia	
Age	1979	1980	lag	cur	lag	cur	lag	cur	lag	cur
16	3.13		3.09	3.08		3.16		3.14	2.76	2.68
17	3.09	3.75	3.28	3.14	3.27	3.18	3.33	3.21	3.14	2.81
18	3.28	3.77	3.47	3.44	3.32	3.79	3.51	3.35	3.59	3.14
19	3.81	4.37	3.62	3.85	3.64	3.94	5.57	3.66	3.46	4.29
20	3.88	4.22	3.70	4.13	3.97	4.23	3.82	4.35	3.38	3.82
21	4.42	4.88	3.97	3.84	4.20	4.13	3.97	4.04	3.78	3.44
22	3.73	4.91	4.41	4.27	4.60	4.54	4.07	4.42	4.72	3.91
23		4.44	4.11	4.75	4.56	5.09	3.88	4.44	3.97	4.81
24				4.33	3.06	4.90	2.44	4.13		4.02
N	110	103	866	919	263	279	376	406	227	234
Weighted Mean Differential	.108		.024		.048		.020		−.001	
Standard Error	(.031)		(.010)		(−.023)		(.013)		(.087)	
Linear Age	.068	.083	.047	.050	.064	.058	.033	.047	.055	.049
	(.016)	(.016)	(.005)	(.005)	(.009)	(.009)	(.006)	(.006)	(.010)	(.010)
χ^2 on Equality of Age Coefficient	.0395		.6331		.464		7.947		1.1937	

Note: Universe for NLS is black youths employed during the survey week in both years, living in SMSAs, and not in the military. Universe for NBER is black youths employed during the survey week and one year earlier. All computations are in logs and converted back to actual-dollar wage ratios for ease of comprehension.

Table A.6　　　　**Actual versus Predicted Portion with a High School Diploma, NBER**

Age	Total		Chicago		Boston		Philadelphia	
	Actual	Predicted	Actual	Predicted	Actual	Predicted	Actual	Predicted
16	.45		1.14		0.0		0.0	
17	1.86	5.86	.00	6.82	.79	2.88	4.62	7.75
18	21.19	30.05	17.27	20.00	20.83	16.54	25.71	41.54
19	43.60	53.13	43.21	39.93	45.58	65.00	43.02	47.62
20	53.44	57.60	45.68	45.45	63.16	66.27	52.22	51.16
21	61.27	57.89	57.69	55.56	74.55	71.05	53.03	54.44
22	60.22	61.27	60.00	48.38	60.42	74.55	60.27	53.03
23	66.67	60.22	58.49	57.69	81.36	60.42	58.49	60.27
24	54.89	60.67	57.35	60.00	64.00	81.36	45.45	58.49

Note: Predicted high school completion rates calculated using youths one year younger than the stated age and assuming all those enrolled in school would complete their current grade.

city. The chi-squared statistics for the test for pooling across the cities were 10.7 and 8.5 for the wage and employment equations, respectively. With six degrees of freedom, these show no sign of a systematic difference across the cities in terms of wage or employment responsiveness to the three explanatory variables.[16] Comparing Boston with each of the other two cities yields chi-squared statistics of 4.7 and 3.2 for the Boston-Chicago comparisons and 4.9 and 3.6 for the Boston-Philadelphia comparisons, with coefficients never differing by more than 10 percent. There is no evidence that any of the regression parameters differs across cities or that Boston is different from the other two cities.

We can address the same issue by using the sample-selection technology. An auxiliary equation can predict who will be in the survey conditional on exogenous variables. Using the proportion of family heads reported in the 1976 Survey of Income and Education for black men in the 16–24 age range and imposing the census age distributions, we can compute a selection equation and then reestimate the wage and employment equations conditional on these probabilities. For the wage equation, the inverse Mills ratio can be used as an explanatory variable. The two-step procedure is preferable to the maximum-likelihood technique because it depends less heavily on distributional assumptions.[17] For the employment equation such a two-step procedure is not available, but it is still possible to write the probit likelihood conditional on a supplementary selection rule and on a cross-equation correlation. The cross-equation correlation captures the nonrandomness of the selection, as does the Heckman term in the linear regression. As long as this correlation is not zero, estimates of the original equation that do not take account of the sampling will be biased.

For wages the estimated cross-equation correlation implied by the inverse Mills ratio is .05, with a t-ratio of .8. For employment the estimated correlation is a trivial .001, but with a standard error of 1.009. Coefficients in the wage and employment equations are negligibly affected and so are not reported here. Thus, there is no evidence of selection biases, but the relevant selection parameters, particularly the one for the employment equation, are poorly estimated. The tests therefore have negligible explanatory power against plausible alternatives.

Conclusion

The foregoing analysis searched for consistent patterns that would suggest sampling biases in the NBER survey data. Although some discrepancies between the NBER and census data and between the current and retrospective data were uncovered, the discrepancies are more easily attributable to differences in the survey instruments than to sampling bias.

Perhaps the strongest evidence for sampling bias lies in Census-NBER comparisons of employment in Boston. Yet Boston showed no discrepancy in any of the other comparisons. Moreover, even if we were to take the census data on Boston as correct, the conclusion we would reach using the NBER data would still be valid. We would be correct in concluding that it was much easier for a young black man to find a job in Boston than in Chicago and in concluding that employment rose with age.

The NBER data are unique; no other survey of inner-city youth of comparable scale or scope exists. The apparent undercount of older youths raises legitimate doubts about possible sampling biases. Yet there is no consistent evidence that the undercount seriously biased the analysis of the key variables studied in this volume.

Notes

1. The NBER survey targeted census tracts in three cities that had at least 30 percent of the population below the poverty line and 70 percent of the population black in 1979. (In Boston the proportions were 20 percent and 60 percent, respectively.) For details of the survey design, see Jackson and McDonald (1981).

2. These percentages are based on birth, death, and net immigration statistics. The assumption is made that there is no illegal immigration, which for blacks may be close to the truth. Details on the estimates can be found in various census publications (see, in particular, U.S. Bureau of the Census [1974; 1982]).

3. Introductions to the work the Census has done in this area can be found in Klein (1970), Johnston and Wetzel (1969), and U.S. Department of Labor (1968). The most serious conceptual problem with these census and Bureau of Labor Statistics surveys is that they may themselves under- or overrepresent a characteristic in the undercount, and so there is no guarantee that they will even be correct in suggesting the right sign on an undercount bias. For example, suppose the nonemployed are those who tend to be missed in the original enumeration. If this is just as true in the postenumeration survey, we will be apt to believe that there is no bias, when, in fact, there is.

4. All details regarding the NBER survey design and implementation can be found in Jackson and McDonald (1981).

5. For amplification on this point see Goldberger (1981), Maddala (1983), and Manski and McFadden (1982).

6. The probable underreporting of criminal activity is discussed in Viscusi (in this volume).

7. Heckman (1979) is the classic reference.

8. See Freeman and Medoff (1982) and Borus, Mott, and Nestel (1978).

9. The comparison I am suggesting is the within versus between comparison, familiar to users of panel data, though not commonly used to test for sampling bias. See Chamberlain (1984) and Hausman (1978).

10. In conception and notation, the equation follows the wage-dynamic literature. Examples are Lillard and Weiss (1979) and Ashenfelter and Card (1984). That literature typically specifies some time-series pattern on ε, with some form of fixed time effects (vintage). The time-series pattern is omitted here for notational convenience, but the

fixed time effects are a necessary restriction, as will become clear below. The sampling and time effects are indistinguishable without information from outside the sample.

11. For notational convenience, the subscripts will be dropped below except where doing so would create confusion.

12. The units of Z are arbitrary. Unit variance is a notationally convenient normalization.

13. $\kappa_t = E(Z|Z < Z_t)$, $\Delta\kappa = \kappa_1 - \kappa_0$.

14. This is the familiar problem that omnibus tests tend to have nebulous explanatory power.

15. The number of older youths heading their own household is strikingly low in the NBER survey. Only 28 percent of 22- to 24-year-olds in the NBER survey headed their own household, whereas the comparable percentage for blacks of the same ages in the 1976 Survey of Income and Education was 53 percent, and for blacks of those ages in the poverty areas of Boston, Chicago, and Philadelphia in the 1970 Census, it was 64 percent.

16. The procedure yields two restrictions each for age, education, and enrollment status. Age is entered as a set of nine dummy variables, but education is still entered linearly. The chi-squared values are again close to their expected values: 25.9 and 19.02, respectively, for wages and employment, for statistics with 20 degrees of freedom.

17. See Olsen (1982).

References

Ashenfelter, O., and D. Card. 1984. Using the longitudinal structure of earnings to estimate the effects of training programs. NBER Working Paper no. 1489

Borus, M. E., F. L. Mott, and G. Nestel. 1978. Counting youth: A comparison of youth labor force statistics in the Current Population Survey and the National Longitudinal Surveys. In *Conference report on youth unemployment: Its measurement and meaning,* 15–34. Washington, D.C.: U.S. Department of Labor, Office of the Assistant Secretary for Policy, Evaluation and Research and the Employment and Training Administration.

Chamberlain, G. 1984. Panel Data. In *Handbook of Econometrics,* vol. 2, ed. Z. Griliches and M. D. Intriligator. Amsterdam: North Holland.

Freeman, R. B., and J. L. Medoff. 1982. Why does the rate of youth labor force activity differ across surveys? In *The youth labor market problem: Its nature, causes, and consequences,* ed. R. B. Freeman and D. A. Wise. Chicago: University of Chicago Press.

Goldberger, A. S. 1981. Linear regression after selection. *Journal of Econometrics* 15: 357–66.

Hausman, J. A. 1978. Specification tests in econometrics. *Econometrica* 46: 1251–72

Heckman, J. 1979. Sample selection bias as a specification error. *Econometrica* 47: 153–61.

Jackson, R., and A. McDonald. 1981. Field documentation, NBER minority youth survey project. Mathematica Policy Research. Mimeo.

Johnston, D., and J. Wetzel. 1969. Effects of the census undercount on labor force estimates. *Monthly Labor Review* 93 (March).

Klein, D. 1970. Status of men missed in the Census. *Monthly Labor Review* 93 (March).

Lillard, L., and Y. Weiss. 1979. Components of variation in panel earnings data: American scientists, 1960–1970. *Econometrica* 47: 437–54.

Maddala, G. S. 1983. *Limited-dependent and qualitative variables in econometrics*. Cambridge: Cambridge University Press.

Manski, C. F., and S. Lerman. 1977. The estimation of choice probabilities from choice based samples. *Econometrica* 45: 1977–88.

Manski, C. F., and D. McFadden, eds. 1982. *Structural analysis of discrete data, with econometric applications*. Cambridge, Mass.: MIT Press.

Olsen, R. J. 1982. Distributional tests for the selectivity bias and a more robust likelihood estimator. *International Economic Review* 23(1): 223–40.

U.S. Bureau of the Census. 1974. *Estimates of the coverage of population by sex, race, and age: Demographic analysis, 1974.* Washington, D.C.: GPO.

U.S. Bureau of the Census. 1982. *Coverage of the national population in the 1980 Census, by age, race and sex: Preliminary estimates by demographic analysis.* Washington, D.C.: GPO.

U.S. Department of Labor, Bureau of Labor Statistics. 1968. *Pilot and experimental program of the urban employment survey.* Report no. 354. Washington, D.C.: GPO.

Contributors

John Ballen
Massachusetts Financial Services, Inc.
200 Berkeley Street
Boston, Massachusetts

George J. Borjas
Department of Economics
University of California, Santa
  Barbara
Santa Barbara, California 93106

John Bound
National Bureau of Economic
  Research
1050 Massachusetts Avenue
Cambridge, Massachusetts 02138

Charles Brown
Department of Economics
University of Maryland
College Park, Maryland 20742

James Cataldo
Employment and Crime Project
Vera Institute of Justice
275 Madison Avenue, 7th Floor
New York, New York 10016

Gary Chamberlain
Center for Advanced Study in Behavioral Sciences

202 Junipero Serra Boulevard
Stanford, California 94305

Jerome Culp
School of Law
Duke University
Durham, North Carolina 27705

Linda Datcher-Loury
John F. Kennedy School of
  Government
Harvard University
79 J.F.K. Drive
Cambridge, Massachusetts 02138

Bruce H. Dunson
Department of Economics and
  Finance
Prairie View A&M University
Prairie View, Texas 77446

Ronald G. Ehrenberg
Department of Labor Economics
Cornell University
P.O. Box 1000
Ithaca, New York 14850

David T. Ellwood
John F. Kennedy School of
  Government
Harvard University

79 J.F.K. Drive
Cambridge, Massachusetts 02138

Ronald Ferguson
John F. Kennedy School of
  Government
Harvard University
79 J.F.K. Drive
Cambridge, Massachusetts 02138

Randall Filer
Department of Economics
Brandeis University
Waltham, Massachusetts 02254

Richard B. Freeman
National Bureau of Economic
  Research
1050 Massachusetts Avenue
Cambridge, Massachusetts 02138

Daniel S. Hamermesh
Department of Economics, Marshall
  Hall
Michigan State University
East Lansing, Michigan 48824

Harry J. Holzer
Department of Economics, Marshall
  Hall
Michigan State University
East Lansing, Michigan 48824

Peter Jackson
413 Hill Hall
Rutgers University
Newark, New Jersey 07102

Jonathan S. Leonard
School of Business Administration
University of California, Berkeley
350 Barrows Hall
Berkeley, California 94720

Robert Lerman
Heller Graduate School for Ad-
  vanced Studies in Social Welfare
Brandeis University
Waltham, Massachusetts 02254

Glenn C. Loury
Department of Economics
University of Michigan
Ann Arbor, Michigan 48109

James. L. Medoff
Department of Economics
Harvard University
Littauer Center, Room 116
Cambridge, Massachusetts 02138

Edward Montgomery
School of Urban and Public Affairs
Carnegie Mellon University
Pittsburgh, Pennsylvania 15213

Samuel L. Myers, Jr.
Graduate School of Public and Inter-
  national Affairs
University of Pittsburgh
3E27 Forbes Quadrangle
Pittsburgh, Pennsylvania 15260

Paul Osterman
Department of Economics
Boston University
270 Bay State Road
Boston, Massachusetts 02115

Michael J. Piore
Department of Economics
Massachusetts Institute of
  Technology
Cambridge, Massachusetts 02139

James W. Thompson
Employment and Crime Project
Vera Institute of Justice
275 Madison Avenue, 7th Floor
New York, New York 10016

W. Kip Viscusi
Department of Economics
Northwestern University
2003 Sheridan Road
Evanston, Illinois 60201

Author Index

Subject Index

Absenteeism, 9, 93, 261–62, 293; blacks and whites compared, 264; and discrimination, 12, 273; and education, 275–77, 284; effected by job characteristics, 264; effects of job status on, 12; effects of wages on, 12; and favoritism, 273; incentives against, 265; incentives for, 264; and job loss, 125; and job security, 281; and school grades, 275–76, 293; theoretical model of, 265–67; and unemployment, 293; and voter registration, 276; and years of schooling, 277, 284

Affirmative action, 3

Age: and crime, 305, 307, 309; and crime income, 324; and employment patterns, 9, 29, 76–79; and job loss rate, 120; relationship to negative effects of welfare programs, 429; and unemployment, 132; and wages, 29

Aid to Families with Dependent Children, 72–73, 404, 406, 412–13, 418, 439

Alcohol abuse: and crime, 310; and inner-city black youths, 8

Alienation, white students compared to black, 246

Annual Housing Survey, 160

Annual Survey of Manufactures, 196

Attitudes, effect on job success, 13

Burglary, 323, 336

Census Employment Surveys, 164

Census of Manufactures, 196

Chicago, Illinois: Annual Housing Survey, 160; Chicago Area Transportation Study, 159, 186; community areas, 166; commuting patterns in, 159; neighborhoods, 166; Spanish-speaking, 170; and spatial mismatch hypothesis, 158–89

Chicago Area Transportation Study, 159, 186

Childbearing, effects of welfare programs on, 414

Churchgoing activities, 362; and crime participation, 325, 354; effect on behavior, 369, 371–72; effect on productive activities, 364; effect of public housing environment on, 372; and employment of black youth, 6; and escape from inner-city poverty, 13; and presence of both parents, 372; survey questions on, 5

Commuting. See Travel time

Competition, between young and old black men, 206–7

Construction industries, 121

Consumer Price Index, 213

Craft jobs, 45

Crime, 24, 293, 307; and age, 305, 307, 309; and alcohol abuse, 310; and churchgoing behavior, 325, 354; and criminal environment, 324; decision to